The Peruvian Economy and Structural Adjustment: Past, Present, and Future

Edited by

Efraín Gonzales de Olarte

North·South Center Press
UNIVERSITY OF MIAMI

The mission of the North-South Center is to promote better relations and serve as a catalyst for change among the United States, Canada, and the nations of Latin America and the Caribbean by advancing knowledge and understanding of the major political, social, economic, and cultural issues affecting the nations and peoples of the Western Hemisphere.

To order or to return books, contact Lynne Rienner Publishers, Inc., 1800 30th Street, Suite 314, Boulder, CO 80301-1026, 303-444-6684, fax 303-444-0824.

The views expressed in this volume of edited papers are those of the authors, not the North-South Center, which is a nonpartisan public policy and research institution.

Library of Congress Cataloging-in-Publication Data

      The Peruvian economy and structural adjustment: past, present, and future / edited by Efraín Gonzales de Olarte.
          p. cm.
      At head of title: North-South Center, University of Miami.
      ISBN 0-935501-97-5
      1. Peru — Economic conditions —. 1968— 2. Economic stabilization — Peru. 3. Economic Forecasting — Peru.   I. Gonzales de Olarte, Efraín. II. University of Miami. North-South Center.
HC227.P4198 1996   94-771
 338.985—dc20   CIP

Printed in the United States of America

00 99 98 97 96 6 5 4 3 2 1

CONTENTS

INTRODUCTION

Efraín Gonzales de Olarte 1

Chapter I

PERU:
THE CURRENT ECONOMIC SITUATION IN
LONG-TERM PERSPECTIVE

Shane Hunt 11

Chapter II

A LONG-RUN PERSPECTIVE ON SHORT-RUN STABILIZATION:
THE EXPERIENCE OF PERU

Rosemary Thorp 59

Chapter III

THE PERUVIAN ECONOMY CIRCA 1990:
STRUCTURE AND CONSEQUENCES

Daniel M. Schydlowsky 77

Chapter IV

POLITICAL CONDITIONS, ECONOMIC RESULTS, AND THE
SUSTAINABILITY OF THE REFORM PROCESS IN PERU

Teobaldo Pinzás 127

Chapter V

THE ECONOMIC CONSEQUENCES OF THE "PERUVIAN DISEASE"

Elena H. Alvarez and Francisco Joel Cervantes 147

Chapter VI

THE VIABILITY OF ALBERTO FUJIMORI'S ECONOMIC STRATEGY

Carlos Boloña 183

Chapter VII

THE DIFFICULT MOMENTS OF THE FUJIMORI ECONOMIC STRATEGY

Javier Iguíñiz Echeverría 265

Chapter VIII

ECONOMIC REFORM AND THE REAL EXCHANGE RATE IN PERU

John Devereux and Michael Connolly 289

Chapter IX

ALTERNATIVE SCENARIOS FOR THE PERUVIAN ECONOMY

Santiago Roca 315

Appendix

PERU WORKING GROUP CONFERENCE 353

Index 357

INTRODUCTION

Efraín Gonzales de Olarte

This book has its origins in an international seminar entitled "The Peruvian Economy and Structural Adjustment: Past, Present, and Future," which was organized and sponsored by the Peru Working Group of the North-South Center at the University of Miami in June 1993.[1] Outstanding Peruvian, U.S., and British economists were invited to discuss Peru's economy in critical moments characterized by deep social and political changes.

It has been difficult to reach a consensus regarding which economic policies and institutional reforms are the most appropriate for a country like Peru, where attitudes of polarization and exclusion prevail in societal relations. Although differences persist when it comes to economic policies, times are changing, and more tolerant ideological positions are flourishing even in the field of economic diagnoses. In the past, the theoretical controversy between neoclassical and post-Keynesian economists clearly influenced the economic policies of successive regimes. Today, however, even the toughest neoclassical economists agree that state intervention is sometimes unavoidable, albeit undesirable, while the most stubborn post-Keynesians argue that the market is the best assigner of a vast variety of goods and factors. A summary of the diagnoses put forth in various chapters of this volume follows, emphasizing the principal points of agreement with regard to economic policy choices.

Efraín Gonzales de Olarte, Ph.D. in economics from the University of Paris (Pantheon-Sorbonne), is a senior research associate and the former director of the Institute of Peruvian Studies (Instituto de Estudios Peruanos, IEP). He was also a senior research associate at the University of Miami's North-South Center. He is the author of numerous publications, including *Economías regionales del Perú* (IEP, 1982); *Economía de la comunidad campesina* (IEP, 1984); *El péndulo peruano* (co-authored with Lilian Samamé, Consorcio de Investigación Económica/IEP, 1991); and *En las fronteras del mercado: Economía política del campesinado del Perú* (IEP, 1994).

THE PERUVIAN ECONOMY: PAST

Recent economic and political trends in Peru are the result of a series of processes and unfinished experiments. Thus, in order to understand the structural adjustment and the institutional reforms currently taking place, it is necessary to rely on a secular historical perspective that relates the present to the immediate past. This is the end of one historical chapter in Peru and the beginning of a new phase.

In his chapter, "Peru: The Current Economic Situation in Long-Term Perspective," Shane Hunt explores the causes of instability in Peru's long-term economic growth. Hunt maintains that Peru has met most of the preconditions for economic growth as outlined by economist W. Arthur Lewis in his classic work, "The Export Stimulus," namely, a capacity for savings and investment, infrastructure, a highly productive agricultural sector, and the existence of entrepreneurial elites. However, what has been missing, according to Hunt, is the capacity to combine these factors. Peru has lacked a strong state with the ability to integrate the country's economic strengths and assure the continuity and stability of a consistent economic model.

During the past forty years, Peru's alternative has been a populist yet weak state. The state's weakness — a persistent feature of the republican era — rather than its populist character doomed it to failure. Hunt posits that this weakness is as threatening to the neoliberalism that prevails today as it would be to any other alternative. Consequently, even anti-state neoliberalism must advocate the building of a strong state; otherwise, it will be very difficult for Peru to find a development model that fosters sustainable growth.

A strong state, as conference discussant Manuel Pastor asserted, is able to impose social discipline and control over the entrepreneurial sector through legitimacy. Such a state must promote an economic model that permits sustained continuity and stability. To achieve this end, agreements between the various social sectors and political organizations are crucial.

The lack of a consistent development model in conjunction with a weak state has inhibited long-term growth in Peru, as evidenced by persistent cyclical short-term economic crises the country has experienced during the past fifty years as well as by explosive inflationary pressures. Stabilization efforts have proven difficult, and adjustments have become progressively harder. Peruvians have learned that after each failed stabilization attempt subsequent initiatives are even more costly in economic and political terms.

The origin of the cumulative nature of Peru's multiple crises and failed stabilization efforts can be traced to the lack of congruence between short-term (stabilization) policies and long-term (development) policies, as Rosemary Thorp explains in her chapter. Thorp attributes this deficiency to the weakness of the institutions that function as links between civil society and the state — particularly the political parties and the institutions responsible for economic and social policymaking. The solution for economic problems in Peru can only be found outside the economic sphere. Thus, she argues that a radical, if not revolutionary, change is needed regarding the state's role and quality. Stabilization efforts and structural adjustment require two indispensable and inseparable conditions: the technical consistency of economic programs and the credibility of the economic system (the economic model and the state). When the credibility level of an economic system is low, linking short-and long-term policies becomes a difficult endeavor. Investment, a key variable for growth, is dependent on the short-term confidence level of potential investors, which is affected in turn by the credibility of the government and its economic policies.

Thorp points out that the focus of the stabilization programs implemented in Peru during the past forty years has been tied to the nature of the economic problems experienced at the time. During the 1950s and 1960s, the reduction of external disequilibria was emphasized, while there was little concern about inflation, which typically registered low annual rates. During the 1980s, however, inflation rates rose dramatically, and efforts to control them increased. The most elusive problems during periods of stabilization have included achieving the alignment of relative prices (the exchange rate, interest rates, wages, and the prices of public goods and services) and closing of the external, fiscal, and savings-investment gaps. However, during the past twenty years it has not been possible to align prices while maintaining stable macroeconomic equilibria.

In the mid-1960s, the existing primary-export, semi-industrial economic model began to suffer a structural crisis in that investment possibilities became dependent on the availability of foreign currency. This phenomenon, in turn, exerted continuous pressure on the balance of payments. In this context, structural adjustment was required to generate more foreign currency and diminish the external shocks characteristic of primary-export economies. At the same time, the fiscal sector was affected by fluctuations in the international economy inasmuch as its income depended, directly or indirectly, on exports. Adjustment policies were not implemented, however, due to political and economic reasons, which eventually led to General Juan Velasco Alvarado's 1968 military coup d'état.

During the 1970s, substantial international credit became available, allowing the military government to close financial and external gaps through foreign indebtedness. Since this time, the burden of foreign debt, which is public for the most part, has become the most important obstacle to the achievement of macroeconomic equilibrium and the stabilization of relative prices.

Twenty years later, toward the end of the Alan García administration (1985-1990), inconsistent heterodox economic policies implemented by the regime resulted in the exhaustion of macroeconomic populism. At the same time, populism as a political style also became depleted.

THE PERUVIAN ECONOMY IN THE EARLY 1990s

A combination of economic and political pressures advocating change led to the election of President Alberto Fujimori in 1990 and the subsequent implementation of an extreme version of economic neoliberalism, including the much-heralded "Washington-inspired" structural adjustment with its institutional reforms. However, a number of inherited structural and institutional problems threatened to stand in the way of the adjustment's success: 1) the existing industrial structure, 2) fiscal weakness related to the foreign debt problem, and 3) a state apparatus with a deficient operative capacity.

The early 1990s have witnessed the characteristics of the Peruvian economy persisting as long-term problems. As Daniel Schydlowsky suggests in his chapter, the economy is in disequilibrium, lacking foreign currency for growth and exhibiting an excess supply of labor. This surplus of labor produces economic inefficiency, which affects the price system and fails to reflect the relative scarcity of other resources. On the other hand, the persistence of great differences in productivity levels between the exporting and the nonexporting sectors influences the long-term exchange rate, reinforcing the inadequate allocation of factors. In other words, the alignment of relative prices is very difficult inasmuch as their levels depend on structural distortions. This may account for the fact that past stabilization policies could never overcome structural disequilibria.

For this same reason, as long as a surplus of labor persists, an unchecked price system is not an efficient allocator of resources and factors, as neoclassical orthodoxy would wish. In this context, Schydlowsky asserts that the informal sector, which represents 40 percent of the labor force, has had great importance as a redistributive force because it has permitted the survival of vast sectors of the population under conditions of marginal state assistance and with relatively little participation in the formal markets.

Preliminary data indicates that a period of improved income distribution could have occurred subsequent to the García administration. However, achieving growth with redistribution requires the availability of abundant foreign currency as well as successful income distribution policies, neither of which Peru had. Thus, an attempt at income distribution would have resulted in a downward process of social equalization and in the impoverishment of the general population.

The market economy is not sufficiently developed in Peru. A series of economic crises — together with the failure of the stabilization policies — has contributed to the shrinkage of markets. As a consequence, the capacity to allocate resources more efficiently in the future depends on the development of markets. Peru therefore requires a state that vigorously promotes and seeks to create markets rather than a state that simply regulates weak and imperfect existing markets.

In his chapter, former Minister of Economy and Finance Carlos Boloña assigns responsibilities differently, suggesting that the distortion of relative prices is fundamentally a consequence of state actions. The state, he argues, is responsible for the informality, the negative externalities, and price controls. He thus presents a different interpretation of Peru's market-state institutional structure and the origins of its malfunctioning state as well as its market imperfections.

An unexpected component of Peru's economic structure has been the appearance and development of a "coca sector" since 1980. This sector encompasses the cultivation of coca plants, the production of basic cocaine paste, and the refinement, transportation, and marketing of cocaine hydrochloride. Characterized by high profitability due to its illegality, this sector has produced controversial economic results, as Elena H. Alvarez has observed. On the one hand, this sector has provided additional foreign currency, generated employment and income for poor peasant sectors, and stimulated the economy of several regions. On the other hand, it has produced the overvaluation of the exchange rate, corruption, smuggling, and violence. Moreover, it has created what Alvarez terms the "Peruvian disease," a variant of the so-called "Dutch disease" of corruption and insurgency that hinders economic policies and governability. On the supply side, its elimination requires substitution not only by means of the eradication of the coca-leaf crops but also through the implementation of a comprehensive rural-industrial development program. However, as conference discussant Francisco Verdera has suggested, this problem could also be confronted from the demand side by substituting other substances for cocaine or lowering consumption. At present, the coca sector continues to be a cause of the cheap dollar and, consequently, a hindrance to the stabilization of the exchange rate and the promotion of an export model.

Though the exchange rate constitutes one of the key components of the Peruvian economic system, its importance has been chronically overvalued. One of the primary purposes of structural adjustment is to correct the structural causes of exchange rate overvaluation. However, to achieve this end, these causes must be clearly identified. Some analysts argue that overvaluation is related to the differential rent that primary-sector exports (metals and fish meal, for example) enjoy despite the exchange rate overvaluation. John Devereux and Michael Connolly contend that the existence of consumption subsidies, the artificially low prices of goods and services produced by public enterprises, and price controls have been the main contributors to the overvaluation of the real exchange rate in the past.

Neoliberal stabilization and structural adjustment programs — influenced by the Austrian School and Friedrich von Hayek — were launched simultaneously in 1990 by the Alberto Fujimori regime as a broad-spectrum response to Peru's various economic problems and multiple crises. In his chapter, Carlos Boloña affirms that the economic disaster and institutional crisis inherited by Fujimori from Alan García paradoxically proved advantageous because they gave the new administration the opportunity to apply a drastic reform program over a very short period of time, with 923 law-decrees promulgated between March 1991 and December 1992.

The Fujimori administration's short-run economic goal was to stabilize the Peruvian economy by correcting the disequilibria of the main macroeconomic variables. Boloña claims numerous achievements — a dramatic reduction of inflation rates, a great increase in international net reserves, the reduction of the fiscal and quasi-fiscal deficit, and the restraint of monetary emission to rates below inflation. However, these accomplishments were accompanied by recessionary pressures resulting from the constraining nature of the program.

Boloña analyzes the structural reforms designed to deregulate and modernize the Peruvian economy. These included policies to promote 1) stabilization (of inflation, international reserves, and fiscal and monetary discipline); 2) the liberalization of markets (goods and services, capital, and labor); 3) reform of the country's property structure (the privatization of public enterprises, opening to foreign investment, the fostering of private property); 4) reform of the state (including a reduction in the size of government, tax reform, and public expenditures in the areas of health, education, housing, and social support); and 5) institutional reforms (reform of the legislative, judicial, and electoral powers, political parties, and the armed forces).

Boloña also discusses the reinsertion of Peru into the international economic and financial community through the resumption of payments that had been suspended by the García administration. The main steps involved in this process were the conformation of the Support Group (comprised of the United States, Japan, and other countries) and the negotiation of the Rights Accumulation Program with the International Monetary Fund (IMF), the Paris Club, and the Inter-American Development Bank (IDB). The former minister further stresses the importance of maintaining the rule of law currently threatened by terrorist activities, which must be eliminated if any effort to improve and modernize the economy is to succeed and endure. With respect to financing this effort, Boloña suggests a better distribution of the costs between the public and private sectors.

Nonetheless, Carlos Boloña's work remains controversial. Devereux and Connolly contend, for example, that Boloña's drastic reform program was implemented at a pace that even International Monetary Fund officials found excessive. It is clear, however, that the Fujimori administration has adopted a style of decisionmaking that is characterized by implementing adjustment initiatives prior to announcing them; thus, reforms have been based on a "surprise factor."

Unlike other initiatives undertaken in the region, Peru's structural adjustment program has lacked the support of a social program designed to ameliorate the negative impact of the program on the most vulnerable sectors of the population. As a result, poverty levels have increased (in 1991, for example, 55 percent of the population lived in abject poverty), and unemployment and underemployment levels have worsened (currently, only 18 percent of the labor force has adequate employment). Conference discussant John Sheahan would claim that the negative social consequences of the adjustment program were simply not a concern to those who designed and executed the program.

On the whole, the results of the economic program are relatively modest, the reduction of inflation being the one result with high political impact. The verdict on the alignment of relative prices and macroeconomic stability is still pending. According to Peruvian economist Javier Iguíñiz, the program is characterized by internal inconsistency inasmuch as relative prices are working against tradable goods, thereby undermining the goal of promoting an export model. On the other hand, in conference discussant Julio Velarde's opinion, the economic program's relatively poor results are due to deficient coordination and management.

The structural reforms designed to promote a market economy to replace the existing mixed economy are examined by Teobaldo Pinzás, who questions their long-term viability in the context of economic recession and political fragility. He also ponders how long it might take for reforms of this magnitude to create new, credible institutional conditions for investors and other economic agents.

Some reforms, such as trade liberalization, were carried out at high speed (in less than one year in Peru, compared with six years in Chile). This fast pace had negative consequences for the tradables productive sector, causing a large number of enterprises to go bankrupt. Although one of the expected effects of this type of reform is that the less efficient will be forced out of the market, efficiency levels are determined by a series of distorted relative prices, an indication of inconsistency between stabilization and institutional reforms. Instead of augmenting capital stock, which is the scarcest factor in countries such as Peru, structural adjustment policies have diminished it.

Perhaps the severest critic of the economic program in Peru is economist and conference discussant Rudiger Dornbusch, who views the program as an eclectic group of policies lacking a precise economic framework beyond that of a general free market economy. Dornbusch holds that liberalization of the economy with little initial devaluation and subsequent overvaluation of the currency is a perverse formula that makes drug trafficking pay, to a certain extent, for liberalization. Such policies do not necessarily lead to economic growth, especially if inflation rates remain over 40 percent per year. Moreover, the relationship between the short-term program and institutional reforms has yet to foster the necessary conditions for the establishment of a new model for growth.

THE PERUVIAN ECONOMY: PROSPECTS FOR THE FUTURE

Peru is presently completing one long-term cycle and beginning another. Given the present international context, it is highly probable that a neoliberal wave will occupy a preeminent position in the Peruvian economy and society during the next twenty years. Thus, the success of structural adjustment policies is of great import if we are to guarantee the country's return to a path of stable growth and safeguard and strengthen Peruvian democracy in all its manifestations.

In the immediate future, a transition period of five to eight years, two unknowns must become clear:

1. Will stabilization be successful, and if so, how long will this process take?

2. Will structural reforms be sustained despite changes of government?

Success cannot be guaranteed, in my opinion, unless modifications and readjustments are made in the current program. Such changes should be based on agreements between the government and political parties, unions, and entrepreneurial organizations. Nevertheless, it is difficult to make predictions about the future of the Peruvian economy, considering the high levels of risk and uncertainty that institutional reforms still bear as well as the fact that economic stability depends on one person — President Alberto Fujimori.

The most important reform still pending is reform of the state, which thus far has advanced only partially and very slowly. To date, the government has reduced the institutional capacity of the state by closing institutions. However, on a broader scale, the government has yet to devise a formula to strengthen the state, promoting government accountability and mechanisms to discipline society and ensure the universal application of norms.

Using a financial-economic programming model, Santiago Roca has prepared four alternative scenarios for the short-term future, analyzing possible policies that could be implemented to correct the short-term economic program in order to make it less recessionary without boosting inflation. Roca contends that the best scenario would involve a renegotiation of the foreign debt in order to free public finances from excessive dependency on high tax rates and allow investment, thereby progressively reactivating the economy.

Beyond the quantitative results presented by Javier Iguíñiz and conference discussant Bruce Kelley, there appear to be a number of possible alternatives to the neoliberal program. No one could legitimately apply these alternatives without being accused of promoting populism, however. Possibilities for bettering the program in the short term include 1) combining income policy and fiscal discipline in order to lessen recessionary effects; 2) pursuing a flexible money management policy followed by an exchange rate overshooting, combined with several anchors to avoid the boosting of inflation; and 3) fixing the exchange rate following the Cavallo model applied in Argentina. On the other hand, institutional reforms could be implemented at a slower pace or in a sequential manner.

Thus, the future of the Peruvian economy remains uncertain. Admittedly, public opinion favors the structural adjustment program. Consequently, the results must be positive. Neoliberal ideology is as strong today as the Economic Commission for Latin America and the Caribbean's proposals were in the 1960s. Sadly, ideologies create high expectations that are often frustrated in the future, resulting in economic and political instability. Let us hope that this time Peru has better luck.

I

PERU:
THE CURRENT ECONOMIC SITUATION IN LONG-TERM PERSPECTIVE

Shane Hunt

INTRODUCTION

This analysis of the Peruvian economy is both descriptive and diagnostic. The descriptive component examines Peru's long-term growth in order to arrive at generalizations regarding this experience. Thus, it explores numerous questions: How high has the long-run growth rate actually been? How does Peru's growth rate compare to that of other countries or regions? How can this long-run experience best be divided into periods? What criteria should be used to determine these periods? The diagnostic portion, on the other hand, explains the growth experience. It begins with an assessment of the proximate causes of growth — domestic savings rates, domestic investment rates, and foreign capital inflows. The export booms that have given Peru periodic short bursts of growth are discussed in this context. The diagnosis subsequently transcends the scope of savings and investment rates to consider the basic factors or preconditions that give rise to long-term growth. Two sets of preconditions are examined. The first set was developed and implemented by Arthur Lewis to account for the differential growth experience in the tropical world before World War I (Lewis 1970), while the second has been utilized by analysts of political economy in more recent times (Haggard 1990; Vogel 1991).

Shane Hunt is emeritus professor of economics at Boston University and research associate at the Instituto de Estudios Peruanos.

Facts About Long-Term Growth

The first fact worth noting about Peru's long-term growth is that we actually know very little about it. In terms of knowledge about growth, the 172 years of Peru's republican existence (1821-1993) fall into three periods. The most recent forty-three years (1950-1993) are covered by adequate national accounts data. However, the preceding thirty-seven years (1913-1950) have been sketched in using unreliable, backward projections, and the ninety-two-year period prior to that (1821-1912) is essentially a complete blank.[1]

The Nineteenth Century: The Age of Inference

For this earliest period, we must abandon the safety of numbers and make inferences about growth from a number of disparate sources. A national income estimate is available for only one of the one hundred years in the nineteenth century, and this one estimate is unfortunately unreliable. Not only is it based on incomplete sources, but it also lacks the support of appraisals from neighboring years, which might give it greater meaning and reliability.[2]

Substantially greater progress has been made in estimating nineteenth-century economic growth in other Latin American countries. The figures for Brazil and Mexico, for example, span the better part of the century and show stagnation of per capita output in both cases (Maddison 1983). While stagnation seems to have been the norm throughout Latin America, the more developed countries of Europe and North America were growing slowly but steadily in per capita terms, resulting in the opening of a North-South gap, which has become still wider during the twentieth century.

Throughout Latin America, in fact, the general impression is one of economic stagnation during the nineteenth century. This bleak scene is relieved only by indications of renewed growth after 1880, particularly in Argentina and Mexico. During this period, Lewis (1970) identifies growth in many parts of the tropical world. Certainly, Peru conforms to this generalized impression of stagnation. Though 1880 brought renewed growth opportunities for other underdeveloped countries, it brought Peru political and economic disaster from which the country would take at least twenty years to recover. If Peru had any opportunity for growth during the nineteenth century, it must surely have been at an earlier time, namely, during the Guano Age.

Peru's growth experience during its nineteenth-century republican era falls neatly into three main periods. The first, the *caudillo* period, dating from 1821 to approximately 1840, has been viewed as a period of political chaos and economic deterioration. More recently, an underlying political coherence has been identified in this period thanks to the work of Paul Gootenberg (1989); nonetheless, the traditional view of economic backsliding remains. Contemporary observers have lamented the deterioration of both physical capital and the level of economic activity that took place toward the end of the period in Lima as well as in many remote provinces of the *Sierra* (Hunt 1985, 278).

The Guano Age that followed was surely one in which deterioration was arrested. It is less clear, however, whether significant growth occurred. Historians have treated the period as one of economic failure, postulating that an illusion of prosperity was created despite the lack of any significant economic growth (Basadre 1969; Levin 1960). This grim judgment surely arises from a sense of disgust at the chaos of public life and public finances during the Guano Age as well as from a sense of disillusionment triggered by the economic collapse and military defeat that marked the end of the era. Peru's social and economic weaknesses were glaringly exposed by the conflict with Chile (Bonilla 1980). However, these negative assessments of the Guano Age are not based on a cool, quantitative assessment of the evidence of growth because such an evaluation has yet to be made.

Abundant evidence of growth in the Guano Age does exist, however. Sugar and cotton production for export spread through coastal valleys. Mining revived in the highlands. The first banks were founded in Lima, and guano itself produced high income levels that financed the process of urbanization in Lima. The significance of this increased activity in national terms is not clear, however. With an incipient but growing capitalist sector and a large and stagnant subsistence sector, the Peruvian economy at this time corresponded fairly well to Lewis' two-sector model. National economic growth was probably quite low, not because the guano-based capitalist sector was not growing, but because it was still so small.

The third period, lasting from 1880 to the turn of the century, was characterized by economic collapse and war-caused devastation. The collapse was fairly swift, whereas the recovery was gradual. The terminal date of this period is therefore difficult to establish. Available data show that Peru's export production reached a peak in the mid-1870s, fell to a low point in 1881, representing a decline of 77 percent in quantum terms, and did not recover to the earlier peak level until about 1904.[3] Since export dynamism was probably the only source of income growth in Peru at the time, it is reasonable to infer that no income growth occurred in the last quarter of the nineteenth century.

These three periods of Peru's nineteenth-century economic experience therefore constitute an initial period of decline, a second period of modest advance, and a third period of collapse and recovery — a U-shaped trajectory with the end no higher than the beginning. Thus, despite the advances of the Guano Age, Peru most certainly reflects the generalized Latin American condition of economic stagnation during the nineteenth century.

THE TWENTIETH CENTURY: THE AGE OF ESTIMATES

Starting in 1900, annual gross domestic product (GDP) estimates of one kind or another are available for every year. Price indexes begin only in 1913, however, making it possible to estimate a real GDP series only from this later date. In fact, all the estimates for the years prior to 1942 have been developed using formulaic approaches that rely on a stable relationship between GDP on the one hand and one or more available economic statistics (exports, government expenditure, or money supply, for example) on the other. In the most recent of these studies, Carlos Boloña summarizes the earlier efforts and demonstrates by means of a series of tests that his own estimates seem the most reasonable (Boloña 1981, Appendix II). His method is quite Keynesian. He estimates an expenditure multiplier, assumes that the only significant forms of autonomous expenditure are exports and government spending, and multiplies one by the other to arrive at an estimated GDP.

Boloña's estimates for Peru are used by Angus Maddison (1989) in his monumental study of world economic growth in the twentieth century. The Maddison study represents a convenient means not only for examining Peru's growth experience during the twentieth century but also for placing it in international context. The most salient figures are set forth in Tables 1, 2, and 3 below.

The first point to note regarding the figures presented in Table 1 is that Maddison provides a worldwide norm for viewing real economic growth in the twentieth century: 3 percent per year in total GDP and 1.7 percent on a per capita basis. Over the full eighty-seven-year span considered in this table, growth rates in the major regions of the world were remarkably similar. In terms of total GDP, however, Latin America demonstrated a slightly higher growth rate than did the other major regions. As for Peru, its total GDP growth rate was slightly above the world norm, while its per capita rate was slightly below it.

When this century-long growth experience is divided into major subperiods, three additional factors are clearly brought to light. The first involves the remarkable turnabout that occurred in Asia at mid-century. In per capita terms, while Asia remained stagnant during the first half of the twentieth century, it became the region that manifested the highest growth in the second half. This turnabout resulted from a number of factors, perhaps the most important being the consolidation of communist power in China. Nonetheless, the Green Revolution and the export-oriented success stories of East and Southeast Asia also played a role.[4] Also noteworthy is the exceptionally high growth achieved by all regions from 1950 to 1973. Maddison terms this period the "Golden Age," and indeed it was, although most did not recognize it as such at the time. Again, all regions participated in the high growth of this period, which was unprecedented in world history. During the most recent

Table 1.
Real GDP Growth (in Percent)

	1900-87	1900-13	1913-50	1950-73	1973-87
Total GDP					
World	3.0	2.8	2.1	5.1	3.4
OECD	2.9	2.9	2.0	4.9	2.4
USSR	3.3	3.5	2.7	5.0	2.1
Asia	3.2	1.7	1.3	5.4	5.9
Latin America	3.8	3.9	3.3	5.2	2.9
Peru	**3.6**[a]	—	**2.8**	**5.4**	**2.6**
Per Capita GDP					
World	1.7	1.4	1.0	3.3	2.2
OECD	2.1	1.6	1.2	3.8	1.9
USSR	2.3	1.6	2.3	3.6	1.2
Asia	1.3	0.7	-0.2	2.8	3.6
Latin America	1.7	2.1	1.4	2.5	0.8
Peru	**1.5**[a]	—	**1.4**	**2.5**	**0.1**

a = 1913-1987
Source: Angus Maddison, *The World Economy in the Twentieth Century* (Paris: Organization for Economic Cooperation and Development, 1989).

period, from 1973 to Maddison's terminal year of 1987, Asia experienced the fastest growth in its history. On the other hand, all the other regions entered periods of relative stagnation. During this period of diminished economic performance, Latin America declined the most dramatically. Such was the malevolent effect of the Latin American debt crisis.[5] In all the various subperiods set forth in Table 1, Peru appears to be a fairly representative Latin American country, with the exception of the most recent period, when Peru's economic decline was more severe than the norm.[6]

Peru's growth experience is detailed in Tables 2 and 3. In Table 2, long-run growth rates covering most of the twentieth century are shown for Peru and for a selection of Western Hemisphere countries that are most often used as standards of comparison. In per capita terms, the data indicate that Brazil has experienced relatively high growth, while Argentina's growth has been relatively low. The other five countries, including Peru and the United States, have experienced very similar long-term growth rates. Thus, a careful, long-term view of the twentieth century reveals that Latin American growth has been close to the world norm (and to that of the United States). More importantly, Peruvian growth has been close to the Latin American norm. In fact, Peru has been a fairly typical country in terms of economic growth in this century. This observation is certainly a positive one, particularly given the pessimistic visions of Peru and its economic prospects that have been so widely disseminated in recent years.

The century-long average growth rates of the various countries listed in Table 2 do not seem profoundly different from one another. They give the superficial impression that the growth experience of these countries was fairly similar. However, differences do appear after a more careful examination of the data. One difference can be found in the final two columns of Table 2. These columns are intended to demonstrate that a small annual percentage difference, when accumulated over nearly a century, amounts to a large absolute difference. Brazil's per capita growth, for example, exceeded Argentina's by "only" 1.8 percent per year (2.7 percent versus 0.9 percent, respectively); however, this means that per capita GDP increased in Brazil by a factor of more than six as compared to less than two in Argentina. At the same time, per capita GDP nearly tripled in the remaining countries analyzed.

Table 2.
GDP Growth, 1913-1987: Latin America, Peru, United States
(Average Annual Figures)

	Total GDP (%)	Popula- tion (%)	Per Capita GDP (%)	GDP Indexes for 1987 (1913 = 100)	
				Total	Per Capita
Argentina	2.8	1.9	0.9	787.8	186.5
Brazil	5.1	2.4	2.7	3,900.6	656.0
Colombia	4.2	2.4	1.8	2,146.0	378.0
Chile	3.1	1.7	1.4	966.7	270.3
Mexico	3.9	2.3	1.6	1,757.7	324.2
Peru	3.6	2.1	1.5	1,337.6	290.4
United States	3.0	1.3	1.7	898.7	359.3

Source: Angus Maddison, *The World Economy in the Twentieth Century* (Paris: Organization for Economic Cooperation and Development, 1989).

Further variation appears in the growth experience of these countries during different subperiods of the twentieth century. These variations are presented in Table 3, where the subperiods are portrayed more finely than they are in Table 1. The variety of experience is striking. Much of the sociopolitical turbulence of twentieth-century history in these countries clearly manifests itself in their growth rates. The macroeconomic effects of Mexico's struggle to form a new society after its revolution, Chile's trauma of class conflict in the early 1970s, Brazil's "miracle," and Argentina's drift from "Dirty War" to debt crisis can all be appreciated here. The only countries that maintained positive per capita growth in all periods were Brazil and Colombia, but Brazil has faltered badly since 1987.[7]

Table 3 also highlights the periods when the Peruvian economy was growing well in excess of population growth as well as those in which it was barely keeping up. It shows, moreover, two distinct periods of high per capita growth: an early period of *civilismo* and the government of Augusto Leguía (1913-1929) and a later period of export-oriented growth in the 1950s and 1960s. The growth rate of the earlier period might be dismissed as a statistical aberration were it not for the fact that Chile, on the basis of more reliable estimates, is estimated to have reached the same growth rate. These statistics lead to a surprising conclusion: from 1913 to 1929, Chile and Peru were the fastest-growing nations of the Western Hemisphere. One can only surmise the reason for this rapid growth from factors that were common to both economies at that time, namely, the development of copper mining and the opening of the Panama Canal.

The impact of the Great Depression is seen in the average growth rates recorded from 1929 to 1938. The figures are somewhat deceptive, however, inasmuch as all countries were adversely affected. Nevertheless, some countries, such as Brazil and Colombia, recovered more rapidly and therefore posted positive growth over the period. Meanwhile, the United States remained mired in the so-called Roosevelt Recession of 1937-1938. Overall, Latin American countries, Peru included, recovered more quickly from the Great Depression than did the United States (Díaz-Alejandro 1982).

Although Peru's experience in the 1930s seems fairly representative, the table also shows a deviation from the norm from 1938 to 1950. During this period, Peru is the only country in the table that failed to achieve a significant increase in per capita GDP. This may be a statistical aberration; on the other hand, it most likely marks the political and economic turmoil that character-ized the APRA[8]-Bustamante period, which lasted from 1945 to 1948.

After 1950, growth accelerated strongly as Peru, along with most other countries, entered Maddison's "Golden Age." After 1965, however, growth declined sharply in Peru and even more so in Chile, while it continued strongly in the other countries examined. Thus, the Golden Age ended prematurely for

Table 3.
Per Capita GDP Growth by Subperiods, 1913-1987
Latin America, Peru, United States
(Average Annual Figures in Percent)

	1913-29	1929-38	1938-50	1950-65	1965-73	1973-87
Argentina	0.9	-0.8	1.7	1.6	2.8	-0.8
Brazil	1.4	2.5	2.3	2.6	6.0	2.2
Colombia	1.2	2.3	1.3	1.6	3.5	1.9
Chile	2.7	-0.5	2.0	2.0	-1.5	0.2
Mexico	0.1	0.2	2.7	3.0	3.2	0.9
Peru	2.7	1.0	-0.2	3.0	1.4	0.1
United States	1.7	-1.4	3.7	2.1	2.3	1.5

Source: Angus Maddison, *The World Economy in the Twentieth Century* (Paris, Organization for Economic Cooperation and Development, 1989).

these two countries. Shortly after 1965, Peru staggered from fiscal crisis under Fernando Belaúnde Terry to revolution from above under Juan Velasco Alvarado. On the other hand, after 1970 Chile experimented with a revolution of its own under Unidad Popular. In both cases, economic growth was eroded or halted by distributive struggle.

The final period examined in the table, that of 1973 to 1987, is comprised of two distinct subperiods. The first, from 1973 to 1982, was marked by unstable growth with increasing indebtedness. The second, from 1982 to the present day, has been characterized by the debt crisis. All countries suffered during the debt crisis (Colombia perhaps suffered the least); thus, the differences in average growth rates over the whole period are largely determined by the events that took place in the 1970s. The countries posting the lowest growth over the period — Argentina, Chile, and Peru — were precisely the only Latin American countries mired in recessions in the late 1970s, while others such as Brazil and Mexico were enjoying the last heady days of growth with debt.

The Chilean record merits comment. The recent Chilean "miracle" is much noted and even envied these days. A long-term view makes it the more miraculous since this strong recent growth follows sixty years of relative stagnation, including fourteen years after the 1973 coup when per capita growth was essentially nil. The Chilean story demonstrates that neoliberal restructuring is a lengthy process; it takes a long time before positive, long-lasting results can be seen.

SUMMING UP PERU'S GROWTH EXPERIENCE

In the broadest of outlines, Peru's growth experience seems to have been close to the Latin American norm. The Peruvian economy was somewhat stagnant during the nineteenth century. It has grown modestly but appreciably, in per capita terms, during the twentieth. However, a close examination of shorter time periods reveals a distinct and rather more turbulent economic history.

In the twentieth century, the age of estimates, the data for all six Latin American countries treated by Maddison indicate periods of high per capita income growth. In this century, however, all these countries have also suffered periods of economic instability and recession. For some, such as Brazil and Colombia, the periods of setback have not been long enough or frequent enough to have had great effect on overall growth. For others — Mexico, Argentina, Peru, and Chile, for instance — the periods of stagnation have been either long or repeated. The presently developed countries have also suffered from wars and other economic calamities. In this century, the Great Depression is carved like a great scar across the statistical record of the United States. Nevertheless, the data suggest that the presently developed countries of Europe and North America have not grown faster than those of Latin America, but more steadily. This is certainly true since 1950, but it was probably also true of the nineteenth century.

There is no better example of the curse of instability than Peru. Among the fastest growing of Western Hemisphere countries during two substantial periods of the twentieth century, 1913 to 1929 and 1950 to 1965, it also suffered economic stagnation or deterioration in the 1930s, 1940s, 1970s, 1980s, and recently in the 1990s. Some of these adverse experiences were undoubtedly caused externally, as in the 1930s and 1980s. Others were very possibly self-administered, such as those of the late 1940s and late 1970s. As for the Peruvian economy in the nineteenth century, instability was certainly present, perhaps in greater measure. Furthermore, Peru's instability probably ran counter to general Latin American trends. While most of Latin America endured stagnation in the middle half of the nineteenth century, Peru experienced some growth during the Guano Age. But when growth began in the rest of Latin America in the last quarter of the century, the Peruvian economy collapsed.

The most compelling conclusion that can be drawn from this review of the facts is that what needs to be explained is the instability, not the incapability, of growth in Peru.

EXPLAINING PERU'S GROWTH EXPERIENCE

The proximate cause of economic growth is the accumulation of physical capital, skills, and technology and their effective combination and allocation. All these factors have been subjected to analysis in sources of growth studies, but problems regarding both measurement and interpretation often make such studies hard to understand (Seminario 1992). For simplicity, the scope of this analysis is limited to the process of accumulation of physical capital, assuming that the other factors have an implicit effect on the capital output ratio.

In a Harrod-Domar framework, derived from the Keynesian tradition that views savings behavior as insensitive to the interest rate, the growth rate is determined by the savings rate. Investment adjusts to the amount of savings available. This framework is not entirely applicable to an open economy with international capital mobility, however. In this setting, an investment project need not be constrained by the availability of domestic savings if it can instead be financed overseas.

To what extent has capital been internationally mobile in Peru's past? The answer is, of course, to a limited extent. Risk and the lack of information have set limits that have varied over time. For most periods of Peru's republican history, portfolio investment has been considered too risky. Only in the 1820s, 1870s, 1920s, and 1970s were investors so emboldened or memories of past defaults so dimmed that loan money flowed in abundance to the Peruvian government. Aside from the single decade in each of these fifty-year cycles, capital inflow has consisted of direct, not portfolio, investment. Foreign investors have generally preferred to be on the premises, keeping a vigilant watch over their money.

Investment opportunities that paid high returns were, of course, particularly attractive to foreign investors. More often than not, high returns were to be found in exporting. New investment opportunities could in theory arise anywhere in an economy, but the significant new opportunities were likely to lie in exporting because of the sheer size of the potential market, that is, the world market. Investment in primary-product exporting could also unlock substantial natural-resource rents. Foreign investors held a competitive advantage in exporting; they were familiar with marketing requirements, and larger scale operations, particularly mining ventures, played to their ability to mobilize large amounts of capital.

This discussion focuses on the long-term importance of the export cycles that have been much commented upon in Peruvian (and also in Brazilian) history (Thorp and Bertram 1978; Furtado 1963 [1959]). In the short-term thinking of recent decades, export booms have been welcomed because import substitution policies have created foreign-exchange-constrained economies and raised the shadow price of export earnings. But in the longer view, export booms have encouraged foreign investors to invest, thereby raising the domestic investment rate above the constraints established by domestic savings.

While export cycles have been much commented upon in Peruvian historiography, the steady growth that can be triggered by an export stimulus — that is, the staple theory — has not. Developed in Canada, appreciated in Argentina, and generalized by Albert Hirschman, the staple theory has attracted little attention in Peru (Watkins 1963; Caves 1966; Diéguez 1969; Hirschman 1977). This emphasis in Peruvian historiography supports the point made by the statistical review presented above, namely, that economic instability rather than low and steady growth or stagnation requires examination.

To summarize, the proximate determinants of Peru's growth record may be found in the domestic saving rate and in the foreign capital inflows that make it possible for investment rates to exceed saving rates. Foreign capital inflows have been erratic, however, because their two principal destinations, government and exports, have been unstable. Although the instability of the government is evident (from time to time, it has gone broke), the instability of exports is not as apparent.

These conclusions lead to a number of empirical questions. What has the domestic saving rate been? How has it evolved over time? How does it compare with that of other countries? To what extent have foreign capital inflows made it possible for investment rates to exceed saving rates? Why has the export experience of Peru been so unstable? Why has the staple theory attracted so little interest?

SAVING, INVESTMENT, AND EXPORTS

SAVING AND INVESTMENT

Whether they involve international comparisons or long-run trends within Peru alone, statistics on saving and investment are a test of both patience and sanity. For reasons of revision, definition, or just confusion, all sources seem to be at odds with each other. Thus, here is a survey of relevant statistics of the apparently solid reality of international comparisons as published by the World Bank.

The World Bank statistics presented in Table 4 provide a broad international perspective for the Peruvian figures on saving and investment. The countries chosen for comparison have been selected for their intrinsic interest. They are also the same countries that will prove appropriate for the international comparison of tax burdens presented below.[9]

Table 4.
Gross Saving and Investment as a Percent of GDP

	Investment/GDP				Saving/GDP			
	1965	1970	1985	1991	1965	1970	1985	1991
Africa								
Malawi	14	26	16	20	-	11	11	9
Kenya	14	24	19	21	15	24	16	19
Asia								
India	18	17	25	20	14	16	21	19
Pakistan	21	16	17	19	13	9	5	12
Korea	15	25	30	39	7	15	31	36
Singapore	22	39	43	37	10	18	42	47
Europe								
Turkey	15	20	20	20	13	17	16	17
Spain	25	27	19	25	21	26	22	22
U.K.	20	20	17	16	19	21	18	15
France	25	27	19	21	26	27	19	21
Sweden	27	25	19	17	26	24	21	19
Latin America								
Argentina	19	22	9	12	23	22	16	15
Brazil	25	21	16	20	27	20	22	30
Chile	15	16	14	18	16	17	16	24
Colombia	16	20	18	15	17	18	17	23
Mexico	22	21	21	23	21	19	26	20
Peru	34	16	20	16	27	17	25	13
Venezuela	24	33	15	19	34	37	24	23

Sources: World Bank, *World Development Report* (1987), Table 5; World Bank, *World Development Report* (1993), Table 9.

For both saving and investment rates, most countries examined in the table post rates of around 20 percent. Only a number of the poorest countries, such as Pakistan and Malawi, record saving rates that are closer to 10 than to 20 percent. At the other extreme, the high-growth, super-exporter countries of East Asia prove to be as extraordinary in their saving and investment rates as in their better-known export and GDP growth rates. These exporters aside, however, the similarity of saving and investment rates among the major regions of the world is noteworthy.

This similarity can be appreciated more easily in Table 5, which aggregates the country figures presented in Table 4 into simple continental averages. The commonality of the 20 percent estimate seems particularly marked on the side of investment for all regions except Asia, where the rate is still higher. The greater dispersion of rates on the side of domestic saving implies a similar dispersion of experience with foreign saving, that is, net capital inflow. The only large positive numbers for net capital inflow, those recorded recently in Africa and earlier in Asia, must be attributed to foreign aid and foreign borrowing rather than to direct foreign investment. As for Latin America, the largest absolute numbers are the recent negative figures that mark the baleful effect of the debt crisis.

These figures also seem to imply that nearly all the countries of the world have experienced the progression envisaged by Lewis — the transition from being 5 percent to 15 percent savers. However, Lewis was referring to net saving. His framework incorporated a 5 percent growth rate powered by a 15 percent net saving rate and a capital output ratio of three. The numbers in Tables 4 and 5 reflect gross figures, however. To establish comparability, depreciation must be estimated and subtracted. Depreciation estimates, inevitably among the weakest elements in the framework of national accounting, are often expressed as a percentage of GDP. A reasonable figure would be 8 percent.[10] Thus, a 20 percent gross investment rate would imply a 12 percent net rate and a 4 percent growth rate. This is below Lewis' target; except for East Asia, the world has not done very well in the 1980s.

In order to take a closer look at Peru's record of saving and investment, we must turn from international comparisons to national sources,[11] which permit the examination of figures for a broader time span than the four years that are shown in Tables 4 and 5. In fact, beginning with 1950, annual figures are available for a forty-year span. Unfortunately, however, several official figures exist for both saving and investment in any given year. This situation results from discrepancies between the estimates generated by the Banco Central de Reserva del Perú (BCR) and those of the Instituto Nacional de Estadística e Informática (INEI) as well as between current price and constant price series and between old series and revised series.

Table 5.
Gross Domestic Investment, Gross Domestic Saving,
and Net Foreign Saving as a Percent of GDP

	1965	1970	1985	1991
Gross Domestic Investment				
Africa	14	25	18	21
Asia	19	24	29	29
Europe	22	24	19	20
Latin America	22	23	16	18
Gross Domestic Saving				
Africa	15	18	14	14
Asia	11	15	25	29
Europe	21	23	19	19
Latin America	24	21	21	21
Net Foreign Investment				
Africa	-1	7	4	7
Asia	8	9	4	0
Europe	1	1	0	1
Latin America	-2	2	-5	-3

Source: Table 4.

These major discrepancies are illustrated in Tables 6 and 7. The more solid estimates are those representing investment presented in Table 6, where, in current prices alone, five series are listed. The BCR had official responsibility for producing national accounts up to 1974, after which time the INEI assumed the responsibility. Therefore, Columns 1 and 5 represent the official series of these two institutions. After 1974, the BCR continued to produce revisions to the official INEI figures (Columns 2 and 4), while the INEI also generated historical series that revised previous BCR figures (Columns 3 and 5, prior to 1974). From 1986-1987, moreover, the INEI produced a revised investment series that was stunningly different from previous figures. BCR revisions to official INEI figures have never represented drastic changes, so when the INEI changed the basic series, the BCR figures changed as well. (Compare the BCR figures in Columns 4 and 2.)

Table 6.
Peru: Gross Investment as Percent of GDP
(Current Prices)

	Older Series			Revised Series		
Column	1	2	3	4	5	6
	BCR	BCR	INEI	BCR	INEI	World Bank
1950-54	22.3		24.5		20.5	
1955-59	24.2		26.4		25.5	
1960-62	22.2		25.0		24.0	
1963-67	19.5		21.4		21.0	
1968-70	13.4		14.7		15.8	
1971-74	16.0		16.2		19.8	
1975-79		16.3	15.9		21.4	
1980-82		20.8		32.2	30.0	
1983-87		15.9		21.2	22.5	
1988-89				21.7	23.4	
1990-92				16.6		
1965	19		21		20	34
1970	13		15		16	16
1985		14		18	22	20
1991				17		16
Investment Rates in Constant Prices of 1970 or 1979						
1965			19		22	
1970			13		18	
1985		12		16	16	
1991				24		

Sources:
1 = BCR, *Cuentas nacionales del Perú*, 1950-1965, 26, 28; 1960-1969, 18, 20; 1960-1974, 20, 22.
2 = BCR, *Memoria 1983*, 109, 119; *Memoria 1987*, 131.
3 = INE, *Cuentas nacionales del Perú*, 1950-1982, 41, 51.
4 = BCR, *Memoria 1992*, 155.
5 = INEI, *Compendio estadístico 1991-1992*, Vol. 2, 34-37.
6 = Table 4.

Table 7.
Peru: Gross Domestic Saving
As Percent of GDP (Current Prices)

	Older Series			Revised Series		
Column	**1**	**2**	**3**	**4**	**5**	**6**
	BCR	**BCR**	**INEI**	**BCR**	**INEI**	**World Bank**
1950-54	20.7					
1955-59	18.5					
1960-62	22.0					
1963-67	16.8					
1968-70	14.5					
1971-74	13.8		14.3			
1975-79		12.3	11.6			
1980-82		15.1		27.5	23.9	
1983-87		12.6		18.9	19.7	
1988-89				19.5		
1990-92				13.4		
1965	16					27
1970	16					17
1985		15		20	22	25
1991				13		13

Sources:
1 = BCR, *Cuentas nacionales del Perú*, 1950-1965, 26, 28; 1960-1969, 18, 20; 1960-1974, 20-22.
2 = BCR, *Memoria 1984*, 127; *Memoria 1987*, 141.
3 = INE, *Cuentas nacionales del Perú, 1950-1982*, 41, 51. Also, similar data from edition of 1950-1979.
4 = BCR, *Memoria 1989*, 160; *Memoria 1992*, 157.
5 = INEI, *Compendio estadístico 1991-92*, Vol. 2, 34-37.
6 = Table 4.

In Table 6, it can be observed that the revised series resulted in an increase in Peru's gross investment rate of approximately seven percentage points of GDP over the period from 1975 to 1987. This drastic revision naturally tended to discredit the earlier series. However, the revised series also creates suspicions, for reasons that will be explained below. In addition, neither the old nor the new series matches well with the World Bank figures shown in Table 4 and repeated in the last columns of Tables 6 and 7. In particular, support for the World Bank's 1965 investment rate of 34 percent is nowhere to be found in the Peruvian data. Various constant price figures at the bottom of Table 6 also fail to sustain the World Bank figures. These various discrepancies are also repeated on the saving side in Table 7. The figures on saving differ only in that the INEI has not produced retrospective series, largely because its compilation methodology does not lend itself to meaningful disaggregation of saving.

These various grumbles notwithstanding, a few useful conclusions can be made from these tables. The years are grouped so as to highlight the moments of change in saving and investment behavior. Key changes appear in nearly all the series.[12] Both saving and investment rates were high in the 1950s and remained quite high through most of the 1960s. A sharp turning point occurred between 1967 and 1968, however, as both saving and investment rates became significantly lower in 1968 and remained low in subsequent years. This was, of course, a period of fiscal crisis followed first by the coup of October 1968 and then by the uncertain investment environment associated with the Velasco government. Investment picked up in the mid-1970s, helped mightily by mining opportunities in Cuajone, and then slumped badly during the depression of the late 1970s. It accelerated again with the boom in copper prices circa 1980, and then turned down in the later 1980s. Saving followed a similar path.

These cycles are fairly clear. What is much less certain is the long-run trend. This uncertainty is highlighted in Table 8, which consolidates Tables 6 and 7 so that long-run trends can be appreciated more clearly. Two saving series and three investment series are intended to draw attention to the magnitude of change introduced by the INEI's revisions of 1986-1987. The only brief period preserved from previous tables is that of the copper boom from 1980 to 1982, in that it was so sharply anomalous. Aside from that blip, there are four periods shown, each covering approximately a decade.

A number of general trends can be identified based on the data presented in these tables. According to the old, prerevision figures, Peruvian saving rates have been in decline over the past forty years. The picture is not quite as clear on the side of investment, however, largely because the old series was not continued into the 1980s. Nonetheless, investment rates also seem to have declined in the 1950s, 1960s, and 1970s. The new, revised series depicts a very different picture. It posts nothing on the side of saving inasmuch as no long-run series exists. But on the side of investment — the more reliable estimate, it should be remembered — no decline occurred. A slight dip is registered in the 1970s, but this decline is followed by a recovery in the 1980s to levels similar to those of the 1950s and 1960s.

Is this possible? Let us consider the implications. At the bottom of Table 8, the INEI investment series is reaggregated into the time periods used by Maddison. Nevertheless, instead of using Maddison's per capita growth figures (as in Table 3), the corresponding total growth rate is shown for each period. A gross investment rate and a GDP growth rate would imply an incremental capital-output ratio (ICOR), given a knowledge of the depreciation rate. Two reasonable assumptions regarding depreciation are shown to be 6 and 8 percent of GDP. The resulting trend in ICORs is startling. Providing that the INEI investment rate figures are dependable, it must be concluded that Peru's ICOR has gone haywire in the last fifteen years, jumping from under three to over six. Hence, either the INEI investment figures are seriously flawed, or Peru has become a profligate waster of capital.

Table 8 also provides a perspective on the relative importance of foreign capital in national growth. Gross investment is financed by and equal to gross domestic saving plus net foreign saving, that is, the deficit on current account. The foreign contribution is calculated simply by subtracting domestic saving from investment. The conclusion is well known: foreign saving (often called foreign investment) is significant, but not nearly as significant as domestic saving.

Foreign investors should be given a little more credit for their contributions, however. First, foreign businesses often expand by reinvesting profits, thereby contributing to domestic saving. Second, their contribution has been substantial at certain times. The 3.7 percent of GDP that they contributed throughout the 1950s, according to Table 8, might have represented an addition of one percentage point not just to total GDP growth but to per capita GDP growth as well. The impact has been even greater over shorter periods. Net foreign saving averaged 6.5 percent of GDP from 1955 to 1958 and 7.6 percent from 1974 to 1977. These figures reflect the massive investments in the mines of Toquepala and Cuajone.

In summary, the saving and investment figures that have been available since 1950 reveal both positive and negative features. The good news is that Peru's gross investment rate generally exceeded 20 percent (at least in the earlier years), whereas its gross domestic saving rate approximated 20 percent. Net foreign saving made a smaller but nevertheless meaningful contribution. These saving and investment rates, like the resulting growth rate, were reasonably high by international standards. On the negative side, these rates seem to have declined over the past forty years although the perception of decline is unfortunately muddied by problems concerning the quality of investment data. This decline could have been caused by institutional factors such as the increasing bureaucratization of the economy in the 1970s and 1980s (Fitzgerald 1976). It could also be the type of reaction to short-run macroeconomic crisis that is the common coin of economic theories of saving and investment. In Peru's case, however, the short run has been dragging into the long run as crisis has followed crisis.

Table 8.
Peru: Long-Term Trends in Gross Domestic Saving, Gross Investment, Net Foreign Saving as a Percent of GDP
(Current Prices)

	Gross Investment			Gross Dom. Saving		NFS
	Old (BCR)	New (INEI)	New (BCR)	Old (BCR)	New (BCR)	Old (BCR)
1950-59	23.3	23.0		19.6		3.7
1960-67	20.5	22.1		18.8		1.7
1968-79	15.5	19.5		13.4		2.1
1980-82	20.8	30.0	32.2	15.1	27.5	5.7
1983-92		22.8[b]	19.9	12.7[a]	17.4	

	dGDP		ICOR, with Depreciation of	
		GDP	8%	6%
1950-65	22.8	5.8	2.6	2.9
1965-73	18.0	4.3	2.3	2.8
1973-87	23.7	2.7	5.8	6.6

a = 1983-87
b = 1983-89
Source: Tables 6 and 7.

EXPORTS

The export sector has been more unstable than the economy overall. Periods of absolute decline have been sharper and more frequent. This empirical result is illustrated in Table 9, which shows periods of decline for both GDP and export earnings during the period in which independent series for both variables are available, that is, since 1950. Perhaps the most surprising feature of the table is the stability depicted by the GDP series, at least until the onset of the 1980s. The table not only demonstrates when real GDP declined, but it also highlights all instances when it grew by less than 1 percent from one year to the next. It can be observed that the recessions experienced by Peru in the 1950s, 1960s, and 1970s made hardly a dent in the steady increase in GDP.[13] In the 1980s, however, Peru was battered not once but twice. In contrast, substantial year-to-year declines in export earnings are common to all decades, the sharpest and longest downturn ranging from the early to the mid-1980s.[14]

Table 9.
Peru: Declines in GDP and Export Earnings
1950-1992

Years of GDP Growth less than 1%		Declines in Export Earnings (Millions of U.S. $)			
1957-1958	-0.6%		**High**	**Low**	**Decline**
1967-1968	0.4%	1951-53	259	228	-12%
1976-1977	0.4%	1957-58	332	292	-12%
1977-1978	0.3%	1966-67	789	742	-6%
1981-1982	0.2%	1970-71	1,034	889	-14%
1982-1983	-12.6%	1974-75	1,503	1,330	-12%
1987-1988	-8.3%	1980-86	3,916	2,531	-35%
1988-1989	-11.7%				
1989-1990	-5.1%				
1991-1992	-2.8%				

Sources:

GDP: INEI, *Compendio estadístico 1991-1992*, Vol. 2, 34-37. Figures for 1991-1992 are from BCR, *Memoria* 1992, 156.

Exports: Richard Webb, et al., *Perú en números 1990, 827.*

Export data allow for a much broader perspective than was possible with GDP data. Annual estimates go back to 1830.[15] Thus, with the help of Table 10, export growth and instability can be scrutinized over this vastly longer period. In an attempt to make trends more visible, the table does not offer annual data; instead, it presents ten-year averages up to 1880 and five-year averages after that date. Long-term averages tend to obscure fluctuations; nonetheless, some of the adversities suffered by the export sector were so profound and enduring that they are clearly evident even in multi-year averages. The War of the Pacific had a clearly devastating effect, for example; the reduction in export quantum is fully 65 percent even when measured by ten-year averages.[16] The severity of the Great Depression of the 1930s is disguised more effectively, even in five-year averages, due to the fact that recovery was fairly rapid. Thus, for Peruvian exporters, the Great Depression was a three-year crisis, not the decade-long ordeal familiar to North American memories. Nevertheless, it was severe while it lasted; the 1932 export quantum reached only 66 percent of the peak value of 1929, while dollar earnings totaled little more than half what they had been just three years earlier. Other hard times also stand out in the table. Exports slumped during

World War II, which apparently damaged the Peruvian economy much more than World War I had. Exports also languished in the late 1940s and the 1970s, during periods when policy did not particularly favor exporting.

Nevertheless, only a limited amount of cyclical behavior can be established from this table. The crucial message conveyed by these numbers is quite different. Peruvian exports, in the aggregate, have not been intrinsically unstable. The principal fluctuations that they have suffered have not resulted from market instability of particular commodities, but from historical events that affected all the countries in the hemisphere — two wars and a worldwide depression. The table undoubtedly points to some instability from these external sources, but it also reveals a great deal of growth. The most compelling evidence in the table is that of 160 years of growth, which caused the export quantum to expand by a factor of 200.

This long-term vision is expressed more clearly in Table 11, which is a consolidation of Table 10. The three great setbacks — the War of the Pacific, the Great Depression, and World War II — resulted in periods of negative export growth. The other periods — the Guano Age, the República Aristocrática, and the mining boom of the 1950s — evidenced strong annual export growth, which lasted much longer than the periods of decline. Export growth has also been appreciable in the period since World War II, but most of that growth occurred in the initial decade of the period, culminating with the opening of Toquepala. In the last three decades, export growth has been mediocre; it has been well below the 3.7 percent figure that is the long-run average for Peru's entire republican history. This is yet another aspect of the unsatisfactory performance of the Peruvian economy in recent decades.

Regardless of recent disappointments, the growth record of Peru's export sector over the longer term has been strong and reasonably well sustained. It is highly correlated with domestic economic growth, and causation undoubtedly goes in both directions. Nevertheless, it seems reasonable to assume that the stronger chain of causation links exports to GDP. This is the message of various theories: Hirschmanian linkages, the Keynesian foreign trade multiplier, and also the staple theory. In fact, the staple theory fits Peruvian economic history fairly well — an expansion of export staples has induced a parallel expansion of the national economy.

Despite its applicability, the staple theory has not captured adherents because it is generally viewed as a celebration of success. Clearly, few Peruvians think of the republic's economic history as a success story. Too much poverty and unaddressed human need still exist to give much credibility to a theory that tends to sound self-congratulatory. While it may be true that Peru's exports have grown over the long term and that the economy has expanded as a result, the growth has not been sufficient to enable the country to escape from underdevelopment.

Table 10.
Peru: Export Quantum Index and Growth Rate, 1830-1989
(1900 = 100)

Years	Export Quantum	Average Annual Growth from Last Period	Years	Export Quantum	Average Annual Growth from Last Period
1830-39	16		1915-19	289	5.7%
1840-49	31	6.9%	1920-24	346	3.6%
1850-59	64	7.6%	1925-29	568	9.7%
1860-69	84	2.7%	1930-34	541	-1.0%
1870-79	121	3.8%	1935-39	699	5.2%
1880-89	43	-18.9%	1940-44	520	-5.8%
			1945-49	570	1.9%
			1950-54	736	5.2%
1880-84	36		1955-59	1,111	8.6%
1885-89	49	6.0%	1960-64	2,278	15.4%
1890-94	54	1.9%	1965-69	2,746	3.8%
1895-99	76	7.3%	1970-74	2,597	-1.1%
1900-04	110	7.7%	1975-79	2,674	0.6%
1905-09	158	7.4%	1980-84	3,258	4.0%
1910-14	215	6.7%	1985-89 .	3,565	1.8%

Sources: For 1830-1960, Hunt (1973), Tables 9 and 24; for 1960-1989, Webb et al., *Perú en números 1990, 832-33, 842;* for 1991, Richard Webb et al., *Perú en números 1991, 954.* Weights for the year 1900 are used for the period 1830-1900. A chained index is used for 1900-1960.

Table 11.
Peru: Long-Term Trends in Exports

Years	Export Quantum	Years	Number of Years	Average Annual Growth
1831	12	1831-1877	46	5.5%
1877	139	1877-1890	13	-7.8%
1890	48	1890-1929	39	6.8%
1929	622	1929-1949	20	-0.8%
1949	563	1949-1961	12	11.4%
1961	2,053	1961-1988	27	2.0%
1988	3,473			
		1949-1988	39	4.8%
		1831-1988	157	3.7%

Source: See Table 10.

PRECONDITIONS FOR SUSTAINED GROWTH

In his illuminating study of tropical growth during the thirty years preceding World War I, Lewis (1970) takes pains to avoid inferring economic growth (about which he has no data) from export growth (about which he does have data). During that period, much export growth consisted of bringing new resources — either land or mineral deposits — into production. Lewis argues that growth on such a foundation could not be sustained because available new resources are inevitably finite. "Development," he emphasizes, "consists not primarily of exploiting new natural resources, but rather of learning to use existing resources more productively" (29). Sustained growth therefore requires a series of transformations; to the extent that export growth might lead to sustained economic growth, he argues, it would have to be associated with key transformations (29).

Lewis suggests that four key transformations are relevant for any underdeveloped country, not just the particular regions and time period that were his subject of study. These are 1) a sustained increase in agricultural productivity, 2) development of adequate infrastructure, 3) development of a class of entrepreneurs and administrators, and 4) the creation of mechanisms of domestic finance for both taxes and savings. This list may be used as an agenda of preconditions for sustained growth. Lewis calls them "development foundations" (29).

To what extent has the Peruvian economy and society succeeded in accomplishing these key transformations over the past century? Beginning with agricultural productivity, Peru presents a dichotomy between *Costa* (the Coast) and *Sierra*. Coastal agriculture has been technologically progressive for more than a century. The beginnings of modern coastal agriculture date to the height of the Guano Age, in the 1860s and 1870s, when technological improvements in transportation first made it possible to grow cotton and sugar for North Atlantic markets. At least as far back as the early decades of this century, sugar, cotton, and rice cultivation have been undertaken on technologically modern, large-scale coastal estates. This production system has been supported by agricultural experiment stations and by the Universidad Agraria, founded in 1902, and extended in scope by a network of irrigation works. More recently, the scientific approach to agriculture has been applied to other food crops such as hybrid corn and potatoes (Himes 1972; Scott 1981 and 1985).

In contrast, relatively little scientific effort has been devoted to improving agriculture in the highlands. The effort that has been undertaken has generally proven unsuccessful. Highland agriculture is carried out today in the same manner as it has been for at least 100 years. Therefore, Peru is dichotomized into a technologically modern coastal region, much of whose output has been destined for export, and a technologically stagnant highland region, whose food crops are used exclusively for domestic consumption.

This state of affairs, for all its inequity, has been adequate to establish the first precondition for sustained growth. Lewis frequently observed that backward and stagnant technology characterizes domestic food production throughout the Third World. In his view, this forms the most solid explanation for any perceived secular decline in the terms of trade (Lewis 1958 [1954], 440-448). Nonetheless, a stagnant and impoverished food-producing sector was quite compatible with a steadily growing capitalist sector. This was the essence of his surplus labor model. It is difficult to conceive of a country that represents this model better than Peru, particularly in the first half of the twentieth century.

The second precondition posited by Lewis is infrastructure. In this category, Lewis places not only transportation, communications networks, and potable water supply but also social infrastructure, such as schools and public health facilities, and government infrastructure, such as police and courts. Over the three decades before World War I, Lewis sees major advances in infrastructure throughout most of the tropical world. Although the major reforms in education and public health were realized later, they materialized nonetheless. This development pattern is also true of Peru. Much as the recent deterioration of facilities is to be lamented, it must be recognized that infrastructure development has been substantial over the decades. Consistent with Lewis' findings regarding the tropical world, over the past century Peruvian infrastructure development has been adequate for sustained growth.

Regarding the third precondition, the formation of elites, Lewis observes that "tropical countries made more progress in creating administrative than entrepreneurial elites" in large part because major trading activity, the training ground for most entrepreneurship, was controlled by foreigners. He adds, however, "This was not much of a problem in Latin America, where the foreigners tended to be assimilated" (1970, 35). This generalization fits Peru well enough. A small but steady flow of European and Asian immigrants reached Peru throughout the first half of the twentieth century. Indeed, an even smaller flow had arrived during the 1800s. Never large numerically, this immigrant group nevertheless represented a significant source of entrepreneurship — in the form of shops, farms, factories, and trading companies — throughout the economy. Thus, even though access to entrepreneurial opportunity has been extremely unequal, Peru has not suffered from a shortage of entrepreneurs.

It may be more difficult to believe that administrative capability has also improved in Peru. Administrative efficiency has certainly deteriorated over short periods, the recent past being one of them. Nonetheless, over the longer haul, administrative capability has indeed improved in a number of areas, ranging from the quality of budget documents and statistics to the expansion of government services such as police and schools to the remote villages of the *Sierra* (Herbold 1973; Tullis 1970). In the last few years, the deterioration of the quality of government services has been associated with fiscal crises and a sharp decline in the real income of public employees (Webb 1991); in the past few decades, it has been associated with the public sector's assumption of more tasks than it can handle, particularly in the management of public enterprises. These shortcomings should not mask the fact that the Peruvian government's capability to administer basic public services has improved vastly over the past century. Whereas growth may well have been hampered by unwise government policies, it seems hard to imagine that it has been held back by Peru's inability to provide basic public services.

Of the four preconditions that he identified, Lewis is most critical of the tropical countries' performance on the fourth and last of these preconditions — financial capacity, particularly the tropical governments' capacity to collect taxes. Lewis recognizes, however, that low tax rates before World War I reflected preferences rather than capability. He claims, "Tax rates were low because governments' horizons were low. They spent so little on education, public health, agricultural extension, and other public services that most of them could manage their current budgets with as little as 4 or 5 percent of the national income in taxes" (1970, 36). Lewis perceives the modern state as being capable of making the social and infrastructure investments that represent a fulfillment of popular needs and as one that has raised tax collection from that early low level to approximately 20 percent of GDP.

The figures of Table 12, drawn from a sample of less developed countries (LDCs) located in different parts of the Third World, indicate that today even the poorest countries (excluding Nepal) have developed a taxing capability that approaches Lewis' 20 percent target. If "popular ambitions," as Lewis terms them, remain unfulfilled, the source of the trouble is more likely to be found in the way government spends its income than in the amount collected.

Table 12 also reveals that the government revenue share of gross national product (GNP) is significantly higher today than it was in the early 1970s in Asia, Africa, Europe and in some but not all countries of Latin America.[17] In Africa and Asia, the higher figures most likely reflect the extension of educational and social services to rural areas. For Europe, they represent increasing costs of health care and pensions in an aging population. What is most notable about the Latin American figures, however, is their extreme variability. Venezuela's high government revenue share is no doubt an example of the benevolence of petroleum, while Chile's even higher share relies on no such bonanza. Whereas the figures for Chile are surprisingly high and those for Colombia are similarly low, the Peruvian figures are among the most variable. These are examined more fully in Table 13.

Table 12.
Central Government Current Revenue as a Percentage of GNP

	1972	1980	1985	1989	1991
Africa					
Malawi	16.0	20.7	21.1	21.2	23.7
Kenya	18.0	22.6	21.7	22.3	21.2
Asia					
Nepal	5.2	7.8	9.2	9.5	9.5
India	10.2	11.7	14.0	15.4	14.3
Pakistan	12.3	16.4	15.7	17.8	16.9
Korea	13.4	18.3	19.0	18.1	17.4
Singapore	21.0	26.3	28.7	27.5	27.7
Europe					
Turkey	20.2	22.3	18.0	19.0	20.7
Spain	20.0	24.0	28.7	27.5	27.7
U.K.	32.6	35.2	37.9	35.6	37.4
France	33.5	39.4	42.2	40.9	40.9
Sweden	32.5	35.4	41.7	44.4	44.4
Latin America					
Bolivia	7.8	-	4.3	14.1	16.6
Ecuador	13.6	13.5	13.6	14.1	18.1
Colombia	10.6	12.1	-	12.6	13.4
Venezuela	18.5	22.2	31.0	22.8	24.3
Costa Rica	15.3	18.7	23.3	26.1	24.6
Chile	30.2	33.2	32.8	30.8	-
Peru	14.6	17.9	-	6.9	8.3

Source: World Bank, *World Development Report* (1987), (1991), (1993), Appendix, Table 12.

The longer time series for Peruvian data in Table 13 indicates that the government revenue share of GNP increased significantly from the 1940s to the 1970s and then stabilized at about 15 percent for some fifteen to twenty years. It then plummeted in the late 1980s as tax collections were decimated by hyperinflation. Compared to the standards established by other Third World countries, therefore, the Peruvian public sector has always been of modest proportions. It has never reached Lewis' 20 percent target. Nevertheless, 15 percent of GNP did fairly well in terms of providing a national system of education, public health, and roads. Currently, Peru, like Bolivia, finds itself struggling to get back to that level in the wake of hyperinflation.[18] With regard to the ability to collect taxes, therefore, not only Peru but nearly all Third World countries have for several decades been able to satisfy Lewis' precondition stipulating that they have the taxing capability to satisfy "popular ambitions" for public social and infrastructure investment.

With regard to the ability to mobilize savings, recent research has documented the deliberate process whereby a domestic banking system was developed and knitted together by the instruments of central banking (Quiroz 1989 and 1993; Drake 1989). Of course, financial intermediaries can still occasionally run amok (as exemplified by the recent convulsions regarding the Centro Latinoamericano de Asesoría Empresarial, CLAE). Nonetheless, Peru has certainly developed a sufficient financial system.

Thus, over the course of the past 150 years but particularly in the period from 1895 to 1960, Peru acquired all the preconditions required for sustained economic growth, according to Lewis' agenda. The country developed a technologically progressive agricultural sector (in the coastal region); adequate physical, social, and political infrastructure; an entrepreneurial elite; an adequate bureaucracy and financial system, and the capacity to collect approximately 15 percent of national income as taxes. According to Lewis's agenda, Peru should have initiated sustained economic growth during the second half of the twentieth century.

MISSING PRECONDITIONS

Needless to say, sustained economic growth did not materialize. The Peruvian economy, like Peruvian society, has faltered to the point of near collapse in recent decades. The promise of steadily rising incomes has been replaced by the bitter experience of three lost decades, per capita incomes being no higher in 1993 than they were in 1963. It is obvious that other factors, apparently overlooked by Lewis, must have managed to derail the Peruvian economy in the recent past.

The first possible deterrent factor is the terms of trade. This has been investigated on a number of occasions, ever since the 1950s when it was identified by R. Prebisch and other structuralists as the principal factor

Table 13.
Peru: Central Government Revenues as a Percentage of GNP

1942-1945	11.2
1945-1950	11.6
1950-1955	12.7
1955-1960	13.3
1960-1965	16.0
1970-1974	15.4
1980	17.1
1981	17.5
1982	14.2
1983	16.2
1984	13.1
1985	14.1
1986	12.2
1987	9.0
1988	8.2
1989	6.5
1990	7.7
1991	8.2

Sources: Figures for 1942-1965 are from Hunt (1971), 402. Figures for 1970-1991 are from the Inter-American Development Bank, *Economic and Social Progress in Latin America*, various issues.

explaining Latin America's relative backwardness.[19] In the forty years that have elapsed since those early assertions, however, new research and new experiences have made terms of trade effects seem relatively unimportant. The record shows that some countries have sustained high growth despite adverse terms of trade (Korea, for instance), while others, despite favorable shocks, have stagnated in the grip of the Dutch Disease.

The second possibility involves other external factors — imperialism in general and multinational corporations (MNCs) in particular — which have been interpreted by various analysts as the keys to the retardation of Latin American growth. In its boldest form, this view posits that growth under capitalism has been impossible for underdeveloped countries due to the oppressive influence of imperialism (see, for example, Frank 1967). However, with the demise of communism and the rise of peripheral capitalism in East Asia, this perspective has not fared well over time. A subtler view that perceives external influences, MNCs included, as shaping the nature of growth policy and economic structure has received more support. This modern literature on multinationals is not oriented toward explaining stagnation, however. With equal facility, it can explain high growth.[20]

The third possible deterrent, one often favored by economists but disdained by political scientists, is personal error. A recent, oft-cited example is the claim that "García ruined Peru." Although individuals do often have the power to sway the course of history for better or worse, these actors are shaped by social forces that influence their decisions. These forces are much more amenable to social analysis. The individual might be thought of as the residual in a regression equation where the dependent variable is the economic outcome and the independent variables are various social and economic forces. The goal is to estimate the equation and leave the residuals aside.

The fourth possible deterrent is the most immediate and powerful social force that moves these leaders to action: ideology. People do what they do because of their world views. More specifically, according to this thesis, García did what he did because he held the belief that state intervention and partial delinking from the world economy would help create a just and modern society, whereas reliance on market mechanisms would perpetuate injustice and underdevelopment. This widely held ideology has in fact persuaded various leaders in Peru and elsewhere in Latin America to lead their countries into economic dead-ends. Difficulties arise in postulating mistaken ideology as the key explanation for Peru's stagnation of recent decades, however. First, ideology is said to be a significant determinant of economic policy only if the state is autonomous (Haggard 1990). The ideas that drive the leaders of a strong and independent state are influential, but the ideas held by the leaders of a weak state fail to make an impact because these actors lack the autonomy to act on those ideas. The Peruvian state has in fact been chronically weak; thus, the scope for acting on ideology has been limited. A second and related difficulty, one which would be suggested by the proponents of economic determinism, holds that ideology is not an independent variable, but that it is instead an intervening variable that reflects underlying economic interests.[21]

In summary, none of these four potential obstacles to growth seems an adequate explanation for Peru's stagnation in recent decades. There is, however, one final deterrent factor that provides a more convincing explanation. This factor goes by various names — inequality, social conflict, and dependence — all of which refer to aspects of the same phenomenon. To give emphasis to the economic problem of long-run growth, this same factor is described as the absence of a consistent development model. Note that the term "model" is employed here in the sense of political economy, not of formal economics, in that it includes political as well as economic elements. That is, on the economic plane, a consistent development model is a set of economic policies that facilitate an adequate level of savings, accumulation, and growth while avoiding bottlenecks (such as foreign exchange or fiscal revenue) that would bring the growth process to a halt. On the political plane, a consistent development model produces a distribution of rewards (both pecuniary and nonpecuniary), generating sufficient political support for the policy set so that the whole process may be continued. The essence of the consistency of the model stems from the fact that it can be replicated time and time again. At the economic level, the system is neither paralyzed by foreign exchange shortage nor consumed by inflation. At the political level, the policy set is overthrown neither by dissidents who capture the government nor by incumbents who change directions in order to accommodate or preempt dissidents.

When economists deal with concepts as broad as development "models" or "strategies," they have most often drawn contrasts between import substitution and export promotion — "IS" and "EP" in Jagdish Bhagwati's notation (1988). These contrasts have generally been made only at the level of economic consistency, and they entail well-known conclusions, one of which holds that EP is more consistent than IS. However, since economists have preferred to make recommendations to a political system rather than analyze one, questions of political viability have generally been left out of consideration.

For purposes of sustained economic growth, a model gives the assurance of policy continuity because major policy reversals are ruled out by definition. Thus, a consistent model makes rational investment planning possible by reducing the likelihood of major bottlenecks or severe changes in relative prices. It encourages investment by lowering the risk premium. On the political plane, a consistent development model requires either that political competition not challenge the basic elements of economic policy or that political competition be ruled out. In other words, political life must be characterized by dominance — of a dominant state, a dominant class, or a dominant coalition. Such dominance need not last forever; twenty to thirty years is enough to work wonders in terms of the acceleration of growth.

CONSISTENT DEVELOPMENT MODELS

Let us briefly review the nature of consistent development models with associated political dominance in East Asia, Latin America, and Peru.

EAST ASIA

A whole generation of scholars has scrutinized the high-growth countries of East Asia in an attempt to understand their extraordinary economic success of recent decades. Not surprisingly, economists have focused on policy consistency at the economic level, finding a case for the superiority of EP over IS. Since East Asian countries have been atypical in their high saving rates as well as in their rates of export growth, policies to lower consumption and foment saving have also been given some attention. Outstanding performance in education — particularly in the development of industrial skills — has also been given its due in the literature (Amsden 1989).

Aside from these economic accomplishments, at the political level scholars have noted the presence of strong states in all economically successful East Asian countries (Vogel 1991; Haggard 1990; Haggard and Kaufman 1992). In explaining how these states — Japan, Korea, Taiwan, Singapore, and to a lesser extent Hong Kong — have become so powerful, scholars have focused on three principal factors: the absence of powerful class interests, administrative efficiency, and a quality that may be called social discipline.

From the perspective of Latin America, the weakness of labor in East Asia has often been noted. What has been seen less clearly is the weakness of business groups and of landlords in all the so-called Four Tigers — Korea, Taiwan, Hong Kong, and Singapore. In these four cases, strong states developed autonomously in power vacuums left by the departure of colonial administrations. Japanese political life, in contrast, has been dominated by a powerful domestic political coalition, so state strength has come not from autonomy, but from a firm alliance with that coalition.

Given the opportunity to exercise power, East Asian states have further extended their power by efficient performance. Their policy packages have been internally consistent, and when elements of the package have required adjustment in the face of changing external conditions such as the oil price shocks, the adjustments have been undertaken expeditiously. These policy packages have been implemented by a bureaucracy widely perceived as dedicated, competent, and honest.

These bureaucratic virtues are held to be the product of both long tradition and recent experience. The long tradition, described as neo-Confucianism, attributes special importance to a bureaucracy run by a dedicated and meritocratic elite (Vogel 1991). The recent experience relates particularly to Taiwan, where the Kuomintang, realizing that it had lost the mainland in part because its reputation had been so tarnished by corruption, resolved that its island bureaucracy would be honest. To achieve this end, the transplanted Taiwanese government emphasized transparency of decisionmaking, with its relations with business people kept at arm's length and strict conflict of interest rules effectively enforced (Vogel 1991).

The virtue of social discipline involves acquiescence to authoritarian measures dictated by government as well as to demands by managers for long hours of work. Of course, acquiescence is not total, as evidenced by periodic student riots in Korea. Nevertheless, East Asian societies are generally viewed as ordered and disciplined compared to most other social systems.

In order to promote growth, these strong states have established credible policy continuity. In this manner, they have reduced risk for investors and therefore decreased the risk premium that investment would have otherwise required. Naturally, this strategy has had the effect of raising investment demand for any given interest rate. However, the East Asian governments have done much more than this; they have also deliberately distorted prices so as to raise returns. Their objective, successfully pursued, has been to get prices wrong (Amsden 1989). Interestingly enough, the policy instruments that have been used to accomplish this goal have a familiar ring — tariffs, import restrictions, credit subsidies, tax preferences, input subsidies provided by public enterprises, and multiple exchange rates (Bradford 1986). Indeed, these are the same instruments of import substitution that have been so widely used and, more recently, so widely discredited throughout Latin America.

Why should these same policies have had such different results in East Asia? The answer surely lies in the terms upon which concessions have been granted to favored industries. Being relatively autonomous, East Asian states have been able to drive hard bargains with business groups. Reciprocity has been demanded; in return for measures of protection and promotion, favored industries have been required to invest and to grow. A competent, independent bureaucracy has held them to account. At the same time, government has invested mightily in social overhead capital that is complementary to private investment. Although education has been a clear beneficiary of this course of action, massive investments in transportation, communications, and financial institutions have also been undertaken.

Thus, East Asian governments have been able to raise investment in at least four ways:

1. By lowering the risk premium through the assurance of policy continuity;

2. By getting prices wrong so that output prices are raised and input prices are lowered as compared to market-based outcomes;

3. By forcing firms to invest more than they might have wanted, given the price and risk structure actually in existence; and

4. By providing complementary social overhead capital.

All of these outcomes derive directly from the strength of the state.

LATIN AMERICA

Latin America has also been witness to a number of successful development models. Over given time spans, certain Latin American countries have hit upon combinations of economic-policy-package-cum-political-systems that have produced high and sustained economic growth for a decade or more. They have accomplished this feat in various ways, but generally not the East Asian way, inasmuch as few Latin American states have enjoyed the unusual autonomy of a Taiwan or a Korea.[22] Latin American states have had to deal with more strongly articulated class interests. Labor has been stronger in Latin America than in Asia, as has business. Moreover, Latin America has had little tradition of a bureaucratic elite insulated from external pressures. And finally, in Latin America, it has not been possible to invoke an external threat as a means of shoring up social discipline, except in the case of Cuba. Unable to develop strength in the East Asian style of autonomy, Latin American states have found strength in various combinations of authoritarianism and alliance with strong domestic political coalitions. In the majority of these successful instances, the domestic coalitions have been multiclass in scope.

To establish a multiclass coalition in societies in which the inequalities of income, status, and influence are so great is not an easy task. This is, however, the genius of populism. As practiced in Latin America, populism calls for greater social justice while accepting existing class divisions. Thus, it attempts to reconcile the potentially irreconcilable and often does so with fair success by manipulating nationalist symbols, using price distortions to favor politically important groups, and invoking the idea of the state as protector. But at bottom it is government by mirrors. It is hardly surprising that such a system occasionally produces delusions about fiscal constraints, resulting in uncontrolled inflation that brings the formerly successful development model to an unsuccessful end (Dornbusch and Edwards 1991). However, these grim endings should not obscure the success of populist development models in Latin America over many decades, for populism has characterized four decades of successful growth in Mexico, three in Venezuela, and at least one in Brazil.[23]

Other successful Latin American development models challenge the limits of what might properly be described as populist. Colombia, another successful case that spans decades, has had one recent presidency described as populist (Kaufman and Stallings 1991, 29), but this country's peculiarly elitist quality makes its multiclass system sui generis (Berry 1971; Sheahan 1987; Thorp 1991; Roldán 1992). Among Latin America's many military regimes, the two noteworthy cases associated with successful development models were those of Brazil in the 1960s and 1970s and Chile in the 1970s and 1980s. While the Brazilian generals retained some of the salient features of populist economic policy (a large public enterprise sector, for example), the Augusto Pinochet regime in Chile was the antithesis of populism.

By means of authoritarianism (Chile), authoritarianism with a dose of populism (Brazil), populism with a dose of authoritarianism (Mexico), pure populism (Brazil in the 1950s, Venezuela), or an inexplicable multiclass elitism (Colombia), Latin American governments have found a variety of successful formulas for promoting growth. In each instance, a strong state has guided the process. Just as in East Asia, the state has raised the investment rate by increasing the profitability of potential investments, distorting prices so as to raise returns, and reducing the risk of policy disruption. It has also used its strength to neutralize potential opponents who might threaten the continuity of the policy regime. These potential disrupters were either successfully repressed or successfully coopted.

PERU

Peru's policy history over the past fifty years has been quite different from that of these other Latin American nations. The most noteworthy difference is that Peru's import substitution era was very brief and not very successful. It can best be described as encompassing the presidencies of Fernando Belaúnde Terry (1963-1968) and Juan Velasco Alvarado (1968-1975), during most of which time economic policy was in convulsions. Only the first four years, 1963 to 1967, could be considered fairly smooth (Kuszynski 1977; Fitzgerald 1976; Schydlowsky and Wicht 1979).

Peru did, however, have a successful development model from 1949 to the early 1960s. Export oriented and based largely on mining development, it obtained political continuity through military repression at first and through elite control of the electoral process later on. This apparently narrow base of political support was broadened by a common memory of the economic difficulties suffered by many during the interventionist APRA-Bustamante policy regime of 1945 to 1948.[24]

Even as the country enjoyed high growth during this period, many Peruvians viewed the political structure supporting this particular development model as an anachronism, the last gasp of an *ancien regime*. Their views ultimately carried the day as Peru turned to the more "progressive" world of import substitution. Since then, the country has been unable to find a development model that could remotely be called successful. The import substitution regime of Belaúnde was ultimately crippled by political paralysis and unresolved sectoral imbalances (Kuczynski 1977). Then under Velasco came the elaborate articulation of a revolutionary new model, which was ultimately incapacitated by both economic and political inconsistencies that have been exhaustively examined (Lowenthal 1975; McClintock and Lowenthal 1983). Following Velasco, Peru's economy has steadily deteriorated.

In recent decades, Peru has lacked a consistent development model due, in part, to the fact that Peruvian political life has been marked by a complete lack of dominance. No social class has dominated; no political coalition has proved stable. The state itself has become so weak as to appear on the verge of collapse at times. A political consensus that might form the basis for political dominance and consistent economic policy has been ruled out by the acuteness of a social conflict that is fed by the country's intractable economic and social inequalities. Thus, seeing Peru's growth problem as the absence of a consistent development model is tantamount to seeing the roots of the problem in inequality and social conflict.

Let us examine more closely this absence of domination that has characterized Peru's recent history, be it domination by the state, by social class, or by political coalition. Beginning with the state, none of the qualities that has given such strength to the states of East Asia — administrative competence, authoritarian political structures, the absence of well-articulated interest groups — is available to shore up the Peruvian state. Administrative capability, never particularly strong, has been devastated in recent years by the collapse of real wages in the public sector (Webb 1991). Even before the collapse, only a few agencies of the government paid salary levels that made a professional career possible (e.g., the diplomatic service, the Central Bank, and the officer corps of the armed forces). For the rest of the public sector, low salaries have been associated with low status, low levels of preparation, and low morale. Higher-level public officials have been seconded from elsewhere, paid by international agencies, or obliged to run down their own assets, meaning that they stay in public service for only a limited time. A bureaucracy staffed in this way is of necessity penetrated and permeated by external influences; it is the antithesis of an autonomous state.

This fundamental weakness should not be confused with an inability to enact legislation. In fact, the executive has been very strong in the Peruvian congressional system (even before the "Fujicoup"). Since 1968, no serious episodes of gridlock have caused policy paralysis. Although Peruvian governments have generally held enough power to enact policy packages, they have lacked the power to assure policy continuity with successive governments. In various instances, they have not even had enough power to finish out their terms. No wonder recent policy history has been compared to a pendulum (Gonzales de Olarte and Samamé 1991).

The Peruvian oligarchy, moreover, has scarcely survived the expropriations of the Velasco revolution. It might be argued, in fact, that a new industrial-commercial bourgeoisie has come to occupy the political space formerly belonging to the old landowning-mine owning oligarchy. Political events over the past quarter of a century have shown that this group's ability to influence political events has been very limited, however.

As for multiclass political coalitions, there have been too many of them. In recent times, both APRA and Acción Popular are considered populist coalitions. The populist competition of sixty years ago between APRA and Luis M. Sánchez Cerro has been well documented (Stein 1980). The proliferation of populist parties has given rise to fragmented political competition instead of political dominance based on a single strong party. The reasons behind this fragmentation must be left to the political sociologists. However, fragmentation could stem partly from the acuteness of class divisions between the leaders of the different parties and partly from the peculiarly sectarian nature of APRA.

Perhaps the only successful development model in Peru's nearly two centuries of republican history has been the República Aristocrática, with its Leguiista extension and Odriista coda (Burga and Flores Galindo 1979). Before that era, the Peruvian elite was too fragmented and the Peruvian state too underdeveloped to provide the trappings of administrative competence. As a result, the state was worse than weak; it was chaotic. Subsequently, the challenge of other social groups became more strongly felt and less easily controlled.[25]

During the República Aristocrática, the policy regime was quite stable. Private enterprise was respected, as was foreign investment. Selective tariff protection was moderate. Fiscal management was characterized by fiscal responsibility. EP was in. IS was not yet a gleam in an Argentine central banker's eye. It may have been colonial economic development (Birnberg and Resnick 1975), but it worked. Peru grew.

PERU'S CURRENT PROSPECTS IN LONG-TERM PERSPECTIVE

Peru's growth prospects are in many respects very promising. The country has demonstrated the capability for saving and investing a portion of national product large enough to generate a high growth rate. It also satisfies Lewis' agenda of preconditions; that is, it has a history of productivity growth in coastal agriculture, a widely developed infrastructure (although it has also been allowed to deteriorate in the recent past), an administrative and entrepreneurial elite ready to do the job if so asked, and administrative and financial systems that can raise taxes and mobilize savings. The only long-term problem is sociopolitical. Can a viable development model be found? Viability, it will be remembered, requires internal consistency at both the economic and political levels. A viable development model will not blow up due to inflation, collapse in a foreign exchange crisis, or be overthrown by political backlash.[26]

The present Peruvian government is looking for a viable development model in neoliberalism, a model with a proven pedigree extending back to Adam Smith. Its success in any given situation, however, depends on its ability to attract investment by providing the assurance of continuity. This, in turn, requires a strong yet minimalist state, true to the principles of laissez faire (Haggard and Kaufman 1992).

Unfortunately, the Peruvian state is anything but strong. Its weakness can be seen in the deterioration of administrative effectiveness, in the fragmentation of supposedly solid institutions such as the armed forces, and in the ease with which the state has been overthrown in the recent past. The essence of neoliberalism is that economic interest groups cease to gain advantage through their influence with government and instead submit to the discipline of the market. How can so weak a state maintain the neoliberal agenda when the special interest groups start to clamor?

Perhaps a viable alternative scenario does exist for achieving a neoliberal success even in the absence of a strong state. Since 1990, the Peruvian government has embarked on a radical new policy course that would have been politically unthinkable a few years earlier. Instead of opposition, the Fujimori neoliberal agenda has found either support or tolerance from all major segments of public opinion. This is a rare window of political opportunity, a consensus built partly on desperation. Alberto Fujimori never gave a speech as dramatic as Víctor Paz Estenssoro's famous "Bolivia is Dying" speech of 1985, but perhaps he did not have to. After more than a decade of inflation, recession, economic isolation, and terrorism, enough Peruvians feared that Peru, too, was dying. Moreover, with the collapse of communism, socialism and state interventionism had suddenly and dramatically been discredited throughout the world. The neoliberal alternative suddenly changed from unacceptable to unchallenged.

From this point on, the scenario continues on a more speculative basis. The neoliberal program, launched in a moment of opportunity, must now generate political support for its continuation. This support might come from three sources. The first source is constituted by the international financial agencies of Washington, D.C. They are firmly committed to the neoliberal agenda and have unusual power over Peruvian policymaking at the present time because of the fervor of Peru's desire to return to the good graces of the international financial community. Second, if the program is successful during its honeymoon period, the beneficiaries of that success will support its continuation. Third, collective memory of past failure can serve to rally support. It will take a long time for bitter memories to be erased so that interventionist ideologies can return to their former strength. Therefore, lacking an ideologically respectable policy alternative, neoliberalism can survive for a long time even with blemishes on the record.

This scenario may be overly optimistic. It presumes a fundamental change in political behavior. Political life in all past ages has been marked by dissension, the major conflict of the past century being the division between socialism and state intervention on the one hand and capitalism and free markets on the other. On the world stage, capitalism has defeated socialism. In Peru, free markets have defeated state intervention, and now, according to the above scenario, political life can proceed in the future on the basis of consensus and cooperation.

This is the "end of history" vision advanced by Francis Fukuyama to both praise and derision (Fukuyama 1989; Talbott 1989). It is implicit in neoliberal optimism simply because neoliberalism does not address the issues most likely to be the source of future political contention, namely the social and ethnic divisions and the income inequality that have not gone away. If new life is to be breathed into "history," surely these unaddressed issues will be the revivifiers.

If it seems a bit too optimistic to consider that history has ended, then the state must be strengthened. A number of limited, but still useful, possibilities exist for achieving this through institutional changes that protect the state from external manipulation. One measure that has been enacted recently in a number of Latin American countries, Peru included, is a reform of the basic statutes of the Central Bank so as to give it greater autonomy (Bianchi 1992). Another measure, recently accomplished in Peru, is to bolster the Superintendency of Banks (Superintendencia de Bancos) and the National Tax Administration Superintendency (Superintendencia Nacional de Administración Tributaria, SUNAT) by means of changes in personnel policy. More generally, proposals to improve public sector management, perhaps to create an elite civil service corps, would strengthen the state by increasing its administrative capability. Public sector reform must be approached with modest ambitions, however, only by remembering that many similar efforts made at different times in Peruvian history met with some short-run success only to unravel with greater passage of time.

Another means by which to make the state stronger is to make it more authoritarian. However, this tempting path unfortunately contains a few booby traps. Authoritarian governments are sometimes weak, and even when they are strong, they are not always what their early backers had hoped they would be. It is always possible to wind up with a Ferdinand Marcos instead of a Lee Kwan Yew.

Finally, there is the problem of the United States, which currently has a very strong yet inconsistent policy in support of democracy. U.S. policy seems to be that dictatorships are permissible only if they are not in the Western Hemisphere and already established. For a Western Hemisphere democracy, a political policy that turns toward authoritarianism is not compatible with economic policy that seeks reinsertion in the international financial community.

The fact that this paper arrives at a rather sober conclusion should come as no surprise to Peruvians and *Peruanistas*, whose love for Peru is matched only by their conviction that for forecasting accuracy the pessimist will beat the optimist every time. Restated briefly, the conclusion is this: long-term growth requires a consistent development model. Consistency requires a strong state that will ensure continuity and therefore credibility. The Peruvian state as currently constituted is too weak to give assurance that it can maintain its policy line — neoliberalism — or any other policy line. Therefore, Peru has not yet found a viable development model that gives prospect for sustained growth.

Options for strengthening the state are quite limited, moreover. A turn toward authoritarianism would be inconsistent with reinsertion. Institutional reform is useful, but probably of limited significance. The construction of a populist (or social democratic) coalition would perhaps be very useful, but this process has hardly begun. The expectation that success will breed support is no doubt well founded, but it is not clear how enduring that support will be when the economy hits bumps in the road, as it inevitably will. The neoliberal economic program is not in immediate danger, however, inasmuch as the political opposition is utterly disorganized and has not articulated a policy alternative. Thus, Peruvian neoliberalism marches on in a policy vacuum created by the end of History. One wonders, however, about when the next chapter of History will begin.

Notes

1. More exactly, Peruvian national account estimates began in 1942, not in 1950, but subsequent methodological revisions extended back to 1950 only. Therefore, the data for 1942 to 1949 fall into the unreliable category and are more appropriately included in the earlier period of backward projection. Early estimates are in Banco Central de Reserva del Perú 1962 and revisions are in Banco Central de Reserva del Perú 1966.

2. The estimate for 1876-1977 is found in Hunt 1985. Discussion of the methodology and some tentative upward revisions of the figures are in Berry 1990. Boloña (1981, Appendix II) uses the estimate as one means of testing the accuracy of alternative estimates for the early twentieth century. Recent work has improved the quality of sources available for national income estimation. A nineteenth-century price index is developed in Gootenberg 1990, and demographic data are analyzed in Gootenberg 1991.

3. Hunt 1973, Tables 9, 24. The peak year figure of the 1870s is an average for 1874 through 1878.

4. Note that Maddison includes Japan in the Organization for Economic Cooperation and Development (OECD) countries, not in Asia.

5. If the end of this final period were extended from 1987 to the present time, the former Soviet Union and Eastern Europe would undoubtedly be seen as the region most adversely affected during the period.

6. The severity of Peru's decline would be all the greater if the terminal year were extended from 1987 to the present.

7. The first thirteen years of the century, also omitted from the table, were probably a period of economic stagnation for Colombia because of the War of the Thousand Days. It is probably correct to state that every Latin American country has sustained periods of economic setback in this century in addition to the Depression of the 1930s.

8. Alianza Popular Revolucionaria Americana (APRA).

9. Available statistics on tax collection refer to central governments only. Thus, international comparisons make sense only when restricted to countries in which local governments play a minor role in tax collection. This restriction caused countries such as the United States, Japan, and Germany to be removed from consideration. In Asia, Pakistan and India are included because of their size, while Korea and Singapore are included because of the great interest in the East Asian super-exporters. In Africa, Malawi and Kenya were two of the few countries having figures available for the earliest years. In Latin America, the seven largest countries are included in the table.

10. Note that this figure should be consistent with reasonable figures for the average length of life of capital and the average capital output ratio. The average length of life is a balance between short-lived equipment and long-lived construction. Consider average values of twenty years and fifty years. To maintain the existing capital stock in these two cases, annual replacement investment would be 5 and 2 percent of that stock, respectively. With a capital output ratio of three, depreciation as a percent of GDP would therefore be 15 and 6 percent, respectively. The 8 percent figure is within this range, but it implies a length of life closer to fifty years than to twenty or a capital output ratio less than three. In terms of actual figures used in national accounting, the U.S. figure is approximately 10 percent; the Colombian figure is 8.3 percent; and Peruvian figures have ranged between 5.3 percent and 7.6 percent since 1970 (Hunt 1990, 374; Ocampo 1989, 151; INEI 1992, 38-40).

11. The annual reports of the Inter-American Development Bank (IDB) constitute another rich statistical source, providing figures that unfortunately match neither those of the World Bank nor those of national sources. Reasons for the discrepancies are many. For example, the data have been converted to dollar equivalents, and they are in constant prices on a base year that is common to all IDB estimates but different from national constant price series. Perhaps the thorniest issue of comparability, however, has to do with the methodological problem of how to handle foreign debt operations. For example, a major study in the 1985 IDB report, covering the first half of the 1980s, showed the gross domestic savings rate of Chile to be only 1.4 percent in 1982 and nearly that low in nearby years (IDB 1985 Report, 36). Although this rate was more than ten percentage points below the lowest figures of any other major Latin American country, it does not indicate that the Chileans were profligate non-savers, but rather that they were making major debt repayments and that these payments were included in the current account. If the payments had been considered capital transactions instead, then net foreign saving (i.e., the current account deficit) would have been much lower and gross domestic saving much higher.

12. The year groupings also follow those used in the well-known study by Alfredo Thorne (1986, 99).

13. This remark requires two qualifications. First, the table refers to total, not per capita, GDP. Declines have been more frequent and more severe on a per capita basis. Second, the recession of 1976 to 1978 was really more severe than indicated by the figures because the GDP total was bolstered by production from Cuajone, which came on line just as the recession began.

14. It should be noted that the export data are not deflated but are in current dollars. If deflated by a dollar price index to produce an income terms of trade series, the declines would be somewhat more pronounced than those shown.

15. More or less similar estimates are in Bonilla 1967-1968, Hunt 1973, and Thorp and Bertram 1978.

16. That is, $(121.2 - 42.6)/121.2 = 65$ percent. Using annual figures, the loss is measured at 79 percent from 1878 (145) to 1881 (31).

17. The sample of countries is not random. It carefully omits countries having important tax-collecting functions carried out by state and local governments, for example, the United States, Japan, Germany. This is because available figures were for the central government alone. For other countries such as Brazil, the figures were too erratic to be credible.

18.   To enjoy the same level of public services, revenue will have to return to a figure three or four percentage points higher than previously because of the burdens of debt repayment.

19.   For a recent review of structuralist thinking, see Corbo 1988. An early and still masterful critique can be found in Hirschman 1961. Peruvian terms of trade are analyzed in Correa 1993.

20.   The enormous literature on dependency and multinational corporations could usefully be approached through the following: Gereffi 1983; Evans 1979; Sigmund 1980; and Caves 1982.

21.   A third difficulty is that this author's knowledge about the subject is limited, and there is very little by way of literature. The sociology of knowledge in the context of economic policymaking comprises a great void in Latin America.

22.   Augusto Pinochet's Chile and Fidel Castro's Cuba are probably the only exceptions.

23.   This catalog of populist success stories differs greatly from that of Robert Kaufman and Barbara Stallings, who ruled out successes by a subtle difference of definition. They saw populism as an alliance of workers and business against "the rural oligarchy, foreign enterprises, and *large-scale domestic industrial elites*" (Kaufman and Stallings 1991, 16) (emphasis added). To set populists against domestic industrial elites radicalizes the definition, which then finds no success stories. Commenting on their paper, Paul Drake produced an alternative definition that excluded Salvador Allende from the populist pantheon (Kaufman and Stallings had included Allende) and included some success stories (e.g., Brazil in the 1950s). However, charismatic leadership was part of Drake's definition, which thus excluded what might be called institutionalized populism, in the style of Mexico's Partido Revolucionario Internacional (PRI) or Venezuela's Acción Democrática (Drake 1991).

24.   Indeed, the Bustamante-Odría-Prado sequence seems a precursor of the better-known (and more traumatic) Allende-Pinochet-Aylwin sequence through which Chile passed two decades later.

25.   For an illuminating parallel story of a powerful oligarchy that lost political control, see Mary Jean Roldán's impressive study of Antióquia (1992).

26.   Governments may be overthrown during the life of a viable development model, but the policy package cannot be overthrown by definition.

REFERENCES

Amsden, Alice. 1989. *Asia's Next Giant*. New York: Oxford University Press.

Banco Central de Reserva del Perú (BCR). 1962. *Renta nacional del Perú 1942-1960*. Lima: BCR.

Banco Central de Reserva del Perú (BCR). 1966. *Cuentas nacionales del Perú 1950-1965*. Lima: BCR.

Banco Central de Reserva del Perú (BCR). 1976. *Cuentas nacionales del Perú 1960-1974*. Lima: BCR.

Banco Central de Reserva del Perú. N.d. *Memoria*. Lima: BCR.

Basadre, Jorge. 1969. *Historia de la República del Perú*. 6th ed. Lima: Editorial Universitaria.

Berry, Albert. 1971. "Some Implications of Elitist Rule for Economic Development in Colombia." In *Government and Economic Development*, ed. Gustav Ranis. New Haven: Yale University Press.

Berry, Albert. 1990. "International Trade, Government, and Income Distribution in Peru since 1870." *Latin American Research Review*, 2:31-59.

Bhagwati, Jagdish. 1988. "Export-Promoting Trade Strategy; Issues and Evidence." *World Bank Research Observer* (January):27-57.

Bianchi, Andrés. 1992. *Independencia del banco central: principios generales y la experiencia chilena*. Photocopied.

Birnberg, Thomas, and Stephen Resnick. 1975. *Colonial Development: An Econometric Study*. New Haven: Yale University Press.

Boloña, Carlos. 1981. "Tariff Policies in Peru, 1880-1980." Ph.D. diss., University of Oxford.

Bonilla, Heraclio. 1967-68. "La coyuntura comercial del siglo XIX en el Perú." *Revista del Museo Nacional* 35:159-187.

Bonilla, Heraclio. 1980. "El problema nacional y colonial del Perú en el contexto de la Guerra del Pacífico." In *Un siglo a la deriva*. Lima: Instituto de Estudios Peruanos.

Bourricaud, Francois, et al. 1969. *La oligarquía en el Perú*. Lima: Instituto de Estudios Peruanos.

Bradford, Colin. 1986. "East Asian 'Models': Myths and Lessons." In *Development Strategies Reconsidered*, eds. J.P. Lewis and V. Kallab. New Brunswick: Transaction Books.

Burga, Manuel, and Alberto Flores Galindo. 1979. *Apogeo y crisis de la República Aristocrática*. Lima: Ediciones "Rikchay Peru."

Caves, Richard. 1966. "'Vent for Surplus' Models of Trade and Growth." In *Trade, Growth, and the Balance of Payments*, ed. Robert Baldwin. Chicago: Rand McNally.

Caves, Richard. 1982. *Multinational Enterprise and Economic Analysis.* Cambridge: Cambridge University Press.

Corbo, Vittorio. 1988. "Problems, Development Theory, and Strategies of Latin America." In *The State of Development Economics: Progress and Perspectives,* eds. Gustav Ranis and T. Paul Schultz. Oxford: Basil Blackwell.

Correa, Percy. 1993. "Evolución de las exportaciones, importaciones, y términos de intercambio." *Ciencia Económica,* University of Lima, (January /April).

Cotler, Julio. 1978. *Clases, estado y nación en el Perú.* Lima: Instituto de Estudios Peruanos.

Díaz-Alejandro, Carlos. 1982. "Latin America in Depression, 1929-39." In *The Theory and Experience of Economic Development,* eds. Mark Gersovitz et al. London: George Allen and Unwin.

Diéguez, Héctor. 1969. "Argentina y Australia: Algunos aspectos de su desarrollo económico." *Desarollo Económico* (January/March).

Dornbusch, Rudiger, and Sebastian Edwards, eds. 1991. *Macroeconomics of Populism in Latin America.* Chicago: University of Chicago Press.

Drake, Paul. 1989. *Money Doctor in the Andes; The Kemmerer Missions 1923-1933.* Durham, N.C.: Duke University Press.

Drake, Paul. 1991. "Comment." In *The Macroeconomics of Populism in Latin America,* eds. Rudiger Dornbusch and Sebastian Edwards. Chicago: University of Chicago Press.

Evans, Peter. 1979. *Dependent Development.* Princeton, N.J.: Princeton University Press.

Ferrari, César. 1989. "Public Savings and Investment in Peru and the Dominican Republic." In *Economic and Social Progress in Latin America. 1989 Report,* Inter-American Development Bank (IDB). Washington, D.C.: Inter-American Development Bank.

Fitzgerald, E.V.K. 1976. *The State and Economic Development: Peru since 1968.* Cambridge: Cambridge University Press.

Frank, André Gunder. 1967. *Capitalism and Underdevelopment in Latin America: Historical Studies of Chile and Brazil.* New York: Monthly Review Press.

Fukuyama, Francis. 1989. "The End of History?" *The National Interest* (Summer):3-18.

Furtado, Celso. 1963 [1959]. *The Economic Growth of Brazil.* Berkeley: University of California Press.

Gereffi, Gary. 1983. *The Pharmaceutical Industry and Dependency in the Third World.* Princeton, N.J.: Princeton University Press.

Gonzales de Olarte, Efraín, and Lilian Samamé. 1991. *El péndulo peruano.* Lima: Instituto de Estudios Peruanos.

Gootenberg, Paul. 1989. *Between Silver and Guano.* Princeton: Princeton University Press.

Gootenberg, Paul. 1990. "'Carneros y Chuño': Price Levels in Nineteenth Century Peru." *Hispanic American Historical Review* (February):1-56. (Also published in *Economía,* December 1989.)

Gootenberg, Paul. 1991. "Population and Ethnicity in Early Republican Peru: Some Revisions." *Latin American Research Review* 26(2):109-157.

Haggard, Stephan. 1990. *Pathways from the Periphery.* Ithaca: Cornell University Press.

Haggard, Stephan, and Robert Kaufman. 1992. "The State in the Initiation and Consolidation of Market-Oriented Reform." In *State and Market in Development: Synergy or Rivalry?* eds. Louis Putterman and Dietrich Rueschemeyer. Boulder: Lynne Rienner.

Herbold, Carl. 1973. "Developments in the Peruvian Administrative System, 1919-1930: Modern and Traditional Qualities of Government under Authoritarian Regimes." Ph.D. diss., Yale University.

Himes, James. 1972. "The Utilization of Research for Development: Two Case Studies in Rural Modernization and Agriculture in Peru." Ph.D. diss., Woodrow Wilson School, Princeton University.

Hirschman, Albert. 1961. "Ideologies of Economic Development in Latin America." In *Latin American Issues: Essays and Comments,* ed. A. O. Hirchman. New York: Twentieth Century Fund.

Hirschman, Albert. 1977. "A Generalized Linkage Approach to Development, with Special Reference to Staples." *Economic Development and Cultural Change* 25:67-98.

Hunt, Shane. 1971. "Distribution, Growth, and Government Economic Behavior in Peru." In *Government and Economic Development,* ed. Gustav Ranis. New Haven: Yale University Press.

Hunt, Shane. 1973. "Price and Quantum Estimates of Peruvian Exports, 1830-1962." Mimeo.

Hunt, Shane. 1985. "Growth and Guano in Nineteenth Century Peru." In *Latin American Economies: Growth and the Export Sector 1880-1930,* eds. Roberto Cortes Conde and Shane Hunt. New York: Holmes and Meier.

Hunt, Shane. 1990. "Ahorro e inversión en la economía peruana." In *Cómo financiar el crecimiemto,* ed. Alejandro Toledo. Lima: Escuela Superior de Administración de Negocios (ESAN).

Instituto Nacional de Estadística (INE). 1983. *Cuentas nacionales del Perú, 1950-1982.* Lima: Instituto Nacional de Estadística.

Instituto Nacional de Estadística e Informática (INEI). 1992. *Compendio estadístico 1991-1992.* Lima: INEI.

Inter-American Development Bank. 1985. *Economic and Social Progress in Latin America.* Annual.

Kaufman, Robert, and Barbara Stallings. 1991. "The Political Economy of Latin American Populism." In *The Macroeconomics of Populism in Latin America,* eds. R. Dornbusch and S. Edwards. Chicago: University of Chicago Press.

Kravis, Irving, Alan Heston, and Robert Summers. 1982. *World Product and Income: International Comparisons of Real Gross Product.* Baltimore: The Johns Hopkins University Press for the World Bank.

Kuczynski, Pedro-Pablo. 1977. *Peruvian Democracy under Economic Stress.* Princeton: Princeton University Press.

Levin, Jonathan. 1960. *The Export Economies.* Cambridge: Harvard University Press.

Lewis, W. Arthur. 1958 [1954]. "Economic Development with Unlimited Supplies of Labor." In *The Economics of Underdevelopment,* eds. A. Agarwala and S. Singh. Bombay: Oxford University Press.

Lewis, W. Arthur. 1970. "The Export Stimulus." In *Tropical Development 1880-1913*, ed. W. Arthur Lewis. Evanston: Northwestern University Press.

Lowenthal, Abraham. ed. 1975. *The Peruvian Experiment*. Princeton: Princeton University Press.

Maddison, Angus. 1983. "A Comparison of Levels of GDP Per Capita in Developed and Developing Countries, 1700-1980." *Journal of Economic History* (March).

Maddison, Angus. 1989. *The World Economy in the Twentieth Century*. Paris: Organization for Economic Cooperation and Development (OECD).

Malpica, Carlos. 1968. *Los dueños del Perú*. 3rd ed. Lima: Ediciones Ensayos Sociales.

McClintock, Cynthia, and Abraham Lowenthal, eds. 1983. *The Peruvian Experiment Reconsidered*. Princeton: Princeton University Press.

Ocampo, José Antonio. 1989. "Savings, Investment, and Growth: Colombia." In *Economic and Social Progress in Latin America. 1989 Report*. Washington, D.C.: Inter-American Development Bank.

Quiroz, Alfonso. 1989. *Banqueros en conflicto: Estructura financiera y economía peruana, 1884-1930*. Lima: Centro de Investigación de la Universidad del Pacífico.

Quiroz, Alfonso. 1993. *Domestic and Foreign Finance in Modern Peru, 1850-1950*. London: Macmillan.

Roldán, Mary Jean. 1992. "Genesis and Evolution of La Violencia in Antióquia, Colombia (1900-1953)." Ph.D. diss., Harvard University.

Scott, Gregory. 1981. *Potato Production and Marketing in Central Peru*. Ph.D. diss., University of Wisconsin at Madison.

Scott, Gregory. 1985. *Markets, Myths, and Middlemen: A Study of Potato Marketing in Central Peru*. Lima: International Potato Center.

Schydlowsky, Daniel, and Juan Wicht. 1979. *Anatomía de un fracaso económico*. Lima: Universidad del Pacífico.

Seminario, Bruno. 1992. "Ciclos y tendencias en la economía peruana. 1950-1989." Lima: Centro de Investigación de la Universidad del Pacífico.

Sheahan, John. 1987. *Patterns of Development in Latin America*. Princeton: Princeton University Press.

Sigmund, Paul. 1980. *Multinationals in Latin America*. Madison: University of Wisconsin Press.

Stein, Steve. 1980. *Populism in Peru*. Madison: University of Wisconsin Press.

Talbott, Strobe. 1989. "The Beginning of Nonsense." *Time*, September 11.

Thorne, Alfredo. 1986. "The Determinants of Savings in a Developing Economy: The Case of Peru, 1960-1984." Ph.D. diss., University of Oxford.

Thorp, Rosemary. 1991. *Economic Management and Economic Development in Peru and Colombia*. Pittsburgh: University of Pittsburgh Press.

Thorp, Rosemary, and Geoffrey Bertram. 1978. *Peru 1890-1977: Growth and Policy in an Open Economy*. New York: Columbia University Press.

Tullis, F. Lamond. 1970. *Lord and Peasant in Peru*. Cambridge: Harvard University Press.

Vogel, Ezra. 1991. *The Four Little Dragons*. Cambridge: Harvard University Press.

Watkins, Melville. 1963. "A Staple Theory of Economic Growth." *Canadian Journal of Economics and Political Science* (May):141-158.

Webb, Richard. 1977. *Government Policy and the Distribution of Income in Peru.* Cambridge: Harvard University Press.

Webb, Richard. 1991. "Prologue." In *Peru's Path to Recovery*, eds. Carlos Paredes and Jeffrey Sachs. Washington, D.C.: The Brookings Institution.

Webb, Richard and Gabriela Fernandez Baca. 1990. *Perú en números, 1990: Anuario estadístico.* Lima: Instituto Cuánto.

World Bank. N.d. *World Development Report.* Annual.

II

A LONG-RUN PERSPECTIVE ON SHORT-RUN STABILIZATION: THE EXPERIENCE OF PERU

Rosemary Thorp

This chapter is a reflection on stabilization experiences in Peru from a long-run perspective. To this end, I review some thirty-six years of attempts at stabilization, from 1959 to the present day, to identify long-run patterns and shifts in both policies and responses. The story is complicated in the telling by the fact that evolution has occurred at three distinct levels. First, international economic structures and behaviors have evolved with time. Second, there have been shifts in the academic understanding of stabilization issues. And third, certain characteristics of Peruvian economy and society have changed, affecting the modus operandi of stabilization policies. This chapter traces these three threads through each of three periods — the 1950s through the 1970s, the 1980s, and 1990-1993. I have found that for different reasons in different periods the central components of short-term management are radically incompatible with the ingredients of longer-run recovery.[1]

TYPES OF STABILIZATION POLICIES

Before embarking upon a historical discussion, it may be helpful to describe the most prevalent types of stabilization policies and their functioning. Two basic types of stabilization policies will be considered. The first comprises the traditional orthodoxy that was prevalent from the 1950s to the 1970s and was consistently recommended by external agents such as the International Monetary Fund (IMF). The second involves Exchange-Rate-

Rosemary Thorp is a lecturer in Latin American economics at the University of Oxford. She has published widely in books and scholarly journals and is co-author of *Peru 1890-1979: Growth and Policy in an Open Economy* (The Macmillan Press, 1978) and author of *Economic Management and Economic Development in Peru and Colombia* (The Macmillan Press, 1992).

Based Stabilization (ERBS), which became increasingly popular over the periods discussed here. ERBS was extended in the 1980s to incorporate the so-called "heterodox shocks."

A preliminary issue concerns what is to be stabilized. The focus of stabilization itself has shifted over time. There are typically two components to macroeconomic disequilibrium: the balance of payments and the price level. In traditional orthodoxy, the balance of payments was usually the focus in practice. The proximate reason for stabilizing was usually the conditionality imposed by the IMF if a standby credit was to be granted. As inflation worsened over time, it came to be more important as a target in itself. We shall see that this is part of the reason for the increasing resort to ERBS.

"Orthodox" policies, therefore, were typically developed under the supervision of the IMF, which would then offer standby credit. Packages required a rigid pattern of fiscal and monetary restriction and steps to restore the free market. Devaluation was used to secure an overshooting of the exchange rate and a new parity, although there was no focus on the anchoring role of the exchange rate in orthodox stabilization.

In the case of Peru, what in retrospect seem to be relatively low rates of inflation — 10 or 12 percent — were perceived as high in the 1950s. At that time, Peru had a relatively open economic structure; thus, it was anticipated that appropriate management of the external sector would help to restrain internal price increases. However, the modus operandi of such policies in Peru (and indeed throughout Latin America) involved extensive negative feedback mechanisms, which undermined the efficiency of orthodox measures as stabilization tools and made them politically unviable. The factors affecting the strength of feedback mechanisms during stabilization are listed in Table 1 and will be referred to in the remainder of this discussion.

Point A of Table 1 lists technical internal characteristics tending to lead to feedback mechanisms which undermine stabilization measures. The first two factors reflect the history of import-substituting industrialization (ISI). By the 1960s, most large or medium-sized Latin American countries had substantial industrial sectors, which were also highly import dependent. They had used up easy substitution possibilities without having created the infrastructure and technological capacity to provide short-run supply responsiveness to exchange rate changes on either the export or import side. Thus, these characteristics create negative feedback; the typical response to devaluation tended to be cost-push inflation with low supply-side response instead of increased exports and decreased imports. The third factor, the financial structure of firms, became more significant in the 1970s, as individual firms became more heavily indebted due to the increase in lending to Latin America. This negative feedback mechanism worked as follows: given weak financial infrastructure and recession, financial costs often

Table 1.
Feedback Mechanisms During Stabilization

A. *Technical internal:*
- Degree and pattern of industrialization
- Degree of elasticity of supply
- Financial structure of firms
- Fiscal vulnerability to recession, inflation, devaluation

B. *Behavioral internal:*
- Wage pressures
- Sensitivity of inflationary expectations

C. *Structural political economy:*
- Coherence, efficiency, legitimacy of state
- Political will, instruments to enforce

D. *Behavior of external transfer*

E. *Size of initial disequilibrium*

constituted a very high proportion of firms' total direct costs. In consequence, with stabilization measures, cost-push pressures from higher interest rates had a significant impact on firms. The fourth factor, fiscal vulnerability to recession, inflation, and devaluation, depends on a) the volume of foreign trade, which falls with recession; b) the level of domestic productive activity, a decline which reduces sales tax revenue; and c) the degree of inflation-proofing in the tax system. The more sensitive the tax structure is to each of these factors, the more tax revenue would fall with stabilization, which would lead to further negative feedback.

Point B of Table 1 lists internal, dynamic political economy variables — in particular, wage pressures and other bargaining responses to rising prices plus inflationary expectations — the strengths of which are a product of past history. These responses were formed by the structural factors highlighted in A, but they also interact with the factors listed under C, namely, the structural political economy characteristics. These are summarized as the coherence, efficiency, and legitimacy of the state and the element of "political will." Taken together, these factors enable both the creation and the use of new instruments; for example, the Bolivian government had both the means and the willingness to repress labor unions.

Interacting with these political economy factors are two sets of external factors. The first involves the behavior of the external transfer. It is extremely difficult to find a case of successful orthodox stabilization which is not facilitated by a positive external transfer. Positive transfers were crucial, for instance, in Chile, Bolivia, and Indonesia. Obviously, the size of the initial disequilibrium is also important, and it affects the credibility of the program and expectations.

The second type of stabilization policy, ERBS, became more popular in the 1980s, not only in response to a growing understanding of the ineffectiveness of orthodox measures but also because of the changing nature of the problem and the context, as analyzed below. ERBS, as is obvious from the name, uses the nominal exchange rate as an anchor. The logic behind this strategy turns on the role of the exchange rate in costs but also more fundamentally on expectations. The specific variety developed in Peru in the 1980s had a second major component, namely, an attempt at a widespread price freeze similar to that attempted in the Plan Austral and the Plan Cruzado. Unfortunately, policies based on ERBS tend to encounter devastating problems of their own, the chief complication being that unless the policies are accompanied by severe orthodox measures, they bias relative prices in favor of nontradables, which is singularly counterproductive. Insofar as they also incorporate more or less radical price freezes, such policies further debilitate the financial position of state enterprises and limit the development of financial markets. Also, being by nature interventionist, they rely on a state capacity that they are sometimes undermining. The example of Peru will illuminate these points.

"ORTHODOX" STABILIZATION EXPERIENCES: 1959-1979

The various stabilization experiences of 1959 to 1979 are summarized in Tables 2, 3, and 4. The tables show the degree of disequilibrium faced at the start of the stabilization effort, the impact of the main instruments, and the principal developments in prices and output.

The first stabilization program was initiated in 1959 by Minister of Finance Pedro Beltrán with strong backing from the IMF. Beltrán implemented a severely orthodox and seemingly successful program. The key element which determined the "success" of the Beltrán program, however, was the simultaneous recovery of exports as a result of long-run reasons rather than Beltrán's policy itself. However, his policy did have subsidiary benefits. The tax reform Beltrán implemented contributed to the program's success, as did a wage constraint. However, the most important contributing factor was the recovery of exports, which halted the various vicious circles described above. Public expenditure, which was concentrated on investment, was reduced, but because of the rise in exports, the level of productive activity did not fall. This, plus the tax reform and the rise in profits tax with the entry into production of the Toquepala copper mine, resulted in an actual increase of tax revenue, and the goals of the program were accomplished with relative ease. With the recovery of the balance of payments, the main goal of the

Table 2.
Indicators of Degree of Crisis at the Start
of the Stabilization Effort

	Inflation Average Annual and Change	Balance of Payments as Percent of Export		Public Sector Deficit Percent GDP
		Current Account Balance	Basic Balance	
1958	7.95	-42.25	-8.88	n.a.
1967	9.79	-37.96	-25.13	n.a.
1976	33.51	-79.94	-32.07	8.82
1978	57.83	-8.32	14.20	5.41
1985	163.40	4.20	27.40	2.39
1990	7481.70	-19.81	-5.62	2.69

Sources: Webb, et al., *Perú en números 1991*, Tables 11.1, 20.1, 22.3, 24.2, and 24.4; Banco Central de Reserva del Perú, *Boletín* (September 1991).

Table 3.
Impact of Stabilization Instruments
(Absolute Change in Number of % Points of GDP)

	1958-60	1966-68	1975-77	1978-79	1985-89	1990-91
Liquidity contraction percent GDP	n.a.	-1.6	-4.1	-0.2	-5.3	-0.8
Public spending percent GDP	-4.2	0.0	-0.4	-2.7	-8.2	-1.2
Public investment percent GDP	-4.2	-1.3	4.1	-0.8	1.1	-0.2
Tax revenue percent GDP	1.9	5.6	-0.4	1.3	-6.3	-0.4
Public sector deficit percent GDP	-5.8	0.0	0.6	-4.5	4.3	-1.8
Real wages change over period	0.2	-0.2	-7.4	-4.5	-41.9	n.a.

Sources: Webb, et al., *Perú en números* (Lima: Cuánto S.A., 1991), Tables 11.1, 20.2, 21.2, 22.3, 22.4, 22.13, and 23.2; Banco Central de Reserva del Perú (BCR), *Boletín* (Lima: BCR, September 1992); Banco Central de Reserva del Perú (BCR), *Cuentas nacionales del Perú* (Lima: BCR, 1960-1973); Instituto Nacional de Estadística e Informática (INEI): *Compendio estadístico (1991-1992)*, (Lima: INEI, 1993).

Table 4.
Behavior of Output, Inflation, and Real Exchange Rate
(Average Annual Change)

	1958-60	1966-68	1975-77	1978-79	1985-89	1990-92
GDP	4.1	4.0	1.6	1.3	0.5	-2.2[1]
GDP per capita	1.3	1.1	-1.2	-1.3	-1.5	-3.4[2]
Industrial output	7.5	4.5	1.7	0.0	0.9	-2.6[1]
Cost of living	9.7	12.5	31.7	62.8	878.6	2653[1]
Real exchange rate – percent change over period[3]	-4.4	13.5	25.8	-3.5	-70.2	-28[1]

Sources: Webb, et al., *Perú en números*(Lima: Cuánto S.A., 1991), Tables 11.2, 11.8, 20.1; Instituto Nacional de Estadística e Informática, *Compendio estadístico (1991-1992)*, (Lima: INEI, 1993); Banco Central de Reserva del Perú (BCR), *Boletín* (Lima: BCR, September 1992); International Monetary Fund (IMF), *International Financial Statistics* (Washington D.C.: IMF); U.S. Wholesale Price Index.

1 = Until September 1992.
2 = 1990-1991.
3 = Nominal exchange rate divided by domestic inflation and multiplied by U.S. Wholesale Price Index.

Beltrán program was immediately accomplished (the rate of inflation was never the main preoccupation, and was not affected by the program).

The second stabilization episode was more complex and indeed does not qualify as a "program." During the 1960s, the state was increasingly pressed to assume an active role in development. However, it lacked a clear political mandate to do so, and the Alianza Popular Revolucionaria Americana (APRA)-dominated Congress resisted an adequate increase in taxation. Thus, the state instead increased its internal and foreign borrowing to the extent that by 1967, with exports slackening, the economic situation was nearing a crisis point. The Central Bank (Banco Central de Reserva del Perú, BCR) apparently hoped that an appeal to the IMF for credit would bring effective external pressure for tax reform, solving the political problem. However, at this time, Peru was still within its first tranche of credit, and the IMF mission came and went without playing the role Peruvians had hoped for. The ensuing measures never amounted to a full "orthodox" program. In 1967, the measures comprised devaluation and little else. In early 1968, a number of rather unorthodox measures, such as controls on imports and on local borrowing by foreign firms, were introduced. Weak attempts were made at credit restriction and the control of expenditure. Finally, in mid-1968, APRA leaders realized that in addition to provoking financial chaos by refusing to increase taxes, they might be provoking military intervention. The government was then granted emergency powers, and a major tax reform was rushed through. It was too late to prevent the coup of October 1968, however.

The military government established in the wake of the 1968 coup was initially able to avoid short-term economic pressures due to favorable terms of trade. Later, the increased availability of loans from abroad held short-run pressures at bay. However, by 1975 the degree of macro imbalance was such that the new government of General Francisco Morales Bermúdez was forced to introduce a "second stage," with repeated efforts at monetary and fiscal restraint and relative price adjustments. The subsequent return in stages to constitutional government from the middle of 1978 was associated with a renewed attempt at an orthodox program. This program was fortuitously rescued as Beltrán's had been by export revenues — in this case, the surge in copper prices in 1979.

From a long-term perspective, a number of conclusions can be drawn with respect to this twenty-year period of Peruvian economic history. First, Table 2 demonstrates that the disequilibrium grew significantly larger over the period. This progressive worsening of the disequilibrium was partly the result of underlying economic and societal trends. More consequential, however, was the fact that disequilibria were allowed to persist for increasingly long periods of time before action was taken.

Among the underlying trends that worsened the disequilibrium were a stagnation in export volume and a downslide in private sector investment, both of which developed in the course of the 1960s and were merely concealed by the events of the early 1970s. These trends, documented for the long run in Table 5, can be attributed to the collapse of the preceding model of accumulation in the 1960s.[2] This model had been based on an oligarchic political system and a relatively easy expansion of the supply of primary exports, assisted by a symbiotic relationship with foreign capital and requiring only a limited role for the state. The model therefore generated an economic elite accustomed to heavy dependence on foreign capital and a state that had limited experience in economic management. The oligarchic political system was being challenged by new political forces at the same time as the easy expansion of export supply came to an end. The new challenges in the export sector required that either the state or the private sector or both together act entrepreneurially in a way for which they were not prepared. Meanwhile, foreign capital was not willing to play its previous role given the new level of political uncertainty and indefinition.

The resulting stagnation in the volume of exports, the growing import needs of an inefficient and poorly coordinated industrial sector, and the increasing food imports were all making for a structural balance of payments problem. This problem could be concealed by terms of trade, loans, and the

Table 5.
Long-Run Trends in Investment and Export Volume, 1960-1992
(Annual Averages)

	Total exports (US$ millions)	Traditional exports[1] quantum index (1978=100)	Investment as a percent of GDP	
			Private	Public
1960-1964	550	92.0	20.4	1.4
1965-1969	787	110.8	15.4	2.0
1970-1974	1,097	101.6	15.2	2.6
1975-1979	2,009	94.5	18.7	2.1
1980-1984	3,324	106.2	21.3	3.2
1985-1989	2,869	109.5	19.1	2.6
1990-1992	3,280	n.a.	19.3[2]	1.9[2]

Sources: Webb, et al., *Perú en números* (Lima: Cuánto S.A., 1991), Tables 11.1, 11.7, 24.2, and 24.39; Banco Central de Reserva del Perú (BCR), *Boletín* (Lima: BCR, September 1992).
1 = In 1970, traditional exports were 97 percent of total exports; by 1990, this percentage was around 70 percent.
2 = 1990-1991.

belated achievement of several large export projects in the early 1970s, but only temporarily. The "underlying" fiscal gap was likewise growing. As private investment declined, the state initially attempted to fill the gap but was not able to command a serious, stable internal source of savings.

In addition, with the collapse of the old model came the demise of a political base for orthodoxy. In the 1950s, openly orthodox measures were supported by a political consolidation on the right, which facilitated their implementation to the degree that even tax reform was permitted (Dragisic 1971). By the 1960s, however, the political spectrum was far more complex, as evidenced by President Fernando Belaúnde's mix of orthodox and unorthodox measures. He appeared to lack the political base needed for a clear shift in policies either to the right or to the left. Again, the same situation was reflected in the hesitant application of measures in 1975, which allowed the crisis to fester until it eventually necessitated much more severe efforts.

Another important reason leading to the tolerance of a high level of disequilibrium was the possibility of external borrowing. It is hard to imagine that the public sector deficit would have risen as it did from 2 percent of gross domestic product (GDP) in 1969 to 10 percent by 1975 had external borrowing not been possible.

At the same time, the various types of negative feedback identified in Table 1 were becoming stronger. First, fiscal restraint was becoming more difficult. With the negative feedback following the 1976-1977 stabilization efforts, tax revenue actually fell in 1977 as a percentage of GDP. This drop was a result of the growth of the informal sector. Survival strategies forced people into informal activities, and tax evasion was aggravated. Secondly, investment was becoming more difficult to cut. Considering the example of the 1930s, fiscal orthodoxy could have been pursued by the wholesale abandonment of projects. Even in the 1950s, cuts would still have been possible. However, by the 1970s, international practices among construction firms and corporations were such that the high penalties for ending projects made it unviable to do so. Nonetheless, funding was often not available to provide the means for the completion of projects. This situation of partial payment without completion, the worst of all worlds, became more marked in the 1980s. Thirdly, defense spending had risen, fueled by foreign borrowing, and could not be cut easily, while interest payments had risen with the debt. If revenue could not be raised, serious compliance with the rules of the game required cutting public sector wages and salaries.

Operating on the external disequilibrium was becoming more difficult, moreover. This difficulty was associated with the fiscal problem inasmuch as by the mid-1970s 50 percent of imports were being transacted by the public sector. Of the remainder, some, such as food, were untouchable. The bulk of the economies had to center on industrial inputs, and of these, just three sectors — chemicals, food, and vehicles — account for the majority. Using generalized recession to reduce the import bill was inefficient and decidedly expensive in the long term.

The difficulty of achieving fiscal adjustment increasingly put the burden of adjustment onto the private sector, therefore. More emphasis had to be put on monetary restriction, as Table 3 shows. Fiscal spending actually rose during the Morales Bermúdez program, while the liquidity squeeze became tighter. This shift began to interact more and more with the underlying political economy problem described above, of course. As the burden fell more heavily on the private sector, the tendency toward an uncooperative relationship between the public and private sectors increased. Hence, it became more difficult to mount a credible, convincing program, and the economy's vulnerability to capital flight increased. These trends became much more marked in the 1980s, yet they were already observable in 1977.

We can summarize this section in terms of Table 1. Point A highlights the basic characteristics of the economic structure which are responsible for negative feedback. In our period, cost-push feedback worsened as the rigidities in the industrial sector which are a product of import substituting industrialization grew, while financial costs became more important. The various components of negative fiscal feedback became more pronounced. Point B reflects the internal political economy variables; as inflation persisted and moved to higher levels, these propagation factors became more deeply entrenched and difficult to manage. Points C and D identify the size of the disequilibrium and the sign of the external transfer as interacting with internal factors: the internal and external disequilibrium grew with time. Thus, Peru's attempts to stabilize using orthodox policies from 1957 to 1979 were increasingly ineffective. All of these developments paled, however, in contrast with the events of the 1980s.

THE 1980s: THE DECADE OF NONADJUSTMENT

The decade of the 1980s was increasingly hostile to successful stabilization in a number of ways, some of which were quite beyond the control of the Peruvian policymakers. Internationalization of the economy proceeded, with technological developments in communications (telex and fax) bringing new segments of the population into the international arena. As a result, the moving of savings internationally was no longer the custom of only the very wealthy. As these new behavior patterns became ingrained, a new sensitivity to interest rates and exchange rates developed, leading to more volatile expectations. Moreover, with Mexico's declaration of nonpayment of debt, at a stroke, the region's positive net external transfer became negative in 1982. What is more, the international growth of trade in drugs sucked Peru into its center, providing dollars but also contributing to the expansion of an informal and illegal economy. By the end of the decade, cocaine was Peru's largest export.

Growth in "dollarization" gradually took more and more of the economy out of reach of Peruvian monetary policy. Continued resort to restrictive credit policies eventually generated a parallel system beyond the reach of BCR instruments. In addition, the expansion of informality and illegality undermined the paying of taxes in a fundamental way; smuggling and evasion became the norm. As lending was withdrawn and Peruvian banks and firms became financially debilitated, the dependence of firms on bank credit and the unwillingness of banks to refinance made the impact of increases in the rate of interest on cost structures very great. Thus, vulnerability to the various types of negative feedback outlined in Table 1 increased sharply.

Given this dim scenario and the declining effectiveness of and political support for orthodox stabilization, it is not surprising that the 1980s witnessed the demise and eventual abandonment of such programs in Peru. However, the program that took its place was no answer at all, and it led to the situation depicted in Table 4, which was considerably worse than the first.

Throughout Latin America in the 1980s, the increase in dollarization and the practice of indexing many domestic prices to the dollar produced enthusiasm for ERBS despite the unfavorable effects these measures had generated in the Southern Cone in the 1970s. This enthusiasm coincided with an intellectual evolution. Academic analyses attested to the ineffectiveness of orthodox stabilization measures and developed an empirical understanding of the shifting structures. These theses inspired further intellectual effort, spearheaded by the Catholic University (Pontificia Universidade Católica, PUC) in Brazil, to expound a logical basis for a "heterodox" price-freeze program, an extreme form of ERBS.

THE POLICIES OF THE BELAÚNDE AND GARCÍA GOVERNMENTS

In fact, the Fernando Belaúnde Terry government avoided adjustment by borrowing until this was no longer possible. A brief effort was made at ERBS in early 1981, backed by an orthodox monetary and fiscal policy and also by a British-Labor-government-style income policy coordinated by Central Bank President Richard Webb and Alfonso Grados, the minister of labor. However, this brave effort lacked the necessary institutional framework and political commitment and thus did not prevail. In August 1981, the policy shifted toward devaluation, the reduction of subsidies, and more severe orthodoxy in demand management, and yet borrowing abroad continued. Policies underwent a severe decline in credibility as the short-term borrowing strategy of public-sector enterprises was revealed. As the BCR put it, "[p]art of the difficulty is that nobody knows how much the state-owned companies have borrowed."[3]

The international rise in interest rates, the reduction in available international money, and the boom in imports with trade liberalization all contributed to a crisis of economic management. The Minister of Economy and Finance, Manuel Ulloa, was replaced by Carlos Rodríguez Pastor. A new effort at traditional orthodoxy was undermined not only by the familiar pressures examined in this analysis but also by drought, floods, the fall in the price of cocaine, and negative attitudes expressed by foreign bankers. The chaos and incoherence that followed led to several standbys being signed but not observed. The degree of recession did permit some accumulation of reserves, however.

Under the leadership of Alan García, Peru's attempt to deal with the negative external transfer issue combined a famous effort at ERBS with the new president's attempt at a price freeze and his radical declaration of the intent (never carried out) to devote no more than 10 percent of export revenues to debt repayment. Unlike a restrictive monetary and fiscal policy, reactivation, it was hoped, could harness the very high level of excess capacity and reverse various forms of negative feedback.

The results of this experiment are well known. García achieved the worst of all worlds with the external transfer, considering that he actually paid as much as the previous administration had. García's reactivation policy and short-term success with inflation generated such euphoria that reactivation was carried far too far, while nothing was done to tackle the underlying problems. The contradictions of such policies had become thoroughly evident by 1987. The exchange rate was seriously overvalued, with no compensating action, whereas price controls, also without compensating action, were undermining the position of various state enterprises and generating huge subsidies. Interest rate controls were crippling the already fragile financial sector development. The policy had already lost what credibility it had had when a mismanaged bank nationalization scheme completely alienated the private sector. The imperative of relative price realignment led to a disastrous year of *paquetismo*,[4] whereby every three months a package of price increases failed to restore confidence and real incentives and merely accelerated inflation. In the final few months leading up to the elections of April 1990, the leadership tried to buy popularity through an irresponsible price policy that included completely nonfunctional price distortions. The new administration was handed a gravely distorted economy with inflation running at over 2,000 percent.

Of course, the failure to stabilize through the 1980s has had further effects on the nature of the stabilization problem. The principal as well as the most obvious consequence was that the Peruvian economy, which at the end of the 1970s boasted a moderate inflation rate, had gone from an average annual inflation of 49 percent between 1976 and 1979 to 94 percent under Fernando Belaúnde Terry and to 2,775 percent in 1989 under Alan García. This staggering increase had radical effects in changing the economic "culture" (the elements listed in Table 1, Point B) and contributed to the further undermining of the state via the collapse of revenue. Tax revenue, which totaled 15.8 percent of GDP in 1980, had plummeted to 6.2 percent by 1989. The collapse of state revenue precipitated a deterioration of the quality of state institutions and the morale of civil servants. Concurrently, the state experienced a further erosion of credibility, leading to a resistance to invest on the part of the private sector. Most public investment ceased. Clearly, the underlying problems of exports and investment remained as grave as ever.

THE PENDULUM SWINGS OUT OF SIGHT: 1990-1993

The increasingly poor returns from orthodoxy and the consequences of poorly managed ERBS thus led to what Richard Webb has graphically described as "the withering away" of the state.[5] Where did this governmental atrophy leave the new administration of Alberto Fujimori when it took office in mid-1990?

The intellectual context that prevailed at the time was one of sharp disillusionment with heterodox thinking. Even the opponents of orthodoxy conceded that a heterodox strategy needed elements of orthodoxy. The experience of the one remaining relative success in Latin America, Mexico, supported this conclusion. Meanwhile, the move to radical restructuring to permit markets to work had gained enormous force and respect on many fronts throughout the 1980s, with Chile providing the constant reference point. These developments — especially the dominance of the Chilean "success" coupled with Fujimori's conviction that orthodoxy was the way to achieve external financing — constituted the initial intellectual support for the option advocated by the new administration.

Fujimori's option has consisted of a form of orthodoxy that is based on a radical return to the market and a severe recession that was far more extreme than any Peru had ever previously experienced. The logic has been that in the absence of state capacity, we have only the market. Unfortunately, however, the market needs the state. Therefore, the solution has to be both more complex and more politically challenging. Paradoxically, the new policy has short-circuited many of the old negative forms of feedback that had plagued orthodoxy in the pre-1980 era only to encounter a new vicious circle of its own. The option was for an exchange rate "determined by the market," though oddly enough with an initial, pre-announced devaluation, which led to an unnecessary inflationary explosion. This strategy has been combined with a radical policy of spending only what is in the kitty, tight credit controls, and trade liberalization plus numerous policies attacking the obstacles to market forces. The latter were slow to begin functioning but were beginning by February 1991.

The old problems related to actually implementing policies such as fiscal orthodoxy have been resolved by a decisive will to accept the consequences, including, it seems, any necessary level of state sector pay. The feedback of the recession on tax revenue has been reduced by a genuine reform of tax administration and enforcement for the first time in many years. This has been aided by the beneficial effect of a substantial reduction in levels of inflation. The need for endless recession to restore external equilibrium has been eliminated by the simple fact of drug money plus the ideological decision to leave both exchange rates and interest rates "to the market." This decision, however, leads to a new vicious circle.

Before the 1990 presidential election, firms quite reasonably gambled on a real devaluation's occurring following the election; they survived by going heavily into debt, relying on devaluation to enable them to repay. But with the shock, the level of activity dropped to almost nothing, while the liquidity squeeze was such that everyone had to remit dollars just to survive. The combination of low levels of activity and inflows of dollars meant that the dollar market rate could not possibly improve in real terms. Having risen somewhat in the interim period before Fujimori took office, the dollar market settled at essentially the same real level after the August price explosion. The lack of real devaluation left firms with huge financial problems, and in the ensuing months, their need for refinancing pushed high interest rates even higher as monetary rigidity continued. Hence, the "circle" with which we are now so familiar was created as ever higher interest rates and scarce liquidity have led to more dollars coming into the economy and more pressure toward overvaluation. The old problem of the recession being the sole, albeit inefficient, tool to limit imports has simply not been an issue.

However, although inflation has been reduced considerably, the new vicious circle has been deadly inasmuch as it rules out a recovery in either exports or investment, the two essential ingredients of longer-run recovery. Thus, we return via a different route to precisely the same conclusion reached at the close of the previous period: the central components of short-term management are radically incompatible with the longer term. The present situation results from the deep crisis of credibility and the new fragility produced by extremely narrow national currency markets. It has been exacerbated by the recent high propensity to move money internationally. One major advance upon prior efforts is that this time the government purports to have a long-term policy based on many ambitious efforts to reform land markets, customs, ports, and so on. It is tragic that so much effort is not enough. After the abdication of state responsibilities in the course of the 1980s, huge deficits abound in infrastructure, education, technical training, support roles to management, and areas such as the identification of new export markets. These same areas require new, more flexible, and efficient roles for the state in collaboration with civil society.

Unfortunately, these circumstances lead to a conclusion that is of necessity quite radical. The manner in which the underlying characteristics of the Peruvian economy and society have evolved between the 1950s and the present, together with international factors such as the greater fluidity of capital movements, has created an intensely complex situation. Relative stabilization has been possible, but the means used to achieve this goal conflict with long-term needs. It is not that a technically effective alternative has been ignored or that a policy which used to work could be reinstated. The only clear short-run alternative would be that proposed by C. Paredes and J. Sachs (1991) — an overshooting of the exchange rate, followed by ERBS backed by severely orthodox monetary and fiscal policy. Lacking measures to restore confidence and credibility and given the narrowness of money markets and the modus operandi of expectations, this strategy, too, would have led to a vicious circle.

Hence, the need is precisely to operate in the long term in a way that accommodates and counterbalances some of the necessary consequences of short-term stabilization and provides coherence and credibility through the obvious relevance and effectiveness of the measures for the long term. This would, however, entail a radical change in the quality of the state's role and, above all, in the way the state interacts with civil society. Richard Webb's masterly summary makes it clear that both the problem and the solution extend far beyond economics: "The government is boxed in: its only hope for financial recovery lies in the laborious and time-consuming route of broad economic development. Likewise, the recovery of governmental authority and enforcement means accepting and working with the multitude of organizations and groups that make up the new polity. Both politics and economics are pushing the state into a partnership with the rest of society."[6] Even though this partnership would clearly amount to a revolution in light of Peruvian history, the realization of its necessity and import can go far to stimulate the detailed constructive thinking and institutional development needed to begin to make this route a reality.

NOTES

1. This analysis draws on a number of earlier works that provide further detail and documentation. See in particular Thorp and Whitehead 1979; Thorp and Whitehead 198; Thorp and Bertram 1978; and Thorp 1992.

2. See Thorp and Bertram 1978 for an explanation of the long-run trends at work here.

3. See *Andean Report* 1983.

4. The practice of implementing a package of economic reforms. *Ed.*

5. See Richard Webb 1991, 1.

6. Webb 1991, 2.

REFERENCES

Andean Report (Lima). 1983. February.

Banco Central de Reserva del Perú (BCR). 1991. *Boletín*. Lima: Banco Central de Reserva del Perú.

Banco Central de Reserva del Perú (BCR). N.d. *Cuentas nacionales del Perú*. Lima: Banco Central de Reserva del Perú.

Dragisic, J. 1971. *Peruvian Stabilization Policies, 1938-1968*. Ph.D. diss. University of Wisconsin.

Instituto Nacional de Estadística e Informática (INEI). N.d. *Compendio estadístico*. Lima: Instituto Nacional de Estadística e Informática.

International Monetary Fund (IMF). N.d. *International Financial Statistics*. Washington D.C.: International Monetary Fund.

Paredes, C., and J. Sachs, eds. 1991. *Peru's Path to Recovery: A Plan for Economic Stabilization and Growth*. Washington, D.C.: The Brookings Institution.

Thorp, Rosemary. 1992. "Reflecciones sobre el programa de largo y corto plazo del gobierno peruano." *Moneda* (Lima).

Thorp, Rosemary, and G. Bertram. 1978. *Perú 1890-1977: Growth and Policy in an Open Economy*. New York: Columbia University Press.

Thorp, Rosemary, and L. Whitehead. 1979. *Inflation and Stabilization in Latin America*. London: Macmillian.

Thorp, Rosemary, and L. Whitehead. 1987. *Latin American Debt and the Adjustment Crisis*. London: Macmillan.

Webb, Richard. 1991. "Prologue." In *Peru's Path to Recovery: A Plan for Economic Stabilization and Growth*, eds. C. Paredes and J. Sachs. Washington, D.C.: The Brookings Institution.

Webb, Richard, Teresa Lamas, and Gabriela Fernández Baca. 1991. *Perú en números, 1991: Anuario estadístico*. Lima: Cuánto S.A.

III

THE PERUVIAN ECONOMY CIRCA 1990: STRUCTURE AND CONSEQUENCES

Daniel M. Schydlowsky

Policy, to be effective, must be grounded in a realistic assessment of the initial conditions in which it will operate. This chapter will examine the structure of the Peruvian economy as of mid-1990 to identify these initial conditions and to derive their consequences for policy formation.

Peru's economy in 1990 presented a particularly complex picture. A set of underlying long-term relationships had built up over several decades of largely self-defeating economic policy, and an overlay of short-term reaction functions had come strongly to the fore over the preceding two years, largely as a response to the rising hyperstagflation of the last years of the administration of President Alan García Pérez (1985-1990).

The long-term underlying relationships comprised the following principal items:

1. The country's resource balance, that is, the fit among the availabilities of labor, capital, natural resources, and foreign exchange;

2. The secular functioning of the price system, that is, the extent to which it fulfilled its allocative function by providing a good measure of resource scarcity, as well as the extent to which it fulfilled its distributive function by generating an acceptable income distribution;

3. The dispersion of real productivity across sectors, that is, the extent to which Peru's product mix departed from static comparative advantage; and

4. The secular evolution of public finances, with regard to both the buoyancy of fiscal revenue and the effect of the expenditure mix on fiscal drag.

Daniel Schydlowsky is professor of economics at American University, Washington, D.C.

The short-term reaction functions comprised the following principal topics:

1. The determinants of the level of activity and the structure of production;
2. The determinants of the rate of inflation and of relative prices;
3. Feedback mechanisms leading into vicious circles and resulting in inert areas[1] of hyperstagflation from which it is hard to break out; and
4. Severe deterioration of the state's managerial capacity.

To the observer in 1990, short-term functions tended to obscure long-term relationships, and policy tended to be discussed almost exclusively in terms of targeting the short term. However, if the long-term underlying relationships were neglected for an extended time, the policy adopted would not prove to be sustainable. Therefore, in this chapter, these long-term underlying relationships will be reviewed first in order to keep them clearly in mind when examining the short-term features of the Peruvian economy in 1990. This sequence will also make it possible to point to the impact of long-term relationships on short-term functions as the latter are discussed. Finally, the consequences for policy of both long- and short-term structural features will be explored.

LONG-TERM UNDERLYING RELATIONSHIPS IN THE PERUVIAN ECONOMY, CIRCA 1990

RESOURCE BALANCE

Peru is a severely foreign-exchange-constrained economy. The foreign exchange earned by traditional exports, non-traditional exports, and coca are not enough to run the economy at "normal" levels of capacity utilization, let alone at full capacity utilization, and even less at full employment, even though foreign debt service is held to the minimum minimorum (in other words, even the World Bank and the Inter-American Development Bank are not getting paid). If debt service were at normal levels, absent massive refinancing (which would only postpone the problem), the level of output would have to be squeezed even further.

This situation is the consequence of a classic case of development through import-substituting industrialization (ISI). Industrialization was adopted as a development strategy by Peru in the late 1950s and was applied with ever-increasing vigor through the mid-1970s. Productivity and cost differentials between the traditional primary sectors and industry were bridged through import restrictions (mostly tariffs, sometimes also licensing and prohibitions). As a result, industrial production was for the domestic market and foreign exchange using, while the primary sectors were foreign exchange producing.

This pattern of growth was unsustainable, and the corresponding *structural* balance of payments crisis erupted in 1975. Unfortunately, this crisis was misdiagnosed, and the therapy applied did not cure the structural imbalance in the pattern of production and investment.[2]

While export promotion was formally initiated with the Certificate for Reimbursement of Taxes upon Export (Certificado de Reintegro Tributario a las Exportaciones, Certex) legislation in 1969, it was not pursued with any degree of vigor until the mid-1970s. Even so, these efforts were not sufficiently strong or stable to make a lasting difference, and they became ever more precarious during the 1980s.[3]

The appearance of coca-based exports in the 1980s added a new productivity differential between primary products and manufacturing and added an Innovational Dutch Disease to the pre-existing Evolutionary Dutch Disease affecting Peru's exchange rate.[4] On the other hand, the increase in foreign exchange earnings coca provided could have raised the sustainable level of domestic output substantially, except that along with this new source of supply, a new source of demand for foreign exchange also appeared, namely, the requirement to service the debt.

In addition, Shining Path (Sendero Luminoso) activities had made operating mines or farming much more expensive in large parts of the country. The consequent reductions in productivity narrowed the traditional differential between these sectors and manufacturing, even though manufacturing was also affected by Sendero's attacks, particularly through the repeated disruption of the electricity supply.

Thus, in 1990 it was still true that Peru did not earn enough foreign exchange from its exports to run its domestic productive capacity at full utilization, much less to provide full employment. A substantial imbalance existed between the availability of foreign exchange and the domestic factors of production. Accordingly, the country's output level was depressed.

Peru's employment situation was correspondingly poor. Starting with the balance of payments crisis of 1975, Peru's modern sector grew only sporadically and only marginally increased its demand for labor. However, Peru's labor force continued to grow. The economy had to make space for those who could not be hired by modern firms constrained in their growth by the consequences of the balance of payments restriction. The solution was spontaneous: those who could not find wage employment went into business themselves and competed with established firms. In the process, they differentiated the products they sold from those of established firms on the basis of location, ancillary services, or the absence of fixed prices. The informal sector grew very quickly in the late 1970s and through most of the 1980s (except for the García boom years). In the process, more and more activities were "informalized" (for example, auto mechanics began making muffler repairs in the street), and the geographical coverage of the informal sector spread throughout Lima and to smaller cities. While the informal sector has been celebrated for its entrepreneurial content,[5] most of its participants have been pushed unwillingly into this sector and are substantially underemployed.

At 1990 levels of activity, Peru clearly had a labor surplus. In addition, it appears highly unlikely that Peru could have achieved full employment even at full use of existing installed capacity if enough foreign exchange had been available to operate it.[6]

SECULAR FUNCTIONING OF THE PRICE SYSTEM

A well-functioning price system accomplishes two important purposes. First, it accurately reflects the true scarcity of resources and thereby provides a reliable guide to resource allocation. Second, it provides a distribution of income between buyers and sellers that is regarded as reasonably equitable. Unfortunately, Peru's price system was not characterized by accurately measuring scarcity. In addition, it distorted allocation of resources in quite specific ways that reinforced the balance of payments constraint and aggravated the surplus of labor. On the other hand, the price system functioned in a way that assured all members of society *some* income, ensuring that surplus labor did not starve but, rather, shared the existing poverty. Thus, the price system was a poor allocator of resources but had some redeeming distributional properties. Moreover, as will be argued below, only some of these features were the result of deliberate public policy, whereas others were well beyond the direct reach of that policy.

PRICES AS MEASURES OF SCARCITY

The major factor prices in the Peruvian economy — the exchange rate, wage rate, and interest rate — exhibited substantial deviations from both marginal social costs and marginal social utility. As a result, costs and prices of most goods and services were distorted. It is useful to review the situation of each of the major prices in turn.

The exchange rate. Peru has traditionally had a managed exchange rate, set at a level sufficiently high (in *soles* per dollar) to make traditional export production reasonably profitable.[7] In addition, the country has operated with significant and increasing levels of import protection since the late 1950s. Furthermore, in boom times, export taxes were levied (for example, in the period between 1978 and 1981), and in bad times import licenses were imposed (during most of the 1970s and the second half of the 1980s). In different periods, one exchange rate operated for the current account and another for the capital account, while during the latter part of the García presidency, a quite complex pattern of multiple exchange rates was developed.

The implication of this confluence of exchange rate policy and trade taxation is that, for all practical intents and purposes, production and sale of different products in different markets (for example, domestic versus export) faced different net exchange rates. These differences resulted mostly from the existence of trade taxes that needed to be added to or subtracted from a single exchange rate to derive the net figure. At times, however, the differences were increased further because of the existence of explicit multiple exchange rates. Whatever the situation, Peru has operated for its recent economic history with a de facto multiple exchange rate system. It follows that the financial exchange rate, that is, the rate normally quoted by the bank, reflects neither the cost of earning a dollar's worth of value added nor the willingness to pay for an additional dollar's worth of imports on the part of consumers.[8]

The marginal social utility of foreign exchange is further affected, however, by the reliance of Peru's balance of payments adjustment mechanism on changes in the level of activity to control the volume of imports. This income adjustment mechanism means that an additional dollar leverages the level of activity and sustains more than one dollar's worth of domestic value added and economic welfare. As a result, even the consumers' willingness to pay for a dollar's worth of imports does not accurately measure the marginal social utility of a dollar; the externality involved in the activation effect must be taken into account.[9]

On the other side of the market, the marginal social cost of production of a dollar is only given by market costs if the wages of labor and the return to capital are accurate reflections of the true scarcity or abundance of these factors. Since this is not so, as will be argued in some detail below, even an exchange rate based on export costs of production at market prices does not measure the true cost of earning foreign exchange. In addition, much foreign exchange is "earned" by saving it in import-substituting production, for which the effective exchange rate is increased due to the existence of protection. Once again, factors of production must be costed at the marginal social cost and not at their market remuneration.

It follows, then, that for a very long time the market exchange rate in Peru has reflected neither the marginal social utility nor the marginal social costs of foreign exchange.[10] Indeed, the most recently available study on the shadow price of foreign exchange places that value at 2.85 times the Mercado Unico de Cambios (MUC) rate in 1986.[11] The qualitative situation was not different in 1990 from 1986, although the numerical difference may have been greater because of the divergence between the MUC exchange rate, the other official rates, and the street rate.

The wage rate. Within most skill levels, but particularly in the low-skill and unskilled categories, Peru's labor market has long been segmented along a number of dimensions. The most notable of these segmentations divides the market between the "formal" or "protected" market, where minimum wage legislation, hiring and firing rules, and mandated fringe benefits apply (and where social security and other taxes are paid); and the "informal" or "unprotected" market, where people make whatever arrangements they can, basically without the benefit of paternalistic state intervention and without paying a share to the tax collector.

In the formal sector, there is a clearly identifiable wage paid, even if there is some wage dispersion for the same skill level. This wage is always below the cost of labor to the firm because of the substantial fringe benefits the firm must fund above and beyond the cash wage paid.[12] Thus, the wage is below the private marginal product of labor. However, since the market price of the output can be greater or less than the shadow price of that output, depending to a large extent on whether export- or import-substituting production is involved,[13] it can only be said for sure that the wage paid will not correctly measure marginal social productivity of the labor employed in the modern sector.

On the supply side of the formal market, wage earners' take-home pay is below the wage since social security and other taxes are withheld. Moreover, since the present value of the corresponding benefits is (correctly) recognized to be worth less than the amounts withheld,[14] labor suppliers' perceived income is below the wage. Correspondingly, it is this lower net income that is compared to labor suppliers' other alternatives: unemployment or work in the informal sector.

The informal sector, in turn, comprises a number of subsectors, with the most important division occurring between those who are wage laborers in the informal sector and those who are in business for themselves, often hiring others to work for them. Naturally, insofar as workers have a choice of subsectors to enter, returns to effort must be approximately equal. However, barriers to entry are not entirely absent between these subsectors nor, indeed, between finer classifications within them. These barriers arise in part from so-called social assets — that complex of information, reputation, and contacts that causes one person to be considered and hired for a job, while another does not even have a chance.[15] A further contribution to market segmentation is made by the capital market, for entering into many vending activities requires either owning some capital or having the connections to be provided with working capital in the form of merchandise to sell.[16] All these elements cause differential access to various parts of the informal labor market, resulting in dispersal of incomes and the obtainment of significant differential rents.

A further element of fundamental importance in the income formation mechanism is the nature of competition in the product markets where those workers who have decided to be independent entrepreneurs sell. It has already been noted that in order to compete with established business, informal sellers differentiate their products. They deliver goods to the home, perhaps even on the requested day (recreating the fruit and vegetable *casero* [door-to-door vendor] of yesteryear), allow closer inspection of the products, provide them at a more opportune time of the day (such as after regular business hours), or provide them at a price open to bargaining. The crucial element here is product differentiation, for this drastically changes the nature of competition and market equilibrium.

With entry reasonably open and products differentiated, the market form is that of monopolistic competition.[17] Two central results of equilibrium under monopolistic competition are 1) excess capacity and 2) prices equal to average cost rather than marginal cost. The first property tallies very well with the observation of extensive underemployment of labor in the informal sector; the second indicates that the Pareto conditions for a welfare optimum will be systematically violated.[18]

We can now summarize. In the formal sector, the wage paid is not equal to the marginal social product of labor because of the wedge introduced by fringe benefits and because of divergence between the market price and shadow price of output. Nor is the income in the informal sector equal to the marginal social product of labor, for both sectors sell at product prices that diverge from their shadow analogues. Finally, labor income in the informal sector is not equal to the marginal cost of labor, for both the existence of rents on social assets and access to product sales under monopolistically competitive price formation introduce a wedge between the value of leisure and the marginal revenue from labor effort.

For 1986, the ratio of the shadow cost of unskilled labor to the private cost of such labor (wage plus fringes and other costs paid by the employer) in the formal sector was found to be 0.11, the corresponding ratio for skilled workers was found to average 0.08, the ratio for office workers was found to average 0.06, the ratio for professionals was found to average 0.05, and the ratio for managers was estimated to be 1.55.[19] Some of these ratios may seem rather low, particularly those for skilled workers and above. The explanation lies in the finding that numerous higher-skilled workers had taken jobs for which they were overqualified. As a result, when they were hired away from these jobs, others with fewer skills replaced them. These in turn were also replaced by less-skilled people who could do the jobs they were vacating, and so on. All along the line, no important training cost was incurred, and only at the end of the job ladder did the economy incur the cost of using an unskilled worker, who is, of course, quite inexpensive in a labor surplus economy. Since the economy in 1990 was much more depressed than it was in 1986, it is hard to believe that these ratios would have gotten any better.

The interest rate. The visible interest rate in Peru is well known to reflect only activity in a limited segment of the economy, while a much larger part of economic activity is served by onlenders through the wholesale and retail trade as well as by the so-called "informal credit market." Moreover, formal lending has been limited by legal requirements of various sorts, including the need to have proper title to provide security as well as by government regulation. Finally, the ownership structure of the financial sector has provided considerable incentives to preferential lending to associated productive enterprises, along the German or Japanese models. As a consequence, Peru's visible interest rates, that is, those charged and paid by banks, have not been representative of the nation's time preference nor of the marginal productivity of capital.

Inequality of the social time preference and banks' "passive" interest rate[20] becomes obvious in light of the limited number of Peruvians who save in banks. These Peruvians could indeed be expected to adjust their consumption and savings behavior until tangency occurs between the market interest rate and their intertemporal indifference curves.[21] However, the same cannot be said of the large number of Peruvians who save and invest outside the banking system, most of them directly in merchandise and physical assets. These people presumably adjust their consumption and savings behavior directly to the return afforded by those assets, which must be presumed to be higher than the bank interest rate, or they would not be at a zero corner solution with regard to saving in banks. It follows that private time preference, on average, is likely to be above the banks' passive interest rate.[22] However, the *social* time preference is generally held to lie below the private time preference,[23] hence the social time preference may lie either above or below the banks' passive rate.

On the other hand, the banks' active rate is not a good measure of the marginal social productivity of capital for several reasons. First, the active rate cannot be greater than the private after-tax rate of return, or entrepreneurs would not borrow.[24] However, the marginal product of capital has to be taken based on gross taxes.[25] Second, the private marginal product of capital is based on the market prices of outputs and inputs, as well as on the market price of labor in the formal sector. However, much of the output comprises traded goods, the private prices of which differ from their social analogues because the shadow price of foreign exchange differs from the particular net exchange rate determining their prices. Thus, output is either under- or overvalued compared to its marginal social utility. A similar distortion is introduced by pricing inputs, many of them traded, at their private prices. Finally, the cost of labor is substantially overstated by taking it at the protected sector wage. The general equilibrium of the price system comes home to roost and signifies that the marginal social product of capital will differ substantially from the marginal private product.[26] Moreover, it may be larger or smaller, depending on the precise interaction, on average, among the different elements involved.[27]

In the empirical calculations for 1986, social time preference was taken at 10 percent, whereas the annual marginal social product of capital was estimated to be 23.2 percent.[28] Given the intervening crisis and lower economic growth, in 1990 social time preference may well have declined. Similarly, given the intervening depression, the marginal product of capital is likely to be lower as well.

Summary. The preceding discussion leads to the conclusion that in mid-1990 Peru's price system was not a good indicator of economic scarcity for a large number of reasons, some resulting directly from government action, while many were the consequence of Peru's state of development and imbalance of resource endowments. Thus, one can attribute to state intervention the distortions in the foreign exchange market arising from trade taxation and the existence of several exchange rates, the distortions in the labor market arising from labor legislation, and the distortions in the capital market arising from interest rate regulation. At the same time, one must recognize that to the extent that market and shadow prices of foreign exchange diverged because the balance of payments mechanism relied heavily on changes in the level of activity, this was in large measure a consequence of the private sector's elasticities and reaction functions. Likewise, socioeconomic structure and the free will of the citizenry were expressed in the monopolistically competitive structure of informal market pricing and in the nature and role of social assets. These crucially affected the labor market. Furthermore, the segmentation of the capital market, in the face of imperfect information and other transaction costs, was as much a product of private sector action as it was of government regulation.

Hence, even if the government removed all its own deliberate or accidental distortions, Peru's markets in mid-1990 would still not have produced prices that were good measures of scarcity. Only the gradual integration of markets, the expansion of information, and the absorption of surplus labor through growth would make market prices increasingly reliable guides for efficient allocation. But this process takes a long time.

THE DIRECTION OF PRICE DISTORTION

The price system in Peru was not randomly distorted; rather, it pushed economic activity in very specific directions and in ways that can be clearly identified. Three are particularly notable and worthy of discussion.

Anti-export bias. It is not surprising that Peru's price system should have included an anti-export bias; all countries following an ISI policy build this feature into their price systems. What is more surprising is that the extensive analyses of the problems of ISI that became current from the early 1970s on did not produce more policy changes in Peru.

Peru's main export promotion instrument, the Certificado de Reintegro Tributario a las Exportaciones (Certex), was created in 1969, not much later than Colombia's Certificado de Ahorro Tributario (CAT). But whereas Colombia, despite maintaining an import licensing system through 1990, systematically pushed non-traditional exports from the late 1960s on, combining the CAT with a managed crawl in the exchange rate, Peru always treated the Certex and other lesser export promotion devices as stepchildren. Accordingly, the Certex was reduced whenever export revenue rose and came into its own only when balance of payments problems grew very serious.

Thus, the Certex was reinforced in the second phase of the military government of the 1970s, when foreign exchange was scarce, to be severely cut back at the start of Fernando Belaúnde Terry's second administration, even though its upper reaches were populated with well-trained economists who knew the literature on inward-looking and outward-looking growth. As the balance of payment problems loomed large again, later Belaúnde cabinets restored the Certex to some degree. Thereafter, during much of García's regime, export profitability was neglected, even though the key technicians were fully steeped in the lore of foreign exchange restrictions throttling Latin American growth. Only from 1987 on, and for brief intervals, did García introduce a pro-export bias into the exchange rate system. Indeed, during part of the succeeding years, the export exchange rate was considerably higher than the import rate for raw materials and intermediate goods. However, the general confusion during this period was such that no stable export drive could result from this incentive.

In 1990, the basic structure of the exchange rate system still included a strong anti-export bias, even though some effective export incentives existed, such as for clothing. Much of any pro-export bias, however, was the result of the multiple exchange rate system on the input side, which provided exporters with low-cost imported inputs. However, this must be thought of as a short-run phenomenon, slated to revert to anti-export bias as soon as the multiple rate structure collapsed into a single rate.

Anti-capacity utilization. The issue of Peru's secular underutilization of installed industrial capacity has been a matter of debate, public policy concern, and business preoccupation since the late 1970s.[29] The fundamental point of the various analyses is that the relative price of labor and machines, the relatively greater availability of credit for fixed assets as compared to working capital, and the depreciation regulations all act together to tilt profitability toward larger installations of machinery working fewer hours in comparison to a smaller number of machines working with multiple shifts. Moreover, these profitability distortions are reinforced by entrepreneurial perceptions about the difficulties of managing shift work, about labor relations problems such practices entail, and about personal efforts that may be involved.[30]

Throughout the 1980s, Peru's entrepreneurs became fully sensitized to the desirability of using installed capacity as much as possible. Moreover, during the first two boom years of García's government, the expansion was based on capacity utilization. Thus, managers developed actual experience in using their capacity more intensively. However, the bias against utilization remained, although it was not as strong. By 1990, the level of activity had been falling drastically since late 1988; accordingly, the issue of long-term capacity utilization had been pushed again into the background.

Anti-labor intensity. The bias in favor of using capital-intensive processes in Peru's "formal" business sector has been long-standing. In this sector, minimum wage laws and other labor legislation have raised the market cost of labor well above its marginal social cost. On the other hand, low or no tariffs for the import of capital goods, combined with a low financial exchange rate, provided for machinery costs below their social opportunity cost. In addition, publicly sponsored availability of low-cost, long-term credit for the purchase of machinery[31] and various tax incentives reinforced the tilt in relative prices toward the profitability of capital-intensive processes of production. Finally, the regime of labor tenure (*estabilidad laboral*) along with labor's sharing of profits and property (*comunidad laboral* [32]) provided some very strong incentives to labor-saving investment.

During the 1980s, businesspeople learned to live with the *comunidad laboral*, while the tightness of work tenure was relaxed on the one hand by the creation of service companies that provided workers that were not on the employers' direct payroll and, on the other, by a decree from President García that provided a regime of temporary employment not subject to tenure rules. However, this regime was of dubious constitutional legality, and businesspeople continuously pointed out that they were using it at their peril.

Thus, by 1990 some of the most salient anti-labor intensity features of the labor regime had been softened. However, the basic discrepancy between market wage and shadow price of labor was still very much in evidence, despite a fall in the real wage of the modern sector. The informal sector had grown; thus, the income floor it provided had become more important. By the same token, a larger part of the labor force was now underemployed, with additional work hours available at very low marginal social cost but under a market structure that required paying a substantially higher market wage.

Some change had also occurred on the cost of capital side, where interest rates had become only slightly negative or perhaps even slightly positive when adding in all the banks' hidden charges. However, the purchase of machinery was still relatively more attractive at private than at shadow prices. Thus, insofar as any investment took place, it continued to be biased to the capital intensive side.

There was substantially less bias in the informal sector. Here, none of the labor legislation was applicable or enforced. Moreover, in many instances, expansion could occur with the labor on hand, which involved a consideration of the cost of their own unproductive time to the entrepreneurs themselves. This meant that the marginal private cost of some labor was very close to the marginal social cost. On the other hand, both capital and foreign exchange were much more costly to the informal than the formal sector. However, the private prices of capital goods and foreign exchange to the informal sector were probably still well below the corresponding marginal social costs. Thus, although the incentives were for the informal sector to be relatively more labor intensive than the formal sector, even the informal sector was not facing the correct relative shadow prices.

THE INCOME DISTRIBUTION EFFECTS OF THE PRICE SYSTEM

To give a proper assessment of the distribution effects of Peru's price system requires setting up an alternative as benchmark against which to compare the actual system. Depending on what benchmark is chosen, the distributional effects of the actual system will look good or bad, and discussion then moves to whether or not the benchmark chosen is relevant or plausible.

Rather than pursue this route, what will be done here is to point out some distributional features of the Peruvian price system that are desirable, *ceteris paribus*. This is not to imply that Peru's income distribution is anywhere near optimal nor that one could not have done better. It is intended to establish only that there are some redeeming distributional features that offset the allocational drawbacks to Peru's long-term price system.

The sharing of poverty through the informal sector. Given Peru's imbalance of factor endowments, with labor in substantial surplus, a competitive labor market would cause real wages to be substantially below even the low levels of 1990.[33] In comparison with this outcome, the existence of an informal labor market characterized by segmentation, the exploitation of barriers to entry generated by social assets and other spontaneous action of labor suppliers, and interconnected through self-employment with an informal market of goods and services characterized by monopolistic competition signifies a distinct distributional improvement. The informal market generates an income floor for a large part of the labor force, albeit at the cost of raising the wages for some (through segmentation of the labor market) and reducing the market for goods or services of formal suppliers (through the competition of informal sector sellers). Thus, the structure of the labor market generates a net income transfer from rich to poor. It therefore constitutes a positive market adaptation of the Peruvian economy to the income distribution needs of the country's society.

The transfer of income from landowners and mine owners to industrial workers and consumers through the ISI price structure. At the time of its adoption of ISI or, indeed, at various later points, Peru could have decided to replace its tariff structure with free trade at a correspondingly higher exchange rate (in *soles* per dollar). If such a devaluation had been enough to keep Peruvian industry producing, it would have also substantially raised the rent accruing to landowners and mine owners while increasing the prices of all low-duty imports, mainly food and raw materials. It would also have made it profitable to expand the production of primary goods and to export manufactures. There would thus have been a very strong initial income distribution effect in favor of land and mine owners, plus a later efficiency effect on the product mix.[34]

Peru chose instead to go with the ISI policy, later complemented with the Certex and other export promotion measures, intended to offset, at least in part, the anti-export bias on the industrial side. The policy mix, therefore, was one oriented to prevent a massive distribution of income in favor of landowners and mine owners.

It is ironic in this context to note that the reforms implemented during the regime of General Juan Velasco Alvarado (1968-1975) removed much of the justification for this policy. Post-Velasco, the large land holdings had passed, at least theoretically, into the hands of the farm workers, while the large mines, except Toquepala and Cuajone, were all owned by the state. Thus, post-Velasco, the distributional consequences of adopting a set of relative prices that did not extract some of the Ricardian rent[35] from the primary sector would have been fine; poor farmers and the state would have benefited. The state could have funded its social expenditure or its investment with that revenue, much as Chile has done with its revenue from the government-owned copper mining company (Corporación Nacional del Cobre de Chile, CODELCO).

This rather "happy" coincidence between allocation and distributional desiderata has once again been undone through the expansion of the coca-producing sector. Rents accruing to this sector do not stay in the hands of the landowners or growers, but rather get passed on to the buyers, who are strong monopsonists in this market. Therefore, devaluations just reduce the dollar price Peru receives for basic paste and, given an inelastic demand, also reduce the total revenue of foreign exchange from these exports. It follows that the choice of an ISI-type relative price system such as the one Peru implemented in 1990 implicitly redistributes income from foreign drug buyers to Peru's urban consumers and industrial workers.[36]

DISPERSION OF REAL PRODUCTIVITY ACROSS SECTORS

Whenever a country adopts an ISI strategy, one expects to find dispersion of protection and consequently dispersion in productivity. However, it is important to be clear that differences in protection cannot be taken to measure differences in productivity, just as ability to compete against imports without protection is not an adequate benchmark of efficiency.

The central differences between competitiveness at market prices and national economic efficiency arise because market prices differ from shadow prices. When market prices do not measure scarcity of resources properly, market-priced indicators such as competitiveness also cannot measure true efficiency.[37]

Efficiency needs to be measured at shadow prices. Moreover, it is desirable to assess it on a disaggregative basis, at the level of different value-added producing activities, in order to differentiate properly the effectiveness of distinct stages of production. Such a procedure, in turn, ties in very well with the availability of trading opportunities and unifies efficiency measurement with the analysis of comparative advantage.

Accordingly, we can measure national economic efficiency by the (direct) domestic resource cost of foreign exchange (DDRC) and consider as efficient all activities having a DDRC no greater than the shadow price of foreign exchange. These will also be the activities in which the country has a comparative advantage. In turn, activities having a DDRC greater than the shadow price of foreign exchange are inefficient,[38] and in them Peru does not have a comparative advantage.[39]

The DDRC is defined as follows:

$$DDRC = \frac{\text{Labor x SH. P. of L.} + \text{CAPITAL x SH. P. of K.}}{\text{NET FOREIGN EXCHANGE EARNED}}$$

This indicates the social cost of per unit of output measured by the net foreign exchange earned. The inverse of this cost measure is a productivity measure, for it tells us how much product (foreign exchange) has been generated per unit of composite labor and capital input used. Therefore, national economic productivity would be written as follows:

$$\text{NAT. ECON. PRDTVTY.} = \frac{\text{NET FOREIGN EXCHANGE EARNED}}{\text{LABOR x SH. P. of L.} + \text{CAPITAL x SH. P. of K.}}$$

The most recent calculations of the domestic resource cost of foreign exchange for Peru are for 1984-1985 and cover the manufacturing sector in detail.[40] Unfortunately, no similar calculations exist for other sectors.

The DDRC calculations available are presented in two time frames: a short run in which production occurs on the basis of existing installed capacity and a medium run in which capacity must be expanded but the production function is otherwise unchanged. Consequently, there are two differences between these calculations: 1) the short-run figures include no cost for the use of fixed assets, whereas the medium-run ones do, and 2) the shadow prices used for the two time frames vary somewhat, with factor costs being higher and the shadow price of foreign exchange lower in the medium term compared to the short run.

The sectoral averages obtained are reproduced in Tables 1 and 2. Each table shows, in addition to the ISIC sectoral classification number and the sector name, the highest, average, and lowest establishment level DDRC found in the sector (DDRCSMAX or DDRCMMAX, DDRCS or DDRCM, DDRCSMIN or DDRCMMIN, respectively), the number of establishments in the sample (NUM), the number of establishments with comparative advantage (NUMS or NUMM), and the percentage of sample output with comparative advantage (PCTS or PCTM). The numbers shown represent shadow costs in *intis* per dollar. The corresponding shadow price of foreign exchange is 39.6 in the short run and 29.2 in the medium term. Accordingly, production at DDRCs below these amounts is efficient and above these amounts, inefficient. In addition, it should be noted that negative DDRCs signify highly inefficient production because they imply a negative denominator and hence indicate that the inputs used are worth more foreign exchange than the output generated with them.

One of the salient facts portrayed by these tables is the wide dispersion of productivity, both within and between sectors. Thus, for instance, although there are four sectors that on average do not have short-run comparative advantage, each of these sectors at least includes one establishment that does have comparative advantage. On the other hand, sectors with comparative advantage on average include establishments that are highly inefficient and show foreign exchange losses rather than gains (i.e., negative DDRCs).

On the whole, however, these findings indicate that Peru's industrial production is remarkably efficient. In the short run, there are thirty-three sectors in which all establishments are efficient, whereas out of 436 establishments in the sample, 396 are efficient producers and represent 87.5 percent of the sample's total output. In the medium term, efficiency is naturally lower due to the inclusion of fixed capital costs as well as to the difference in shadow prices. In this time frame, there are only 18 sectors where all establishments are efficient and eight sectors that show average DDRCs that indicate inefficiency. Overall, in the medium term, out of the 436 establishments in the sample, 348 are found to be efficient, representing 72.6 percent of the sample's value of output.

The changes that occurred in the Peruvian economy between 1984 and 1990 do not change the general picture emerging from these numbers. First, the shadow price of labor may have fallen a bit, and the shadow price of foreign exchange certainly rose; this means that the range of efficient,

Table 1.
Direct Domestic Resource Cost (DDRC) At Sectoral Level
Short Run (Idle Capacity)

	ISIC	Sector	DDRCSMAX	DDRCS	DDRCSMIN	NUM	NUMS	PCTS
1	3112	Milk products	-3.92	4.51	0.57	4	3	0.80
2	3113	Canned fruit & vegetables	-3.57	-8.53	0.69	9	8	0.75
3	3115	Oils & fats	-20.58	6.89	0.65	9	7	0.95
4	3116	Milled products	-19.83	-24.69	7.32	9	5	0.38
5	3117	Bakery products	54.57	2.98	1.13	11	9	0.91
6	3119	Cocoa, chocolate, & candy	-21.99	2.32	0.95	12	11	0.99
7	3121	Various food products	-1.44	2.25	0.42	9	8	0.78
8	3122	Animal feed	-43.85	-4.06	31.26	7	1	0.29
9	3131	Alcoholic beverages	18.07	2.21	0.69	9	9	1.00
10	3132	Wine	4.25	2.52	2.07	3	3	1.00
11	3133	Malt & malt-based beverages	3.98	1.71	0.24	10	10	1.00
12	3134	Nonalcoholic beverages	7.54	3.73	1.79	10	10	1.00
13	3135	Ethyl alcohol	0.72	0.72	0.72	1	1	1.00
14	3140	Tobacco	3.08	2.88	1.85	2	2	1.00
15	3211	Spinning, weaving & finishing	-427.93	2.66	0.50	26	23	0.96
16	3213	Knitwear	10.67	2.26	1.62	9	9	1.00

Table 1—*Continued*

No.	ISIC		DDRCSMIN	DDRCSMAX	DDRCS	NUM	NUMS	PCTS
17	3214	Carpets & rugs	-14.03	3.01	2.61	2	1	0.91
18	3215	Ropes	4.99	2.23	1.47	4	4	1.00
19	3220	Clothing except footwear	-55.28	1.46	0.24	18	17	0.99
20	3231	Tanning & finishing	-39.92	46.66	1.31	10	5	0.35
21	3240	Shoes except rubber	12.39	3.46	2.78	3	3	1.00
22	3311	Sawmills	3.49	1.17	0.39	5	5	1.00
23	3320	Non-metallic furniture & access.	4.75	2.26	0.82	7	7	1.00
24	3411	Wood pulp, paper & cardboard	-8.92	7.47	1.67	3	2	0.42
25	3412	Containers & boxes of paper & cardboard	5.64	1.59	0.66	8	8	1.00
26	3420	Printing & publishing	1.52	1.52	1.52	1	1	1.00
27	3511	Basic chemicals except fertilizer	-6.76	1.32	0.77	17	16	0.99
28	3512	Fertilizer & pesticides	9.14	1.15	0.32	7	7	1.00
29	3513	Resins & synthetic fibers	-5.17	2.18	1.34	9	8	0.93
30	3521	Paint, varnish & lacquer	7.41	3.27	2.43	7	7	1.00
31	3522	Medicines	7.42	2.82	1.08	16	16	1.00
32	3523	Soap & toiletries	26.92	1.45	0.99	11	11	1.00

ISIC = Import-Substituting Industrialization Classification
DDRCSMAX = Maximum Short-Run Direct Domestic Resource Cost
DDRCS = Average Short-Run Direct Domestic Resource Cost
DDRCSMIN = Minimum Short-Run Direct Domestic Resource Cost
NUM = Number of establishments in sample
NUMS = Number of establishments with comparative advantage
PCTS = Percentage of sample output with comparative advantage
nes = Not elsewhere specified

Continued on next page

Table 1—*Continued*

	ISIC	Sector	DDRCSMAX	DDRCS	DDRCSMIN	NUM	NUMS	PCTS
33	3529	Chemical products nes	-6.54	1.98	0.95	16	14	0.95
34	3551	Tires & inner tubes	1.62	1.34	1.14	2	2	1.00
35	3559	Rubber products nes	3.44	3.14	2.40	2	2	1.00
36	3560	Plastic products nes	19.97	2.72	0.99	24	24	1.00
37	3561	Plastic footwear	3.38	3.38	3.38	1	1	1.00
38	3610	Objects of clay & porcelain	648.59	10.82	2.43	3	2	0.47
39	3620	Glass & glass products	-26.03	3.27	0.66	8	7	0.84
40	3692	Cement, calcium & plaster	7.56	2.32	1.45	3	3	1.00
41	3699	Nonmetallic minerals	7.56	1.57	0.54	6	6	1.00
42	3710	Basic iron & steel	21.13	1.98	0.78	10	10	1.00
43	3720	Basic non-ferrous metals	-42.99	1.43	0.24	8	7	0.80
44	3811	Hardware	-9.48	3.07	1.69	4	4	1.00
45	3812	Metal furniture & accessories	-1.76	7.94	1.98	5	4	0.98
46	3813	Structural metal products	3.59	3.25	3.05	2	2	1.00
47	3819	Metal nes except machinery & equipment	-17.01	2.71	0.60	17	16	0.64
48	3822	Agricultural machinery & equipment	5.06	4.91	4.74	2	2	1.00

Table 1—Concluded

49	3829	Machinery & equipment nes except electrical	20.18	4.37	2.15	11	11	1.00
50	3831	Electrical machinery & industrial equipment	11.49	4.10	2.30	8	8	1.00
51	3832	Communications equipment	-13.50	3.57	1.37	11	10	0.94
52	3833	Domestic appliances	2.80	2.32	2.16	3	3	1.00
53	3839	Electrical equipment nes	3.61	1.66	1.07	6	6	1.00
54	3843	Automobiles	266.26	15.28	2.70	7	6	0.83
55	3844	Motorcycles & bicycles	3.15	2.07	1.64	3	3	1.00
56	3851	Scientific equipment	6.85	3.24	1.49	6	6	1.00

Table 2.
Direct Domestic Resource Cost (DDRC) At Sectoral Level
Medium Run (New Investment)

	ISIC	SECTOR	DDRCMMAX	DDRCM	DDRCMMIN	NUM	NUMM	PCTM
1	3112	Milk Products	-28.04	31.06	17.91	4	2	0.77
2	3113	Canned Fruit & vegetables	-46.60	-97.37	3.01	9	4	0.50
3	3115	Oils & fats	-41.82	26.16	1.63	9	5	0.57
4	3116	Milled products	-163.71	-186.91	27.94	9	2	0.09
5	3117	Bakery products	-3340.23	27.59	16.74	11	6	0.75
6	3119	Cocoa, chocolate, & candy	-63.03	20.49	5.23	12	8	0.79
7	3121	Various food products	-10.79	10.94	3.33	9	8	0.78
8	3122	Animal feed	-58.37	-11.54	54.68	7	0	0.00
9	3131	Alcoholic beverages	74.36	14.93	12.50	9	8	0.91
10	3132	Wine	20.82	14.41	11.76	3	3	1.00
11	3133	Malt & malt-based beverages	59.76	18.41	6.01	10	8	0.93
12	3134	Nonalcoholic beverages	47.01	25.12	10.04	10	7	0.46
13	3135	Ethyl alcohol	14.38	14.38	14.38	1	1	1.00
14	3140	Tobacco	8.90	8.69	8.64	2	2	1.00
15	3211	Spinning, weaving, & finishing	-131.04	13.65	3.15	26	22	0.92
16	3213	Knitwear	61.86	10.75	5.76	9	8	0.87

Table 2—*Continued*

	ISIC		DDRCSMAX	DDRCS	DDRCSMIN	NUM	NUMS	PCTS
17	3214	Carpets & rugs	-182.00	15.93	14.19	2	1	0.91
18	3215	Ropes	30.69	10.93	7.62	4	4	0.96
19	3220	Clothing except footwear	-54.60	5.96	2.50	18	17	0.97
20	3231	Tanning & finishing	-426.27	95.63	5.84	10	4	0.32
21	3240	Shoes except rubber	49.35	14.81	12.78	3	2	0.97
22	3311	Sawmills	75.72	17.65	3.25	5	4	0.75
23	3320	Non-metallic furniture & access.	17.39	10.48	6.43	7	7	1.00
24	3411	Wood pulp, paper & cardboard	-49.92	69.70	10.99	3	2	0.42
25	3412	Containers & boxes of paper & cardboard	55.21	8.86	4.59	8	7	1.00
26	3420	Printing & publishing	4.88	4.88	4.88	1	1	1.00
27	3511	Basic chemicals except fertilizer	-20.96	12.94	3.17	17	15	0.98
28	3512	Containers & boxes of paper & cardboard	20.28	5.98	2.04	7	7	1.00
29	3513	Resins & synthetic fibers	-24.86	16.26	6.47	9	6	0.69
30	3521	Paint, varnish & lacquer	27.03	13.28	6.49	7	7	1.00
31	3522	Medicines	23.30	10.54	4.80	16	16	1.00
32	3523	Soap & toiletries	128.61	7.10	4.08	11	10	0.99

NUM	=	Number of establishments in sample
NUMS	=	Number of establishments with comparative advantage
PCTS	=	Percentage of sample output with comparative advantage
nes	=	Not elsewhere specified

ISIC	=	Import-Substituting Industrialization Classification
DDRCSMAX	=	Maximum Short-Run Direct Domestic Resource Cost
DDRCS	=	Average Short-Run Direct Domestic Resource Cost
DDRCSMIN	=	Minimum Short-Run Direct Domestic Resource Cost

Continued on next page

Table 2—*Continued*

	ISIC	SECTOR	DDRCMMAX	DDRCM	DDRCMMIN	NUM	NUMM	PCTM
33	3529	Chemical products nes	-800.71	9.15	3.09	16	13	0.93
34	3551	Tires & inner tubes	11.27	9.81	8.84	2	2	1.00
35	3559	Rubber products nes	13.13	10.85	9.98	2	2	1.00
36	3560	Plastic products nes	70.55	16.23	9.32	24	22	0.89
37	3561	Plastic footwear	14.18	14.18	14.18	1	1	1.00
38	3610	Objects of clay & porcelain	117.16	43.52	6.97	3	2	0.19
39	3620	Glass & glass products	-109.71	28.17	5.04	8	7	0.76
40	3692	Cement, calcium & plaster	155.67	46.33	36.98	3	2	0.00
41	3699	Nonmetallic minerals nes	32.87	15.70	4.01	6	6	0.91
42	3710	Basic iron & steel	95.77	13.54	6.12	10	9	1.00
43	3720	Basic non-ferrous metals	-330.87	7.64	1.58	8	6	0.70
44	3811	Hardware	76.47	20.02	6.58	4	3	0.93
45	3812	Metal furniture & access.	-8.22	22.34	5.82	5	3	0.73
46	3813	Structural metal products	17.18	16.91	16.75	2	2	1.00
47	3819	Metal nes except machinery & equipment	-35.71	13.75	3.52	17	15	0.59
48	3822	Agricultural machinery & equipment	30.13	24.98	19.98	2	2	0.42

Table 2—*Concluded*

49	3829	Machinery & equipment nes except electrical	-14,256.50	18.04	9.65	11	8	0.83
50	3831	Electrical machinery & industrial equipment	34.66	13.70	6.79	8	8	0.96
51	3832	Communications equipment	-15.98	11.55	4.24	11	8	0.84
52	3833	Domestic appliances	9.11	7.31	5.71	3	3	1.00
53	3839	Electrical equipment nes	16.78	8.74	6.43	6	6	1.00
54	3843	Automobiles	127.86	38.77	10.61	7	5	0.13
55	3844	Motorcycles & bicycles	9.45	5.84	4.50	3	3	1.00
56	3851	Scientific equipment	24.90	18.06	4.11	6	6	1.00

comparative advantage activities increased. Second, international prices changed, but not in any systematic direction in favor or against Peru's comparative advantage in selected manufacturing activities. Third, productivity during this period was subject to conflicting pressures. On the one hand, the general deterioration of the economic environment as well as high inflation promoted laxity and made supervision by means of quantitative indicators very difficult, while the high level of uncertainty created a high level of confusion regarding the proper target for managerial effort. On the other hand, the shrinking market, as well as the prospect for eventual trade liberalization, generated considerable pressure for streamlining of production techniques, lowering costs (particularly for export production), and shedding unneeded labor. On average, therefore, one can expect productivity not to have changed much, although there surely must have been changes in individual productive establishments.

Since these data do not pertain to the primary sectors, they do not shed light on the crucial productivity difference between the primary and the industrial sectors. One would expect to find medium-term DDRCs for primary sectors to be lower than those for industry. However, this may well not be the case for short-run DDRCs, which in industry are based on idle labor and idle fixed capital, unless there is also underutilization of land, machines, or people in the primary sectors. In addition, it is necessary to consider that Sendero Luminoso has driven up the real costs of production in both mining and agriculture while having much less of an effect on industry and thus narrowing the differential between the sectors. Finally, the appearance of coca cultivation — which surely has the lowest medium-term DDRC of all — must be taken into account.

THE SECULAR EVOLUTION OF PUBLIC FINANCES

Public finances have been systematically squeezed by Peru's development strategy. On the revenue side, the tax base has comprised fundamentally international trade and the production of modern industrial goods. Thus, import substitution has eroded the import duty tax base, particularly as successive domestication of additional products has shifted the remaining imports to ever-lower duty categories.[41] When the foreign exchange constraint then forced Peru's growth to stop, the domestic tax base stopped growing as well. The subsequent rapid growth of the informal sector reduced the market share of taxpaying enterprises, adding the next twist to the fiscal screw. The secular decline of tax revenue as a percentage of gross national product (GNP) was thus a natural byproduct of the growth strategy and could only be partially countered by repeated increases in the rates of easily collected taxes, such as those on fuel.

The structure of the tax base had a further long-term consequence, which was to tie the fiscal fortunes to the relative prices of traded to non-traded goods. While the government's revenues depended on traded goods, much of its expenditures went for non-traded goods, particularly wages. Thus, as the domestic terms of trade shifted toward traded goods, the government's revenue went up proportionally to its expenditures as a result of the positive effect of its own terms of trade. The opposite occurred when the terms of trade shifted the other way.

Since domestic terms of trade are closely connected to the real exchange rate, devaluations also would improve the government's terms of trade. However, insofar as devaluations were accompanied by domestic recessions, there would be a recessionary reduction in tax base, thus countering the positive effect of the terms of trade gain. During the 1980s, economic expansion has been accompanied broadly by increasing overvaluation of the real exchange rate, while higher real exchange rates have gone along with recessions. It is this offsetting of effects that has obscured the identification of the impact of the domestic terms of trade on government finances.[42]

Public enterprises have played a role in this evolution. They produce almost entirely traded goods and public services. The former are directly dependent on the exchange rate, and both their prices and their revenues have moved cyclically with it. Public services, on the other hand, including the domestic operations of Petroperú, were managed most of the time with a view toward their contribution to the government's anti-inflationary policy. This role was most evident during García's last two years, although it has a long history going back almost to the Velasco government's acquisition of the enterprises through nationalization. In addition, various public enterprises were used as effective obtainers of foreign loans, both public and private. Thus, the business role of the public enterprises was largely overshadowed by their use as instruments of stabilization policy and as vehicles of foreign loan procurement.

On the expenditure side, there have also been important compositional changes with major macroeconomic consequences. As the 1980s progressed, Peru's obligations to service its foreign debt represented increasing shares of its public expenditure. Accordingly, as the government used tax revenue (which reduced private expenditure) to service the foreign debt, it increased the fiscal drag inherent in the balanced budget multiplier. Put another way, taxes collected were sterilized on the expenditure side through the balance of payments. The consequences were as depressive as any other leakage from the expenditure stream.[43]

In terms of growth in the face of a foreign exchange constraint, the increasing share of government expenditure devoted to foreign debt service was equivalent to an increase in the average foreign exchange intensity of domestic aggregate expenditure and, thus, meant that a given amount of foreign exchange could only sustain a lower level of GNP. To keep the level of activity up and GNP growing then required either more borrowing (as in the early years of Belaúnde's second administration) or less debt servicing (as at the end of that administration and during all of García's term).

SHORT-TERM REACTION FUNCTIONS IN THE PERUVIAN ECONOMY CIRCA 1990

DETERMINANTS OF THE LEVEL OF ACTIVITY AND THE STRUCTURE OF PRODUCTION

From an analytical point of view and for policy purposes, it is useful to divide Peru's productive sectors into two groups: 1) those in which output is determined fundamentally by the position of the supply curve and 2) those in which output is determined fundamentally by the position of the demand curve.

SUPPLY-DETERMINED SECTORS

These sectors have upward sloping supply curves and on the demand side confront a mix of domestic demand and export demand or, in some cases, domestic demand and import supply. Accordingly, price in these sectors is largely determined by the world price, as modified by the applicable exchange rate(s) and by export taxes and subsidies or import duties and other restrictions. The domestic price cannot deviate much from the world price plus trade regime, except insofar as producers are able to act effectively as discriminating monopolists or if there are very significant quality differences between the product sold in the domestic market and that exported or imported.

This group of sectors comprises mining (both oil and mineral), export and import competing agriculture, and export fishing (canned fish and fish meal). Since 1985, these sectors have faced an almost continuing reduction in their product-specific real exchange rates, which has driven their equilibrium output down along their supply curve. Lagged prices for some key inputs, such as fuel, and preferential exchange rates for some of the imported inputs served to slow down the deterioration of the applicable real exchange rates but did not succeed in stopping it altogether. At the same time, the cost curve for many of these sectors was drastically shifted upward as a consequence of the activities of Sendero Luminoso. For mining, Sendero increased the costs directly by demanding — and receiving — payoffs in money and dynamite. For agriculture, Sendero signified demands for restrictions in marketed output, the loss of terrorized workers through migration, and the loss of major cadres of technical and managerial personnel, both through induced outmigration and assassination. For both sectors, transportation and energy costs were increased by terrorist actions. Only the fishing sector was spared the impact of Sendero.

By mid-1990, mining output had declined somewhat due to reductions in the output of the large mines, but much more as a result of closures of middle and small mines that found the pincer movement of Sendero and the real exchange rate too overwhelming to resist. Accordingly, a number of mining companies and many more individual miners were technically bankrupt and just holding on to their concessions in the hope that a turnaround would come with the new government.

Agriculture was not in much better shape. The security situation in the country's major agricultural areas was abysmal, with Sendero roaming at will. Accordingly, planting for the market was dangerous. Only the Northern and Southern coasts were largely free of Sendero, with Cajamarca and Arequipa having a fluctuating mix of safe and unsafe provinces. Moreover, the high rates of inflation and the devaluation made planning virtually impossible for the farmer. In consequence, many of them put their government loans for working capital into foreign exchange hoards instead of buying seed and fertilizer. This not only depressed agricultural output but also increased the demand for foreign exchange in the street market, thus contributing to drive up the rate and fuel the inflation. Agricultural output may thus be thought of as being "repressed" by very short-run factors. In consequence, agricultural quantities supplied for export were down, as were even more the supplies of food that directly or indirectly determined Peru's food import requirement.

DEMAND-DETERMINED SECTORS

These sectors operate in the flat or downward-sloping part of their supply curves, and they confront mostly domestic demand. The position of this demand curve is such that at equilibrium, substantial additional supply is available at the same or lower prices.[44]

The sectors in this group include manufacturing and most services. Ever since the crisis of 1975, these sectors have tried to break out of a vicious circle in which their costs are continuously pushed up by various inflationary elements, while the demand curves they face move inward and outward in tandem with government policy and the export cycle. Accordingly, as many enterprises as found it profitable have tried to break into export markets based on the correct notion that this market will prove to be more stable than the domestic market.[45] Unfortunately, the anti-export bias in the exchange rate system made it impossible for many companies to cross the cost threshold into export sales. For others, the lagging real exchange rates as well as the instability of the export promotion incentives have made export selling a roller coaster ride.

In mid-1990, the domestic market was depressed. Alan García's golden period, from December 1985 to July 1987, had shown how quickly supply could respond when demand was there. It had even shown to what extent high levels of activity generate support for a policy as well as investment plans. However, the nationalization of the private banking system, announced on July 28, 1987, created an abrupt change in direction. Once it was clear that the nationalization announcement was not a call to government-private sector negotiations over new rules of the game, but an outright challenge to a test of strength, expectations and economic decisions in the private sector changed abruptly. The most important change was a dramatic reordering of the risk attached to different assets in the private sector's portfolio. Foreign exchange was strongly upgraded, particularly for the short and medium terms, while real investment, particularly in fixed assets but even in inventories, was downgraded. All the way up and down the income distribution, the purchase of goods and services was postponed and the acquisition of foreign exchange undertaken instead.

The result was a sharp increase in the demand for dollars on the street market and a corresponding reduction in domestic effective demand. As the fall in effective demand showed up in increased unsold inventories, production was reduced, and the shelving of investment plans undertaken for political reasons was confirmed by economic reasons. Domestic inflation accelerated, but real profits fell. Effective demand spiraled downward, and demand for foreign exchange increased further. As the exchange rate rose, the judgment that "going long dollars" was profitable was confirmed, and it led to further movements into dollars.[46]

Through perhaps the third quarter of 1988, it could be argued that the level of output was constrained by foreign exchange availability and that import licenses held back output. However, after that date, the shift in aggregate demand impacted strongly, while the regulations increasingly allowed imports with "own" foreign exchange, that is, at the free rate.[47]

Along with the fall in the private demand came a fall in public demand as the government reacted to the reduction in its revenues with repeated cuts in expenditure. Ironically enough, the recession itself was causing the tax base to shrink through two mechanisms: 1) it caused a direct contraction of the base as a consequence of lower output in the whole economy, and 2) as formal employment fell, more workers were pushed into the informal sector, which caused a spate of innovation in informalizing additional sectors of the economy, even while it created more pressure on the informals in established sectors. The net result was a loss of markets on the part of formal producers, thus reducing their tax base more than proportionately.

Further compounding the fiscal problem was an Olivera-Tanzi effect caused in part by the incomplete indexing of tax debt and in part by the curious custom of having the government pay its private suppliers a VAT (valued-added tax)-inclusive price, only to receive the VAT payments back some 45 days later in devalued currency.

Thus, by mid-1990, the level of output of Peruvian industry and services was not constrained by the lack of foreign exchange. It is true that official foreign exchange reserves were exhausted, but private reserves were more than plentiful. Rather, the level of output was determined by a very depressed demand, which in turn reflected the judgment that in these very uncertain times, and particularly with inflation raging, it paid to keep consumption to a minimum and raise dollar accumulation to a maximum.[48]

DETERMINANTS OF INFLATION AND RELATIVE PRICES

Peru's inflation was 15 years old in 1990. During this time, Peru's businesspeople, wage earners, informal sector workers, and just plain consumers learned a number of important lessons on how to survive with high and uncertain inflation and how to minimize their loss of real income.

Up to 1975, Peru's inflation was of the order of 15 percent *per year*; between 1975 and 1982, annual inflation stepped up to about 75 percent per year. Then, in 1983-1985, a new plateau of around 130 percent was established. Even more important, the first half of 1985 saw *monthly* inflation exceed 10 percent almost every month. García's "heterodox" stabilization program brought inflation down to 3.5 percent per month in September 1985, and after hitting a low of 2.7 percent per month in December of that year, it settled in the range of 3.6-5.5 percent per month through July 1987. After the nationalization of the banks, the rate started climbing again, going to the teens per month in the first half of 1988, to 30-40 percent per month in the second half, to then following a winding path between 25 and 40 percent through June 1990.

Sustained inflations of an unstable variety have substantial implications for the price system. First, the information content of prices is much diminished. It is not clear that the price at a particular moment in time actually conveys true scarcity; it could simply be that the seller has not yet gotten around to changing it. Second, prices do not stay put long enough to have an effective function in the minimization of costs, for by the time a round of comparative shopping has been completed, the prices of the suppliers canvassed first will have changed. Hence, buyers must restrict their choices and limit the amount of comparative shopping undertaken. This, in turn, implies that as the market becomes more segmented, competition becomes more imperfect, and demand elasticities faced by particular sellers are lowered. Third, business risk increases enormously for sellers, who have as much difficulty calculating their replacement costs as consumers have in guessing what will happen to the prices they pay. However, if a business miscalculates its replacement costs, it may find its equity wiped out. Hence, under these circumstances, markups rise as a precautionary measure. Fourth, while price elasticities are recognized by sellers to have become substantially reduced, considerable uncertainty exists about the extent of buyer "price resistance," that is, the actual magnitude of the price elasticity of demand. Thus, it is better for the seller to begin with a high posted price that can always be reduced "for a particular client" than to start with a lower price that cannot be raised. In other words, not only is monopoly power recognized and used, but there is every incentive for sellers to become discriminating monopolists. On the other hand, buyers can play this game, too. Hence, temporary bilateral monopolies are common, always, however, behind the facade of high posted prices and negotiated discounts.

The upshot of all this is that both sellers and buyers need a rule of thumb for pricing. This rule of thumb is provided by a simple indexation rule to the most visible price of all, the exchange rate. However, when other important inputs into a product exist, such as fuel, credit, or wages, the indexing system can become more complex and include shifting weights, depending on which price is leading or lagging and how long that discrepancy is expected to last.

The general system of price determination can thus be described as one of indexation to the expected future exchange rate at the time of replacement of stocks, modified by a widening of margins to account for the increased risk and further reinforced by a general tendency to overshoot the required price adjustments, since discounts can always be given on a discriminatory basis.

This price determination system applied not only to established business with its sophisticated managers. It applied equally to the suppliers in the informal market, who understood the concept of replacement cost superbly well and who knew that if they charged below replacement cost they would quickly lose what little capital they owned. The suppliers of both segments of the market were thus working with the same price-setting mechanism, to the detriment of competition between them.

Moreover, since prices in the informal sector were indexed to the exchange rate (and the other major price benchmarks such as gasoline), a large part of labor incomes were so indexed. However, indexation of informal labor incomes was not complete, for these incomes depended not only on the price of the goods sold, which could be fully indexed, but also on the volume sold, which was falling throughout this period, in part due to the general recession and in part through additional migration of labor from the formal sector to the informal sector. Thus, real informal incomes per person were falling. In turn, the formal sector market, operating an imperfect arbitrage link to the informal sector, also saw the supply price of labor become only partially indexed.

Generalized indexation implies that all relative prices are fixed and any exogenous price increase can set off an inflation. Things were not that rigid in Peru in mid-1990. Prices as a whole were indexed to the free exchange rate. That rate was under continued pressure due to expectational demand for dollars as precautionary hoards. Even more, the expected free exchange rate was under pressure due to government attempts to slow the rate of devaluation, thus perversely generating price increases to cover expected future devaluations, which generated indices of devaluation lag, which fed expectations of even larger impending devaluation, which caused further price increases, and so on. In addition, inflation was fueled by occasional adjustments in government-controlled prices (bread, noodles, gasoline). Whenever the government raised these prices "to make them more realistic," they generated cost push. When they were not adjusted, however, they generated expectations of devaluation because the fiscal cost of keeping them constant inflated the fiscal deficit.

Credit creation and fiscal deficits played a dual role in this context. On the one hand, against a drumbeat of monetarist interpretations of the inflation, expectations of inflation and of devaluation were affected by published or rumored figures of both the size of the deficit and its increase.[49] On the other, the increased availability of domestic currency fed the demand for dollars and drove the exchange rate up, thus raising the main indicator against which prices were being set.

The picture on ·inflation is not complete without mention of two important pillars of government intervention: the Mercado Unico de Cambios (MUC), or low tier of the exchange rate, and the price control of selected products. Both were leftovers from the first two years of García's administration, when inflation had been slowed successfully from 10 percent a month at the end of Belaúnde's government to 3.5 to 5.5 percent through mid-1987. By early 1990, the MUC provided cheap dollars only for the import of medicines and food, while price controls on these products were intended to prevent profiteering. Keeping these prices down, along with those of fuel and some basic public services, was designed to dampen the inflationary spiral. However, the ability of these measures to slow inflation was very limited. Instead, they had an enormous effect on relative prices, skewing them very strongly against the preferentially imported foods and medicines and against fuel prices and public services.[50]

Relative prices, then, were primarily affected by government intervention through the MUC and what remained of effective price controls. The remainder were set by the market. However, the price response of different sectors was not uniform to the fluctuations of aggregate demand induced by the government's repeated attempts to implement anti-inflationary monetary policy in late 1989 and early 1990. In food agriculture, flex prices continued to operate, and falls in demand tended to depress relative prices. In industry and services, falls in demand tended to raise prices as the widening of margins was used to offset lower volumes.[51] These differences in behavior were consistent with the changes in market structure and the increase in temporary monopoly power generated by the inflation itself, as noted above.

The composite result of roaring inflation, different market adjustment mechanisms in different parts of the economy, and haphazard government intervention produced a generalized conviction that relative prices were very much out of line. That consensus no doubt contained much truth. But to go beyond it and identify what the "right" set of relative prices might be was much more difficult.

FEEDBACK MECHANISMS AND THE APPEARANCE OF INERT AREAS

Under the circumstances in mid-1990, a number of behavioral interactions resulted in vicious circles and made it hard to design appropriate policy to move the economy forward. In what follows, three such categories are discussed: 1) perverse reaction functions in the foreign exchange market, 2) perverse interaction between private sector decisionmaking and public sector interpretation of the ensuing consequences, and 3) the appearance of policy conundrums leading to inert policy areas. We examine each in turn.

PERVERSE REACTION FUNCTIONS IN THE FOREIGN EXCHANGE MARKET

In a normal foreign exchange market, a higher exchange rate (in number of *soles* per dollar) will bring forth greater supply and reduce demand. For several components of Peru's foreign exchange market in mid-1990, this relationship was reversed, as explained below.

Supply of foreign exchange from coca exports. Peru was at that time strictly a producer of raw materials and first-stage transformation — that is, of coca leaf and coca paste. Moreover, producers in Peru were numerous and not organized in any kind of global syndicate, Sendero's efforts notwithstanding. On the other hand, the buyers were members of the Colombian syndicate, operating effectively as a monopsony. Given the inelastic demand for the product, the *higher* the exchange rate, the *less* the foreign exchange earned. As a consequence, in this segment of the market, the supply of foreign exchange was *forward falling.*[52]

Supply of foreign exchange from remittances. Peru's deepening economic crisis on the one hand strongly pushed emigration, particularly to the United States, and on the other pressed Peruvians living abroad to substantially increase the support they provided to relatives back home. Remittances from Peruvians thus gradually became an important item in foreign exchange inflow.[53]

The motivation of remitters is twofold: to provide a reasonable standard of current living and to allow the acquisition of certain durables, such as housing and house furnishings, including in some cases consumer durables.

How many dollars have to be remitted to meet that target depends naturally on the real exchange rate. The lower the rate, the greater the required remittance. Hence, once again, the supply curve of foreign exchange in this segment of the market was *forward falling*.

Hoarding and dishoarding of foreign exchange. The effect of the exchange rate on hoarding and dishoarding was much more complicated, in part because hoarders and dishoarders were active at the same time and in part because the motivations were not symmetric on different sides of the market nor independent of expectations.

The main motivation for hoarding was to acquire an asset that was a safe store of value. Thus, it made sense to hoard in foreign exchange insofar as there was an expectation that the real exchange rate would rise. From this point of view, the lower the rate, the greater the probability that it would rise, and therefore the greater the quantity of foreign exchange demanded. So far, the demand curve would be negatively sloped. However, insofar as a rise in the rate was taken as a signal that devaluations would continue, it became more attractive to buy even more foreign exchange. Hence, a rise in the rate would increase the quantity demanded rather than reduce it, which implied an *upward sloping demand curve!*

Dishoarding, on the other hand, was largely motivated by the need to cover current expenditure (largely for consumption) insofar as there was a cash deficit from insufficient income. In this case, the lower the real exchange rate, the greater the quantity of dollars that needed to be sold. Once again, there was a *forward falling supply curve.*

While there were parts of the market that had normally shaped supply and demand curves, the relative importance of the segments of the market with perversely shaped curves was large. In particular, the share of the market accounted for by hoarding and dishoarding had grown very large indeed, as the very high inflation and erratic movement in the exchange rate often made it attractive to hold foreign exchange even for very short periods of time, such as a few weeks or even a few days. Accordingly, the global stability of the foreign exchange market was in question.

PERVERSE INTERACTION BETWEEN MARKET BEHAVIOR AND POLICY INTERPRETATION

Policy decisions are usually based on what decisionmakers perceive the condition of the economy to be. However, the statistical record shows outcomes rather than the motivations leading to them. Thus, when the same outcome can be the result of alternative motivations, there is a risk of data misinterpretation and erroneous policymaking. To avoid such errors, it would be necessary systematically to search for alternative explanations and then identify data to distinguish between them. The first of these is normally resisted by policymakers who view alternative explanations as challenges to their diagnoses and policies. The second usually confronts data problems and also considerable delays. For these reasons (and surely also others), several such misinterpretation cycles were at work in Peru's economy in 1990.

Buoyancy of non-traditional exports. The natural interpretation when export levels bear up in the face of declining real exchange rates is to conclude that profitability levels must have initially been quite high, perhaps even excessively so. In any case, the squeeze resulting from the lower real rate only serves to make producers try to cut costs, but in no way endangers their financial survival.

In Peru in mid-1990, however, exports overall were holding up not because they were profitable but for three quite different reasons: 1) many companies had long-term export contracts which they needed to continue to honor in order to preserve their market for the future; 2) many companies had entered into export contracts with the government pursuant to which they had imported machinery with lower duties; if exports did not continue at an established level, these duties would become due, at large cost to the respective firms; and 3) the local market had gotten so bad that exporting was the only game in town even if it, too, was not particularly profitable.[54]

The policy consequences of this alternative explanation are substantially different from the standard interpretation. In the standard case, one concludes that there has been fluff in the exchange rate for a long time and that the newer real rate is much closer to equilibrium and to pressing business to raise productivity. Thus, it is fine to let the real rate continue to revalue. In the alternative explanation, one sees business hanging on to avoid bankruptcy, squeezed by a revalued real exchange rate, overseas markets that can easily be lost, and domestic tax penalties for falling below established export targets. With this view, it is urgent to raise the real exchange rate; otherwise, one will wake up one day to find that numerous firms have gone broke.

Which explanation corresponds to reality can be ascertained, albeit with some difficulty, by the analysis of data at firm and establishment level. However, this analysis involves critical questions about what constitutes a "proper" or "fair" return on investment as well as regarding the reliability of firm-level accounting information. Moreover, considerable delay is unavoidable in obtaining results; such a lag may well prove fatal to at least part of the "patients."

Repatriation of capital by domestic firms. As the recession deepened and the domestic interest rate rose in real terms, numerous companies obtained lines of credit at Miami banks and substituted expensive Lima-based credit for cheaper Miami-based credit.

One possible interpretation is to welcome the reentry of Peru into the world credit markets and celebrate the capital inflow occurring. Based on this reading, the tight money policy is doing its work by strengthening the capital account of the balance of payments. Another interpretation is to recognize the capital flow as resulting from Peruvians' bringing in their own money from Miami, via back-to-back arrangements with Miami banks, in order to keep their sinking firms afloat until Peru's economy stabilizes. On this reading, the capital flow is a clear danger signal and far from something to rejoice about. If the second interpretation is true but the first is acted upon, the domestic screws can be tightened further in the mistaken belief that the private sector can easily stand the treatment, until a large part of the private sector abruptly collapses into bankruptcy.

Discriminating between these two alternative views again hinges on what firm-level data are to be believed and on views regarding appropriate levels of profitability, given Peru's economic situation.

CONUNDRUMS AND INERT AREAS

A number of government actions in mid-1990 could be expected to have contradictory effects, thus being partially or totally self-defeating. As a result, the unstable hyperstagflation tended to get perpetuated. Among these conundrums were the following.

The hyperstagflationary effect of tax increases. There was general agreement that government revenue needed to be raised. This was mostly held to signify an increase in tax collections. However, the most collectible taxes and those generating a significant part of the revenue were indirect taxes: the general sales tax (Impuesto General a las Ventas, IGV), the fuel tax, and import duties. All of these would raise prices and, via the existing indexation, push inflation. At the same time, they would siphon purchasing power away from the private sector. Expenditures would fall, and the demand restriction would tighten. Hyperstagflation would get worse.

The one bright spot in this picture could be a reduction in the demand for dollars, consequent to lowered private purchasing power. However, with inflation increasing, the desire to shift into dollars could only increase. In addition, any momentary pause in the rate of devaluation would be seized upon as a good time to buy. Thus, private expenditure would shift further away from local goods and services and into foreign exchange, further deepening the depression and reducing the tax base. The tax increases were thoroughly entrapped.

The revaluation effect of raising controlled prices. There was general agreement that government-controlled public service prices were far too low and needed to be adjusted. However, insofar as this was done, the domestic price level would rise, surely pushing inflation and certainly making the exchange rate appear even more overvalued. This would cause further expectations of devaluation and fuel further price increases of traded goods, thus annulling, at least in part, the price correction attempted. If public sector prices had been adjusted further, the inflationary spiral would have been given a further push.

The price distortionary effect of devaluation. Not only was the MUC in need of devaluation, the market exchange rate was also believed to be undervalued. Devaluation, in turn, would raise the relative prices of traded goods, further increasing the lag in public service prices. In addition, devaluation would open a yawning fiscal gap on account of food imports and oil prices. On the other hand, if these prices were raised along with the devaluation, it was most likely that inflation would further accelerate, with little relative price correction accomplished. Once more, policy was boxed in.

DETERIORATION OF THE STATE'S MANAGERIAL CAPACITY

In mid-1990, there was widespread agreement that the state was a bloated, inefficient, and ineffective bureaucracy, capable of managing little, if anything. The last time exasperation with the operational capacity of the public sector had been this visible was in the later 1970s, when the expansionary phase of Velasco's regime had collapsed into stagflation and balance of payments problems. "Phase III" of the military regime, under the leadership of Javier Silva Ruete and Manuel Moreyra, put order into public administration, and the issue subsided but did not go away.

Belaúnde's second administration expanded public employment substantially, partly, it was said at the time, as a reward to his party's adherents. García did the same, and an acceleration of hiring was clearly in evidence toward the end of his tenure. Table 3 puts this growth into perspective. It is remarkable to note that the increase in the total for García's term (1990 minus 1985), at 150,000, was no larger than the increase in three out of Belaúnde's five years (1985 minus 1982). Such a reduction in the rate of increase of public employment from Belaúnde to García stands in stark contrast to what was generally believed in mid-1990.

Table 3.
Employment in Peru's Public Sector

	Sector	1982	1985	1988	1990
1.	General government	495,649	614,837	713,065	730,000
	Central government	385,523	493,530	558,669	561,000
2.	State enterprises	107,742	142,953	172,000	172,000
	Totals	*603,391*	*757,790*	*885,065*	*902,000*

Source: Moore 1990, Table 1.

The situation in mid-1990 differed from previous periods of exasperation with the functioning of the state in several important respects:

1. The García administration had significantly increased the role of state intervention in the economy. Thus, as regulatory difficulty increased after mid-1987 and intervention became ever more complex in 1988 and 1989, the inadequacy of the administrative apparatus to respond to its task was increasingly obvious and had immediate and strong effects on a range of economic agents.

2. Since mid-1987, Peruvian economic (and political) developments had been largely framed within the context of a head-on collision between President García and the private sector, caused by the attempted state takeover of privately owned banks. In this battle, little quarter was given by either side, and therefore there was little tolerance among the public for even "normal" inefficiency of government operations.

3. The increase in public sector employment during the García period was accompanied from 1988 on by a dramatic collapse in the real wage of public servants, perhaps by as much as two-thirds in 1988 and 1989 alone. The cause of this fall lay in the collision of the desire to provide jobs with the fall of tax revenue in the context of a rapidly rising price level. While such a containment of government expenditure may have been justified on macro grounds, at the micro level it forced government employees to confront very basic survival needs. The resulting pressures only increased corruption and moonlighting. The existence of extensive government regulation and the requirement to obtain many permits and licenses provided fertile ground for corruption, while the impact of real wage compression contributed to a supervisor's understanding attitude if supervisees worked short hours to accommodate other income-producing activities.

Sendero Luminoso also contributed its share to complicate the picture further, since Sendero systematically targeted local authorities and leaders, thus substantially hobbling another layer of public administration. Moreover, since real pay in the military had also declined, the counterinsurgency effort necessarily suffered from the corresponding morale problems.

POLICY IMPLICATIONS OF THE STRUCTURE OF PERU'S ECONOMY CIRCA 1990

Peru's economic structure had quite fundamental implications for the main objectives of economic policy in 1990: stabilization of prices, reestablishment of Peru's balance of payments viability, recovery of fiscal viability, and, last but certainly not least, recovery of real personal incomes. The major elements of these implications are sketched out below. However, before focusing on specific policy needs, it is important to highlight the fundamentals emerging from Peru's resource imbalance and from the structure of the price system.

RESOURCE BALANCE

Peru's imbalance between its labor endowment and the other cooperating factors — capital, land, and foreign exchange — could only be righted by a policy mix emphasizing 1) export-led growth (with some judicious and efficient import substitution thrown in) to break the tightest constraint, the shortage of foreign exchange; 2) capacity-utilizing growth, to make use of past savings to the maximum extent possible and then to extract as much output from new savings as could be obtained on a triple shift basis; and 3) labor-intensive growth, not only in order to use the plentiful factor, but to generate well-distributed earned income.

In the absence of such a strategy, the growth of the informal sector would be the only refuge for the economy. And while this sector uses a factor mix more closely approximating the factor endowments than the formal sector, it nonetheless represents a social and economic market adaptation oriented to share poverty and make tolerable a situation of stagnation or insufficient growth. Even during the first years of an effective growth strategy, the informal sector would continue to be of enormous importance in the economy, centrally affecting the functioning of the price system and shaping the economy's adjustment to macro pressures.

A policy which delayed the generation of foreign exchange from new exports and import substitution or a policy which did not attempt to maximize the salvage value of Peru's existing capital stock would only postpone unnecessarily the day when Peru would emerge from its imbalance of resource endowment.

FUNCTIONING OF THE PRICE SYSTEM

Peru's market prices differed from shadow prices in part due to inappropriate government intervention (particularly in foreign exchange), in part due to resource imbalance (particularly in the labor market), and in part due to externalities (particularly in the foreign exchange market and in the capital market). The government could, in principle, control its own policies, although in practice it would be subject to severe limitations due to the distributional consequences of reversing some of its interventions. However, sources of inadequacy in the price system not caused by the government would only disappear as a result of a very substantial amount of economic growth. It would, therefore, take a long time until Peru was blessed with a well-functioning price system that gave correct allocative signals.

It is most important that this point be fully recognized: *until Peru had had a lot of growth, its free markets would not produce good allocation of resources even if the government removed all the distortions it had introduced.*

Distorted price signals (i.e., market failure) required offsetting government intervention. Unfortunately, in mid-1990, the Peruvian government was not well situated for such intervention from an administrative point of view nor in terms of the confidence its intervention would inspire in the private sector. Nonetheless, to believe that "getting the government out of the way" would lead to good allocation of resources was contrary to what was known about the functioning of Peru's markets. The objective, then, had to be a viable and judicious mix of free markets and government management.

With these fundamentals stated, it is now possible to turn to the more specific policy objectives.

PRICE STABILIZATION

The multiple indexation of Peru's price system signified that any attempt at stabilization would require a policy involving multiple anchors. It would not be enough to use an exchange rate anchor because an important number of public prices needed to be raised, thus risking continued domestic price rises that would make the exchange rate anchor untenable in short order. On the other hand, using a public price anchor was not credible, since these prices were widely believed to be too low, and they were, in any case, closely tied to the exchange rate. In turn, a monetary anchor was also not good enough because tight money had proved to be stagflationary. While no anchor would be sufficient on its own, a combination of exchange rate, public price, wage, and monetary anchors could conceivably do the job.

BALANCE OF PAYMENTS VIABILITY

Viability required the availability of international reserves, an increase in traditional and non-traditional exports, and the reestablishment of normal relations with creditors.

The first of these fundamentally involved a voluntary transfer of private dollar hoards to the government, presumably in exchange for local currency or other financial assets. At issue was the credibility of a stabilization program and of the solidity of the alternative financial assets. Since the stabilization program itself would be more credible if it were backed by official international reserves, the creation of a solid, but governmental, financial asset for individuals to hold instead of their dollars was a viable way to break a vicious circle. Candidates for that kind of paper were external "dollar" bonds, with backing in kind or guarantees of third parties such as the Andean Development Corporation or the Andean Reserve Fund.

The second objective involved tackling the short-term lack of profitability of Peru's exports. In large measure, these were depressed due to an excessively low real exchange rate. In turn, Peru's import-competing activities could only compete insofar as import restrictions were in force. The real net exchange rate needed to be increased. However, if that were accomplished exclusively through nominal devaluation, it would collide with the stabilization policy. Hence, a range of cost reduction options, which are "devaluation substitutes," needed to be explored, including reduction in port charges and port delays, elimination of electricity outages, red tape reduction, enhanced security for personnel (particularly in mining), and so on. For non-traditional exports, the gamut of promotional instruments needed to be streamlined.

Fundamentally, however, care had to be taken so that as the real exchange rate was raised, too much foreign exchange would not be lost from those suppliers with perversely sloped supply curves. Hence, a market-based differentiation between legal exchange receipts and others, with the former receiving a preferred rate, would be a policy consistent with the structure of Peru's foreign exchange market.[55]

Fiscal Viability

The difficulty of raising taxes on the existing low incomes and the perverse interactions resulting from attempts to raise taxes have already been pointed out. No doubt, it was possible to extract a few additional percentage points of GNP with great effort. However, the level of tax collection was so low that it was essential to tackle the problem at its structural base.

As noted before, Peru's real tax collections had been severely reduced by four interacting factors: 1) fall in the tax base due to recession, 2) fall in the tax base due to induced informalization, 3) fall in the real value of taxes due to Olivera-Tanzi effects of inflation, and 4) fall in the real value of taxes due to adverse terms of trade for the government.

All four of these causes could be subjected to policy action. Economic expansion along with efforts to ease the de-informalization of informal business would effectively address the first two concerns. Proper indexation of tax debt could deal with the third. The fourth required a lasting change in relative prices but was consistent with what was desirable for dealing with the balance of payments problem. Thus, at bottom, government revenue was dependent on the solution of other problems. It was important, therefore, that it not be seen as independently capable of solution, since raising such expectations would only lead to disappointment and frustration and could even get in the way of achieving other goals such as price stabilization and economic reactivation.

RECOVERY OF REAL PERSONAL INCOMES

Real incomes could only recover as economic activity expanded. In turn, such expansion had to be based on raising production in export sectors as well as in sectors supplying the domestic market.

The short-term level of activity in the supply-determined sectors was held down by an overvalued real exchange rate and by Sendero's terrorism. It followed that policy had to be oriented to counteract both these effects. Profitability in the production of traded goods had to be raised, and the security risks involved in producing needed to be reduced.

In the demand-determined sectors, output was being held down by insufficient effective demand, resulting from private preference for being liquid and from governmental paucity of resources. It follows that policy should have aimed at refocusing private decisions away from hoarding foreign exchange and toward a more normal expenditure pattern. Such a policy orientation would be consistent with the stabilization effort and a lengthening of decision horizons. In turn, private sector-led reactivation would produce new tax revenue, allowing the public sector to reestablish some of its required expenditure as well.

PUTTING THE PIECES TOGETHER

Assembling individual policies into a coherent whole required careful meshing of objectives and tools and ensuring of mutual reinforcement among individual policy elements. Uncertainty had to be reduced, horizons lengthened, individual actors' interests and incomes respected and to an extent satisfied, while collective needs such as those represented by target tax revenues had to be tended to. Given the initial conditions of a malfunctioning price system, overlaid by short-term pricing behavior that was uncompetitive and driven fundamentally by expectations based on little more than guesswork about the present and the future, the complex coordination that was required unavoidably implied extensive participation and agreement of the main actors in the economy, business, labor, and government in some sort of "National Pact" incomes policy. Letting the markets operate without any agreed-upon steering would be a prescription for a very long and costly *tatonnement,* during which countless resources would be wasted as risk-averse individual actors very slowly changed their behavior in response to a lagged recognition of changed circumstances. Rather, markets would have to be helped to reach reasonable short-term equilibria quickly so that resources could be put to work productively as soon as possible.[56] This was not an easy requirement, given the status of the state's administrative capacity. In consequence, the private sector would have to be called upon to do its share, on the one hand, by a programmed return to the market, and on the other, through lending of personnel to government agencies to reinforce the implementation of a transition strategy of contained economic and social cost.

Notes

1. The term "inert area" was coined by Harvey Leibenstein to signify an economic decision space which is not optimal but from which, for a variety of reasons, economic agents do not move. See Leibenstein 1976.

2. See Schydlowsky and Wicht 1979 or 1983 for a description of this period.

3. For a detailed analysis of Peru's export promotion efforts and their emasculation in 1982, see Schydlowsky, Hunt, and Mezzera 1983.

4. For a comparison of the origins and nature of Evolutionary, Innovational, and Acute Dutch Disease, see Schydlowsky 1993.

5. See De Soto 1986.

6. The only estimates available on this question are for 1976. For that date, it would appear that the country's unemployed comprised about 7 percent of the labor force, whereas the underemployed totaled about 30 percent. Assuming that the underemployed were one-third employed implies that full-time equivalent unemployment stood at 27 percent. Going to two-shift utilization of installed capacity would employ an additional 8 percent of the labor force, and going to three-shift utilization of installed capacity was estimated to employ an additional 26 percent of the labor force. For 1990, Lima's open unemployment stood at 8 percent, while underemployment had skyrocketed to 73 percent (Instituto Nacional de Estadística 1992, Table 6.4, 575). If the underemployed were one-third employed, these numbers imply a full-time equivalent unemployment of 56 percent. To get to full employment would require putting the economy on a multiple-shift standard and keeping it there for a number of years. See Schydlowsky 1979.

7. Note that owner-operators of agricultural and mining enterprises rarely distinguished clearly between that part of their income which constituted rent, that part which constituted return to created capital, and that part which constituted return to entrepreneurship. Nor did they typically have a clear idea of the value of their natural resource asset and hence of the opportunity return of their investment in it.

8. The former is measured by the domestic resource cost of foreign exchange, while the latter is measured by the consumption weighted average of net import exchange rates.

9. On the role of market adjustment mechanisms in the definition of shadow prices, see Schydlowsky 1973a and 1973b and Ramírez 1980.

10. See, for instance, Schydlowsky 1978 and Schydlowsky, Hunt, and Mezzera 1983, Chapter 4, Appendix B.

11. See Bitrán et al. 1986.

12. A good source for up-to-date information on fringe benefits is the publication *Analisis Laboral.* See Schydlowsky, Hunt, and Mezzera 1983, Chapter 5, for a detailed discussion and numerical evaluation pertaining to the early 1980s. Consult also Schydlowsky 1978 for an analysis of the effect of the *comunidad laboral* on the difference between cost of labor and nominal wage.

13. Export production will have a price determined by the market exchange rate, which is systematically lower than the shadow price of foreign exchange, hence the marginal social product of labor in export production is above the private marginal product. Import-substituting production faces an implicit effective exchange rate equal to the market exchange rate times one plus the effective rate of protection, a net rate which can be above or below the shadow price of foreign exchange. Accordingly, it is not unambiguously clear whether the marginal social product of labor in import-substituting production is above or below the private marginal product.

14. While social security taxes are supposed to fund a range of benefits, from medical attention to retirement pensions, workers correctly assume that they will get little back for their contributions. Indeed, medical services have been steadily deteriorating, and the retirement fund is technically bankrupt. The social security pension obtained in 1990-1992 after a lifetime of maximum contribution was approximately $1.50 a day, a little below what was obtained previously. However, the bulk of modern sector retirement pay came from compulsory, unfunded, company provisions for severance pay upon retirement. Yet workers have always feared that companies would avoid payment when the time came, and indeed Peru's crisis has made it impossible for many companies to comply with their obligations.

15. A good example is the hiring of domestics by recommendation of a friend's domestics. As a result of this practice, family ties as well as a common geographic origin become "social assets." For a detailed discussion of labor markets in which this feature is important, see Papanek 1986. For a more theoretical treatment, see Manove, Papanek, and Dey 1985, while an empirical treatment can be found in Papanek, Wheeler, and Dey 1985.

16. Informal vendors of fruits and vegetables typically have to pay cash for their merchandise, but vendors of shirts and other industrial goods are often given trade credit by the factories and wholesalers that supply them. For a more general analysis of the role of the capital market in creating labor market segmentation, see Mezzera 1981.

17. Recall Chamberlin 1965, Chapter 5.

18. Vilfredo Pareto (1848-1923) developed the concept known as "Pareto optimality," which postulates three conditions that must be met by an economy in order to maximize the economic welfare of the community.

19. See Bitrán et al. 1986.

20. The rate banks pay on deposits is traditionally referred to as the "passive" rate because the banks are the passive element in the depositor-depositee relationship and also because it is the rate paid on the banks' liabilities, *pasivos* in Spanish. In contrast, the "active" rate is the rate on the banks' loans, in which the banks are active players, but it is also the rate charged on the banks' assets, *activos* in Spanish.

21. Further marginal conditions must hold if additional financial or real assets are held by these individuals.

22. If savers do not save in banks because no banking institutions are within reach, as in outlying provinces, then the own-interest rates of the assets in which they save could be below banks' passive rate. Correspondingly, the private time preference of these savers will be below banks' passive rate. Now, while it is unlikely that the savings generated by individuals in this situation constitute an important part of national savings, they may well represent an important part of the population and of income and consequently deserve a substantial weighting in the average national social time preference.

23. The reasons usually cited for this discrepancy are that the private time preference includes "myopia" (the incapacity of the human being properly to project into the future) as well as a limited life expectancy. The social time preference by comparison is held to be based on purposive projections of the future, and society as a whole does not die. In addition, there may well be externalities to simultaneous saving by many, which further lower the social time preference. On these topics, see Eckstein 1957, Frisch 1964, Feldstein 1964, and Marglin 1963a and 1963b.

24. Indeed, given credit rationing, the active rate is ordinarily below the private after-tax rate of return. Moreover, when assessing rates of return to capital, care must be taken to make provision for the return to entrepreneurship, an item sometimes referred to as "normal profits."

25. This point is made forcefully in Harberger 1972.

26. For the original presentation of this "general disequilibrium" approach, see Schydlowsky 1973a and 1973b.

27. For good order's sake, it should also be added that when there is no equilibrium in the capital market, it is inappropriate to measure the marginal product of capital as an internal rate of return; rather, it needs to be taken as the present value of the future return discounted at the social time preference. This issue has been discussed extensively in the project evaluation literature. For an early, clear, and never effectively rebutted statement, see Eckstein 1957.

28. See Bitrán et al. 1986.

29. Early studies on the topic are Millan 1975, Abusada-Salah 1975, and Valdivieso 1978. The implications of under-utilization were drawn out, and the potentials of such utilization were forcefully argued in Schydlowsky and Wicht 1979 and 1983. Further figures on utilization were provided in Schydlowsky, Hunt, and Mezzera 1983, which also analyzed the consequences of excess capacity for export promotion. The macroeconomic consequences of excess capacity were explored in Schydlowsky 1979 and 1981 and in greater modeling detail in Schydlowsky, Hunt, and Mezzera 1983 and in Schydlowsky 1986.

30. Summary statements of these mechanisms can be found in Schydlowsky 1974, 1979, and 1981.

31. Note that, until quite recently, the international financial agencies supported state-owned development banks that lent for long-run purposes at below market rates.

32. For a detailed description and analysis of this regime, see Rabinovich 1985.

33. Indeed, depending on the elasticity of demand for labor, it is conceivable that full employment is not achievable at a positive wage. See Eckaus 1955 for the seminal statement of this possibility.

34. For a more complete discussion of the options faced by developing countries in this context, see Schydlowsky 1991 and 1993.

35. David Ricardo (1772-1823) formulated theories of distribution and comparative advantage.

36. This is not to say that the costs to other exporters from this Dutch Disease-type situation is not considerable — nor is it impossible to do better. For some policy suggestions in this regard, see Schydlowsky 1993.

37. This point was made regarding Peru's non-traditional exports in Schydlowsky, Hunt, and Mezzera 1983, Chapter 4. It is generalized and more forcefully argued in Schydlowsky 1984.

38. Negative DDRCs also indicate comparative disadvantage, for they imply loss of foreign exchange from production.

39. The domestic resource cost of foreign exchange is a measure developed in Israel in the early 1950s to aid in that country's decisionmaking on industrialization. See Bruno 1962 and 1967. For a more recent overview of its uses, see Schydlowsky 1984.

40. See Levy et al. 1986.

41. Along the way, the average import duty collected has become an increasingly poor indicator of the protective impact of the tariff, an effect long recognized by analysts of effective protection, who use domestic production-weighted tariff indices in lieu of import-weighted indices in constructing their estimates.

42. See Seminario, Beltrán, and Sueyoshi 1992, Chapters 4 and 5, for a quantification of the government's terms of trade and the measurement of the deficit in properly deflated real terms.

43. The contractionary effect of government foreign exchange expenditure was first pointed out in Schydlowsky 1981. See Parot and Rodríguez-Salas 1988 for a formalized model. See also Blejer and Cheasty 1991.

44. Note, however, that to the right of equilibrium, marginal revenue falls faster than marginal cost.

45. For an analytical exploration of this proposition, with simulations that show the extent to which it is true for Peru, see Schydlowsky and Rodríguez-Salas 1982.

46. The movements in the real exchange rate were erratic in that period, in part because the number of applicable exchange rates multiplied. What is quite clear is that short-run speculative holding of dollars was widely perceived as being more profitable that regular domestic business activity.

47. There were, as always in confused times, a number of exceptions. For instance, for some number of months, the milk canning industry was able to import powdered milk at the lowest official exchange rate and sell the reconstituted and canned milk to the border towns of Lake Titicaca (for resale across the border) at the

equivalent of the free rate, which stood some six to ten times higher. The milk canning industry was certainly working at full capacity during this time — fulfilling an export demand, but unfortunately one that almost surely caused foreign exchange loss.

48. One might question why there was no flight into goods instead of a flight into foreign exchange. The answer is that there were indeed times when particular goods were a good acquisition. For instance, the price of first-quality Peruvian wines lagged the general inflation at different times during 1988. At other times, it paid to accumulate inventories of gasoline — if one had suitable storage facilities. However, with inflation in the monthly two digits and fluctuating at hard-to- forecast rates, and with relative prices highly unstable, it was far too costly and difficult to devise a sound arbitrage strategy for an inventory of real goods, if it could be implemented at all, to make this a viable proposition for a significant number of people.

49. It is notable that throughout the last two years of García's government, an extraordinary compression of government expenditure took place. According to Central Bank figures, the current expenditures of the public non-financial sector as a percentage of GDP were as follows: 1982, 38.9 percent; 1983, 45 percent; 1984, 37.5 percent; 1985, 38 percent; 1986, 31.3 percent; 1987, 28.3 percent; 1988, 29.9 percent; 1989, 23.6 percent; 1990, 22.0 percent (Banco Central de Reserva del Perú 1992, 166). Capital expenditure shows a similar pattern.

50. In addition, since access to the Mercado Unico de Cambios (MUC) virtually guaranteed enormous profits on imports, the selective award of access to the MUC provided multiple opportunities for corruption, which, according to press reports, were extensively used.

51. See Ferrari 1989 for a discussion of different price-setting modes in different sectors of the Peruvian economy.

52. There were two possible countervailing influences to this "incorrect" slope of the supply curve: 1) Sendero's actions as a cartel formed to oppose the buyers' monopsony and 2) the impact of a devaluation on the cost of production in *soles* via the local currency cost of inputs (not much) and wages (a bit more). Sendero indeed probably raised the price received by growers in the areas it "protected." In addition, it also collected some direct protection money from the drug buyers. However, Sendero only controlled a part of the coca-producing area, and in addition, there is every reason to believe that Sendero's export tax was a constant amount or a constant proportion that would not be adjusted upward to compensate for the terms-of-trade effects of a devaluation. On the other hand, the pass-through of a devaluation onto costs of coca production can at best be partial in view of the large component of rent in the domestic value added of coca leaf and basic paste production.

53. No reliable estimates are available, but some guesses on amounts can be hazarded. Assume only one million Peruvians lived in the United States in 1990, probably most of them illegal. Assume again that they each sent only $20 per month. That would make an annual flow of $240 million, or more than Peru was earning in oil exports. However, a better estimate starts with about 500,000 Peruvian earners in the United States sending as much as $100 per month. That yields $600 million in remittances, almost as much as half of all non-oil mining exports combined, or three times as much as oil exports.

54. "It is better to go broke on the installment plan than all at once!"

55. It should be noted that Colombia operates precisely such a system and taxes all undocumented sales of foreign exchange by some 20 to 25 percent. For many years, Peru has operated a similarly divided exchange system under the name of Certificado de Divisas de Moneda Extranjera, which was introduced by the Klein Sachs Commission in 1949 to unwind a set of multiple exchange rates left behind by the Alianza Popular Revolucionaria Americana (APRA) government in power under President José Luis Bustamante.

56. See Patinkin 1993 for insightful comments on the successful Israeli effort to "jump to equilibrium" by social compact during their mixed ortho-heterodox stabilization program of the mid-1980s.

REFERENCES

Abusada-Salah, Roberto. 1975. *Utilización del capital instalado en el sector industrial peruano*. Boston: Boston University Center for Latin American Development Studies. Processed.

Banco Central de Reserva del Perú (BCR). 1992. *Memoria 1991*. Lima: BCR.

Bitrán, Eduardo, Juan José Fernández-Ansola, and Matilde Pinto de la Piedra, with the collaboration of Daniel M. Schydlowsky. 1986. *Estimación de los precios sociales de los factores básicos en el Perú: 1986-1987*. Boston: Boston University Center for Latin American Development Studies for the Instituto Nacional de Planificación. Processed.

Blejer, Mario, and A. Cheasty. 1991. "The Measurement of Fiscal Deficits: Analytical and Methodological Issues." *Journal of Economic Literature* (December).

Bruno, Michael. 1962. *Interdependence, Resource Use and Structural Change in Israel*. Jerusalem: Bank of Israel.

Bruno, Michael. 1967. "The Optimal Choice of Import Substituting and Export Promoting Projects." In *Planning the External Sector: Techniques, Problems and Policies*. New York: United Nations.

Chamberlin, Edward H. 1965. *The Theory of Monopolistic Competition*. Cambridge, Mass.: Harvard University Press.

De Soto, Hernando. 1986. *El otro sendero, La revolucion informal*. Lima: Instituto Libertad y Democracia.

Eckaus, Richard S. 1955. "The Factor Proportions Problem in Underdeveloped Areas." *American Economic Review* (September).

Eckstein, Otto. 1957. "Investment Criteria for Economic Development and the Theory of Intertemporal Welfare Economics." *Quarterly Journal of Economics* 71 (February).

Feldstein, Martin. 1964. "The Social Time Preference Discount Rate in Cost-Benefit Analysis." *Economic Journal* 74 (June).

Ferrari, Cesar. 1989. *Política económica, teoría y práctica en el Perú*. Lima: Ebert Foundation.

Frisch, Ragnar. 1964. "Dynamic Utility." *Econométrica* 32 (July).

Harberger, Arnold C. 1972. "On Measuring the Social Opportunity Cost of Public Funds." In *Project Evaluation*, ed. A. C. Harberger. London: Macmillan.

Instituto National de Estadística (INE). 1992. *Perú: Compendio estadístico 1991-92*. Lima (May).

Leibenstein, Harvey. 1976. *Beyond Economic Man: A New Foundation for Microeconomics*. Cambridge: Harvard University Press.

Levy, Santiago, R. Parot, and M. Rodríguez-Salas. 1986. *La medición de la ventaja comparativa en el sector manufacturero del Perú*. Boston: Boston University,

Center for Latin American Development Studies for the Instituto Nacional de Planificación.

Manove, M., G. F. Papanek, and H. K. Dey. 1985. "A Theory of Wage Determination in Less Developed Countries." Boston: Boston University, Center for Asian Development Studies. Discussion Paper 30.

Marglin, Stephen. 1963a. "The Social Rate of Discount and the Optimal Rate of Investment." *Quarterly Journal of Economics* (February).

Marglin, Stephen. 1963b. "The Opportunity Cost of Public Investment." *Quarterly Journal of Economics* (May).

Mezzera, Jaime. 1981. "Segmented Labor Markets Without Policy-induced Labor Market Distortions." *World Development* 9 (11/12).

Millan, Patricio. 1975. *The Intensive Use of Capital in Industrial Plants: Multiple Shifts as an Economic Option.* Ph.D. diss. Cambridge: Harvard University.

Moore, Richard. 1990. "Administrative Reform and Reform of the Civil Service." World Bank Working Document. December.

Papanek, Gustav F. 1986. *Lectures on Development Strategy, Growth, Equity, and the Political Process in Southern Asia.* Lecture II, 41-62. Islamabad: Pakistan Institute of Development Economics.

Papanek, Gustav F., D. Wheeler, and H. K. Dey. 1985. "A Labor Income Determination Model for Labor Abundant Countries: Empirical Evidence." Discussion Paper 24. Boston: Boston University, Center for Asian Development Studies.

Parot, Rodgrigo, and Martha Rodríguez-Salas. 1988. "Net Expansionary Effect of the Fiscal Sector." In *IMF Backed Stabilization and Growth: An Inductive Study Based on the Costa Rican Case,* eds. R. Parot, M. Rodríguez-Salas, and D. M. Schydlowsky. Boston: Boston University Center for Latin American Development Studies.

Patinkin, Don. 1993. "Israel's Stabilization Program of 1985, Or Some Simple Truths of Monetary Theory." *Journal of Economic Perspectives* (Spring) 7 (2).

Rabinovich, Catalina. 1985. *Las acciones laborales: Fuente de financiamiento, alternativa de inversión y efectos de distribución.* Lima: Friedrich Ebert Foundation.

Ramírez, Luis A. 1980. "Benefit-Cost Analysis Methodologies: Untangling their Equivalences and Discrepancies." Boston: Boston University, Center for Latin American Development Studies. Discussion Paper 39.

Schydlowsky, Daniel M. 1973a. *Project Evaluation in Economies in General Disequilibrium: An Application of Second Best Analysis.* Boston: Boston University, Center for Latin American Development Studies, and Inter-American Development Bank, Washington, D.C.

Schydlowksy, Daniel M. 1973b. *Methodology for the Empirical Estimation of Shadow Prices.* Boston: Boston University, Center for Latin American Development Studies, and Inter-American Development Bank, Washington, D.C.

Schydlowsky, Daniel M. 1974. "Influencia del mercado financiero sobre la utilización de capacidad instalada." *Desarrollo Económico.* (Buenos Aires) (July/Sept).

Schydlowsky, Daniel M. 1978. "The Design of Benefit/Cost Analysis of Investment Projects in Peru: A Country Specific View." *Industrialization and Development* 2.

Schydlowsky, Daniel M. 1979. "Capital Utilization, Growth, Employment, Balance of Payments, and Price Stabilization." In *Planning and Short-Term Macroeconomic Policy in Latin America,* eds. Jere Behrman and James Hanson. Cambridge, Mass: Ballinger.

Schydlowsky, Daniel M. 1981. "Macroeconomic Situation and Outlook." In *Latin Economic Outlook: Peru,* eds. W. R. Cline, Daniel M. Schydlowsky, and Riordan Roett. Washington, D.C.: International Economic Analysis, Inc., and Evans Economics.

Schydlowsky, Daniel M. 1983. "The Short-Run Potential for Employment Generation on Installed Capacity in Latin America." In *Human Resources, Employment, and Development,* Vol. 4, Latin America, eds. Víctor L. Urquidi and Saúl Trejo Reyes, 311-347. Proceedings of the Sixth World Congress of the International Economic Association held in Mexico City in 1980. Hong Kong: The McMillan Press, Ltd. Also appeared in *Perú Exporta* 85 (August 1981): 44-56; 86 (September 1981): 38-45.

Schydlowsky, Daniel M. 1984. "A Policymaker's Guide to Comparative Advantage." *World Development* (April). Also appeared in *Perú Exporta* 88 (November 1981): 34-41.

Schydlowsky, Daniel M. 1986. "The Macroeconomic Effect of Non-Traditional Exports in Peru, 1978-1980." *Economic Development and Cultural Change* 34 (3) (April): 491-508.

Schydlowsky, Daniel M. 1989. "La eficiencia industrial en América Latina: Mito y realidad." *Pensamiento Iberoamericano* (16) (July-December).

Schydlowsky, Daniel M. 1991. *Savings and Investment and the Synergy of Economic Integration in Latin America.* Buenos Aires: Institute for Latin American Integration (INTAL).

Schydlowsky, Daniel M. 1993. *Foreign Exchange Regimes for Dutch Disease Prone LDCs.* College Park: University of Maryland, IRIS.

Schydlowsky, Daniel M., Shane Hunt, and Jaime Mezzera. 1983. *La promoción de exportaciones no tradicionales en el Perú.* Lima: Asociación de Exportadores del Perú.

Schydlowsky, Daniel M., and Martha Rodríguez-Salas. 1982. "The Vulnerability of Small Semi-Industrialized Economies to Export Shocks: A Simulation Analysis Based on Peruvian Data." In *Trade, Stability, Technology, and Equity in Latin America,* eds. M. Syrquin and S. Teitel. 125-141. New York: Academic Press.

Schydlowsky, Daniel M., and Juan J. Wicht. 1979. *Anatomía de un fracaso económico: Perú 1968-1978.* Lima: Universidad del Pacífico.

Schydlowsky, Daniel M., and Juan J. Wicht. 1983. "The Anatomy of an Economic Failure: Peru 1968-1978." In *The Peruvian Experiment Reconsidered,* eds. A. Lowenthal and C. McClintock. Princeton, N.J.: Princeton University Press.

Seminario, Bruno, Arlette Beltrán, and Ana Sueyoshi. 1992. *La política fiscal en el Perú: 1970-1989.* Cuadernos de Investigación. Lima: Universidad del Pacífico.

Valdivieso, Luis. 1978. *The Distributive Effects of Alternative Policies to Increase the Use of Existing Industrial Capacity.* Ph.D. diss. Boston: Boston University.

IV

POLITICAL CONDITIONS, ECONOMIC RESULTS, AND THE SUSTAINABILITY OF THE REFORM PROCESS IN PERU

Teobaldo Pinzás

The reforms carried out by the Alberto Fujimori government have changed central aspects of economic management in Peru by applying policies which form part of the so-called "Washington Consensus." These policies, which are oriented toward opening, privatizing, and deregulating the economy, are currently being put into practice — with varied success — in numerous developing countries. This chapter briefly reviews the political conditions that allowed the Peruvian government to implement the reforms with practically no opposition, the results to date of two of the main reforms, and the problem of the sustainability of the reform program under democratic conditions. The central argument presented here holds that it was neither necessary nor wise to implement the reforms simultaneously, that simultaneous implementation has created conditions that hinder the adjustment of businesses, and that under democratic conditions economic recovery must be prioritized if the reform program is to be sustained.

POLITICAL CONDITIONS OF THE STRUCTURAL REFORMS

Structural reform processes encounter opposition from all sectors whose interests they affect adversely. These sectors include not only the enterprises that produce importable goods but also organized labor. In both cases, opposition arises because reforms radically change the ground rules, demanding adjustment processes without guaranteeing success.

With the removal of barriers to imports, internal producers must increase their efficiency in order to survive the new competition. Increased efficiency involves the implementation of a series of measures, the first of which is

---

Teobaldo Pinzás is a senior research associate at the Institute of Peruvian Studies (Instituto de Estudios Peruanos, IEP).

personnel cuts. Adjustment demands changes in labor legislation to allow and facilitate worker layoffs. Thus, new labor legislation and higher unemployment are early consequences of economic liberalization.

Internal producers must also accept reduced profit margins, either to cover the high cost of capital, to adjust to international prices, to cover more realistic public service rates charged in the new economic environment, or to devote greater resources to marketing and sales so as to remain competitive in relation to imported goods. In addition, the adjustment must take place in the midst of a recession brought on by the higher unemployment rate and public spending cuts that accompany stabilization policies. As a result, many producers whose survival depends on highly protectionist policies ultimately disappear.[1] Thus, though structural adjustment programs are considered necessary during times of macroeconomic instability, those sectors affected generally resist them vigorously. A recent example, which in today's Latin America seems vaguely anachronistic, is the "*Caracazo*" early in the Carlos Andrés Pérez government. At the same time, political organizations and parties that oppose neoliberalism on ideological grounds combat the implementation of these reform programs with weapons granted them by the democratic system. These pressures often cause political crises for the government, if not its replacement by another, whether de jure or de facto. Changes in high-ranking officials may bring policy setbacks followed by generalized confusion, which erodes the credibility the program requires.[2]

For these reasons, International Monetary Fund (IMF) representatives often praise the "courage" of governments that undertake adjustment programs. It is clear, moreover, that authoritarian regimes find it easier to apply such programs as long as the regimes remain in power long enough to guarantee the continuity of the reforms. The best example of this is the Augusto Pinochet regime in Chile, which was the first country in Latin America to introduce liberalizing reforms and the only one to sustain them through the change of government in 1990.[3]

PROLONGED CRISIS AND POLITICAL CONDITIONS IN PERU

Various foreign observers have commented upon the enormity and radicalism of the reform program currently underway in Peru. They have also made note of the clear lack of political and social opposition to the reforms despite the points mentioned above. Several important considerations help explain this apparent paradox.

1. First, the recent history of Peru's economy and economic policy can be described as a failed stabilization process. Since 1975, one partially implemented stabilization effort has followed another, and each has managed (with increasing difficulty) merely to restore international reserves to a certain level and thus temporarily overcome the crisis, only to find it repeated a number of years later.[4]

2. The effect of these repeated failures has been a kind of "dirty adjustment" evidenced by a progressive decline in public investment and spending and decreasing per capita product, real wages, and levels of adequate employment. Peru's seesawing economic policy (Gonzales de Olarte and Samamé 1991) did not overcome this backdrop of economic decline.

Table 1.
Evolution of Some Macroeconomic Variables
1975-1992

	per capita (in 1986 dollars)		(in 1991 soles)		(1979=100)
	Real GDP	Real Public Spending	Real Wages Minimum	Monthly Wage	Industrial Employment
1975	1,391.60	275.20	27.44	n/a	95.60
1976	1,376.40	276.20	24.73	44.70	99.90
1977	1,325.10	297.00	21.16	32.40	100.60
1978	1,262.60	285.70	21.41	73.70	99.90
1979	1,288.50	262.60	24.20	66.70	100.00
1980	1,324.40	304.40	28.21	60.80	101.90
1981	1,361.40	290.70	31.92	72.70	103.00
1982	1,330.60	269.90	23.50	72.90	101.60
1983	1,128.40	266.40	23.61	125.10	96.20
1984	1,153.80	270.30	21.88	111.50	86.10
1985	1,147.60	257.00	20.84	158.30	85.00
1986	1,244.60	255.20	190.00	62.90	90.10
1987	1,336.80	237.20	206.00	114.50	97.70
1988	1,212.80	171.60	175.00	1,722.00	95.60
1989	1,042.00	148.30	105.00	2,776.00	85.12
1990	997.00	137.23	90.00	7,650.00	82.87
1991	1,021.00	n/a	55.00	139.20	78.70
1992*	977.14	n/a	n/a	56.70	70.65

* = estimated
Sources: Webb, Richard, and Graciela Fernández Baca, *Perú en números 1993* (Lima: Cuanto S.A.); Banco Central de Reserva del Perú (BCR), *Memoria 1993*, (Lima: BCR); Instituto Nacional de Estadística e Informática (INEI), *Compendio estadístico 1989-1992*, (Lima: INEI).

3. This prolonged economic decline resulted in the fracturing of social and economic institutions. In the public sector, the state's capacity to implement policies and regulate the economy fell considerably for several reasons. On the one hand, as public sector salaries declined, so did the qualifications and the efficiency of government bureaucracy. On the other, Peru developed the biggest informal economy, proportionally speaking, in Latin America, a phenomenon that spread tax evasion. The state's weakness went hand in hand with the growth of illegal economic activities (mostly related to narcotics trafficking), which helped fuel the growth of corruption in several state institutions. The true dimension of this process became clear during the chaotic second half of the Alan García administration (1985-1990), as accusations of official corruption, a growing drug trade, and subversive activity rose to a crescendo.

4. The results of the failed stabilization efforts during this period undermined the power of organized labor. The growth of the informal sector and of underemployment, unemployment, and nonstandard employment weakened all labor organizations, which could stop neither the free fall of wage levels nor the changes in working conditions wrought by modes of temporary employment such as the Temporary Employment Program (Programa Temporal de Empleos, PROEM).[5] Work force underemployment reached the highest levels on the continent, and nonstandard employment spread.[6]

5. At the same time, the parties of the legal left (traditional opponents of liberalization policies) also lost force, partly because of internal problems and partly because of repercussions from the international crisis of communism. Meanwhile, business leaders, who had supported President García's macroeconomic policies between 1985 and 1987, later criticized them intensely and worried about the spread of political violence (whose direct impact was a large increase in security costs). Businesses began calling forcefully for a liberal program, looking to the Chilean experience for guidance. This position crystallized in the formation of the Democratic Front (Frente Democrático, FREDEMO) and the presidential candidacy of the writer Mario Vargas Llosa, who ran on a platform of radical liberalization.[7]

6. In addition, public perceptions associated the traditional political elite (including the legal left, which has been represented in Parliament since 1979) with the incapacity to solve critical national problems, the protection of personal interests, and even participation in or suspicious proximity to corruption. Traditional political parties, which had kept undemocratic structures and practices alive, showed signs of internal struggle and factionalism and proved inadequate for the needs of the country.

At the time of the 1990 presidential elections, the potential opponents of an economic liberalization program — organized labor, state bureaucracies, leftist parties, and business groups — had lost much of their strength. At the same time, after the hyperinflation experienced during the García government, most of the voting population understood that the incoming government would have to carry out major policy changes (ones which, they realized, would not be statist or collectivist) in order to attack economic problems such as high rates of inflation, unemployment, and economic stagnation.[8]

The new government therefore encountered a political vacuum that gave it broad discretion in decisionmaking on economic policy. This situation benefited the Alberto Fujimori government, though Fujimori's leadership style blocked the formation of a consensus with the broad sections of the political elite whose support for the FREDEMO platform indicated there existed general agreement with the reforms the executive had begun to implement. This peculiarity of the Peruvian situation is very important. Without powerful opposition forces to fight the liberalizing policies and perhaps block or overcome them, there is no real argument for the fast, simultaneous implementation of reforms.

STRUCTURAL REFORMS NOW UNDERWAY: TRADE LIBERALIZATION AND PRIVATIZATION

THE MAIN CHARACTERISTICS OF THE PROGRAM

Although structural reform programs implemented in less developed countries with the support of international financial institutions contain the same essential elements, these programs are put into practice differently in each country. The most noteworthy characteristic of the principal reforms in Peru may be their simultaneous implementation. In one fell swoop, Peru experienced the liberalization of its internal market of goods and factors, trade liberalization, and the opening up of the capital account of the balance of payments. The government chose this path fully cognizant of the risks it implied for the producers of tradable goods: adjustment processes in other Latin American countries have shown that overvalued national currencies and persistently high interest rates can occur simultaneously. One common argument to justify this path holds that incoming foreign capital can partially neutralize an economic recession by increasing the supply of lendable funds. Another posits that it offsets losses associated with one component of the program with gains from another (Haggard and Webb 1993). If, in addition, the liberalization is fast, the risk that the measures may be overturned is minimal. In Peru, the government decided that this style of reform, followed by inflexible management, guaranteed greater success for the measures' implementation and longevity.

A second aspect of the Peruvian program is that despite its magnitude and radicalism it met with relatively little opposition from the sectors that were most directly affected. As noted above, this lack of opposition arose from the political conditions created by the combination of prolonged macroeconomic instability and political processes specific to Peru.

Third, despite the scale of the reforms and the adjustment program begun in August 1990 and their immediate impact on employment[9] and economic activity, no massive social support programs were established to help absorb the redistributive impact of the adjustment. In this sense, Peru clearly differed from Chile, which is so often used as an example of this strategy. In Chile, a public works program created thousands of jobs during the most critical moments of the adjustment.

Fourth, the degree of conditionality throughout the process deserves mention. Although conditionality is inevitable for less developed countries seeking support from international financial institutions, Peru faced a severe degree of conditionality in its relations not only with all the multilateral institutions but also in bilateral relations.[10] At the same time, the present government's general compliance with established goals to date has won so much recognition from international financial officials that compliance appears to be the policy's lodestar. The risk, of course, is that the government may lose sight of the program's true objectives.

STRUCTURAL REFORMS

Although the Fujimori government announced its intention of introducing liberalizing structural reforms early on, advances were made only tentatively at first. However, with the appointment of Carlos Boloña as minister of economy and finance in February 1991, the process gained impetus, as the first measures to modify the framework of the Peruvian economy appeared in March 1991. The chief modifications introduced by this legislative package were the following:

1. Liberalization of foreign trade, eliminating all restrictions to imports and modifying the tariff system;

2. The start of the privatization process with the elimination of public monopolies (in communications, for instance) and the announcement that twenty-three state-owned companies would be sold;

3. Reform of the financial system through a new banking and financial institutions law; and

4. Deregulation of the exchange and capital markets.

Throughout the year, complementary measures and some additional resolutions followed the March package. In late 1991, a series of decree laws consolidated the liberalization of the Peruvian economy, as agreed upon with the international financial institutions in September of that year.[11] The most important measures can be summarized as follows:

1. A reduced state role in the economy and support for private enterprise in the liberalized areas, including a privatization law;

2. Greater flexibility in the labor market through such measures as the elimination of the labor community (*comunidad laboral*),[12] the prohibition of salary indexations to match increases in the cost of living, and the elimination of job security; and

3. Strong support for private domestic and foreign investment.

In 1992, the structural reform process ran into trouble when the decree laws issued by the executive branch were debated in Congress, where the government party constituted a minority. The resulting bottleneck was one of the reasons offered by President Fujimori to justify his April 1992 *auto golpe* or self-coup, a coup against Congress with the support of the military. Later that year, the government issued decree laws aimed at consolidating the reforms and modifying them slightly in order to speed up some processes or clean up certain markets.

After the self-coup, the privatization process accelerated, as became clear in September 1992, when an IMF Letter of Intent included the sale of seventeen state-owned enterprises before the year's end.

Of the set of reforms which the current government has put into practice, trade liberalization and the promotion of private investment are discussed below.

Trade Reform

One reform accepted and even demanded by the business sector as well as much of the Peruvian population was trade reform. The high level of effective protectionism of the manufacturing sector, reduced only briefly early in the 1980s (during President Fernando Belaúnde Terry's second administration), had an important impact on resource use in the Peruvian economy. As a result, an inefficient sector that produced mainly for the internal market expanded. High levels of protectionism gave producers high profit margins despite their inefficiency. Subsidized credit policies, tax benefits, and the oligopolistic structures typical in the sector also pushed profits up. Nevertheless, these profits were not reflected by high rates of investment or growth nor by improvements in product quality.

In this context, it appeared that reduced protection would have positive effects on efficiency and well-being by subjecting the sector to greater competition. It was also expected that trade liberalization would affect inflation by reducing producers' discretion in setting prices. However, although the electoral debate in 1990 did not touch upon this point,[13] it was also expected that trade liberalization would be a step-by-step process in which the goals of reduced protection would be reached within a previously established, realistic time frame. This fundamentally pragmatic consideration takes into account that each country is different and that a successful reform effort must recognize the rhythm at which individuals and organizations can adjust (Corbo and de Melo 1987). The experiences of Chile and Colombia in liberalizing their foreign trade are two useful references in this sense (Corbo and de Melo 1985a and 1985b; Fanelli, Frenkel, and Rozenwurcel 1990).

There is also the question of the sequence of trade and financial reforms, especially with regard to the deregulation of interest rates and the opening up of the capital account of the balance of payments. Without the monetary authorities' setting their limits, interest rates tend to rise in real terms during reform processes, attracting capital from abroad and sometimes causing the national currency to be overvalued. This gives the business sector mixed signals, which are different from those intended, and exposes it to foreign competition in adverse conditions, making the adjustment process more difficult. In addition, these situations stimulate increased imports of consumer goods, which can produce a balance of payments crisis that in turn affects the continuity of the reforms.

Table 2 presents the evolution of Peru's balance of payments and real exchange rate from 1990 to 1993. Trade liberalization helped increase imports, especially of consumer goods, while exports remained constant. The negative balance in the current account is equilibrated by the balance of capital accounts, particularly the short-term capital account. This phenomenon has been interpreted as deriving from an influx of so-called *capitales golondrinos* ("swallow" capital), short-term capital attracted by the high real interest rates prevailing in the deregulated financial system. Consequently, the real exchange rate decreased despite the fact that after the April 1992 self-coup the government tried to push it up with Central Bank (Banco Central de Reserva del Perú, BCR) dollar purchases, a policy that was halted in the first trimester of 1993, when inflation began to rise. Additional factors for the *sol's* appreciation could be repatriation of Peruvian capital and income from the narcotics trade within the context of recession.

In any case, the overvaluation of the sol joined high interest rates and the recession to make the adjustment process a difficult one for business. Indeed, the resulting situation has generated a dangerous instability insofar as business insolvency has made the financial sector very fragile. Under these circumstances, a run on Peruvian banks could have truly critical macroeconomic effects. At the same time, the continuation of an adjustment process with no light at the end of the tunnel gives rise to growing pressures from the most severely affected business sectors, especially as elections approach. The resulting panorama is a complicated one for economic policymaking.

Table 2.
Balance of Payments, Inflation, and Real Exchange Rates

	90.III	90.IV	91.I	91.II	91.III	91.IV	92.I	92.II	92.III	92.IV	93.I
Commercial Indicators (Indices)											
Exports	100	91.8	93.4	100.2	92.6	87.0	95.7	97.2	95.6	102.0	n.d.
Traditional exports	100	85.9	93.3	98.8	87.7	81.6	95.4	94.7	91.6	93.8	n.d.
Nontraditional exports	100	108.5	93.6	104.3	106.4	102.1	96.6	104.3	106.8	125.2	n.d.
Imports	100	82.4	104.1	121.4	131.3	142.3	151.4	136.0	144.3	147.0	n.d.
Consumer goods	100	147.2	330.6	419.4	486.1	538.9	708.3	619.4	500.0	508.3	n.d.
Intermediate goods	100	98.7	121.7	130.0	137.0	143.3	137.0	134.7	158.7	163.7	n.d.
Capital goods	100	72.0	71.2	98.3	106.3	119.5	123.3	116.9	119.5	114.8	n.d.
Balance of Payments (Millions of Dollars)											
Commercial balance	192	242	104	44	-93	-220	-206	-85	-157	-119	n.d.
Non-financial services	-156	-167	-162	-178	-204	-180	-214	-215	-221	-200	n.d.
Current account balance	-145	-113	-265	-336	-464	-519	-560	-449	-548	-472	n.d.
Long-term capital	196	178	82	192	-32	463	156	164	199	93	n.d.
Short-term capital	532	197	308	516	721	585	518	386	521	510	n.d.
Balance of payments	583	262	125	372	225	529	114	101	172	131	n.d.

(Real exchange rate not adjusted for external inflation)
Source: Central Reserve Bank (BCR), *Nota semanal*, (Lima: BCR, 1990-1993), various issues.

Continued on next page

Table 2—Continued

	90.III	90.IV	91.I	91.II	91.III	91.IV	92.I	92.II	92.III	92.IV	93.I
Prices (Indices)											
Nominal exchange rate	100	163.4	189.5	261.1	277.6	338.1	335.4	393.7	446.9	551.2	605.4
Inflation	100	179.7	269.5	334.0	422.1	483.3	549.2	624.2	687.1	758.0	852.3
Tradable	100	172.6	225.6	262.4	308.0	343.2	397.0	434.3	472.0	546.6	618.1
Non-tradable	100	185.7	308.8	398.8	525.3	605.5	688.0	798.0	884.0	950.8	1065.8
Real exchange rate	100	90.9	70.3	79.2	65.3	70.0	61.1	61.5	65.0	72.7	71.0

PRIVATIZING STATE ENTERPRISES

The privatization of state enterprises is another issue on which a broad consensus exists. Except for very reduced sectors (among them the state employees, whose working conditions were once much better than those of other workers, and laid-off employees), the vast majority of the population agrees with the need to eliminate, through privatization, the vices and inefficiencies of government-owned businesses. This, then, was another "easy" issue for the reformers, even more so than trade reform because the public enterprises were not organized into pressure groups and have always been dependent on the government in power (which is precisely their greatest weakness).

What is important in the case of privatization is to define and achieve a majority agreement on the areas and functions that should remain in state hands. In the current government's view,[14] the state should limit itself to the traditional functions of education, health, public order, and defense. The criteria that guide the privatization process are 1) to sell all state-owned enterprises and 2) to do so as quickly as possible (Pinzás 1993). We can make the following two general observations about these criteria:

1. The decision to sell off all public enterprises fails to distinguish among different economic sectors and thus ignores natural monopolies, nor does it recognize the state's regulatory shortcomings, especially under current circumstances, when the state apparatus has enormously reduced its size without improving its quality.

2. Selling all the companies as quickly as possible would not appear to be a correct proposition from the standpoint of revenues, program credibility, and the operative capacity of the privatizing body. When the goal is to make a fast sale, obtaining the best conditions for the public treasury takes a back seat.[15] Moreover, Peru is still considered a high-risk country for investment (although it has made great strides in this sense), and many potential domestic buyers prefer to wait and see how the economy performs in the medium term. At the same time, it is difficult for the small privatization team to process several different operations within a short time. Privatizing everything as soon as possible may lead to erosive failures or to auctioning off state-owned assets under terms unfavorable to the public treasury.

Thus, during 1993, progress on privatization has been very slow. The last three important cases (Petrolera Transoceánica and two paper factories belonging to Sociedad Paramonga) have not been sold in the first auction, and Sociedad Paramonga's sale has been put on hold. At this point, it is clear that Peru will not meet the goals proposed to the IMF in the Memorandum on Economic and Financial Policy.

Table 3.
Privatization (In Millions of Dollars)

Company	Base Price	Sale Price	Assets	Annual Sales
1991				
1 Sogewiese Leasing S.A.	1.00	1.00		
2 Buenaventura Mines	2.30	1.50		
Total	**3.30**	**2.50**		
1992				
3 Condestable Mining	2.20	1.30		
4 Banco de Comercio	5.37	5.37		
5 Gas stations[1]	25.00	38.49		
6 Inasa	1.74	0.81	1.50	
7 Quimpac[2]	6.00	6.6	12.00	18.00
8 Solgas S.A.	6.10	7.33	10.10	45.80
9 Enatru Peru (452 buses)	13.02	11.07		
10 Minpeco USA	5.50	4.10		
11 Hierroperú	22.00	120.00	114.00	53.00
12 Quellaveco[3]	9.00	12.00		
Total	**95.93**	**207.07**	**137.60**	**116.80**
1993				
13 Aeroperú	41.00	54.00	54.00	87.00
14 Renasa	2.20	2.93	3.00	6.50
15 Petromar[4]	—	—	38.00	103.00
Total	**43.20**	**56.93**	**95.00**	**196.50**
Total (1991, 1992, 1993)	***142.43***	***266.50***	***232.60***	***313.30***

Companies that could not be sold:[5]
16   Conchán Refinery (1992)
17   Banco Popular (1992)
18   Ecasa warehouses (1992)
19   Petrolera Transoceánica (1993)[6]
20   Storage module for recycled paper fiber (Paramonga) (1993)[7]
21   Paper recycling plant (Paramonga) (1993)[7]

1 = Seventy-eight of 82 stations offered were sold.
2 = This sale took place in two auctions; the figure given represents the sum of both.
3 = The concession will be paid off in three stages; as of mid-1993, only one payment had been made.
4 = No price was set; instead, the concession was leased for 20 percent of production and an annual payment.
5 = Companies put up for sale, but not placed.
6 = As of mid-1993, a first auction had taken place, and a date for a second auction had not been set (by law, it should offer a base price lowered by 15 percent).
7 = Two Paramonga warehouses could not be sold in the first auction; the sale of the third was postponed pending the selection of a new form of sale.
Sources: Comisión de Promoción de la Inversión Privada (COPRI); *Gestión* (Lima), several issues; *El Comercio* (Lima), several issues.

In the case of the state oil company, Petróleos del Perú (Petroperú), the privatization model recommended to the Commission to Promote Private Investment (Comisión para la Promoción de Inversión Privada, COPRI) produced media debate that in effect halted the operation for the first time in the process.[16] This case has shown that though there is a broad consensus on the expediency of privatizing state companies, differences remain in regard to the limits of the process and the manner in which to privatize certain enterprises. While the sale of a chemical plant or a state bank faced little opposition, the same cannot be said of companies like Petroperú, which large segments of the population consider important to the national interest.

The privatization experience suggests that it is preferable to be less ambitious in this initial stage and to proceed gradually, seeking majority agreements and avoiding issues which may be too divisive. Seeking to accelerate the process to the maximum may be counterproductive, leading to greater delays and even halting the process, with adverse effects for the credibility and stability of the reforms.

THE SUSTAINABILITY OF STRUCTURAL REFORMS

The success of a structural reform program is measured by its effects on macroeconomic stability and the rate of economic growth. According to both criteria, Chile can today be considered an example of a successful reform program. The Chilean experience suggests that in order to have an effect on the efficient use of resources in the economy, the reforms should give the economic agents the right signals and remain in vigor the length of time necessary. To achieve this end, the program must be constantly evaluated in order to make corrections as they become necessary.

Chile's implementation of reforms benefited from two events unique to that country's political history. The first was the experience with the Popular Unity government, which tried to initiate a peaceful transition to socialism. The second was Augusto Pinochet's authoritarian regime, which lasted seventeen years. The political process prior to Pinochet persuaded many in business to accept the liberalizing reforms, though they knew that doing so meant losing their privileged positions. For nearly two decades, Pinochet's iron-handed leadership assured that the reforms would not stop and eliminated the possibility of backsliding. In this fashion, the country passed through its most critical stages around 1982, when open unemployment reached roughly 25 percent.[17]

Currently, the greatest challenge in Latin America is that structural reforms must be carried out within a context of democratic regimes that must be consolidated. Generally, this means much less discretionary power for designing and applying policies than that held by Pinochet's government in Chile. The restriction lies in the fact that the reforms must generate noticeable economic growth and greater attention to the problem of poverty.[18] Otherwise, the proponents of alternative policies may increase their own electoral backing, leading to processes whose outcome may be far from democratic (Lowenthal and Hakim 1992).

The sustainability of a liberalizing reform program depends on the balance between the advance of liberal policies and the resulting macroeconomic stability (Rodrik 1990).[19] As Vittorio Corbo and Jaime de Melo have pointed out, this means, on the one hand, that the program

> ... needs a realistic timetable — and what is realistic may vary from one policy area to another and from one country to another. Any reform package which ignores the rhythm at which individuals and organizations can adapt — a variable partly determined by political circumstance — runs the risk of failure and undermines the credibility of future reforms (1987, 128).

However, the liberalizing impulse must also be moderated when the reforms may effect more damage than is necessary in the macroeconomic context. Ignoring this tension leads the policy reformer to self-deceit. Achieving a favorable political context (like that of Peru in 1992 following the self-coup) and massively promulgating reforms does not mean that they will all be put into practice nor that the process may not backfire.

In Peru's case, the García government and the hyperinflation it unleashed convinced many people of the need for profound changes in economic policy. This was, perhaps, the positive side of a very negative experience, but at the same time García's chaotic government, with the help of commentators too willing to use labels, debased several political terms and styles. Sadly, "gradualism," a way of implementing reforms progressively over time but without backsliding, was one of those terms. In reality, the conditions created by Peru's peculiar political and economic process in recent decades allowed and even required a gradual process that took Peru's specific situation into account.

The simultaneous implementation, at any cost, of the reform package ignores this specificity and causes excessive damage, especially when the distortions the package seeks to eliminate (the recession's persistence) are maintained if not increased at first. The sol's overvaluation and the elevated interest rates form an environment in which even the best businesses find survival difficult. The weakness of the private sector and the drastic personnel cuts in the public sector are reflected in an increase of the already high levels of unemployment and underemployment and in the growth of the segment of the population living in poverty. In such a context, it is surprising to find no massive employment or social support programs, which are indispensable not only for reasons of fairness but also because of a fall in aggregate demand.

Fiscal restrictions undoubtedly exist, yet in 1992 the so-called "fiscal overadjustment" reached approximately $200 million. At the same time, the executive branch has clearly not given the same attention to an employment program, implemented with domestic resources or international cooperation, that it has given to relations with foreign creditors.

According to opinion polls, Fujimori's popularity withstands these problems and continues to be high (his performance generally receives more than 60 percent approval ratings), but the economic policy invariably receives much less public support. In late 1992, one poll among businesspeople showed that 84 percent of those interviewed believed that the first priority was job creation.[20] The president, for his part, has repeatedly called on businesses to invest and on banks to lower their interest rates. The answer has been that the problem lies in the recession and that measures without reactivation will not solve the problems.[21] There is still a feeling (and there are public statements) that the economic program is on the right track, and criticism is generally reserved for the program's "managerial" deficiencies. Overall, however, the situation is fragile, and the time for elections is close. There is nothing to reassure us that the reforms will survive the elections.

FINAL COMMENTARY

The option of maintaining "The reforms have been made, so let the market do its job" seems inadvisable in Peru today. In Bolivia, such a policy has brought "stability at the bottom of the barrel," a situation that has already lasted eight years and that has been maintained thanks to international cooperation and the coca economy. In Peru, the scale is greater and the political outlook is different.

The stability of the liberalization process depends on its short-term success. In our judgment, given the distortions and current economic stagnation, deliberate state intervention to reactivate the economy is needed. This intervention may be broad based. In the public sector, it should include increased public investment expansion, job programs to rehabilitate the productive infrastructure, and salary increases for state employees. In the financial arena, beyond exhortations to bankers, the government should seek more direct ways to bring interest rates down. The reactivation of the productive apparatus would rebound in larger tax collection, improvements in the financial sector's portfolio of bad loans (easing pressure on interest rates), and a recovery of the exchange rate.

The implementation of an initiative of this kind demands great state effort on various fronts. The most important concern is to solve the fiscal shortage, which would require a review of Peru's commitments on servicing the official foreign debt in addition to the utilization of resources from multilateral lenders. It is also important to take actions that, without implying subsidies, help expand exports (commercial information, tax refunds, and so on). Observers will note that this task is made more difficult by the extreme weakness of the state's technical teams.

As for the remaining initiatives on the reformers' agenda, the most rational path would be not to insist they be implemented at this time in order to avoid opening new fronts and therefore creating greater confusion. We have the example of educational reform. Launched in great haste and with much noise, the program was recently halted by President Fujimori, signaling the probable fate of further liberalization efforts.

NOTES

· I am grateful to Carolina Trivelli for her assistance and to John Sheahan and Richard Weisskoff for commenting on an earlier version of this chapter.

1. Corbo and de Melo 1985a and 1985b provide an interesting review of private sector experiences with adjustment programs in Argentina, Chile, and Uruguay during the 1970s and early 1980s.

2. Corbo and de Melo 1987 review failed adjustment efforts in the Southern Cone from 1975 through 1985.

3. An overall look at the characteristics of the Pinochet period can be found in Whitehead 1990. Interestingly, the government of Renovación Democrática (Democratic Renovation), the opposition bloc which succeeded Augusto Pinochet, has not changed the central features of the economic system set up by its predecessor.

4. Kuczynski (1977), Thorp and Whitehead (1979), and Pinzás (1981) describe various failed stabilization efforts. See Iguíñiz, Basay, and Rubio 1993 for a review of the main stabilization policies from 1975 onward.

5. PROEM was a program introduced during the government of Alan García, allowing employers to hire workers for a period of up to two years without giving the workers job stability, as existing law would have required.

6. See Verdera 1992.

7. Dornbusch and Larraín 1989 mention some aspects of the formation and weakening of political or6anizations during the second half of the García government, though they overestimate the weight of the United Left on the national political scene at that time.

8. In this sense, Peru in 1990 more closely resembled Bolivia at the end of the Popular Unity government (1985) than Salvador Allende's Chile (1973).

9. For example, public sector personnel cuts directly due to the reforms cost 50,000 jobs.

10. An Inter-American Development Bank (IDB) disbursement of $50 million, for example, was conditioned on the elimination of tariff surcharges on imported agricultural products. The IDB's opposition to maintaining the National Bank instead of liquidating it like all the other state development banks was also clear. In general, the multilaterals' policy is to divide disbursements and condition each one on meeting certain very specific policy goals.

11. IMF negotiations during the second half of 1991 ended with the signing of a Referential Economic Program for 1991-1992. The government signed an agreement with the Inter-American Development Bank in September. Both accords included a program of structural reform, emphasizing trade and financial liberalization.

12. A form of worker participation in decisionmaking, profit sharing and, progressively, ownership of industrial enterprise which was established during General Juan Velasco Alvarado's government (1968-1975).

13. There was no debate on the issue because while one presidential candidate proclaimed the need for a liberalizing "shock," the other (the winner) presented himself as the "no- shock" candidate. As a result, no concrete proposals for each reform were discussed, and the elected president supported "on hearsay" the measures which his ministers of economy and finance proposed.

14. In fact, this is the interpretation of the Commission to Promote Private Investment (Comisión para la Promoción de la Inversión Privada, COPRI), which we assume represents the government's view, though on several occasions President Fujimori has made statements distancing himself from this position.

15. Peru's privatization process has produced relatively modest figures. In recent statements, President Fujimori recognized that in 1992 the government had spent $140 million to ready state companies for sale; total income from privatization that year was $207 million (Table 3).

16. The consulting firm of Booz-Allen & Hamilton recommended dividing Petroperú and selling each part separately (oil pipeline, refineries, and so on). Petroperú itself proposed transferring part of the company's activities to the private sector and then privatizing the company as a whole.

17. The problems which arose at that time in Chile were solved by a new economic team which modified specific policies but maintained the liberal orientation of the macroeconomic policy.

18. Beyond massive employment programs, poverty merited little concern in the Pinochet period. Officials of the current Chilean government claim that the population living in conditions of extreme poverty exceeds five million people.

19. This observation resembles the "pragmatic state" proposed for Latin American nations in Amadeo and Banuri 1990. This state creates the institutional conditions so that different organized groups can cooperate with each other and which maintains some barriers to international financial flows and certain control and influence over the national financial sector.

20. Poll by APOYO S.A. of businesspeople at the Annual Conference of Executives (CADE) in 1992 (See APOYO 1992).

21. See Instituto de Estudios Peruanos N.d.

REFERENCES

Amadeo, Edward, and Tarik Banuri. 1990. "Política económica y manejo de conflicto." In *El Trimestre Económico* 22, 57(1), (January-May): 241-276.

APOYO S.A. 1992. *Gestión* (Lima). December 9.

Arriagada, Pedro. 1985. "Adjustments by Agricultural Exporters in Chile during 1974-1982." In *Scrambling for Survival: How Firms Adjusted to the Recent Reforms in Argentina, Chile, and Uruguay,* eds. Vittorio Corbo and Jaime de Melo. World Bank Staff Working Papers 764. Washington, D.C.: World Bank.

Banco Central de Reserva del Perú (BCR). *Nota Semanal.* Lima: Banco Central de la Reserva del Perú, various issues.

Corbo, Vittorio, and Jaime de Melo, eds. 1985a. *Scrambling for Survival. How Firms Adjusted to the Recent Reforms in Argentina, Chile, and Uruguay.* World Bank Staff Working Papers 764. Washington D.C.: World Bank.

Corbo, Vittorio, and Jaime de Melo. 1985b. "Adjustments by Industrial Firms in Chile during 1974-1982." In *Scrambling for Survival. How Firms Adjusted to the Recent Reforms in Argentina, Chile, and Uruguay,* eds. Vittorio Corbo and Jaime de Melo. World Bank Staff Working Papers 764. Washington, D.C.: World Bank.

Corbo, Vittorio, and Jaime de Melo. 1987. "Lessons from the Southern Cone Policy Reforms." *World Bank Research Observer* 2 (2).

Corbo, Vittorio, and Jaime de Melo. 1992. *Development Strategies and Policies in Latin America: A Historical Perspective.* Occasional Papers 22. N.p.: International Center for Economic Growth.

Cuánto S.A. 1992. *Perú en números.* Lima: Cuánto S.A.

Fanelli, José María, Roberto Frenkel, and Guillermo Rozenwurcel. 1990. *Growth and Structural Reforms in Latin America: Where We Stand.* Document No. 57. Buenos Aires: CEDES.

Fischer, Stanley. 1986. "Issues in Medium-Term Macroeconomic Adjustment." *World Bank Research Observer* 1 (2): 163-182.

Gonzales de Olarte, Efraín, and L. Samamé. 1991. *El péndulo peruano.* Lima: Instituto de Estudios Peruanos.

Government of Peru. 1993. "Memorandum de política económica y financiera del gobierno del Perú para el período de enero de 1993 a 31 de diciembre de 1995." Lima: Government of Peru.

Haggard, Stephan, and Steven Webb. 1993. "What Do We Know about the Political Economy of Economic Policy Reform?" *World Bank Research Observer* 8(2): 143-168.

Hamilton, C. 1989. "The Irrelevance of Economic Liberalization in the Third World." *World Development* 17(10): 1523-1530.

Iguíñiz, Javier, R. Basay, and Marcial Rubio. 1993. *Los ajustes: Perú 1975-1992.* Lima: Fundación Friedrich Ebert.

Instituto de Estudios Peruanos (IEP). N.d. *Argumentos, Boletín de coyuntura política y económica* 7. N.p.

Instituto Nacional de Estadística e Informática (INEI). 1992. *Compendio estadístico. Vols. 2 and 3.* Lima: Instituto Nacional de Estadística e Informática.

Lal, Deepak, and S. Rajapatirana. 1987. "Foreign Trade Regimes and Economic Growth in Developing Countries." *World Bank Research Observer* 2 (2): 189-217.

Lowenthal, Abraham, and Peter Hakim. 1992. "Latin American Democracy in the 1990s: The Challenges Ahead." In *Evolving U.S. Strategy for Latin America and the Caribbean,* ed. E. Kjonnerdod. Washington, D.C.: National Defense University Press.

Meller, Patricio. N.d. *Revisión del proceso de ajuste chileno de la década del 80.* Colección Estudios Cieplan 30, 5-53.

Mosley, Paul, and J. Harrigan. 1987. "Evaluating the Impact of World Bank Structural Adjustment Lending: 1980-87." *The Journal of Development Studies* 27(3): 63-94.

Petrei, H., and Jaime de Melo. 1985. "Adjustments by Industrial Firms in Argentina during 1976-1981." In *Scrambling for Survival. How Firms Adjusted to the Recent Reforms in Argentina, Chile, and Uruguay,* eds. Vittorio Corbo and Jaime de Melo. World Bank Staff Working Papers 764. Washington, D.C.: World Bank.

Pinzás, Teobaldo. 1993. "Privatización y nuevo rol del Estado: Algunos aspectos conceptuales con referencia al caso peruano." Working paper 43. Documentos de Política 1. Lima: Instituto de Estudios Peruanos (IEP).

Quijandría, Jaime. 1993. *El futuro de la empresa del Estado: El caso del sector petrolero.* Working paper No. 49. Documentos de Política 3. Lima: Instituto de Estudios Peruanos (IEP).

Rodrik, Dani. 1990. "How Should Structural Adjustment Programs be Designed?" *World Development* 18(7): 933-947.

Thorp, Rosemary, and Laurence Whitehead, eds. 1979. *Inflation and Stabilisation in Latin America.* New York: Holmes and Meier Publishers.

Velarde, Julio, and M. Rodríguez. 1992. *Los problemas del orden y la velocidad en la liberalización de los mercados.* Working paper. Lima: Universidad del Pacífico/Consorcio de Investigación Económica.

Verdera, Francisco. 1992. "Peru: Temporary and Part-time Employment in Metropolitan Lima, 1984-1989." In *Circumventing Labour Protection: Non-standard Employment in Argentina and Peru.* Research Series 88. Geneva: International Institute for Labour Studies.

Webb, Richard. 1993. "The Political Economy of Policy Reform. Peru 1980-1985." Paper presented at the Conference on Policy Reform, Institute for International Economics, Washington, D.C.

Whitehead, Lawrence. 1990. "Political Explanations of Macroeconomic Management: A Survey." *World Development* 18(8): 1133-1146.

V

THE ECONOMIC CONSEQUENCES OF THE "PERUVIAN DISEASE"

Elena H. Alvarez
Francisco Joel Cervantes

INTRODUCTION

Although Peru is currently considered to be a calmer country than it was in the early 1990s,[1] at a seminar held at the Library of Congress in 1990, one of the panelists compared the economic and political situation of this Andean nation to that of a country concomitantly experiencing the Civil War, the Great Depression, and Prohibition.[2] Indeed, since 1980, Peru has experienced political violence, economic decline, and a significant expansion in the illicit coca trade.

In this chapter, several arguments are developed regarding the nature of the "Peruvian disease," a combination of Dutch Disease (DD), drug trafficking, and insurgency, all of which are related to the expansion of the illicit coca/cocaine sector in Peru. While the production and commercialization of coca leaf and its by-products have generated large inflows of foreign exchange, creating conditions conducive to DD symptoms in Peru, different societal groups, including drug trafficking and guerrilla organizations, joined forces in the late 1980s to fulfill their common goals, namely, the procurement of revenues and the forceful and active opposition to the Peruvian state. In so doing, these groups strengthened their positions and increased the country's political instability, which in turn further deteriorated the country's investment environment.

Elena H. Alvarez is a research associate professor with the University Center for Policy Research (UCPR) at the State University of New York at Albany and a senior research associate at the University of Miami's North-South Center. Francisco Joel Cervantes is a Ph.D. graduate student in economics at the State University of New York at Albany. He is currently on leave from the Centro de Estudios Monetarios para Latinoamérica (CEMLA).

Several "building blocks" will be posited to characterize the nature of the "Peruvian disease." To this end, this analysis has been divided into four sections, the first two of which examine the economic significance and the characteristics of the coca sector in Peru and the impact of political instability on the investment environment in the country. In the final two sections, we identify DD-type symptoms that have flourished in the Peruvian economy based on preliminary empirical evidence.

THE COCA SECTOR IN PERU

The coca plant plays an important role in Andean culture; it has been cultivated in the Andean region for hundreds of years.[3] When the illicit consumption of cocaine boomed in the late 1970s and 1980s, Peru and Bolivia — producers of high quality varieties of coca leaf, the major raw material in the production of cocaine — responded by allocating hundreds of hectares to its cultivation. The coca leaf has great value as an export crop inasmuch as it contains the alkaloid used as the basis for the manufacture of cocaine, an addictive substance whose illegal distribution in most countries has reached alarming proportions.[4]

The production process begins with crude cocaine or coca paste, a mixture of alkaloids that is approximately two-thirds cocaine. Coca paste is produced by dissolving dried leaves in sulfuric acid and precipitating the alkaloids with sodium carbonate. The paste is then converted into a salt by solution in hydrochloric acid and further treatment to remove the other alkaloids. Cocaine base, a transparent crystalline substance, requires further purification.[5] Peru and Bolivia are increasingly exporting cocaine hydrochloride. Nonetheless, they continue to export cocaine base to Colombia, where it is further processed.

FACTORS CONTRIBUTING TO THE EXPANSION OF THE COCA SECTOR

COMPARATIVE ADVANTAGE

Peru's ecological conditions and geographical location provide the Andean nation with a comparative advantage in the production of coca leaf and its derivatives. Ecological conditions allow the production of a leaf with a high alkaloid content. Moreover, the remoteness and difficulty of accessing coca-producing areas in Peru (and to a lesser extent in Bolivia) make the illicit harvesting of the coca leaf relatively impermeable to police action.

RURAL POVERTY AND HIGH PROFITS

Income levels in the Andean region are generally very low. The majority of the farms are agricultural units smaller than five hectares in area; these are referred to as *minifundios*.[6] Income data for 1994 indicate that annual per capita income in the rural highlands was roughly $470, which was one-third of the national average (approximately $1600) for the same period.[7] Thus, it is often the case that people with limited income potential are willing to do almost anything to survive, including work in illicit activities.

Coca leaf and its illegal derivatives generate high profits. These steep profits are associated with the high premium paid for the risk of participating in the illegal industry. However, recent estimates, as shown below, seem to confirm that the bulk of the high incomes is not destined for rural workers. High profits are received by traffickers — both foreign and national — who market the Peruvian cocaine base and also by others who collaborate in the trafficking of the drug and assist in money laundering activities. The elevated profits generated by the illicit industry together with the low incomes characteristic of rural Peru constitute the primary driving forces behind the coca industry, therefore.

INSTITUTIONAL CORRUPTION

Needless to say, a large illicit sector such as this requires the collaboration of many actors in the licit sector so as to permit the agents associated with the illegal activity to operate freely. Recent U.S. Drug Enforcement Administration (DEA) publications regarding Peru report increasing involvement of some members of the peacekeeping forces, particularly those stationed in the Amazon region of the country. Peruvian investigative journalist Gustavo Gorriti has confirmed the connection between the military and coca growers. He has documented the fact that military officials received bribes from traffickers in exchange for allowing them to operate freely in the coca and illicit drug producing areas (Gorriti 1994). This connection had the effect of neutralizing the "controlling" forces of the country. Although the United States Department of State's Bureau of International Narcotics Matters stresses that "corruption of narcotics enforcement personnel is individual, not institutional," Bureau officials also assert that "corruption is endemic in virtually all GOP [Government of Peru] institutions" (United States Department of State Bureau of International Narcotics Matters 1993, 124).

CHANGING FOOD CONSUMPTION PATTERNS

Food consumption patterns have changed drastically in Peru. The consumption of rural, essentially Andean food products — potatoes, barley, soft maize, soft wheat, and other Andean crops — has gradually been replaced by the more Westernized diet prevalent in urban areas: rice, white potatoes, chicken, dairy products, bread, noodles, and other processed foods. As a consequence, in recent decades, Andean food producers have faced a declining domestic market for the type of foodstuffs they can produce within the ecological zones of the Andes (Ferroni 1980; Alvarez 1980, 1983a, and 1983b; Hopkins 1981; Figueroa 1984; Escobal 1992). This shrinking domestic market became a primary driving factor in motivating producers to switch to coca production as a livelihood.

FAILED LAND REFORM

The agrarian reform of 1969 affected Peru's best land —about ten million of the total 30 million hectares in farm properties — and transferred assets to former hacienda and modern plantation workers (Caballero and Alvarez 1981). However, this significant agrarian reform process excluded transfers to Andean *minifundistas* (owners of *minifundios*), who constituted the vast majority of the poor agricultural producers in the country.

Many factors contributed to the failed agrarian reform of 1969. First, most of the *minifundistas* and landless peasants were left out of the reform process because there was not enough agricultural land to go around (Caballero and Alvarez 1981). Second, the institutional framework created to manage the reform sector was too rigid, thereby hindering the management of new enterprises and the expansion of employment opportunities (McClintock 1981; Scott 1981; Matos Mar and Mejía 1980; Velazco 1992). Third, most of the agricultural policies devised and implemented by the Juan Velasco Alvarado/ Francisco Morales Bermúdez military regime were colored by a strong urban bias. In particular, measures that applied to agriculture were intended to increase the welfare of the urban population, either directly or indirectly, by supplying cheap foodstuffs for the urban areas (Alvarez 1983a). The principal effect of this bias was to lower the profitability of most agricultural activities.

ADMINISTRATIVE INEFFICIENCY

Coupled with the low profitability of alternative crops such as rice and corn, government delays in processing loans and organizing the marketing of foodstuffs undoubtedly fostered the growth of coca production in Peru. Administrative inefficacy in the processing of loans to agricultural producers often resulted in the producers' missing planting or harvesting seasons. Moreover, public enterprises were often tardy in paying growers for harvested crops, a situation that created severe cash flow problems for small producers in particular.

MIGRATION TO THE JUNGLE

Rural poverty and the declining market for Andean foodstuffs motivated a continuous rural-to-urban migration from the Peruvian Andes to the coastal region until the late 1960s. However, as a result of the agrarian reform process and the inefficiency of government policymaking, the direction of migration later changed: migrants from the Andean highlands began to settle in the Amazon jungle region (Aramburú 1989; Martínez 1985; Ferrando 1985; Bedoya and Verdera 1987).

The Amazon region, an area of colonization since the first Fernando Belaúnde Terry administration (1963-1968), initially provided opportunities for the production of numerous food items that the urban areas required — rice, yellow corn to be used for chicken feed in the expanding poultry industry, and palm oil used in the manufacture of cooking oil. However, in the mid- and late 1970s, exports soared; thus, the jungle, a region which had never previously been very significant in terms of agricultural production, became the second most important agricultural region in Peru in the 1980s.

The significant external demand for coca by-products and the comparative advantage of producing coca in Peru combined to bring about a massive expansion in the export of these products. In sum, these two factors were aided by the following conditions:

1. The low income levels in the Andes and the high profits associated with coca/cocaine production;

2. Institutional corruption;

3. The gradual loss of domestic urban food markets;

4. The effective exclusion of Andean peasants from the 1969 agrarian reform program;

5. The low profitability of agricultural activity;

6. Government inefficiency in serving agricultural producers in the jungle; and

7. A change in the pattern of internal migration.

Thus, coca production became the best, if not the only, alternative available to those Andean peasants and rural workers who aspired to improve their standard of living. Moreover, in spite of the fact that the data indicate that the profitability of coca is declining compared to that of other crops, illegal coca production is still more profitable than legal economic alternatives (Alvarez 1993a).

Figure 1 presents estimates of coca sector exports for Peru for the period 1979-1992 on a quarterly basis. It must be stressed that these are preliminary figures that should be interpreted as mere approximations. It is expected that these estimates will be further refined as better data become available. Inasmuch as many unknowns still exist regarding the coca sector, it would be presumptuous to claim development of the "definitive" coca figures.[8]

Figure 1. Coca Exports
1979.1 - 1992.4

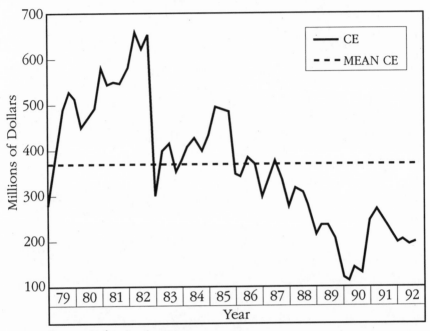

Source: Authors' estimates.

With respect to the production of cocaine derivatives, reasonable assumptions have been made, given the information available, regarding allocation of land, land productivity, and technical coefficients. Price data for the different cocaine derivatives have been furnished by the official organizations responsible for monitoring this activity, such as the Drug Enforcement Administration (DEA), the United States Agency for International Development (USAID), and the United Nations International Drug Control Programme (UNDCP).

Several different estimates have been made regarding the size of the coca sector in Peru; these estimates have been analyzed elsewhere in the literature (Alvarez 1992a, 1992b). Two estimates — one low, the other medium — have been developed based on this analysis of the existing information, field trips to coca-growing areas, and consultation with many experts. These estimates have a low bias, which makes them somewhat conservative. Annual growth rates for hectares planted are derived from the U.S. Department of State's *International Narcotics Control Strategy Report* (INCSR) estimates, which are the most conservative available. These growth rates are used in the medium estimates herein.

Coca sector data show that income in the coca-producing sector is declining. This downturn is due to the sharp decreases in the prices of coca leaf and all of its derivatives. The workings of the cocaine industry itself do not clearly account for this price behavior. Recent studies conducted by the United Nations Development Programme (UNDP) demonstrate that leaf, paste, and base production have increased significantly in Colombia, thereby reducing the importation of Peruvian coca products (Uribe 1995). In addition, high expectations regarding the profitability of coca products may have encouraged too many economic agents to engage in this activity, resulting in an increased supply which, in turn, contributed to price declines. In the short term, price decreases are most likely due to interdiction or control policies, which reduce the demand for coca leaf, paste, and base. In turn, this slump in demand creates temporary gluts in the market.

Although declining, the share of the coca sector in Peru's gross domestic product (GDP) is nonetheless significant.[9] Estimates for 1985 show that coca amounted to between 10 and 14 percent of Peru's GDP. For 1992, in contrast, the same indicator accounted for from 1.4 to 2.1 percent of GDP (Alvarez 1993b). It should be noted, however, that the effects of the coca/cocaine industry on Peruvian employment are high.

Coca: Few Backward Linkages

According to Javier Núñez and Rolando Reátegui (1990), the ratio of the value of inputs to the gross value of production in the coca sector is low; that is, the sector makes very few purchases (or backward linkages) from the remainder of the economy in order to produce cocaine paste, base, and hydrochloride. Input-output calculations (Alvarez 1993b) show that the value of the coca sector's purchases from other sectors ranged from 1 to 5 percent of the sector's total intermediate demand. The major implication of these findings is that the coca industry has limited importance from an interindustrial perspective.[10]

Value Added and Employment in the Coca Sector

In 1992, value-added estimates for the coca sector (the income received by each factor of the production process) were as follows: coca leaf, $707 million; cocaine paste, $324 million; cocaine base, $106 million; and cocaine hydrochloride (HCl), $101 million (Alvarez 1993b). Thus, the largest share of value added is appropriated at the coca leaf stage. This finding should not be surprising considering that the majority of workers are employed at this stage.

An important question that remains concerns the distribution of income in the coca sector. Using budget and cost of production information for each stage of the cocaine manufacturing industry, Instituto Cuánto has estimated annual income per capita based on the following assumptions: 200,000 hectares planted in coca; an average coca farm size of 5.2 hectares; 160 person workdays (*jornales*) to farm one hectare of coca; and individual worker contributions of 300 person workdays annually (Alvarez 1993b). The data indicate that the producers of cocaine base and hydrochloride receive the highest incomes, approximately $2 million per capital annually. Furthermore, if cocaine base and hydrochloride manufacturers are considered to be the same group of producers (a reasonable assumption), the income of these producers may be even higher, perhaps roughly $4 million per year. In contrast, the estimated income per capita for coca growers or *cocaleros posesionarios de tierra* (those who have access to land regardless of its property status) totals approximately $15,000 per year, an income well above the national average, though significantly lower than the traffickers' income. Wage laborers working in coca leaf and paste processing obtain between $1,350 and $4,540 per year, respectively. These figures are significantly lower than the traffickers' income but higher than both the average income earned in rural areas[11] and the national average income. Moreover, inasmuch as coca leaf wage laborers are often also coca paste processors, their total income is likely to be higher than the estimated $1,350 per year.

These figures clearly demonstrate that the agricultural laborer in the coca industry earns the smallest income, whereas the trafficker profits greatly from this activity. These estimates support the thesis that poverty, extremely low wages in alternative legal activities, and profits (an "extra profit" is paid for the risk entailed by the activity) constitute important driving forces behind the illicit drug sector. An additional implication of the data discussed in the previous section is that the coca sector generates high revenues, making possible the payment of bribes to members of the peacekeeping forces and other collaborators in civil society.

The employment effect of the coca sector in the Peruvian economy is also quite significant. In 1992, the sector as a whole directly employed approximately 175,000 people (Alvarez 1993b, 41-42). This accounted for roughly 7 percent of the agricultural labor force of the country and 2 percent of Peru's total economically active population. Needless to say, these percentages would have been substantially higher if indirect employment had been considered.

IMPACT OF POLITICAL INSTABILITY ON THE INVESTMENT ENVIRONMENT

Peru witnessed high levels of political violence during the 1980s and early 1990s. Although this situation changed significantly as of 1994, investors considering Peru in the 1980s and early 1990s were deterred by the violent and unstable political situation that prevailed in the country (Thorp and Bertram 1978; Degregori 1990; Gorriti 1990). Indeed, according to a special

Peruvian Senate committee report, losses of fixed capital and physical infrastructure related to violence during the period 1980-1991 were estimated at approximately $20 billion (Senado de la República del Perú 1992, 72).

Contrary to what might be expected, political violence did not deter private investment altogether; however, it changed the composition of investment in a way that was not conducive to strong economic development, however. Investment projects were concentrated in two areas (Gonzales de Olarte 1991, 23-24). One area consisted of risk-averse activities, such as investments in real estate, which partially replaced investments in transportation equipment and industrial machinery. The other comprised new investments in very small and micro enterprises in the informal sector, where overhead costs are low.

Inasmuch as political violence and its effects discouraged private investment, their eradication was of crucial importance for the economic future of the country. Guerrilla activity and changes in government policy undoubtedly contributed to an uncertain business environment. As a result, even the most adventurous entrepreneurs had good reason not to undertake productive investment in Peru. Investment projects concentrated instead on speculative, short-term operations, such as real estate, and small-scale, informal enterprises.

Although the role played by Peru's guerrilla movements in drug trafficking has generally been characterized as that of a friendly alliance with the traffickers, not one of direct participation in the industry, there is growing evidence that both the Shining Path (Sendero Luminoso) and the Tupac Amaru Revolutionary Movement (Movimiento Revolucionario Tupac Amaru, MRTA) have been actively involved in drug processing and trafficking. It has been noted that both the MRTA and the Shining Path drew upon the coca leaf growers as an excellent source of revenue; the guerrillas served as a private "army" for the growers, thereby effectively extracting protection money from them. Assuming, for illustrative purposes, that in its role as "protector" the Shining Path received a total of 5 percent of the coca leaf and coca paste revenues, a projection based on a conservative estimate for 1988 data (Alvarez 1993a) reveals that the guerrillas would have taken in between $13 million and $56 million in revenues. This is a conservative estimate; considering that the guerrillas could have been directly involved in trafficking, as discussed earlier, their profits could very well have been significantly higher.

In addition, some observers (Reid 1989; Gorriti 1988; ECONSULT 1986; Bedoya 1990) have identified the bribing of coca producers by government officials and the USAID crop substitution project as indirect causes of the alliance between the Shining Path and the coca growers. Thus, the political violence generated by the Shining Path can partially be attributed to the illegal drug trade, and in turn, drug trafficking contributed to the deterioration of the political situation in the country. It is important to note, moreover, that even though insurgency has declined since 1994, the major guerrilla groups remain active, particularly in coca-producing areas, and they continue to profit from drug trafficking (Valenzuela 1995). In short, as long as there is drug trafficking in Peru, there may be guerrilla activity in the country.

DEFINING DUTCH DISEASE-TYPE SYMPTOMS

The literature on Dutch Disease (DD) is extensive and growing. The term "Dutch Disease" was first used to refer to the adverse effects on Dutch manufacturing of the natural gas discoveries of the 1960s, essentially through the subsequent appreciation of the Dutch real exchange rate.[12] This analytical framework has been used to analyze export booms in developing countries and to devise appropriate policies to manage these booms effectively. Thus, it constitutes a useful tool for analyzing situations in which large, prolonged foreign exchange inflows are affecting the productive structure of a country, necessitating adjustments that entail high economic costs, such as the draining of the stock of reserves (Cambiaso 1993) (see Figure 2).

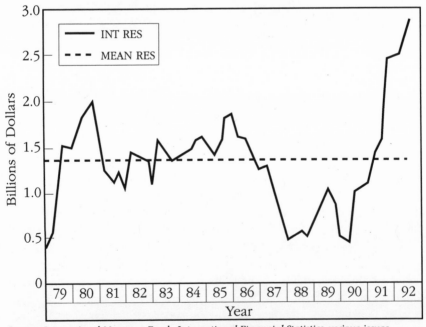

Figure 2. Total International Reserves Minus Gold
1979.1 - 1992.4

Source: International Monetary Fund, *International Financial Statistics,* various issues.

Proper assessment of a boom's temporal duration under normal circumstances is important so that effective policy actions can be implemented accordingly. Considering that it is not easy to arrive at a proper assessment for legal export commodities, it is certainly more difficult to do so for illicit activities. Given this uncertainty, economic authorities must assess the convenience of allowing the absorption of these resources through the appreciation of the foreign exchange rate, which in turn affects the competitiveness of the external sector. If adjustment measures increase the relative value of the national currency, for example, commercial flows will be negatively affected. Furthermore, if economic agents expect the foreign exchange inflows to be temporary, they may develop expectations of devaluation. Such expectations can induce instability in the foreign exchange market and aggravate uncertainty in the economy (Cambiaso 1993) (see Figures 3, 4, 5, and 6).

The capacity of Latin American economies to absorb significant inflows of external funds into productive activities is limited (Cambiaso 1993, 5) due to the developing nature of these economies. Therefore, extraordinary inflows of foreign exchange can fuel inflationary pressures. Inflation, in turn, can frustrate the achievement of critical growth and economic goals that depend on a dynamic, diversified external sector. Large foreign exchange inflows tend to increase the stock of reserves in central banks and seriously complicate monetary policy management, particularly if inflationary pressures continue on the rise, increasing nominal interest rates. Moreover, large inflows of foreign exchange can appreciate the real exchange rate, decrease export competitiveness, and encourage nonproductive imports (see Figure 6).

In addition, large foreign exchange inflows typically generate an unexpected increase in the money supply, which can hinder the competitiveness of the exportable sector (see Figure 7). Such an excess of liquidity induces an increase in domestic expenditure (see Figures 8 and 9) that can be partly absorbed through higher prices for nontradable goods and services and an increase in imports, thereby reducing and transferring the inflationary pressures to the rest of the world. If the import leakages turn out to be relatively small, the result is an appreciation of the real exchange rate. In the case of illicit outflows of foreign exchange, these resources can encourage capital flight, the hoarding of foreign exchange, or investment in securities in the stock market (see Figures 10, 11, and 12). The permanency of the external stimulus tends to produce a reallocation of productive resources from the tradable to the nontradable sector; thus, prolonged inflows hinder potential export-led growth.

Figure 3. Index of Real Exchange Rates
Seven Main Commercial Partners — 1979.1 - 1986.4

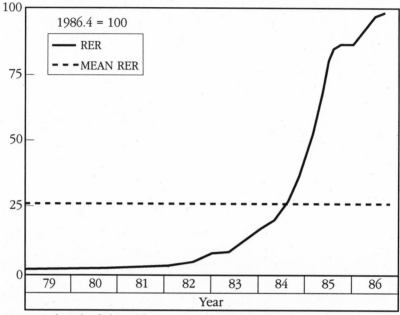

An increase in the index (below 100) represents a (decreasing) real appreciation of the currency.
Source: Authors' estimates.

Figure 4. Index of Real Exchange Rates
Seven Main Commercial Partners — 1987.1 - 1992.4

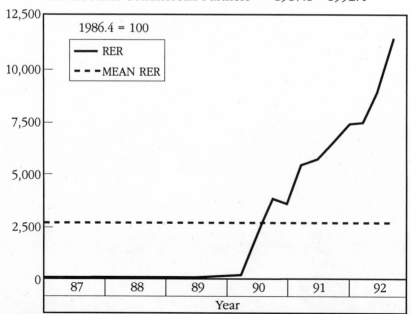

Source: Authors' estimates based on data from the International Monetary Fund.

Figure 5. Index of Bilateral Real Exchange Rate

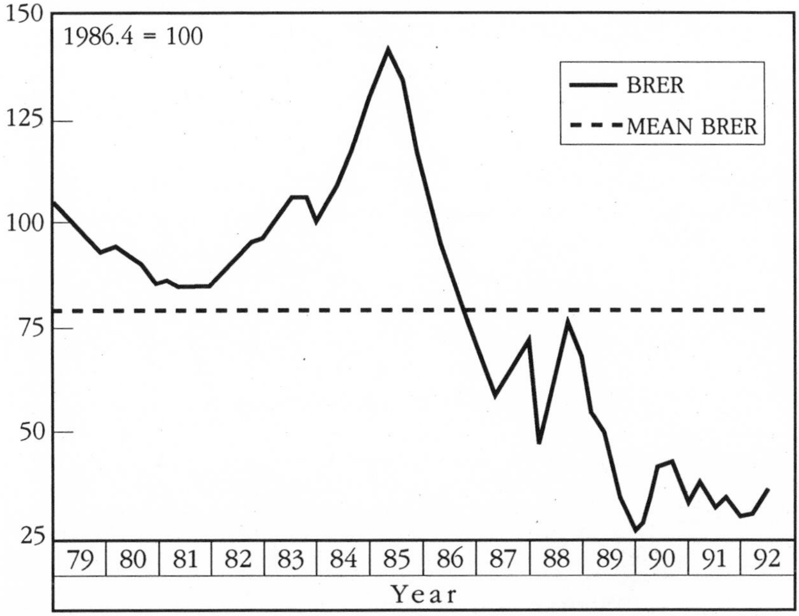

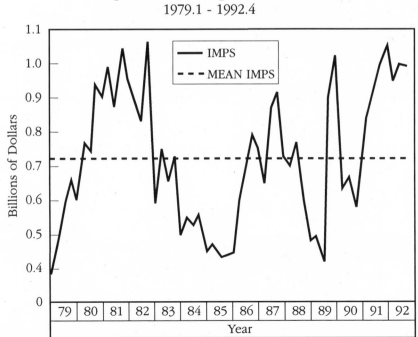

The real exchange rate is the product of the exchange rate and the ratio of foreign to domestic prices.
Source: International Monetary Fund, *International Financial Statistics,* various issues.

Figure 6. Total Imports of Goods
1979.1 - 1992.4

Source: International Monetary Fund, *International Financial Statistics,* various issues.

Figure 7. Money (M1)
1979.1 - 1986.4

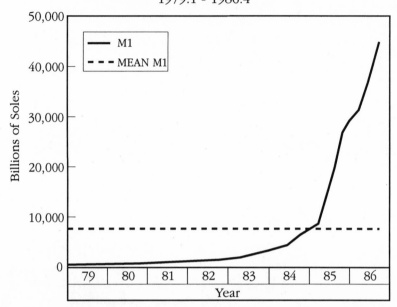

M1 = Currency outside banks and demand deposits other than those of the central government.
Source: International Monetary Fund, *International Financial Statistics,* various issues.

Figure 8. Velocity of Circulation of M1
1979.1 - 1986.4

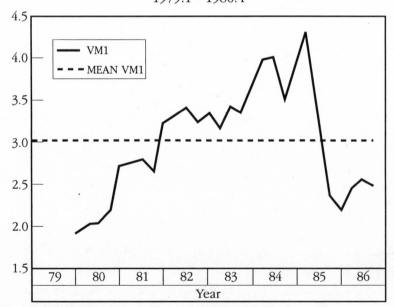

VM1 = Nominal GDP/M1
Sources: Webb and Femández Baca, *Perú en números,* various issues.
         International Monetary Fund, *International Financial Statistics,* various issues.

Figure 9. Velocity of Circulation of M1
1987.1 - 1992.3

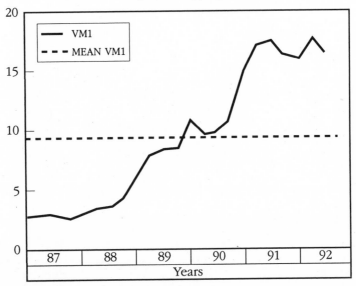

VM1 = Nominal GDP/M1.
Sources: Webb and Fernández Baca, *Perú en números,* various issues.
　　　　 International Monetary Fund, *International Financial Statistics,* various issues.

Figure 10. Real Interest Rate Differential
1979.1 - 1986.4

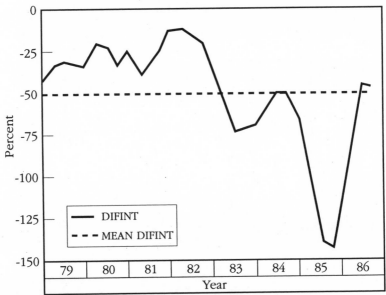

DIFINT = Peruvian real savings deposit rate minus U.S. real Treasury bonds rate.
Sources:　Webb and Fernández Baca, *Perú en números,* various issues.
　　　　　International Monetary Fund, *International Financial Statistics,* various issues.

Figure 11. Real Interest Differential
1987.1 - 1992.4

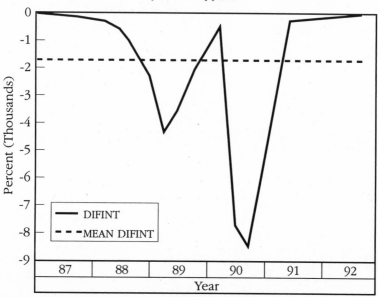

DIFINT = Peruvian savings deposit rate minus U.S. Treasury bond rate.
Sources:　Webb and Fernández Baca, *Perú en números,* various issues.
　　　　　International Monetary Fund, *International Financial Statistics,* various issues.

Figure 12. Capital Flight
1979.1 - 1992.4

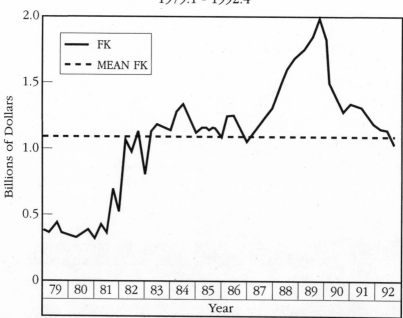

FK = Liabilities to Peruvian residents reported by all kinds of depository institutions and banks in the U.S.
Source: *Federal Reserve Bulletin.*

EMPIRICAL EVIDENCE OF DUTCH DISEASE
SYNDROME IN PERU

ASSESSING THE FACTS[13]

The results that associate the Peruvian coca boom with some of the typical symptoms of Dutch Disease are discussed in this section.[14] Though declining, coca was an important export commodity during the period under study, 1979-1992. A preliminary methodology has been developed with which to improve our understanding of the economic impact of the coca boom in Peru. This analysis and the data used require further refinement, however.

In tracing the Dutch Disease problem, a necessary initial condition must be met, namely, an extraordinary inflow of foreign exchange. Therefore, the first task of the analysis consisted of the collection of a quarterly series of international reserves comprising the first quarter of 1979 (1979.1) through the fourth quarter of 1992 (1992.4) (see Figure 2). An observation of this time series reveals that reserves mostly remained above their historical average from the fourth quarter of 1979 (1979.4) to the fourth quarter of 1986 (1986.4) and that they varied in several quarters by more than one standard deviation. Subsequently, reserves dropped below their average level until the first quarter of 1991 (1991.1) and skyrocketed thereafter. Thus, the data suggest (see Figure 2) that during the periods 1979.1 to 1986.4 and 1991.2 to 1992.4, there was indeed an extraordinary inflow of foreign exchange in Peru.

The next task was to determine whether coca exports followed a pattern similar to that of international reserves. The data indicate that they did.[15] As can be seen in Figures 1 and 2, both variables demonstrated a behavior that was higher than average until the fourth quarter of 1986 (1986.4), after which they both dropped significantly.

Among the possible allocations of an extraordinary inflow of foreign exchange are the following:

1. *An increase in productive imports (inputs to increase the social overhead capital) and/or consumption imports* (see Figure 6). The similar increases of productive imports and consumption goods with respect to coca exports from the first quarter of 1979 (1979.1) to the fourth quarter of 1983 (1983.4) seem to be canceled by their collapse during the period 1984.1-1986.1. Thus, the import leakage effect does not appear to be strong enough to boost GDP growth and export inflationary pressures to the rest of the world.

2. *Capital flight* (see Figure 12). The outflow of financial resources seems to be determined by the default, interest, taxation, and credibility risks, uncertainty, and strong yield differentials between the domestic economy and the rest of the world. Capital flight is also

strongly correlated with the degree of development of the financial sector. Although capital flight is difficult to register, the analysis of the deposits made by Peruvian residents in U.S. financial and banking institutions, which were on the rise until the fourth quarter of 1989 (Board of Governors of the Federal Reserve System), indicates that in 1988, $396 million in deposits were made. This figure represents 33 percent of our own estimates of coca exports or 40 percent of Macroconsult's (1990a) estimates for that year.

3. *Particular conditions of the Peruvian economy.* In the Peruvian economy, there appear to be risk factors, bottlenecks (rural migration and differences between coca-growing regions, among others), a low capacity of absorption of the capital infrastructure of the economy, and a strong deterioration of the terms of trade (See Figure 16).[16] Given these adverse factors, the extraordinary inflow of foreign exchange, partly compensated by capital outflows, appears to have been monetized, inducing a significant increase in the money supply and therefore an increase in the inflation rate that was higher than proportional.[17] Consequently, the difference in domestic and foreign inflation rates widened significantly, creating strong expectations for the appreciation of the real exchange rate, which in turn restricted the needed expansion and diversification of the tradables sector. This excess supply of money prompted an excess demand for nontradable goods which manifested itself in a significant increase in the velocity of circulation of M1[18] (see Figures 8 and 9) and the reallocation of productive resources from the tradable to the nontradable sector. In this respect, the construction and service sectors experienced a significant growth in 16 out of 28 quarters (55 percent) from the first quarter of 1980 to the fourth quarter of 1986 (see Figures 13 and 14).

All these developments point to the fact that Peru was indeed experiencing Dutch Disease Syndrome,[19] which was further complicated by indexation schemes and a monetary expansion/inflation/devaluation spiral.

The next task was to determine whether a correlation existed between coca exports and international reserves. For this purpose, we applied an econometric analysis based on the variables shown below.

In this stage of the analysis, econometric practice suggests the building of a correlation matrix so as to choose the set of variables with which to build a reasonable structural model to obtain impact multipliers and be able to judge not only direct effects but also second-, third-, and fourth-round effects among the variables. The correlations were obtained for the periods 1979.1-1986.4 and 1987.1-1992.4 (see Tables 1, 2, and 3).

Figure 13. Real Gross Domestic Product — Services
1980.1 - 1991.4

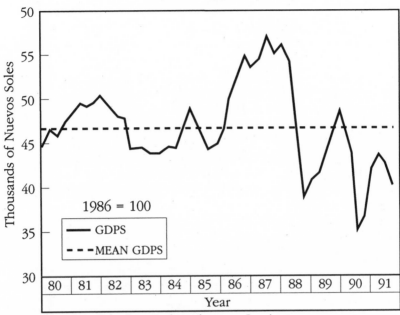

1986 = 100

— GDPS

- - - MEAN GDPS

Source: Webb and Fernández Baca, *Perú en números,* various issues.

Figure 14. Real Gross Domestic Product — Construction
1980.1 - 1991.4

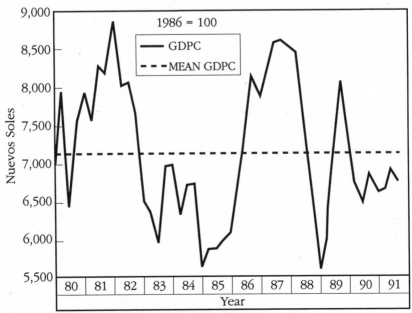

1986 = 100

— GDPC

- - - MEAN GDPC

Source: Webb and Fernández Baca, *Perú en números,* various issues.

Figure 15. Real Gross Domestic Product
1980.1 - 1993.3

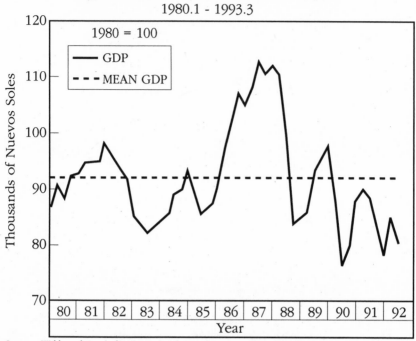

Source: Webb and Fernández Baca, *Perú en números,* various issues.

Figure 16. Terms of Trade

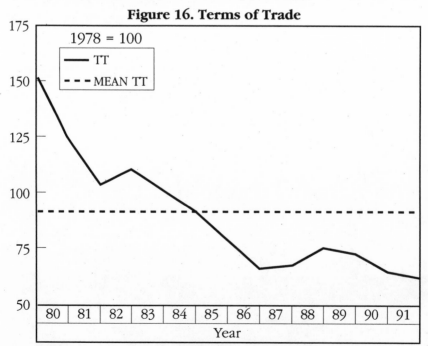

TT = Traditional exports price index/foreign imports price index.
Source: Webb and Fernández Baca, *Perú en números,* various issues.

Description of Variables

BRER = Bilateral real exchange rate. BRER equals the product of the exchange rate and the ratio of foreign to domestic prices.

Δ = Rate of variation.

DIFINF = Difference in rates of inflation of the consumer prices between Peru and the United States.

DIFINT = Difference of real interest rates between Peru and the United States. For Peru, the official rate of interest for saving deposits was considered. For the United States, the rate of treasury bills was taken.

DIFVM2 = Absolute change of the velocity of circulation of M2.

GDP = Gross domestic product.

GDPC = Real GDP of the construction sector.

GDPS = Real GDP of the service sector.

IMPS = Imports.

INFC = Rate of change of the price of cocaine quoted in Chicago.

INFP = Inflation in Peru.

INSTRS = Instruments used in the Two-Stage Least Squares (TSLS) estimation.

M1 = currency outside banks and demand deposits other than the central government's.

M2 = M1 plus time, savings, and foreign currency deposits of resident sectors other than central government.

REC = Rate of change of coca exports.

RER = Sum of weighted cross exchange rates. The cross exchange rate is the number of domestic currency units per one unit of foreign currency (dollar, mark, pound, and so on). The weights are given by the share of imports coming from seven main commercial partners within total imports of goods. 1986.4 = 100.

RFK = Rate of change of the liabilities to foreigners (Peruvian residents' deposits) reported by all kinds of depository institutions (as well as brokers and dealers) and banks in the United States payable in U.S. dollars.

RGDPR = Rate of change of real GDP.

RIMPS = Rate of change of imports of goods.

RIR = Rate of change of international total reserves (U.S. dollar value of monetary authorities' holdings of Special Drawing Rights, reserve position in the Fund, foreign exchange) minus gold, that are available to adjust a disequilibrium in the balance of payments.

RM2 = Rate of change of M2.

RRER = Rate of change of the multilateral real exchange rate.

TT = Terms of trade.

TT = ratio of traditional exports price index to foreign imports price index (in figures).

VM1 = Nominal GDP/M1.

VM2 = GDP/M2.

Table 1.
Matrix of Correlations of Variables Associated with Dutch Disease Syndrome:
Peru[1] — 1980.2-1986.4

	REC	RIR	RM2	DIFINF	DIFINT	RRER	DIFVM2	RGDPR	RIMPS	INFC	RFK
REC	100.0	36.9	20.2	-1.1	5.5	-6.5	2.8	18.1	43.5	0.1	41.7
RIR	36.9	100.0	42.3	10.2	-10.5	2.6	-54.0	-9.5	29.8	-1.5	5.4
RM2	20.2	42.3	100.0	54.5	-38.5	45.7	-67.4	-13.5	9.0	-34.8	26.1
DIFINF	-1.1	10.2	54.5	100.0	-92.5	43.1	-8.5	-2.1	-20.5	-50.0	-12.1
DIFINT	5.5	-10.5	-38.5	-92.5	100.0	-18.1	1.8	0.6	5.4	46.8	13.2
RRER	-6.5	2.6	45.7	43.1	-18.1	100.0	-11.9	-56.8	-39.8	-8.7	5.6
DIFVM2	2.8	-54.0	-67.4	-8.5	1.8	-11.9	100.0	26.9	-14.5	18.5	-42.4
RGDPR	18.1	-9.5	-13.5	-2.1	0.6	-56.8	26.9	100.0	46.5	-1.0	-5.2
RIMPS	43.5	29.8	9.0	-20.5	5.4	-39.8	-14.5	46.5	100.0	7.2	44.6
INFC	0.1	-1.5	-34.8	-50.0	46.8	-8.7	18.5	-1.0	7.2	100.0	-6.9
RFK	41.7	5.4	26.1	-12.1	13.2	5.6	-42.4	-5.2	44.6	-6.9	100.0

Sources: Webb and Fernández Baca, *Perú en números*, various issues; International Monetary Fund, *International Financial Statistics*, various issues; authors' estimates.

1 = Consult the Description of Variables list.

Table 2.
Matrix of Correlations of Variables Associated with Dutch Disease Syndrome:
Peru[1] — 1987.1-1992.3

	REC	RIR	RM2	DIFINF	DIFINT	RRER	DIFVM2	RGDPR	RIMPS	INFC	RFK
INFC	0.1	-1.5	-34.8	-50.0	46.8	-8.7	18.5	-1.0	7.2	100.0	-6.9
REC	100.0	45.7	7.9	32.8	-37.4	-4.4	-1.3	14.5	14.0	-33.7	25.0
RIR	45.7	100.0	54.2	48.4	-47.5	43.7	-45.3	-31.3	-8.3	4.9	-14.3
RM2	7.9	54.2	100.0	70.4	-60.5	94.4	-11.2	-48.9	-8.1	31.3	-20.2
DIFINF	32.8	48.4	70.4	100.0	-98.3	59.3	18.1	2.2	4.2	-12.3	-16.9
DIFINT	37.4	-47.5	-60.5	-08.3	100.0	-51.0	-18.0	8.1	7.3	27.9	7.8
RRER	-44.4	43.7	94.4	59.3	-51.0	100.0	-14.7	-63.2	-17.9	23.0	-15.5
DIFVM2	-1.3	-45.3	-11.2	18.1	-18.9	-14.7	100.0	40.1	5.7	-7.6	20.8
RGDPR	14.5	-31.3	-48.2	2.2	-8.1	-63.2	40.1	100.0	23.4	-21.1	-23.9
RIMPS	14.0	-8.3	-8.1	4.2	-7.3	-17.9	5.7	23.4	100.0	-2.9	36.6
INFC	-33.7	4.9	31.3	-12.3	27.9	23.0	-7.6	-21.1	-2.9	100.0	-33.0
RFK	25.0	-14.3	-20.2	-16.9	7.8	-15.5	20.8	23.94	36.6	-33.0	100.0

Sources: Webb and Fernández Baca, *Perú en números*, various issues; International Monetary Fund, *International Financial Statistics*, various issues; authors' estimates.

1 = Consult the Description of Variables list.

Table 3.

Matrix of Correlations of Variables Associated with Dutch Disease Syndrome:

Peru[1] — 1980.2-1992.3

	REC	RIR	RM2	DIFINF	DIFINT	RRER	DIFVM2	RGDPR	RIMPS	INFC	RFK
REC	100.0	40.5	5.0	18.7	-22.0	-5.2	1.1	13.3	27.8	-21.8	33.2
RIR	40.5	100.0	46.4	39.6	-39.5	36.6	-41.6	-26.9	4.7	3.7	21.3
RM2	5.0	46.4	100.0	76.8	-68.7	93.8	-5.7	-46.5	-4.3	23.7	-7.7
DIFINF	18.7	39.6	76.8	100.0	-98.6	66.2	20.6	-7.0	2.6	-8.5	-10.6
DIFINT	-22.0	-39.5	-68.7	-98.6	100.0	-52.1	-21.3	1.7	-4.8	21.3	8.0
RRER	-5.2	36.6	93.8	66.2	-52.1	100.0	-9.1	-6.2	-16.8	19.1	-8.1
DIFVM2	1.1	-41.6	-5.7	20.6	-21.3	-9.1	100.0	34.5	2.8	-5.3	-1.1
RGDPR	13.3	-26.9	-46.5	-7.0	1.7	-6.2	34.5	100.0	29.1	-17.4	6.1
RIMPS	27.8	4.7	-4.3	2.6	-4.8	-16.8	2.8	29.1	100.0	0.2	36.1
INFC	-21.8	3.7	23.7	-8.5	21.3	19.1	-5.3	-17.4	0.2	100.0	-11.8
RFK	33.2	21.3	-7.7	-10.6	8.0	-8.1	-1.1	6.1	36.1	-11.8	100.0

Sources: Webb and Fernández Baca, *Perú en números*, various issues; International Monetary Fund, *International Financial Statistics*, various issues; authors' estimates.

1 = Consult the Description of Variables list.

The empirical implication that can be derived from these tables tends to support the existence of certain relations, but not strict causality, among variables that led to the fulfillment of DD Syndrome:

1. The rate of change in coca exports (REC) is reasonably correlated with the change in international reserves (RIR). That is, coca exports contributed to the extraordinary inflow of reserves within the designated time frame:

   $\Delta REC \Rightarrow \Delta RIR$

2. The change in reserves is reasonably correlated with monetary expansion, suggesting that reserves were monetized:

   $\Delta RIR \Rightarrow \Delta M1(M2)$

3. Monetary expansion is highly correlated with the difference between domestic and foreign inflationary rates (DIFINF) and with the change in the real exchange rate (RER) — especially during the period 1987.1-1992.4, when the monetary expansion/inflation/devaluation spiral took place:

   $\Delta M2(M1) \Rightarrow \Delta DIFINF \Rightarrow \Delta RER \Rightarrow \Delta M2(M1)$

The correlation matrix reveals that the crucial variables involved in DD Syndrome are highly collinear; that is, their influences on RER are not independent of each other. Therefore, it is necessary to attempt to solve the simultaneous equation bias. In this respect, an initial attempt was made by using the Two-Stage Least Squares (TSLS) estimating procedure.

At this point of the analysis, the cross influence of the chosen variables was tested using simple Least Squares (LSQ) and Two-Stage Least Squares estimating procedures. The results are shown in Table 4.

Considering the estimates, the assumed "causality" would run as follows:

$\Delta REC \Rightarrow \Delta RIR$

$\Delta RIR \Rightarrow \Delta RM2(M1) \Rightarrow \Delta INFP \Rightarrow \Delta DIFINF \Rightarrow \Delta RM2...$

$\Delta INFP \Rightarrow \Delta DIFVM2(M1) \Rightarrow \Delta DIFINF$

$\Delta DIFINF \Rightarrow \Delta RER$

$\Delta DIFINT \Rightarrow \Delta RER$

$\Delta DIFVM2(M1) \Rightarrow \Delta RER$

$\Delta RM2 \Rightarrow \Delta RER$

$\Delta RER \Rightarrow -\Delta RGDPR$

$\Delta RER \Rightarrow -\Delta EXPORTS$

Finally, it must be stressed that a full simultaneous model is required to analyze all the cross effects and not just the first round effect of the impact of

Table 4.
The Impact of Coca Exports on the Real Exchange Rate[1]
(Preliminary Estimates from Regression Analysis) — 1979.3-1992.4

	REC	RRER	RIR	INFC	INFP	RM2	RRER	RGDPR	DIFVM2	DIFINT	DIFINGF	R**2	F-STAT	PERIOD
LSQ														
RIR	0.7 (3.0)	0.1 (0.4)										0.32	4.06	79.3-86.4
RIR	0.3 (1.5)	0.1 (4.9)										0.60	9.88	87.1-92.4
RIR	0.5 (3.1)	0.1 (5.3)										0.47	14.77	79.3-92.4
RM2			1.4 (4.2)	3.6 (1.7)	0.03 (5.30)									
DIFINF			-4.7 (-2.6)			13.7 (6.5)	-6.8 (-5.4)	-22.8 (-2.7)	133.8 (1.6)	-1.0 (-378.6)		0.99	745.1	80.3-92.3
TSLS														
RRER	0.5 (1.2)								35.3 (1.1)	0.5 (3.3)	0.5 (3.1)	0.54	4.7	80.3-86.4
RRER	2.0 (20.0)								24.4 (1.7)	-0.1 (-4.4)	-0.1 (-4.8)	0.98	167.1	87.1-92.3
RRER	1.9 (28.4)								24.6 (2.5)	-0.1 (-6.2)	-0.1 (-6.9)	0.98	378.0	80.3-92.3
INSTRS.	REC	RIMPS	RIR	INFC	INFP	RM2	RFK	RGDPR	DIFVM2	DIFINT	DIFINGF			

Sources: Webb and Fernández Baca, *Perú en números*, various issues; International Monetary Fund, *International Financial Statistics*, various issues; authors' estimates.

1 = Consult the Description of Variables.

coca exports on the real exchange rate and the rest of the economy. Also, the evidence suggests that it is not fair to dismiss the sizable impact of coca exports by merely looking at its changing (decreasing) ratio over GDP over time.

Another important issue that was tested is the notion that macroeconomic variables tend to follow a random walk process. In this case, the best forecast of tomorrow's value is the immediate past value of the variable since the variable tends to deviate permanently from its trend when impinged upon by exogenous shocks. Variables that follow such behavior cannot be associated across time. This would hinder the possibility of drawing strong conclusions about the existence of Dutch Disease Syndrome. In this respect, preliminary tests were run. The Dickey-Fuller test showed that RER and REC apparently do not follow a random walk behavior. For more definitive results, further analysis and more solid testing will be needed.[20]

To conclude, the empirical evidence obtained by implementing the estimating procedures described above suggest that coca exports exercised a significant, direct influence on the extraordinary inflow of foreign exchange, especially during the period 1979-1986. On the whole, reserves appear to have been monetized and used to increase spending on nontradable goods and services. Given that certain leakages do not fully offset the inflationary pressures of the upsurge in reserves, the difference in inflation rates between Peru and the rest of the world widens and the real exchange rate tends to appreciate. As a consequence of real appreciation and a severe deterioration in the terms of trade, export growth is severely inhibited. The data also suggest that the impact of coca exports is not a "once and for all" effect. After impinging upon the expansion of the buffer stock of reserves, it filters into the rest of the economic structure and affects the expectations and the adjustment velocities of all economic agents, sectors, and markets. Once the impact has taken place, the process seems to fuel its own inertia and become deeply rooted.

CONCLUDING REMARKS

To a great extent, the expansion of the illicit coca sector can be attributed to Peru's inability to improve the living conditions of the rural population in the Andes. The coca sector, which became very important in the late 1970s, was the best income-generating activity in Peruvian agriculture. Although the sector's revenues are currently on the decline, coca is still the best income alternative in the coca-producing areas of the country. Throughout the 1980s, the coca sector exacerbated political and economic instability inasmuch as political violence, which took off in the late 1970s, deterred productive investment in the country. Guerrillas, coca growers, and traffickers formed alliances for tactical purposes, neutralizing the controlling and peacekeeping forces through corruption.

An analysis of coca data in relation to other macroeconomic indicators suggests that the coca sector may have caused Dutch Disease-type symptoms in Peru, especially during the period 1979-1986. Even though the subsequent impact of this sector has been indirect, it remains important and merits further analysis. Without a doubt, the illicit coca sector constitutes a major factor in the analysis of the economic consequences of the "Peruvian disease."

NOTES

The authors wish to thank Francisco Melero and Ana María Vallina for their assistance and useful comments. Jaime Gálvez of Instituto Cuánto also kindly provided information for this paper, and Kathleen Hamman and Cynthia L. Jenney made many valuable editorial suggestions. This analysis of the coca sector is based on research sponsored by the External Grant Program of the University of Miami's North-South Center.

1. See Brooks 1993. Another indicator of this relatively peaceful situation, as discussed with Peru's top official in charge of tourist affairs, is the recent increase of tourist flows into the country.

2. Remarks made by Maureen Taft-Morales, commentator-analyst of Latin American affairs, Congressional Research Service. See *Cocaine Production, Eradication, and the Environment: Policy, Impact, and Options* 1990, 51.

3. For further information, see Mortimer 1901; Morner 1985; and Rostworoski de Diez Canseco 1988.

4. Alkaloids are substances occurring naturally in plants; they are pharmacologically active in animals and humans. Other examples are caffeine from coffee and other plants as well as morphine and codeine from the opium poppy (Grinspoon and Bakalar 1976, 73-75). The intranasal use of cocaine hydrochloride and smoking of cocaine base produce quite different psychological and pharmacological experiences from the traditional mastication of coca leaves (Grinspoon and Bakalar 1976, 217-222; Mortimer 1901).

5. Cocaine base can be purified using two different methods. One method involves processing with petroleum ether, methanol, and hydrochloric acid, while the other utilizes a mixture of acetone and benzene (Grinspoon and Bakalar 1976, 73-75).

6. A hectare (ha) is equivalent to approximately 2.4 acres.

7. Preliminary data processed by Cuánto S.A. for the National Survey for Measurement of the Standard of Living (Encuesta Nacional Sobre Medición de Niveles de Vida, ENNIV) conducted in 1994. For further information, see Instituto Cuánto 1995.

8. The coca production data were developed for Bolivia and Peru for a research project funded by an external grant from the North-South Center of the University of Miami. The methodological details of the development of these estimates as well as research findings are presented in Alvarez 1993b.

9. The coca sector is unquestionably more important in Bolivia than in Peru. Our calculations for 1985 show that the sector amounted to between 7 and 11 percent of Bolivian GDP. For 1992, the coca revenue for Bolivia as a share of GDP amounted to between 4.6 and 9.0 percent (see Alvarez 1993b).

10. A similar situation is found in Bolivia. In fact, according to the calculations made by the Unit for the Analysis of Economic Policy (Unidad de Análisis de Políticas Económicas, UDAPE) in the report of the Presidency of the Republic of Bolivia (1990, 26-27), $1.00 in the coca circuit generates $.04 in intermediate demand for inputs, while $1.00 in construction generates $.61; in industry, $.31; and in modern agriculture, $.27.

11. According to Cuánto S.A., income for rural areas ranged between $470 and $720 in 1994. These figures are based on preliminary data processed by Cuánto S.A. for the ENNIV 1994 survey. See Instituto Cuánto 1995.

12. Corden and Neary 1982 and Corden 1982 reprinted in Corden 1985 have become classic surveys on the subject.

13. Details of the econometric analysis are available from the authors upon request.

14. Vega and Cebrecos (1991) deny the existence of Dutch Disease in Peru because of preexisting domestic price rigidities and other structural disequilibria. For other alternative analyses of DD in Peru, see Cruz-Saco, Revilla, and Seminario 1994. The latter work, however, seems to contain several analytical and factual inconsistencies which do not provide solid basis for their claim that there is no relationship between the illicit coca foreign exchange inflows and DD in Peru.

15. Due to the difficulty posed by the underregistration of the true levels of coca exports, our figures are underestimated by about 40 percent compared to the point estimates of other sources such as Macroconsult's for the year 1988 ($1.89 billion versus our average figure of $1.196 billion).

16. See Webb and Fernández Baca 1992.

17. For example, within our Dutch Disease period, from 1983.2 to 1986.1, inflation reached an average thre-digit rate of 131 percent.

18. See Description of Variables, p. 167.

19. In other words, numerous symptoms of Dutch Disease were present in the economy.

20. Additional testing was done through Johansen's procedures. This analysis for the period 1979.1-1992.4 suggested that the illicit coca export revenues and the real exchange rate seemed to be cointegrated in the long-run. Thus, even though the coca sector share of GDP is declining, this does not mean that its multiple impact can be ignored, overlooked or diminished, Cervantes 1995.

REFERENCES

Alvarez, Elena H. 1993a. *Illegal Export-Led Growth in the Andes: A Preliminary Economic and Socio-Political Assessment.* Report prepared for the United Nations Research Institute for Social Development.

Alvarez, Elena H. 1993b. *The Political Economy of Coca Production in Bolivia and Peru: Economic Importance and Political Implications.* Report prepared for the North-South Center of the University of Miami in collaboration with Instituto Cuánto and the Centro de Estudios Bolivianos Multidisciplinarios.

Alvarez, Elena H. 1992a. "Coca Production in Peru." In *Drug Policy in the Americas,* ed. Peter Smith. Boulder: Westview Press.

Alvarez, Elena H. 1992b. *Opportunities and Constraints to Reduce Coca Production: The Macroeconomic Context in Bolivia and Peru.* Report prepared for the U.S. Congress, Office of Technology Assessment.

Alvarez, Elena H. 1991. *La economía ilegal de la coca en el Perú.* Lima: Fundación Friedrich Ebert.

Alvarez, Elena H. 1990. "Reasons for the Expansion of Coca Exports in Peru." In *Cocaine Production, Eradication, and the Environment: Policy, Impact and Options.* Washington, D.C.: Congressional Research Service, United States Government Printing Office.

Alvarez, Elena H. 1988. *The Economics and Political Economy of Coca Production in the Andes: Implications for U.S. Foreign Policy and Rural Development in Bolivia and Peru.* Albany: Nelson A. Rockefeller Institute of Government, State University of New York.

Alvarez, Elena H. 1983a. "Government Policy and the Persistence of Rural Poverty in Peru, 1960-1980." Ph.D. diss. New York: New School for Social Research.

Alvarez, Elena H. 1983b. *Política económica y agricultura en el Perú, 1969-1979.* Lima: Instituto de Estudios Peruanos.

Alvarez, Elena H. 1980. *Política agraria y estancamiento en el Perú, 1969-1977.* Lima: Instituto de Estudios Peruanos.

Aramburú, Carlos. 1989. "La economía parcelaria y el cultivo de la coca: El caso del Alto Huallaga." In *Pasta básica de cocaína,* eds. Federico León and Ramiro Castro de la Mata. Lima: CEDRO.

Bedoya, Eduardo. 1990. *Las causas de la deforestación en la Amazonía peruana: Un problema estructural.* Binghamton: Clark University and Institute for Development Anthropology.

Bedoya, Eduardo, and Francisco Verdera. 1987. *Estudio sobre mano de obra en el Alto Huallaga.* Lima: Ronco Consulting.

Board of Governors of the Federal Reserve System. Several years. *Federal Reserve Bulletin.* Washington, D.C.: Publication Services.

Brooks, J. 1993. "In a Calmer Peru, Braver Bulls and Fewer Bombs." *The New York Times*, December 8.

Caballero, José, and Elena H. Alvarez. 1981. *Aspectos cuantitativos de la reforma agraria (1969-1979)*. Lima: Instituto de Estudios Peruanos (IEP).

Cambiaso, Jorge. 1993. "Síntomas de mal holandés por la vía de la cuenta de capital." *Monetaria* (Centro de Estudios Monetarios Latinoamericanos) 16 (January-March): 2-26.

Cervantes, Francisco J. 1995. *"Are Purchasing Power Parity Components Cointegrated? How long should the long-run be? The Cases of Mexico and Peru."* Paper prepared for *"Advanced Times Series Analysis"* Course, Department of Economics, University at Albany, State University of New York, Spring.

Cocaine Production, Eradication, and the Environment: Policy, Impact, and Options. 1990. Washington, D.C.: United States Government Printing Office.

Corden, Warner. 1985. *Protection, Growth and Trade. Essays in International Economics*. New York: Basil Blackwell.

Corden, Warner. 1984. "Booming Sector and Dutch Disease Economies: A Survey." Oxford Economic Papers, 36 (November): 359-380.

Corden, Warner, and J. P. Neary. 1982. "Booming Sector and De-Industrialization in a Small Open Economy." *Economic Journal* 92 (368), (December): 825-848.

Cotlear, D. 1987. "La economía campesina en las regiones modernas y tradicionales de la Sierra." Paper presented at the Peruvian Association of Agricultural Economics Conference, in Lima, July 9-10.

Cruz-Saco, María Amparo, Julio Revilla, and Bruno Seminario. 1994. "¿Es relevante la coca? Narcodólares y tipo de cambio real." *Apuntes* 35: 53-75.

Degregori, Carlos. 1990. *El surgimiento de Sendero Luminoso*. Lima: Instituto de Estudios Peruanos (IEP).

Degregori, Carlos. 1986. *'Sendero Luminoso': Lucha armada y utopía autoritaria*. Lima: Instituto de Estudios Peruanos (IEP).

Degregori, Carlos. 1985. *'Sendero Luminoso': Los hondos y mortales desencuentros*. Lima: Instituto de Estudios Peruanos (IEP).

DESCO and Comisión Andina de Juristas. 1989. *Violencia y pacificación*. Lima: Comisión Andina de Juristas.

ECONSULT. 1986. *Informe final de la evaluación del proyecto AID No. 527-0244. Desarrollo del área del Alto Huallaga*. Lima: ECONSULT.

Edwards, Sebastian. 1989. "Determinantes reales y monetarios del comportamiento del tipo de cambio real: Teoría y pruebas de los países en desarrollo," In *El trimestre económico* (Mexico) 56: N.p.

Escobal, José. 1992. "La agricultura peruana en el contexto internacional" In *Perú: El problema agrario en el debate/SEPIA IV*, eds. Carlos Degregori, José Escobal, and Benjamín Marticorena. Lima: SEPIA.

Ferrando, Delicia. 1985. "Situación demográfica." In *La Selva peruana: Realidad poblacional*, ed. Asociación Multidisciplinaria de Investigación y Docencia en Población. Lima: AMIDEP.

Ferroni, Marco. 1980. "The Urban Bias of Peruvian Food Policy: Consequences and Alternatives." Ph.D. diss. Cornell University.

Figueroa, Adolfo. 1984. *Capitalist Development and the Peasant Economy in Peru*. New York: Cambridge University Press.

García Sayán, Diego, ed. 1990. *Narcotráfico: Realidades y alternativas.* Lima: Comisión Andina de Juristas.

García Sayán, Diego. 1989. *Coca, cocaína y narcotráfico.* Lima: Comisión Andina de Juristas.

Gonzales, José. 1989. "Perú: Sendero Luminoso en el valle de la coca." In García Sayán, ed. *Coca, cocaína y narcotráfico.* Lima: Comisión Andina de Juristas.

Gonzales de Olarte, Efraín. 1991. *Una economía bajo violencia.* Working Paper No. 40. Lima: Instituto de Estudios Peruanos (IEP).

Gonzales de Olarte, Efraín, and Lilian Samamé. 1991. *El péndulo peruano.* Lima: Instituto de Estudios Peruanos (IEP).

Gorriti, Gustavo. 1994. Interview by Elena H. Alvarez. Miami.

Gorriti, Gustavo. 1990. *Sendero. Historia de la guerra milenaria en el Perú.* Lima: Apoyo.

Gorriti, Gustavo. 1988. "Democracia, narcotráfico y la insurrección de Sendero Luminoso." In *Democracia, sociedad y gobierno en el Perú,* eds. L. Pasara and J. Parodi. Lima: CEDYS.

Grinspoon, Lester, and Joseph Bakalar. 1976. *Cocaine. A Drug and its Social Evolution.* New York: Basic Books.

Gutiérrez Noriega, Carlos, and Víctor Zapata. 1947. *Estudios sobre la coca y la cocaína en el Perú.* Lima: Ministerio de Educación Pública.

Hopkins, Raúl. 1981. *Desarrollo desigual y crisis en la agricultura peruana, 1944-1969.* Lima: Instituto de Estudios Peruanos.

International Monetary Fund (IMF). Several issues. *International Financial Statistics (IFS),* Washington, D.C.: International Monetary Fund.

Instituto Cuánto. 1995. *Retrato de la familia peruana. Niveles de vida, 1994.* Lima: Instituto Cuánto and Fondo de las Naciones Unidos para la Infancia (UNICEF).

Instituto Cuánto. 1992. *El impacto de la coca en la economía peruana: informe de avances.* Report prepared for USAID. Lima: Instituto Cuánto.

Instituto Cuánto. 1991. *Ajuste y economía familiar: 1985-1990.* Lima: Instituto Cuánto.

Instituto de Defensa Legal. 1992. *Perú hoy: En el oscuro sendero de la guerra.* Lima: Instituto de Defensa Legal.

León, Federico, and Ramiro Castro de la Mata, eds. 1989. *Pasta básica de cocaína.* Lima: CEDRO.

Macroconsult. 1990a. *Impacto económico del narcotráfico en el Perú.* Lima: Macroconsult.

Macroconsult. 1990b. *Análisis de la producción de coca y de los principales productos legales en cuatro áreas de selva alta.* Lima: Macroconsult.

Martínez, Héctor. 1985. "Migraciones internas." In *La Selva: Realidad poblacional,* ed. Asociación Multidisciplinaria de Investigación y Docencia en Población (AMIDEP). Lima: AMIDEP.

Matos Mar, José, and José Mejía. 1980. *La reforma agraria en el Perú.* Lima: Instituto de Estudios Peruanos (IEP).

McClintock, Cynthia. 1981. *Peasant Cooperatives and Political Change in Peru.* Princeton, N.J.: Princeton University Press.

Morales, Edmundo. 1989. *Cocaine: White Gold Rush in Peru.* Tucson: University of Arizona Press.

Morner, Magnus. 1985. *The Andean Past.* New York: Columbia University Press.

Mortimer, Weil. 1901. *Peru: History of Coca.* New York: Vail.

Murra, John. 1986. "Notes on Pre-Columbian Cultivation of Coca Leaf." In *Coca and Cocaine. Effects on People and Policy in Latin America,* eds. D. Pacine and C. Franquemont. Boston: Cultural Survival.

Núñez, Javier, and Rolando Reategui. 1990. *La economía cocalera en el Alto Huallaga: Impacto económico.* Unpublished thesis. Universidad del Pacífico.

Otarola, Manuel. 1992. "Estocacidad y no estacionaridad en las series de tiempo económicas. Un análisis de cointegración en torno al tipo de cambio informal en el Perú." *Ciencia económica* (Lima)(January-April): 79-114.

Pacine, D. and C. Franquemont, eds. 1986. *Coca and Cocaine: Effects of People and Policy in Latin America.* Boston: Cultural Survival.

Plowman, Timothy. 1986. "Coca Chewing and Botanical Origins of Coca (Erythroxylum spp.) in South America." In *Coca and Cocaine: Effects on People and Policy in Latin America,* eds. D. Pacine and C. Franquemont. Boston: Cultural Survival.

Plowman, Timothy. 1980. "Aspectos botánicos de la coca." In *Cocaína 1980,* ed. F. R. Jeri. Lima: Pacific Press.

Presidency of the Republic of Bolivia. 1990. *National Strategy for Alternative Development 1990.* La Paz.

Reid, Michael. 1989. "Una Región Amenazada por el Narcotráfico." In *Coca, Cocaína y Narcotráfico,* ed. Diego García Sayan. Lima: Comisión Andina de Juristas.

Rostworowski de Diez Canseco, María. 1988. *Conflicts over Coca Fields in Sixteenth Century Peru.* Memoirs of the Museum of Anthropology 21, Ann Arbor: University of Michigan.

Salazar, Alvaro. 1990. "Análisis económico de cultivos alternativos a la coca en la región del Alto Huallaga." Report for United Nations Development Project AD/PER/86/459. Lima: United Nations Drug Control Program.

Salehi-Esfahani, Haideh. 1988. "Informational Imperfect Labour Markets and the 'Dutch Disease' Problem." *Canadian Journal of Economics* 21 (August): 617-624.

Schuldt, Jürgen. 1994. *La enfermedad holandesa y otros virus de la economía peruana.* Lima: Centro de Investigación, Universidad del Pacífico (CIUP).

Scott, Chris. 1981. "Agrarian Reform and Seasonal Unemployment in Coastal Peruvian Agriculture." *Journal of Development Studies* 17 (4): 282-306.

Senado de la República del Perú. 1992. *Violencia y pacificación en 1991.* Lima: Centro de Investigación Legislativa del Senado.

Smith, Peter, ed. 1992. *Drug Policy in the Americas.* Boulder: Westview Press.

Thorp, Rosemary, and Geoffrey Bertram. 1978. *Peru 1890-1977. Growth and Policy in an Open Economy.* New York: Columbia University Press.

U.S. State Department, Bureau of International Narcotics Matters (BINM) 1993. *International Narcotics Control Strategy Report.* Washington, D.C.: Bureau of International Narcotics Affairs, United States Department of State.

Uribe, Sergio. 1995. Interview by Elena H. Alvarez. Santafé de Bogotá. June 28.

Valenzuela, Cecilia. 1995. Interview by Elena H. Alvarez. Lima. July.

Vega, Jorge, and Rufino Cebrecos. 1991. *La enfermedad holandesa y la economía peruana*. Research Monograph. Lima: Instituto de Estudios Económicos y Mineros (IDEM).

Velazco, Jaqueline. 1992. "Azúcar: verdad y mito de una prolongada crisis." In *Perú: El problema agrario en el debate/SEPIA IV*, eds. Carlos Degregori, José Escobal and Benjamín Marticorena. Lima: SEPIA.

Webb, Richard, and Teresa Lamas. 1987. "Aspectos metodológicos y macroeconómicos de la ENARH." In *Hogares rurales en el Perú*, ed. J. Portocarrero. Lima: GAPA/PADI and Friedrich Ebert Foundation.

Webb, Richard, and Graciela Fernández Baca de Valdez. 1994. *Perú en números 1994*. Lima: Cuánto S.A.

Webb, Richard, and Graciela Fernández Baca. 1993. *Perú en números 1993*. Lima: Cuánto S.A.

Webb, Richard, and Graciela Fernández Baca. 1992. *Perú en números 1992*. Lima: Cuánto S.A.

Webb, Richard, and Graciela Fernández Baca. 1991. *Perú en números 1991*. Lima: Cuánto S.A.

Webb, Richard, and Graciela Fernández Baca. 1990. *Perú en números 1990*. Lima: Cuánto S.A.

World Bank. 1992. *Annex: Consequences of Coca Production*. Washington, D.C.: World Bank.

World Bank. 1988. *Policies to Stop Hyperinflation and Initiate Economic Recovery*. Washington, D.C.: Latin America and the Caribbean (LAC) Regional Office.

World Bank. 1987. *World Bank Atlas*. Washington, D.C.: International Bank for Reconstruction and Development (IBRD).

VI

THE VIABILITY OF ALBERTO FUJIMORI'S ECONOMIC STRATEGY

Carlos Boloña

INTRODUCTION

This chapter analyzes the economic and political changes experienced by Peru during the early 1990s.[1] After having served as Peruvian minister of economy and finance for more than twenty-two months, I am writing my reflections for the purpose of advancing an understanding of the philosophy, direction, and orientation of the economic revolution which began during my term with the support of the president of the republic. I believe it is important to delineate the ground already covered and to highlight the objectives that still need to be accomplished.

On December 30, 1992, it was decided that I should not continue occupying my post at the Ministry for "political reasons." This notwithstanding, I decided to continue advocating and defending the economic stabilization process, structural reform, and the reinsertion of the country into the international economic community. I have remained in Peru in order to fulfill my commitment to these initiatives. The effort and sacrifice we Peruvians have made since July 28, 1990, cannot and must not be wasted, nor should we permit the progress we have made to be eroded. I am convinced that the course we have embarked upon will bring well-being to all Peruvians, especially to the poorest sectors of our society.

Carlos Boloña served as minister of economy and finance during the first Alberto Fujimori administration. He is also the director of the Instituto de Economía de Libre Mercado in Peru.

POLITICS FOR CHANGE

AN OVERVIEW

M y taking office as Peruvian minister of economy and finance at a time
when economic stability had deteriorated and public finances had
collapsed offered me a number of advantages that may not be immediately
obvious. Paradoxically, a crisis as severe as that faced by Peru in 1990 provides
an ample operating margin due to the existence of widespread popular
support for reform. I accepted this crucial post knowing full well that other
countries had surpassed crises worse than Peru's and with the conviction that
old liberal principles could be applied advantageously in the existing context
as they had always contributed to overcoming crises and fomenting development. In addition, I was able to capitalize on the fact that those analysts who
had advocated a return to the inflationist past had suffered a complete loss of
prestige, and I had the firm backing of a president who enjoyed vast and
sustained popular support.

I addressed my first conference as minister of economy and finance on
May 27, 1991, in Trujillo, Peru. On that occasion, I presented the four great
pillars which would serve as the foundation of the economic program for the
1990s: 1) economic stabilization, 2) modernization of the economy, 3)
reinsertion into the international economic and financial arenas, and 4) the
restoration of law and order. On this occasion, I met former Chilean minister
and presidential candidate Hernán Büchi, and both our lectures were later
published in the volume *Boloña y Büchi: Estrategas del cambio.*[2]

The first pillar, that of economic stabilization, was aimed at achieving an
equilibrium among the principal macroeconomic variables. Restoring macroeconomic equilibrium is a challenging task that takes time. The greater the
disequilibrium, moreover, the more difficult it is to achieve stability. It is
impossible for a country to grow without macroeconomic equilibrium, and if
the imbalance is not solved in the short run, it will never be solved. Not to
stabilize a country because of the excessive social costs that the stabilization
process involves is a great mistake given that instability is far more costly than
adjustment. Achieving macroeconomic equilibrium is a complex process, and
it is often based on the application of a series of measures using the "trial and
error" method.

After more than forty years of errors, Peru committed the greatest
possible economic sin in Latin America. The country fell into a hyperinflationary
spiral it still cannot control and generated a tremendous balance-of-payments
problem that also remains unsolved. And, as is well known, the more heinous
the sin, the greater the penitence.

During my twenty-two and one-half months at the ministry, however,
we made progress toward achieving macroeconomic equilibrium. Inflation

was reduced from a staggering 7650 percent in 1990 to 57 percent. Net international reserves grew from (minus) -$100 million to $2 billion, and the fiscal (and quasi-fiscal) deficit was reduced from more than 16 percent to 2.5 percent of the gross national product (GNP). In addition, the money supply grew at rates lower than inflation. Needless to say, economic growth did not show positive figures for 1991-1992, which was the price paid in order to eradicate hyperinflation. However, it would be utopian to think that in just twenty-two months it would have been possible to stabilize the economy, consolidate growth without inflation, and solve the problems of the balance of payments and the fiscal deficit. Such high expectations could only be held by those who are unaware of the fact that Peru has lagged behind and become increasingly more impoverished for more than forty years and that today it is a country that is struggling to overcome bankruptcy.

The second pillar of the reform process encompasses structural reforms — policies designed to deregulate and modernize the economy, thereby permitting significant growth due to increased investment. These structural reforms are of a microeconomic nature; they aim toward the liberalization of markets. Other important reforms relate to property, the state, and institutions. These structural reforms serve as the foundation for the new order to which this economic model leads. They are what remains, what endures, provided they are given a chance to bear fruit. Though economic stabilization is necessary, it is not sufficient for growth. In addition, stabilization is the condition that provides the least political return to a head of state simply because all appreciate it when they lose it, but few do so when they reap its benefits.

From the time I assumed office on February 15, 1991, my convictions and my aim were clear: to carry out an integral package of structural reforms that would lay the foundation for future growth. I was convinced not only that the reforms had to parallel the stabilization process but also that they had to be completed in as short a time as possible (that is, in less than three years). Reforms not made in the first difficult moments of the stabilization process are never made. Thus, during the first three weeks of my administration, a small team of ten people and I devoted ourselves to the preparation of the first wave of structural reforms, which I unveiled to the public in my message to the nation on March 11, 1991.

An argument often used to justify not applying structural reforms holds that these reforms undermine "acquired rights." However, in the name of those same rights, enterprises, economic sectors, governments, and countries often become bankrupt. What kind of rights provide 10 percent of the labor force job stability at the expense of the other 90 percent who are unemployed or underemployed? What kind of rights allow the social security system to pay 90 percent of retirees a retirement allowance of $60 a month, while 10 percent, due to privileges, receive retirement benefits (which are often superior to those of active workers occupying similar posts) after having paid into the system for only five years? What kind of rights permit the Agrarian Bank (Banco Agrario) to assume the payroll for a few farmers, thereby turning them into bureaucrats who receive a subsidy from the state for working only four hours a day?

The structural reforms were implemented in three great waves. The first wave began on March 12, 1991, and lasted until April of the same year. A total of sixty-one presidential decrees were approved, twenty-three of which pertained to foreign trade, eight to the exchange market, three to the financial market, fourteen to the fiscal sector, five to public enterprises, and eight to labor regulations. This first wave included policies which dictated the reduction of tariffs and the elimination of tariff-like barriers, the liberalization of the exchange and labor markets, and the elimination of public monopolies as well as the first decree to promulgate the privatization of public enterprises. Due to pressure and opposition from members of the Cabinet who had socialist tendencies, the original list of eighty companies to be privatized was reduced to twenty-three. Nonetheless, this first wave got the changes underway and persuaded a multi-party Cabinet as well as the Peruvian people that this was the appropriate strategy to follow.

The second wave of structural reforms was effected between May 18 and November 15, 1991. This wave consisted of 117 decrees which delegated power to legislate in matters related to peacekeeping and the promotion of investments and employment. The third wave of structural reforms was implemented between April 5 and December 30, 1992. In this third stage, 745 law decrees were issued, 281 of which took effect in December. The reforms were oriented toward the commercial, public, productive, and social sectors and the restoration of constitutional guarantees.

One vital structural reform, one which many do not consider important, is that which pertains to the so-called "privatization of the private sector," that is, preventing business interests from making a living based on monopolistic practices, returns on investments, and fees assigned by regulation. This implies the elimination of protections, including the subsidies on credit, the dollar, and fuels in addition to the capitalization of enterprises with money that does not belong to the owners. These vices, which have been common practice in Peru for the last four decades, are difficult to correct in two years. Nevertheless, it is indispensable to do so in less than five years; otherwise, it will be very difficult for the structural reforms to be effective. The challenge is to create a real private sector inasmuch as the existing sector is extremely undercapitalized and thus unable to respond; it has, moreover, numerous mercantilist biases that should also be corrected. One could even say that within the formal sector we do not have a real private sector; instead, we have "para-statal enterprises" that apply the "golden rule" of privatizing profits and socializing losses.

Among these structural reforms, we also included the Social Emergency Program (Programa de Emergencia Social), which was intended to alleviate or mitigate extreme poverty in the short and medium terms until stabilization and modernization allowed the country to grow, generate employment, and emerge from underdevelopment. On the whole, the structural reforms which were implemented have permitted us to modernize the country, liberate markets, and give consumers the freedom of choice. For instance, between 1985 and 1989, the cheapest automobile sold in the country cost $25,000, a sum which had to be paid in cash at the time of purchase. Today, cars run around $7,000 and can be purchased over a three-year period at a rate of approximately $250 a month. During the period 1985 to 1989, moreover, foreign investments scarcely reached $15 million, whereas from 1990 to 1992 investments totaled $600 million. As for public transportation, the liberalization of routes and tariffs has permitted a substantial increase in supply. Peruvians no longer need to form lines to board deteriorated units, fares are competitive, and transportation strikes have all but disappeared.

The third pillar of the economic program relates to the reinsertion of the country into the international economic and financial markets. This step presupposes the normalization of foreign relationships regarding debt payments in order to promote credit, investment, and technology. Peru's nonpayment policy had closed access to credit and foreign capitals. The demagogic argument that was used to justify nonpayment was the need to provide for the "internal social debt" before paying the "external debt." The results were catastrophic, and the Peruvian people became even more impoverished. Thus, in September 1990, we resumed payments to the multilateral entities. A year later, in September 1991, the reinsertion of Peru was accomplished with the formation of the first international support group, the Rights Accumulation Program (RAP) with the International Monetary Fund (IMF), the Paris Club, and the first credit obtained from the Inter-American Development Bank (IDB) after arrears had been cleared.

With the resumption of external debt payments, Peru became a member of the international financial community once again after having been an economic "pariah" for more than seven years. However, the events of April 5, 1992, endangered this reinsertion, and Peru found itself on the brink of becoming a political pariah. This situation was avoided as a result of President Fujimori's compromise in the Bahamas on May 18, 1992, when he announced that an election would be held to form a Constitutional Congress. I took part in the formulation of this idea, together with Hernando de Soto. This compromise kept the doors of reinsertion half open until December 30, 1992, at which time the Constitutional Congress was installed.

The second international reinsertion began with negotiations conducted with the IMF in October 1992 in order to obtain an Agreement of Amplified

Facility, which would permit the clearing of arrears with the World Bank and the International Monetary Fund. It also required the establishment of a second support group, renegotiation with the Paris Club, and negotiation with the international commercial banking system. This time, it was not my responsibility to complete these tasks.

The fourth pillar of the economic program concerns the maintenance and strengthening of democratic governability in the country. Without law and order, political stability cannot exist; without political stability, there can be no judicial stability. All three conditions are necessary in order to ensure the success of an economic program, and it is the state's duty to guarantee them. Constitutional law and order must be achieved within a context of economic and political freedom. That is to say, individual rights and the balance of power between the branches of the government must be respected. We must remain wary of abuses of power involving not only the economy but also civil rights. The government must be subordinate to the individuals it governs, not the contrary.

Terrorism is the foremost nemesis of democratic governance in Peru. None of the other three pillars of the economic program can function successfully unless terrorism is controlled and defeated. The eradication of terrorism requires the dismantling of the subversive structure by means of intelligence work, military operations, civilian initiatives, and the mobilization of the general population. The fight against terrorism also requires an adequate distribution of costs between the public and private sectors as well as the promulgation of legal reforms regarding the trial, sentencing, and punishing of terrorists. Awareness campaigns on the ideological level are also vital.

Drug trafficking is another enemy of democratic governance in the country. The illicit production and trafficking of drugs distorts economic activity and corrupts people, institutions, and the society as a whole. If this illegal activity is not controlled and eradicated in the medium term, it will end up controlling us.

THE FIVE GREAT STRUCTURAL REFORMS: EMERGENCY TREATMENT

OBJECTIVES, INVESTMENTS, AND KEY PRICES

Inflation, recession and unemployment, a deficit in the balance of payments, a fiscal deficit, monetary emission, and an imbalance between savings and investments constitute symptoms which can be used to determine the relative "health" of an economy. Once a critical condition has been diagnosed, the first step of the cure is to take the "patient" to the emergency room so as to put an end to the unpredictable and uncontrolled evolution of variables.

In a neoliberal prescription, the keystone of economic stability is to control inflation, while interventionist policies aim to avoid recession and unemployment. Keynesian theories favor further state intervention through public expenditure and monetary emission. These strategies were in fashion in the 1930s in an attempt to avoid economic depression and widespread unemployment. The members of the Austrian School, however, having experienced times of hyperinflation in their country, knew that Keynesian policies would bring about further inflation, which in turn would generate more recession and unemployment in the long run. These results were experienced in both post-war periods as well as during the decade of the 1980s in the capitalist countries and in the decade of the 1990s in Eastern Europe following the collapse of socialism.

The object of economic stability is to control inflation and avoid recession and unemployment in order to achieve economic growth in the medium and long terms. To achieve this end, macroeconomic accounts must be balanced, which implies having a viable balance of payments, an equilibrium in treasury and monetary accounts, and an equilibrium of income in relation to expenditure or savings and investment. Economic stability is measured by means of a number of economic policy objectives, explicitly enumerated and quantified for the Peruvian case as follows:

1   Control of inflation. Controlling inflation means reaching international levels, that is, an inflation rate lower than 10 percent per year or 1 percent a month.

2   Economic growth and unemployment. The aim is to achieve gross domestic product (GDP) rates of higher than 4 percent per year in the short run in order to achieve growth rates higher than 7 percent per year in the medium and long terms. The unemployment rate should be reduced to less than 3 percent of the labor force.

3   Adequate level of net international reserves (NIR). This entails procuring net international reserves equivalent to six months to one year's import needs, which totals an amount greater than $3 billion.

4   Fiscal discipline. The fiscal deficit must be financed with external rather than internal credit and must not exceed 2.5 percent of the GDP. In the medium term, the goal should be fiscal equilibrium.

5   Monetary discipline. Monetary emission in a stable economy must be concordant with increases in the GDP. Moreover, it must be below the level of inflation, and the Central Bank must not give credit to the public or private sectors.

The instruments of economic policy are oriented toward achieving the goals mentioned above. These instruments can be managed according to a market economy scheme or in accordance with the principles of state intervention. Inasmuch as the first method is the most relevant, I will explain it in detail. The economic policy instruments the government manages include fiscal, monetary, commercial, exchange, wage, and pricing policies. Fiscal policy includes mechanisms such as public expenditure, taxes, and external and internal indebtedness, whereas monetary policy includes instruments such as money supply, reserve requirements, rediscounts, and open market operations (the purchase and sale of government securities by the Central Bank). Commercial policy takes into account importation rights, while exchange policy includes the establishment of the exchange rate and exchange regulations (managed or determined by the market). Price policy involves the determination of managed prices fixed by the government by virtue of its monopolistic position. We are referring to prices of goods and services such as fuel, electricity, water, and telecommunications. Finally, wage policies include the determination of salaries in the public sector and the definition of norms for their establishment in the private sector.

Key macroeconomic prices are those that balance the principal markets, that is, the market of goods and services, the money market, and the labor market. The prices that balance these markets are the exchange rate, the prices charged for goods and services, and the managed prices of interest rates and salaries. Under a neoliberal program, the exchange rate, the interest rate, and salaries should be determined by the free market, while managed prices determined by the government should be calculated under market criteria. A guideline could be established, for instance, specifying that the latter should approach international prices.

INFLATION: THE WORST OF ALL EVILS

How Inflation Is Generated

Inflation, the generalized and sustained increase of prices in the economy, is a very dangerous disease. When inflation runs out of control and turns into hyperinflation, it can destroy a society. Inflation is a monetary phenomenon generated by an increase of the money supply which is greater than the growth of production. Inflation determines the internal value of the national currency, and the exchange rate determines its external value.

Inflation is generated by the government by means of an accelerated growth of the money supply, which in turn responds to an accelerated increase in public expenditure through reactivation policies of the government or mistaken policies of the monetary authority, the Central Reserve Bank (Banco Central de Reserva del Perú, BCR). If public expenditure is financed with taxes, internal indebtedness (agreed to by the public) or external indebtedness, it does not generate inflation. However, establishing taxes or acquiring debts has its limits, and this is not the type of policy politicians are willing to implement because it often leads to a loss of voter support. The only way in which to finance public expenditure without losing public support is to issue more currency, which is achieved through credits from the BCR to the Ministry of Economy and Finance, the state banking system, or the financial system. Spending more without levying taxes may indeed be attractive for presidents or legislators; nonetheless, it is fatal and irresponsible for the economy.

Some economists also hold that it is possible to come out of recession by injecting more money into the economy. For instance, Alan García issued currency in order to reactivate the Peruvian economy after 1985. When García took office, he aspired to reactivate production by stimulating demand. To this end, he lowered interest rates, controlled prices, raised salaries, and interfered with the exchange rate. He believed, therefore, that boosting demand would stimulate production. If consumers did not buy, he argued, factories and cultivated land would be abandoned. García naively believed that it was sufficient to create a program of massive employment in order to expand the purchasing power of the unemployed and thus increase demand and sustain production. Utilizing the unused capacity of the productive sector, uncontrolled emissions, and the dollars in the net international reserves of the BCR, García attempted to boost production, employment, salaries, exports, and imports. He considered that increased public expenditure would generate production and employment, while taxes would have the reverse effect. However, the opposite actually occurred: spending more and issuing money to get out of recession only injected higher doses of inflation into the economy, causing it to plunge into a deeper recession.[3]

The Banco Central de Reserva can also foster inflation by implementing mistaken policies, such as those aimed at controlling the interest or the exchange rates. The BCR, in fact, should only manage the money supply injected into the economy. Let us suppose, for instance, that after issuing more domestic currency or *soles,* the BCR decides to purchase more dollars in the market in order to raise the exchange rate, which is tantamount to devaluation. At the beginning, the nominal exchange rate is devalued, and the rate of interest in *soles* might decrease. This increases the inflation rate, which in turn reduces the real exchange rate (the exchange rate minus inflation) as well as the real interest rate, thereby producing a loss of parity in the exchange rate and a decline in the profitability of savings. In this way, the situation of the exporters and of those who have savings worsens in comparison to their original condition.

The additional amount of money issued by the BCR is equivalent to a tax on the people's money. For this reason, it is called an "inflation tax." However, this is the most unjust tax the government can impose since people with lower incomes do not have the mechanisms to protect themselves from the loss of purchasing power that this tax implies.

THE GREAT INFLATIONS

Hyperinflation, according to Philip Cagan (1956), initiates in the month in which inflation surpasses 50 percent and terminates when it reaches levels inferior to 50 percent per month and remains that way for more than a year. There have been many cases of hyperinflation throughout the world, especially during post-war periods. The highest hyperinflation rate occurred in Hungary in 1945, with a monthly average of 20,000 percent, followed by the cases of Greece in 1943 with 365 percent and Germany in 1922 with 322 percent. From 1988 to 1990, the hyperinflation rate in Peru ranked among the eight highest in the world. It was higher than that experienced in Russia and was the second longest in duration.

In Peru, in fact, hyperinflation has occurred on two occasions. The first period of hyperinflation took place between 1879 and 1883, as a consequence of the war against Chile (la Guerra del Pacífico). At this time, inflation registered levels of 1200 percent as a result of the overflow of paper money and the abandonment of the gold standard. The second period occurred between 1988 and 1990, when inflation reached 4 million percent.

Inflation takes years to generate; likewise, it takes years to control. The relationship between a higher rate of monetary emission and a higher rate of inflation is not immediate. Thus, in the United States or Great Britain, for instance, an increase in monetary emission takes between six and nine months to augment production and to reduce unemployment. Moreover, it takes from 12 to 18 months for this effect to translate into higher inflation, destroying the initial beneficial effect. For Peru, in contrast, these periods can be reduced by one-half or one-third. In any case, the higher the inflation rate, the shorter the time required to translate the effects of adjustments in the money supply to changes in inflation.

INFLATION IS A DRUG

Inflation can be compared to drug addiction in that a small amount of the drug (inflation) produces a pleasant sensation (reactivation) at first. However, increasingly higher doses (hyperinflation) are required to continue producing the same effect, which can ultimately lead to death (or social chaos). Once drug addiction is in an advanced state (hyperinflation), the cure takes a long time and has painful side effects. In the economy, these include reduced economic growth, high levels of unemployment, and the slow reduction of inflation. During periods of hyperinflation, some benefit while others suffer. Those who benefit desire to continue exploiting the situation, but this damages productive activity. Profit can be generated through speculation and returns on investments, without the country's engaging in a great deal of productive activity. Those who suffer from this situation, of course, are those who have less.

The only cure for drug addiction is to stop consuming the drug, which is easier said than done. Success depends on the addict's determination and the perseverance of those in charge of the cure. In the same way, the only cure for inflation and hyperinflation is to reduce the monetary supply, which is also a difficult task. Decreasing inflation requires a great dose of political determination.

INFLATION AND UNEMPLOYMENT

Price and salary controls neither cure nor control inflation. In fact, they have the opposite effect inasmuch as they distort the price structure. These are bad substitutes, being both temporary and inadequate, for fiscal and monetary discipline. Price and salary controls produce positive effects for a short period, after which time they fail due to the fact that they raise inflationary expectations and thus result in higher inflation. Ultimately, the only effect these controls have is to increase the state's intervention in the economy.

The only way to curb inflation is to control the increase in the amount of money in the economy. This adjustment immediately produces severe unemployment, but this, in the Peruvian case, is a result of bad investments that were made during the inflationary years. "The great inflation in Austria and Germany," according to Friedrich A. von Hayek, "interested us because of the connection between changes in money and changes in the level of unemployment. It showed us in particular that employment created by inflation started to decrease as soon as inflation began to fall and that putting an end to inflation always produced what came to be called a stabilization crisis, with severe unemployment" (1979, 34).[4]

The side effects result from lowering inflation because, in reducing the money supply, "static" is introduced into the information transmitted through the price system. This static is translated into inappropriate responses by economic agents. Thus, inflation cannot be reduced without incurring unemployment and recession. von Hayek states this concept very clearly after explaining why it is impossible to avoid the consequences of inflationist irresponsibility: "There is no possible choice between inflation or unemployment, just as there is no possible alternative between gluttony and indigestion. For a while, the glutton can abandon himself to the pleasure of taste; later, however, he will forcibly have to suffer the painful syndrome of indigestion" (1979, 73).[5] These effects can be mitigated through a gradual but determined lowering of inflation by means of the gradual reduction of the money supply in a pre-announced and realistic fashion.

INFLATION IN PERU

Between 1950 and 1972, yearly inflation averaged 7 percent. During the period 1968 to 1977, the inflation rate hit 17 percent, and from 1983 to 1990, it skyrocketed to 1400 percent. From 1991 to 1992, annual inflation averaged 98 percent.

Inflation grew from 61 percent in 1980 to 158 percent in 1985 and then experienced a decrease to 63 percent in 1986 due to price controls. It subsequently escalated to 115 percent in 1967, 1700 percent in 1988, 2800 percent in 1989, and 7650 percent in 1990. After the implementation of the current economic program, however, inflation declined to 139 percent in 1991 and 57 percent in 1992.

Peru entered the hyperinflationary process in September 1988. This period lasted until August 1990, that is, twenty-four months. During 1991, the monthly inflation rate was reduced from 18 percent in January to 4 percent in December. During 1992, inflation ranged around 3.5 percent per month, including a peak of 7.4 percent in March due to the tax reform package and a low of 2.6 percent in September. Hyperinflation was generated because the monetary supply grew by 116 percent in 1987, 440 percent in 1988, and 2400 percent in 1989. The harmful effects of this hyperinflationary process are clearly evidenced in the erosion of the tax base, which dropped from an average of 15 percent in the early 1980s to 6 percent in 1989. The ill effects of hyperinflation are also demonstrated by the distortion of relative prices — the exchange rate, interest rates, salaries, and controlled prices — as well as of prices in general. The demand for money experienced a progressive reduction from 18 percent of the GNP in 1980 to 5 percent in 1989, while production fell 24 percent between 1988 and 1990.

RECESSION AND UNEMPLOYMENT

THE BUSINESS CYCLE

The business cycle leads to expansion, which is followed by generalized economic contractions which cause recession and unemployment. John M. Keynes proposed the "fatal idea" that unemployment is caused by insufficient demand and that the state, via expenditure and monetary emission, can reactivate demand. This, however, was an inflationary policy which provided politicians a fast and cheap method to alleviate human suffering as well as a way to eliminate the burdening restrictions that prevented them from gaining popularity. Hence, expenditure and deficit budgets were suddenly considered virtuous. It was argued, even persuasively so, that continued state expenditure was meritorious since it promoted the utilization of unused resources and that this did not represent any costs for the community, only net profit (von Hayek 1979, 42). Keynesian policies therefore created a dislocation of the real supply and demand and the consequent disorder of prices relating to the different factors of production.

According to von Hayek, moreover, unemployment is the consequence of rearranging investment within a new and healthier economic environment:

> The true, though not verifiable, explanation for massive unemploy-
> ment is the discrepancy between the distribution of the labor factor

(and other production factors) in industries (and in the localities) and the distribution of the demand for their products. This discrepancy is caused by a distortion of relative prices and salaries in the system. And that can only be corrected by changing those relationships — that is, establishing in each economic sector such prices and salaries that will result in equality of supply and demand. In other words, the cause of unemployment is a deviation from the prices and salaries equilibrium that would have been established in a free market with stable currency (1979, 41).[6]

Intervention in the market by means of increasing the monetary supply creates distortions in the natural tendency of the market because of the inflation this adjustment generates. According to Taylor,[7] the problem with inflation is that it affects the essence of the market process, producing in the best case cyclic, intermittent, disturbing movements and in the worst, the disastrous cessation of market interchange which has been observed in highly industrialized societies (1989, 121).

SOURCES OF GROWTH

Growth is the result of the long-term effects of physical capital formation (or investment), an increase in the labor force (or human capital), and technological change. These should take place in the context of a market economy in order to obtain higher levels of growth and higher returns on production factors. In addition, economic growth is affected by fluctuations in the terms of trade, that is, the purchasing power of exports compared to imports. Exports are also an important source of growth. Unlike goods destined for domestic consumption, they provide resources for imports and investments.

Countries that have a reduced capacity to generate internal savings and thus exhibit low levels of internal investment must resort to foreign investment as a source of growth. Foreign investment is especially crucial considering that foreign capital has more capability than domestic capital and that it also incorporates the most recent technological innovations. In order to attract foreign investment to Peru, it is necessary to break taboos regarding its presumed perverse nature as well as the belief that foreign investment is a form of imperialistic exploitation. These prejudices were raised and nourished by the Left, populism, and "bureaucratism" during the 1970s and 1980s, and a number of politicians still advocate these theses.

IMAGINARY EMPLOYMENT

The periods of high growth that were achieved in the Peruvian economy between 1900 and 1979 were associated with increased exportation, the presence of foreign investment, favorable terms of trade, or a combination of these elements. During the period 1951 to 1990, economic growth can be attributed to an increment in exports, a hike in domestic investment, and increased productivity.

It would be erroneous to think that it is possible to promote sustained growth by utilizing mechanisms such as higher public expenditures, an increased money supply, or the artificial fixing of key prices (such as exchange rate or interest rate) in order to boost exports and investment. These are unhealthy policies that ultimately result in higher inflation and price distortions.

Although figures regarding employment patterns in Peru are not very reliable, open unemployment is more relevant than underemployment. The latter is not a very exact concept as it depends on the minimum wage or some other reference point upon which calculations are based. We know that when minimum wages are fixed, unemployment grows because such salaries are generally above market levels. Aside from this, the active labor force in Peru totaled 7.5 million people in 1990. From 1980 to 1991, unemployment dropped from 7 to 6 percent, while underemployment experienced a substantial increase from 26 to 79 percent.

During the first two years of President Fernando Belaúnde Terry's administration (1980-1985), unemployment decreased to 7 percent. Later, during the crisis of 1983-1984, it rose to 10 percent. The Alan García administration (1985-1990) subsequently implemented a policy of reactivation based on higher expenditures financed with monetary emission. This strategy lowered unemployment from 1986 to 1987; however, the country later fell into a recession, which increased unemployment considerably during the hyperinflationary period.

MACROECONOMIC ACCOUNTS

NET INTERNATIONAL RESERVES AND THE BALANCE OF PAYMENTS

Net international reserves are assets one government is willing to accept from another as payment for debts acquired. These reserves are obtained from the difference between international assets and liabilities, and their variation is determined by the balance of payments — that is, the difference between the income and expenditures of foreign currency resulting from the trade of goods and services as well as from the movement of capital. International reserves increase when income is higher than expenditure.

The central banks of many countries keep a stock of international reserves in order to cushion fluctuations or imbalances between income and expenditure in foreign currency and to stabilize the exchange rate. These stocks make it possible for the country to maintain a stable exchange rate even in the case of a surplus or deficit in the balance of payments. More importantly, they make it possible to keep the domestic economy stable when there are external shocks in the balance of payments. The principal characteristic of international reserves is their liquidity; hence, they must be kept in dollars or strong foreign currency that is internationally accepted, such as Special Drawing Rights[8] from the IMF and gold. The composition of these reserves must make it possible to cover the needs of international trade and investment with liquid reserves so that other reserves can render higher revenues. According to John Williamson, the total amount of the reserve stock depends on four factors: 1) the vulnerability of the balance of payments to external shocks, 2) the consequences of running out of reserves, 3) the opportunity cost to maintain the reserves, and 4) the speed and dependability of balance of payments adjustments (1991, 165-175).

A crucial element utilized in determining the desired level at which to maintain reserves is the exchange policy, specifically, the exchange regime. Under a fixed exchange rate system, a significant amount of reserves is required to prevent fluctuations of the exchange rate and avoid external shocks that may negatively affect the domestic economy. Milton Friedman and R. V. Roosa suggest that international liquidity problems disappear under a system characterized by a free or floating exchange rate (1967, 16). Thus, it is not necessary to accumulate international reserves because if foreign currency is scarce, the private sector will react to an increase in the exchange rate, providing the reserves that are needed.

A flexible exchange rate allows for the orientation of the country's fiscal and monetary policies toward internal stability without its having to deal with balance of payments problems. Critics of the free exchange rate argue that it generates instability, but the fluctuations caused by controlled exchange rates have always been greater than those generated by a free exchange rate strategy.

INTERNATIONAL RESERVES IN PERU

In 1980, the Central Bank's net international reserves (NIR) reached a level of $1.48 billion. In the following years, reserves fell to roughly $1 billion, but they later recovered, approximating their 1980 level of $1.493 billion. During the García administration, however, international reserves plummeted to the negative sum of (minus) $-352 million. During the Fujimori administration, reserves rose to $531 million in 1990, $1.304 billion in 1991, and $2.001 billion in 1992. This increase in net international reserves has been the result of the implementation of the economic program in the early 1990s.

The level of net international reserves reached in 1992 was the highest recorded since 1980 and represented approximately 50 percent of the annual import requirements. However, it is important to note that not all the reserves on deposit in the Banco Central de Reserva del Perú are available for use as the foreign currency deposits owned by Peruvian residents form part of the NIR. If we deduct short- and long-term obligations to residents (which totaled

$1 billion and $500 million, respectively, in 1992), we obtain the exchange position, or the amount of cash available in dollars. The exchange position totaled (minus) $-1.434 billion in 1988, (minus) $-315 million in 1990, (minus) $-55 million in 1991, and $311 million in 1992. Consequently, only in 1992 did Peru achieve a positive exchange position, which is fundamental in terms of promoting confidence in the economic program.

It is important for Peru to be able to show positive net international reserves and positive exchange balances as these foster confidence and external credibility for the country and the program. After Peru ran out of dollars, the economic agents needed to see a significant amount of backing returning to the country. In the medium term, the exchange policy that is to be implemented ideally approximates the free exchange rate and progressively distances itself from the "dirty flotation" scheme (that is, the BCR's intervention in the currency exchange market in order to achieve a goal with respect to the level of reserves) that is currently in effect. This currency exchange policy would permit a reduction in net international reserves. In the meantime, Peru must maintain a high level of international reserves and improve the exchange position in order to inspire confidence in the country, both internally and externally.

Having $2 billion in net international reserves creates risks in that politicians and economic agents often want to make use of these funds for expenditures, public works, or credits for the private sector. Utilization of these funds is not possible inasmuch as the real amount available is $311 million. Secondly, these funds have been generated through the purchase of foreign currency by the BCR, financed via emission, not fiscal savings, which means that their use would be inflationary.

It has often been alleged that Peru has a large balance of payments deficit and that this deficit has worsened from 1991 to 1993, reaching levels of 4.6 to 6 percent of the GNP (between $2.2 and $2.7 billion). According to some critics, this situation will lead to the failure of the current economic program. However, this prediction will not come true provided that 1) the economic program continues to be implemented the way it was designed, 2) the currency exchange rate and the exchange policy continue to be free, and 3) the country gradually moves away from the "dirty" flotation scheme and the temptation to fix or anchor the currency exchange rate.

DISCIPLINE IN FISCAL ACCOUNTS

It is a healthy practice for individuals or governments not to spend more than they have. A country that abandons this practice should do so only via indebtedness (domestic and foreign). Even in that case, the period of indebtedness cannot be too long. There is a time limit after which economic problems begin.

In order to spend more money than it possesses (that is, more than it appropriates from taxes), a government requires internal and external credit. Internal credit can be obtained either through bonds that the government offers voluntarily to the private sector through the stock market or by the coercive imposition of bonds or credits that it places in the central bank, increasing the money supply and consequently inflation, as explained above.

During 1985, the fiscal deficit in Peru totaled 6 percent of the gross domestic product. Ninety percent of the GDP was financed by not repaying the foreign debt (García's policy) and 19 percent, through BCR money issue. By 1988, the deficit had reached 16 percent of the GDP, of which 23 percent was financed by not paying the foreign debt, while the remaining 77 percent was financed internally via BCR's money issue. As we have seen, these deficit levels and the manner in which they were financed generated hyperinflation that rose to 7650 percent in 1990.

The fiscal discipline that was applied in the second half of 1990 reduced the deficit to 6 percent of the GDP, of which 60 percent was financed externally by not repaying the foreign debt and 40 percent was internally financed. By 1991, a solid fiscal discipline had finally been established. The deficit was reduced to 3 percent of the GDP, and external financing was obtained for the whole either by foreign credit or negotiated nonpayment relief. For 1993, the projected deficit should be 2.9 percent of the GDP with zero internal financing. To reduce the deficit, expenditures must decrease, whereas tax income must increase. Regarding increasing taxes, Peru augmented its tax pressure from 5.5 percent of the GDP in 1989 to 9.5 percent in 1992.

DISCIPLINE IN MONETARY ACCOUNTS

The government has great responsibility in monetary matters. Monetary emission, coining, and bill printing must be subject to clear, stringent norms, and these decisions should not be left to the discretion of monetary authorities. Once inflation is under control, the amount of money issued must be equal to the growth of production. When inflation levels are high, monetary emission must be equal to the real growth plus the value of expected inflation, necessarily much lower than existing levels of inflation. Emission variations in Peru and their relation to inflation can be seen in Table 1.

It is important to mention that when emission occurs at an accelerated rate, it is surpassed by the rate of inflation. When the rate of emission is reduced, inflation follows, but with some delay.

SAVINGS AND INVESTMENT ACCOUNT

Investment is a determining factor for growth. Higher investment rates are associated with higher growth rates. Thus, to the extent that investment

Table 1.
Monetary Emission and Inflation
1987 - 1992 (Percent Variation)

	Emission	Inflation
1987	11	115
1988	439	1,722
1989	1,783	2,766
1990	5,214	7,650
1991	96	139
1992	62	57

productivity increases, growth increases as well. Investment can be public or private, and the latter can be either domestic or foreign. Foreign investment is characterized by its capability to mobilize more capital and by its higher productivity in comparison to domestic investment.

Between 1980 and 1984, public investment in Peru represented roughly 8 percent of the gross national product. Between 1985 and 1989, it accounted for 4 percent, whereas in 1990, it was reduced to 1.7 percent. Public investment subsequently increased to 2.4 percent in 1991 and 3 percent in 1992. These lowest levels in decades were the result of hyperinflation. On the other hand, private investment represented 18 percent of the GNP between 1980 and 1984, 13 percent in 1990, 14 percent in 1991, and 13 percent in 1992.

Investments financed by savings can come from abroad by means of credit or foreign investment. Investments can also be financed internally through savings accumulated by individuals, corporations, or the government. In Peru, savings have originated abroad through credit or García's policy of nonrepayment, or they have come from the private sector. The public sector's savings were reduced because of the fiscal deficit. Total savings in Peru have shrunk from 25 to 16 percent of the GDP between 1980 and 1992. For purposes of comparison, savings levels during the same time period totaled 35 percent of the GDP in the People's Republic of China, 30 percent in Malaysia, and 26 percent in Thailand.

Savings are determined by the people's present and future income level as well as by earnings from savings. With positive real interest rates (higher than inflation), individuals are willing to save more; thus, more funds are available for loans. Greater volumes of investment can be financed, fueling increased growth. For this reason, positive real interest rates are associated with higher rates of economic growth in the countries where they occur.

MARKET LIBERALIZATION

Macroeconomic stability is a necessary condition for markets to function and for structural reforms to be successful. Markets are unable to transmit the right signals to economic agents in an inflationary context. The market reform program in Peru is based on the economic liberalization of each market in which structural reforms are applied: the markets of goods and services, the money market (including foreign currency), values and credits, and the labor market. The purpose of this liberalization is increased efficiency, production, and productivity. Additionally, the program endeavors to reduce the size of the state and its intervention in the economy. What can be done by the private sector must not be done by the public sector. The market reforms aim at a successful transition from stabilization to economic growth.

THE MARKET OF GOODS AND SERVICES

The purpose of reforming the market of goods and services is to liberalize it not only for goods and services produced domestically but also for those that come from abroad. Not only are prices liberated, but market controls, regulation, and the price fixing of domestic goods and services by any other mechanism than the market itself are eliminated. Subsidies to economic activities and any monopolies created by law are also eliminated. In addition, tariffs and restrictions to imports are reduced to levels that are compatible with international standards in order to foster competition between domestic and imported goods.

THE MONEY MARKET

THE MONEY MARKET IN GENERAL

The objective of money market reform is to obtain a financial system that is efficient, profitable, competitive, open to foreign markets, and characterized by solvency and prudence. These reforms aim to eliminate financial repression and create a new system that covers financial needs in the short and long runs. We also seek to develop a capital market that can play a significant role in the financing of businesses. The financial sector must be an efficient private savings intermediary so that both private and public savings finance the different economic sectors. The financial system is the basis for economic growth.

To achieve these objectives, it is necessary to liberalize interest rates, eliminate quantitative and qualitative controls, and reduce the required reserve ratio to normal levels. Similarly, we must facilitate the financial institutions' access to the market as well as eliminate monopolies in the financial system.

THE FOREIGN CURRENCY MARKET

The economic program aims to unify the exchange rate and encourage its determination by the market. An alternative to this is to implement a flotation system with restricted intervention from the Banco Central de Reserva based on international reserves and monetary goals. Another alternative is the free flotation of the exchange rate, which is preferable. In addition, the right to convert domestic currency and to possess and trade foreign currency is ensured. Foreign currency controls are eliminated from transactions in current and capital accounts. The shipment of profits abroad is unrestricted, as are royalties and patents.

THE LABOR MARKET

FLEXIBILITY OF THE LABOR MARKET

The reform of the labor market aims to achieve flexibility in this market by means of the freedom to increase or cut personnel, to determine salaries, and to reduce labor costs. It is necessary to put a halt to the monopolistic power exercised by labor unions in the negotiation of working conditions and the use of the strike as a negotiation tool. In addition, monopolies sustained by the occupational licensing system and by professional associations must be eliminated.

REFORM OF THE RETIREMENT SYSTEM

One significant expense within the labor sector is the retirement system, which also required structural adjustment. The reform creates a retirement system based on freedom of choice, market mechanisms, and management by the private sector. This private retirement system should be managed and operated by various retirement fund administrators, and it should be regulated and supervised by a superintendency.

The most salient features of this private retirement system are the following:

1. Workers have individual retirement accounts.
2. Workers are issued a savings book with which to manage the funds in their account.
3. Contributors' obligatory payments are deposited in their individual accounts, the beneficiaries of which are the contributors themselves.
4. The numerous, competitive administrative institutions are privately managed.
5. Workers select the institution in which to open their accounts.
6. Coverage includes retirement, disability, death, and funeral fees.

REFORM OF THE PROPERTY STRUCTURE

THE PRIVATIZATION OF PUBLIC ENTERPRISES

Given that state-run businesses exist for political rather than technical reasons, the transfer of public enterprises to the private sector is both necessary and convenient. Privatization should be carried out efficiently and transparently. Insolvent enterprises should be liquidated.

Public enterprises must be eliminated regardless of their level of profitability. If privatization is postponed to avoid political backlash or to obtain better prices, the state-run businesses will never be sold. The benefits of privatization include not only the sale value that is obtained but also an end to money loss, the collection of taxes, and the fostering of reinvestments, new management, and new technology.

In order to be effective, the privatization strategy should include the following components:

1. The initial sale of the smallest enterprises followed by the marketing of the larger corporations in order to gain experience and thus avoid jeopardizing the process.

2. A clear and flexible legal framework which permits sufficient freedom of action so as not to hinder the process.

3. A central privatization committee and other special committee responsible for carrying out the process in a centralized manner.

4. The restructuring of large enterprises to divide them into smaller units before privatizing them.

5. The cash sale of all enterprises to ensure that they do not return state ownership and that the private sector assumes all risks.

6. The dismantling of monopolies and the revocation of privileges.

7. Appraisals should not be permitted to impede a sale. Although the appraisal of the state-run enterprises can begin with their book or economic value, their real value is determined by the market. Therefore, the stock market is the clearest and most adequate mechanism to carry out the privatization process.

8. Worker participation in the ownership of the enterprises to be privatized.

9. The channeling of the resources obtained from privatization into investments (social or productive), not current expenses, inasmuch as these resources provide a one-time income opportunity.

10. A public awareness campaign to convince the Peruvian people of the advantages of the process so as to ensure popular support.

OPENING TO FOREIGN INVESTMENT

Investment in physical capital is a necessary requirement for economic growth. Investment can come from domestic or foreign sources. In order to attract foreign and domestic investment, we must legislate the opening of markets to private, competitive international investment. A clear normative framework, together with a series of measures and initiatives that promote investment and do not discriminate on the basis of origin, is required to achieve this end. Moreover, all impediments to foreign investment must be eliminated, and guarantees must be established to protect all vested interests.

PROPERTY STRUCTURE BY SECTORS

Private property in the different economic sectors must be the foundation of economic behavior. Any practices that restrict the use, disposal, or transfer of property must be eliminated, together with expropriatory dispositions that fix prices or amounts in the markets. These principles should be applied in sectors such as agriculture, industry, and housing, among others.

REFORM OF THE STATE

The purpose of this particular reform is to reduce the size of the state along with the state's intervention in the economy. Reforming the state implies restructuring, tax reform, reform of public expenditure, and attention to the poorest sectors of society.

DOWNSIZING THE GOVERNMENT

It is necessary to reduce the size of public administration and bureaucracy in Peru. Ministries should exercise functions that are more normative than executive. The number of ministries and decentralized public organisms must be reduced, and displaced government employees should be relocated.

TAXES

Tax reform is aimed at modernizing the tax system and exercising better control over the collection of fiscal income. Taxes that permit a higher rate of collection must be levied. All taxes must be neutral, meaning that they should not favor one economic activity over another. In addition, they should be simple and easy to manage.

PUBLIC EXPENDITURE

Public expenditures designated in the national budget must follow the principle of general funds. The system of designated incomes must be eliminated. Expenditures must be made rationally and efficiently, prioritizing investment over current expenses and giving special emphasis to social expenditure to alleviate extreme poverty.

Public investment, to be implemented by the private sector, must be restructured on a cost-benefit basis. National priorities should determine that the greatest expenditures be made on basic infrastructure such as roadways, potable water, electrification, and sanitation.

ATTENTION TO EXTREME POVERTY

The purpose of this reform is to reduce state intervention in the social sectors considering that such intervention has not produced the desired effects and has instead created distortions and privileges. The "benefactor state," which aspires to "socialize" education, health, housing, and welfare, should be replaced by a small and efficient state that allows the pursuit of these objectives, wherever possible, through private sector participation.

REFORM OF THE SYSTEM OF EDUCATION

The objective of education reform is to foster investment in human capital through the use of market mechanisms and private sector initiatives. State intervention in the management of education has caused waste and the poor utilization of the taxpayers' money, resulting in a low-quality, centralized, bureaucratized, and socialized system.

Education is a revenue-producing economic activity which can generate profits. Thus, it should not be allowed tax exemptions. Moreover, private investment should be guaranteed free access to the education sector. Most importantly, education must be fomented through the free market; a state monopoly must be avoided in the sector.

State-owned basic education centers must be transferred to municipalities and private enterprises. Such centers would receive monthly payments from the state in the form of a subsidy (a voucher or education bond) for each student who attends school regularly. However, this subsidy should be allotted only within the poorest sectors of society.

The great advantage of this system is that it eliminates the odious and unjust discrimination by which the poor are condemned to low levels of education, while those who can afford private education obtain superior levels that enable them to fulfill the demands of the labor market. This scholarship system permits the poor and the wealthy access to the same educational services, offering similar levels of quality with respect to teaching, methodology, and didactic materials.

Higher education — university, vocational, and professional — must not be free. The state will establish an educational credit system that will not discriminate against public or private institutions. The higher education subsidies which favored students with higher incomes in the past are not advisable. Higher education for all is a very praiseworthy goal, provided students pay tuition either while completing their studies or afterward in the manner of repaying a credit or an investment in shares or securities (that is, as a percentage of the income they generate). Repayments of this educational credit can be made simultaneously with income tax payments.

Another option would be to grant educational vouchers, similar to those described above for basic education, which could be used in any institution of higher education. In this scheme, students would compete for vouchers according to preestablished criteria, whereas institutions, both public and private, would compete with each other for students. In this way, equal treatment of public and private institutions would be achieved. It is important to subsidize students, not educational institutions, inasmuch as the subsidizing of institutions creates distortions.

Tax-deductible donations to the education sector are a hidden subsidy from which some institutions benefit, creating corruption and privileges. Consequently, the state often allots more resources to some private institutions than it provides for public universities. Moreover, this system fostered corruption in the trading of donation certificates. A real black market was created, and ultimately universities received only a small amount of the total that was subject to exemptions. Thus, an educational voucher would be fairer and more efficient.

While striving for quality in all aspects of education, it is also important to foment vocational orientation and training. In addition, parents should have greater control and influence regarding the type of education their children receive; parental control could be exerted directly or indirectly (for example, via local government).

REFORM OF THE HEALTH CARE SYSTEM

Health care reform is aimed at incorporating the private sector into the health care arena, thereby providing the individual the option to choose from among private and public services. To achieve this goal, it is necessary to create instruments for decentralization, to introduce incentives for efficiency in the state system, and to establish subsidies in inverse proportion to income. Primary health care should be prioritized as well as obstetrics, pediatrics, and attention to the physically challenged and the poor.

REFORM OF THE HOUSING SYSTEM

Housing reform aims to create a private system of savings and credit for housing which would replace the obsolete state system. The goals of the program are to create a long-term financing system for housing, to preserve the purchasing power of contributed revenues, to assist low-income contributors, to foment construction, and to promote do-it-yourself homebuilding. The new housing system would feature individual accounts, a private financial system, mandatory savings, and market-determined interest rates.

ALLEVIATION OF EXTREME POVERTY

The greatest relief for extreme poverty is inflation control. However, relief can also be achieved through temporary programs that define a target population and specify methods to reach this goal. Assistance can be provided in different ways, including 1) the distribution of food (the provision of school breakfasts and lunches, the creation of soup kitchens, and so on); 2) the distribution of basic medicines (vaccines, for example); 3) employment; 4) the development of and investment in basic community infrastructure; 5) the distribution of capital goods to the communities that use them; and 6) the distribution of information and methods for family planning. Suitable managers for these programs would be the municipalities, religious groups, and private organizations.

ENVIRONMENTAL PROTECTION

The absence of real, clear property rights has permitted the predatory exploitation of our natural resources, favoring the system of privatizing profits and socializing losses. By instituting clear property rights and transparent institutional frameworks, we aim to conserve the environment by reducing and preventing pollution due to sewage, garbage and rubbish, mining residues, coca refining, and toxic wastes. We also seek to protect endangered vegetable and animal species (such as the vicuña) and to put a halt to the overexploitation of vegetable and animal species (the anchovy, for example).

INSTITUTIONAL REFORMS

CONSTITUTIONAL FRAMEWORK

The 1979 constitution was the result of political negotiation between the parties of the Left, the Alianza Popular Revolucionaria Americana (APRA), and the Partido Popular Cristiano (PPC). The result was a constitution that consolidated the interventionist and socialist structural reforms of the Juan Velasco Alvarado regime and that incorporated lyrical concepts of a social market economy without any concrete foundation upon which to develop effective prescriptions.

INSTITUTIONAL FRAMEWORK

REFORM OF THE LEGISLATIVE BRANCH

The legislative branch must be restructured in order to create a modern, autonomous body which not only legislates but also checks the performance of the executive branch. Congressional immunity must be guaranteed. The efficiency of this branch could be improved by means of the application of a system that guarantees the rapid passage of laws as well as the quality of legislation.

In addition, congressional lobbying should be reduced through the ratification of broad regulatory norms rather than dispositions that address particular cases. The plan for Multiple Electoral Districts (Distrito Electoral Múltiple, DEM) should be implemented in lieu of the Unique Electoral District (Distrito Electoral Unico, DEU) plan in order to guarantee elections that are more open and accessible to all citizens. Conditions and mechanisms should be established in order to alleviate pressures in Congress regarding expenditures, regulation, and the budget.

REFORM OF THE JUDICIAL BRANCH

The judicial branch must be decentralized. Decentralization should address not only the physical location of the courts but also the increased allotment of resources for the arbitration of cases of an economic nature, among others. In addition, courts should be "municipalized." Special tribunals and summary judgment processes should be established for terrorism cases, and paralegal technicians should be employed in order to alleviate the judges' workloads.

The judiciary branch must be depoliticized, held to higher moral and professional standards, and modernized. Depenalization policies should be implemented. Private or public services should be contracted in order to provide increased security for prisons. Moreover, professionals should be encouraged to become notaries so as to prevent the development of monopolistic control of the field.

REFORM OF LOCAL AND REGIONAL GOVERNMENTS

Local and regional governments must be downsized. They must decrease their intervention in the economy of the regions and municipalities they govern. They must be financially self-sufficient, while avoiding the levying of excessive taxes. In addition, these governments should totally privatize the services they provide their respective communities.

REFORM OF THE ELECTORAL COLLEGE

The electoral college (Jurado Nacional de Elecciones) must be modernized and computerized. The use of an official identification card (*cédula única de identidad*) should be instituted.

REFORM OF POLITICAL PARTIES

Political parties should apply the principles of market economy to political processes. In this way, the concentration or monopolization of power would be avoided. Access to membership in political parties should be liberalized, thereby ensuring that these political organizations are more democratic. Greater political competition by means of primary elections would promote the renewal and modernization of political parties. Needless to say, all reforms must respect the right of freedom of assembly and political organization.

REFORM OF PROPERTY RIGHTS

Access to private property must be facilitated through the expeditious and inexpensive issuance of urban and rural property deeds. Property rights must be guaranteed. Administrative procedures related to the creation of private businesses and enterprises, bureaucratic transactions, and the obtaining of documents must be simplified. Also needed are regulation, decentralization, and the reduction of costs for the informal sector.

REFORM OF THE PEACEKEEPING FORCES

The peacekeeping forces should be restructured so as to merge those institutions which perform similar functions, thereby achieving a more rational use of security personnel. Furthermore, all enterprises owned and run by these forces (Entramsa, Fable, and Indumil, for example) should be privatized and liquidated. Select fixed assets belonging to the defense forces should be sold so as to capitalize on their value (for example, the sale of military headquarters located on prime property in business and financial districts and the relocation of these headquarters to more appropriate, economically rational zones).

Additional reforms should be aimed at rationalizing and limiting the purchase of weapons and armaments. Those arms purchased should be destined for the fight against terrorism. It is also necessary to implement transparent bidding and purchasing procedures for all expenditures related to defense and peacekeeping. Moreover, the moral character of the various peacekeeping entities must be upgraded, emphasizing, in particular, the elimination of corruption in their ranks.

THE IMPACT OF THE REFORMS

At a macroeconomic level, we can analyze the structural reform package by dividing the economy into three great markets: the market of goods and services, the labor market, and the money market. In reality, these markets are not independent of one another, but interrelated. The economic agents that operate within these markets can be classified as consumers, producers, and the government.

Before the implementation of the economic program of the 1990s, the market of goods and services was hampered by price controls and restrictions on the supply and demand of goods through regulations and administrative practices. Price controls produce scarcity, rationing, and black markets. At the same time, they reduce the total level of production and employment. When these markets and foreign trade are liberalized, prices rise initially, but the supply and demand for these products increases, scarcity disappears, and competition prevents prices from overflowing or generating monopolistic margins.

Before 1990, the labor market was characterized by a series of restrictions and regulations such as the minimum wage, collective negotiations, and a multitude of strikes, all of which were instrumental in raising the price of labor. The practices of occupational stability *(estabilidad laboral)* and workers' community *(comunidad laboral)* also contributed to this price increase. Together, these factors resulted in wage levels that were above the market equilibrium, which caused the unemployment rate to rise. Labor practices that increase the cost of labor diminish both the demand for and the availability of labor, thus causing production to fall.

The structural reform of the labor market seeks to liberalize the market and eliminate the minimum wage as well as the practices that increase the cost of hiring workers. These initiatives should produce positive results in the medium term. The cost of creating a new position should drop; as a consequence, both employment and production will increase overall.

The money and loan market, on the other hand, was formerly characterized by financial repression. Interest rates were controlled and thus below inflation, credit was subjected to quantitative controls, a poor linkage existed between financial assets and income, the banking industry was underdeveloped, and the development of the capital market was limited. When a money market is liberalized, the demand for money increases because the funds available for loans can be transferred from less profitable activities to those that promise higher profitability. The money supply increases as a result of the financial mechanisms that are created. The costs of intermediation (the spread between the interest rate collected on loans and that paid on deposits) are reduced although one would expect that the interest rate for loans would drop, while the rate for deposits would rise. Finally, the average interest rate would be expected to rise.

The foreign currency market, a subsector of the money market, was overregulated and controlled. The exchange rate was fixed below its equilibrium level. The demand for foreign currency was inhibited by the implementation of tariff-like policies and restrictions on foreign trade, while the supply of foreign currency was also depressed because of these controls, capital flight, and so on. Upon liberalizing the exchange markets, the demand for and availability of foreign currency would increase, and the exchange rate could devaluate or revaluate, depending on the displacement of foreign currency supply and demand curves. There is a possibility that a devaluation would result from this liberalization, but if the interest rate in the money market is high enough to attract capital inflows from abroad, the supply of foreign currency will surpass demand, producing a revaluation of the exchange rate.

Downsizing the government, whether by means of restructuring or privatizing public enterprises and services, initially causes increased unemployment due to personnel displacement and a decline in the national income precipitated by the reduction of public expenditure. However, downsizing ultimately generates additional activity for the private sector, which becomes more efficient and productive, thus fomenting higher growth and employment in the medium term.

The mechanisms instituting obligatory savings funds — such as individual capitalization of compensation for service time, retirement funds, and housing funds — transfer these funds from public to private administration in order to insure their security and integrity. This transfer not only increases the supply of funds for loans but also fortifies and develops the stock and money markets, promoting further financing for investment and economic growth.

Indeed, the structural reforms analyzed here can produce unfavorable effects in the short run. In the medium term, however, their effects are positive and contribute to further growth, employment, and a better use of credit funds. The structural reforms improve the availability of foreign currency and facilitate the creation of a small but efficient government.

The Tyranny of the Status Quo

Monopolistic groups can be found among trade unions, professional associations, business organizations, the government, and political groups. These are the groups that are generally most opposed to structural reforms, either on an individual basis or through alliances.

Trade unions, often monopolistic, often fail to reflect the interests of their members but rather benefit at their members' expense. For instance, when a union successfully negotiates a salary increase which surpasses the market rate, this improvement is made at the expense of nonaffiliated workers. Unions also often limit the availability of workers and use violent, coercive methods against both employees and employers. Certain unions, moreover, obtain protection from the government through pressure or negotiation. This protection is effected by means of legislation regulating minimum salaries, maximum working hours, wage scales, and work by minors.

The best protection for workers, however, is the existence of competition for their services, not union affiliation. Unprotected workers are those who have one employer or are unemployed. Workers should have the right to organize unions in order to offer members the services they desire, but these union members must respect the rights of others and not use coercion. Membership and participation in union activities must be voluntary. "Unions of unions" also exist, such as sector-based unions that claim to represent all the workers that belong to a particular productive sector (fishing, mining, and so on).

Professional associations are also often monopolistic in that they restrict their membership in order to generate higher remunerations. They also obtain contributions that the state collects and transfers to them. Thus, these associations finance their activities by raising the costs of transactions or services rendered for the average citizen. On the other hand, business organizations sometimes become monopolistic with the purpose of lobbying and obtaining profits and privileges from the state or maintaining those already in existence. In many cases, these associations are not truly representative; they associate merely to reduce lobbying costs for the benefit of an entrepreneurial elite. Another monopolistic group can usually be found within the government itself. This faction may be managed by a group of bureaucrats with clear interests. Administrative and sector-based unions also exist within the government.

Government business is carried out by bureaucrats who spend other people's money and measure their success by means of the power they acquire. Management costs are widely distributed, while political benefits are centralized in a few hands. The armed forces constitute another important group within the government. We must depend on the armed forces if we are to secure political and economic stability in the country, a fact which has been demonstrated during 172 years of republican history.

Another large monopolistic group is that formed by politicians. These representatives obtain their votes thanks to political campaigns financed with their own money or that of their supporters. They often promise voters advantages that will be paid for by other voters. Some politicians communicate with their constituents only during election time; after taking office, they pay little attention to the mandate they have received from their constituents.

Thus, these three tyrannies — the tyranny of the beneficiaries (including labor, professional, and business associations), the tyranny of the bureaucrats, and the tyranny of the politicians — constitute what Milton and Rose Friedman have called the "Iron Triangle," which protects privileges and acquired rights and impedes the dismantling of state mechanisms for the redistribution of wealth. This triangle constitutes the "Tyranny of the Status Quo," which is very difficult to break because of its strength, consistency, and coinciding interests.

From Theory to Practice

In Search of the Lost Equilibrium: Macroeconomic Reform

The Reference Program with the IMF (August 1990-September 1991)

In August 1990, at the beginning of Alberto Fujimori's term in office, a stabilization program was implemented. Prices were liberalized, subsidies were eliminated, and the quest for macroeconomic equilibrium began. However, after registering some positive initial results, the process went awry in December of the same year, and inflation rose again, reaching 24 percent monthly. This situation, as is well known, prompted Juan Carlos Hurtado Miller's departure from the Ministry of Economy and Finance.

On February 15, 1991, when I was appointed minister of the economy, I found myself confronting a difficult situation indeed. My first priority was to rescue the stabilization program, which had been seriously affected. My second task was to begin the implementation of the structural reforms, an area in which very little progress had been made, particularly with respect to tax reform, which had in fact retrogressed. My third priority was to make advances on the road to international economic reinsertion, which, according to many, had been delayed excessively.

During my first three weeks in office, with the collaboration of the economic team, I formulated sixty-one structural reforms in the areas of commerce, finance, labor, and public administration. These reforms were approved by the Council of Ministers on March 11, 1991, and at 10 p.m., we unveiled the economic program to the nation. It was well received inasmuch as there were no *gasolinazos*[9] or *paquetazos*.[10] Among the reactions I received were that of the president of the Council of Ministers and that of the wife of a painter who was doing some work in my house at the time. Dr. Carlos Torres y Torres Lara approached me after the Council session exclaiming, "This is not a program! It doesn't have a paquetazo!" I didn't believe he was complaining, but somehow he seemed to miss a paquetazo. On the other hand, the painter's wife whispered in tears: "There is no paquetazo. There is no paquetazo."

These economic reforms were not designed with the intention of adjusting the old interventionist model; we intended instead to institute a different model so that the budgetary tendency toward deficit spending could be reversed. We believed that the government needed more adjusting than the people, and this represented a 180-degree turn in the management of economic policy. With respect to stabilization, I made a commitment to the principles of fiscal and monetary discipline. The Central Bank was not going to finance public expenditure; that was a "golden rule." On the other hand, the budget for 1991 had to be restructured because tax pressure had been calculated at 12 percent of GDP, while inflation had been estimated at 28 percent for the entire year. These figures were absolutely unrealistic; tax pressure would not surpass 8 percent of GDP, and as of March, the accumulated rate of inflation had already reached 39 percent.

In early 1991, I appeared before Congress to request supplementary credit because higher inflation would result in the state's having an increased income in soles. The members of Congress were surprised. Boloña wanted credit! Wasn't he going to cut their budget? Had he forgotten his orthodoxy? They seemed to be victims of the so-called "monetary illusion." I do not know if they understood, but what was happening was that inflation was helping me. If inflation reached 90 instead of the estimated 28 percent and if we kept the approved nominal amounts or even raised them via supplementary credit, we would actually be making a tremendous budgetary adjustment. What this supplementary credit would actually do, therefore, was restructure and drastically cut the budget.

The new budget was approved in May 1991. Inflation started to decline. It fell to 7.7 percent in March 1991 and 5.8 percent in April. In addition, the exchange rate that had remained stagnant at 0.55 soles per dollar from January to March 1991 moved to 0.64 soles per dollar in April. Regarding international economic reinsertion, April was a good month. After my trip to Nagoya, Japan, the Japanese began to move more decisively toward the formation of the Support Group. Enrique Iglesias of the IDB, David Mulford of the U.S. Treasury, and Japan's vice minister of economy committed themselves in a more effective manner at this time.

In May 1991, by contrast, the situation became more complicated. First, my public statement announcing small monthly adjustments in the price of fuels angered the president, who declared that due to my lack of experience, as evidenced by my baby face, I had acted naively. His attitude undermined my authority vis-à-vis Congress regarding budget negotiations. This incident prompted my resignation on May 15, 1991. The president rectified his position immediately, however, declaring that I was his "favorite minister"; thus, I continued in my post.

That same month, due to the inadequate intervention of the BCR in the exchange market, the devaluation of the dollar began to accelerate, and the exchange rate hit 0.90 soles per dollar. Credit lines or rediscounts were being given by the BCR to local banks at a monthly rate of 4 percent, and since devaluation exceeded this figure, the banks generated a profit. This inadequate intervention ceased when it was announced that the BCR would participate in the market selling dollars. Thus, the speculative wave came to an end, and the exchange rate decreased to 0.83 soles per dollar. Inflation, on the other hand, increased to 7.6 percent.

The following month, June 1991, was also difficult as a consequence of the "tax war" that I waged against the Congressional Commission on the Economy. The commission did not approve of my modifying or broadening the General Sales Tax (Impuesto General a las Ventas, IGV) and the income tax. Former President Alan García's allies were seeking to validate the policies implemented during the previous five years. They refused to approve a tax increase, making it necessary to finance the budget by not repaying foreign debt or by issuing more money. In addition, the price of fuel increased 18 percent due to fiscal reasons as well as the struggle between the Treasury and Petroperú over the income generated by the sale of fuel. The credibility of the economic program suffered as a result of these increases. For these reasons, inflation continued to increase, reaching 9.3 percent.

Two major protests also took place in June 1991. The first, a teachers' strike, involved 400,000 protestors, whereas the second, in the health care sector, involved 100,000. This situation had an adverse effect on the economic program as protestors were demanding salary increases ranging from 30 to 300 soles, a fiscal impossibility given the nature of the reform program. As long as these strikes continued, so did expectations for continued inflation.

The strikes were resolved in July 1991, when the government granted workers an increase of 70 soles instead of 300, as a result of which the expectations of inflation began to diminish. Inflation dropped to 9.1 percent that month and to 7.2 percent in August 1991, beginning a downward trend that ended in December with 3.7 percent. This drop was achieved because public expenditures were kept in line, taxes were increased, and the monetary supply was reduced.

In August and September 1991, the Support Group was activated, necessitating my traveling to Europe. During my absence, an alternative economic program was orchestrated behind my back with the purpose of implementing a 100 percent devaluation to prevent a number of economic agents who had contracted excessive debts in soles from going bankrupt. This attempt constituted a direct application of the mercantilist principle, "Let us adjust Peru so that a few may benefit." Fortunately, this initiative was stymied.

On the other hand, negotiations with the Congressional Commission on the Economy had broken off by this time. The game Alan García's followers were playing was very clear, so I asked President Fujimori to legislate the necessary taxes by means of emergency decrees. He refused; we therefore had to wait until September 1991, when the president of the Congressional Commission on the Economy was due to step down, to obtain approval for an improvement in the IGV, a key component of tax reform.

September was a gratifying month, crowning a great effort by the Peruvian government. Among the accomplishments made were the formation of the Support Group, the signing of the Rights Accumulation Program with the IMF, the negotiations with the Paris Club, and the procurement of a loan from the IDB after the country's having been an "economic pariah" for seven years. With the application of this program, Peru regained its status as a "serious country" with internal and external credibility. Peru was returned to the Peruvian people. Nevertheless, though these achievements were great, future challenges would be even greater.

The Rights Accumulation Program
(September 1991-December 1992)

The first formal program with the International Monetary Fund, the Rights Accumulation Program (RAP), was signed on September 12, 1991. A mechanism created to promote the recovery of confidence in a country following its application of a unilateral scheme for the repayment of the foreign debt, the Rights Accumulation Program had a duration of fifteen months in Peru, during which time its fulfillment was often in jeopardy.

The statutes of the IMF and the World Bank stipulate that no credit can be granted to a country that has yet to fulfill its payments on previous loans. According to the Rights Accumulation Agreement that Peru adopted with the IMF, no payment for those arrears would be made until the end of 1992. Fulfillment of the program's goals would permit the quarterly accumulation of the right to obtain, at the end of 1992, a loan of $873 million for eight years, including a grace period of three years. At the onset of 1993, Peru would need to obtain a bridge loan in order to cancel all arrears with the IMF; the country would also need the IMF to disburse resources for the same amount in order to cancel the bridge loan. From that moment, Peru would be eligible to receive fresh resources from the IMF in order to finance or support its balance of payments and would begin negotiating an Extended Facility Program for the period 1993-1995, which did in fact happen, although with a delay of three months.

In October, the armed forces exerted a great deal of pressure to augment public expenditure by $350 million on the grounds of an imminent border conflict. The Minister of Defense wrote me two harsh letters, with copies to all general commanders, in which he threatened that I would be "historically responsible" if I did not release the funds. Thus, a conflict developed. However, the minister made the mistake of also sending a document pertaining to the period January-September in which funds were requested to cover travel expenses, photocopies, and medals, all hardly justifiable under the pretext of a war. I reacted harshly, responding that "because of my family heritage and personal code of conduct, I could not permit my patriotism to be questioned·or doubted in any way." I explained that his demands had little to do with preparations for an armed conflict and that I was already handling the necessary requirements directly with the general commanders. Ultimately, the armed conflict did not occur; the issue in question was resolved some months later through diplomatic channels.

In November 1991, a populist initiative, the Emergency Agrarian Law (Ley de Emergencia del Agro), was proposed in Congress. The initiative provided for a series of tax breaks on the importation of seeds and fertilizers, exemption from the Selective Consumption Tax (Impuesto Selectivo al Consumo, ISC) on diesel for those farmers who extracted water from subterranean reserves, the dollarization of the agrarian debt, and the refunding of the General Sales Tax (IGV) to those engaging in agrarian activities. The expenditure involved surpassed $300 million, which would presumably be financed with surcharges on the import duties for agrarian products. In reality, this surcharge would barely have covered 15 percent of the sum that was needed to finance the proposed initiative.

This proposal marked the beginning of the end of the structural reform program in that it deviated from the logic of the tariff policy and generated further fiscal deficit. For this reason, I appeared before the Senate to explain the proposal's inconveniences and attempt to avoid conceding advantages to certain economic factions. I was able to achieve the latter, though the proposal was ratified. The negative effects of this law had to be minimized by means of presidential decrees until it was finally repealed in April 1992 and then replaced by another law which was more neutral vis-à-vis the economic reform program.

December 1991 was a complicated month as well. On December 6 and 7, I appeared at congressional hearings to respond to charges from APRA, the Left, and a number of independents. At approximately the same time, a problem arose between President Fujimori and Congress. The president accused a group of representatives of being in collusion with drug traffickers because they had abrogated numerous articles of a law related to money laundering. The president's accusation caused an angry reaction from the Senate, which proposed to begin impeachment procedures and passed that motion to the Chamber of Deputies at the very moment when I was appearing before the representatives. As Representative Ricardo Letts cooled spirits down, the impeachment motion did not succeed. On Saturday, December 7, 1991, I concluded my testimony. I even came out of it gracefully, answering a question from APRA's Carlos Rivas Dávila with a quotation by Víctor Raúl Haya de la Torre regarding the convenience of foreign investments.

While I was testifying in Lima, the other members of the Andean Group were negotiating the Barahona Act in Bogotá, Colombia. The member countries approved a common external tariff with levels of 0, 5, 10, 15, and 20 percent, which voided the uniform tariff of 15 percent that the Fujimori administration was aiming at and on which the economic reform program was based. It took several trips and various rounds of negotiation during the following six months to prevent the approval of the common tariff. Finally, in June 1992, a solution was reached through Peru's temporary exclusion from the Andean Group.

In addition, December unleashed the budget battle with Congress. Congress had discarded the president's proposal comprised of 100 articles and had prepared its own containing more than 300. These articles named specific beneficiaries, such as those involved with Certificate for Reimbursement of

Taxes upon Export (Certificado de Exportaciones, Certex) payments and other cases; these were later withdrawn as a consequence of discussions and accusations. The most serious problem, however, was the fact that the budget was unbalanced inasmuch as 400 million soles which had originally been allotted for salary increases were reallocated to "public works." In spite of my three letters to Congress explaining the problems involved, the budget was approved on December 15, 1991. It was unbalanced by 1.265 billion soles, equivalent to 2 percent of the GDP.

Indebtedness and financing laws were also approved. The latter included the new income tax, which involved a series of corrections and improvements plus a tax on assets. These laws were approved in a joint session of Congress. However, a number of amendments cutting fiscal income were added, thus creating a serious problem in that they hindered the country's achieving the goal of a tax level of 9.3 percent of GNP. This led to the issuance of Supreme Decree 307-EF-91, dated December 28, 1991, which clearly constituted an amendment to the previous law. Finally, the president vetoed the 1992 budget.

Thus, we started 1992 without a budget, and in January almost no money was spent except for salary expenses. Consequently, Congress convened for a special session and on January 7 approved the 1992 budget without considering the modifications that the president had made. In addition, the administration had paid Christmas bonuses despite the lack of budgeting for this expenditure. Therefore, in the middle of the battle over the budget, I had to go to Congress in order to ask for supplementary credit that validated the payment of bonuses; in lieu of this credit, we would have had to deduct these bonuses from the government employees' salaries. We discussed the issue in the Joint Budget Committee, and I obtained approval for the credit. I subsequently obtained approval from the Permanent Committee. This was a victory in the midst of this war between the executive and legislative branches of the government.

At the end of January, I went to Washington, along with Argentina's Minister of Economics Domingo Cavallo, to attend a meeting at the World Bank to discuss the problems related to exchange overvaluation. The conclusion was clear: in order to implement the Cavallo Plan in Peru, numerous fiscal problems would have to be resolved, and the country would require large amounts of international reserves. Thus, we decided to discard the possibility. At this time, I also met IMF Director Michael Camdessus, who showed concern for the Peruvian economic situation. In his opinion, with the budget that had been passed, the mediated fiscal policies, and the Emergency Agrarian Law that had been approved by Congress, the economic program would not be viable. He offered to help by coming to Peru by mid-February in order to convince the authorities and the Legislature to implement the proper tax policies.

Director Camdessus arrived in Peru on February 12, 1992. Throughout his visit, Camdessus emphasized the need for higher taxes as an expression of increased solidarity. As a result, a tax package was implemented with the aim of raising the tax rate from 7.8 to 9.3 percent in March. This package was based on modifications of the IGV and the income tax as well as the elimination of tax exemptions. These taxes, approved as presidential emergency decrees, were valid for only six months because Congress had limited the president's authority and it was not possible to apply the presidential emergency decrees provided for in Clause 20, which granted the executive the power to modify taxes.

Shortly after the tax package was passed, several ministers forced us to reverse some policies, and I had to slow down. Facing a wave of new taxes, Congress called on me to justify the emergency decrees before the Economic and Constitutional Committees. It seemed to me that I lived in Congress in March 1992. I had meetings every morning and afternoon to discuss taxes, the budget, or the bankruptcy of public and private banks.

In April 1992, when the new Congress convened, Alan García directed his attacks against me and against the economic program with the purpose of destabilizing the administration and becoming the leader of the opposition. García hoped to secure my immediate censure in the April 7, 1992, congressional session, without giving me any opportunity to defend myself. He was collecting signatures for that purpose. A few days before that date, I responded strongly, accusing him of being responsible for the country's bankruptcy and comparing him to Iraq's Saddam Hussein. García and Saddam, I claimed, were the only leaders in the world who, after ruining their countries, continued to have political force, bizarre as this might seem. I was preparing to confront my censure, and I had learned during my December hearings that the best defense is to launch an attack.

Before Congress was installed on Sunday, April 5, 1992, at 9:30 in the evening, I was summoned by President Fujimori to a meeting with all the ministers at the "Pentagonito,"[11] where he informed us, only 30 minutes prior to his address to the nation, of his decision to dissolve Congress. The moments that followed were extremely tense and difficult. I had to make a fast and definite decision about whether or not to continue collaborating with the administration. At that moment, my staying in office was critical to the government, especially on the external front. However, how could I support the disruption of constitutional rule? And on the other hand, what would happen to the economic reform program? Would constitutional rule and the reform program both be lost?

Finally, I chose the lesser of two evils. Constitutional norms had already been violated, but if I left — I thought then and do still — the orientation of the reforms would be at risk as well. In addition, I reasoned that since the economic reinsertion process depended to a great extent on the credibility of the government, I could work from within the Cabinet for the return to institutional normalcy.

I had witnessed how difficult it was for the country to begin changing course after forty years of mercantilism and interventionism. Distortions arose not only from Congress and an institutional organization that was inadequate at its very roots but also many times from within the executive branch itself. Among those who remained in the government, were there any officials who could and would maintain the stabilization program and especially the economic reforms?

In general, I surmised that the pragmatism that prevailed in the executive branch would be conducive to any shift in orientation. An authoritarian temptation might be imposed upon the economy, which would return us to the old interventionist ways. On the other hand, I knew that the economic reforms that had been implemented had effectively led to greater political and democratic liberalization.

I do not mean to suggest that I saw these issues as clearly then as I do now. I had mixed feelings and some confused ideas. Nonetheless, the difficulties that had been encountered in defending the economic program were so great that it became clear to me, above all, what should not be done. I believed then as I do today that on April 5, 1992, much more than democracy was put at risk; the very foundation of our civil society had been jeopardized. If this government failed — with Sendero Luminoso[12] leader Abimael Guzmán still at large, Alan García's sabotaging every effort to modernize the country, and the country's lacking a definite arrangement with the multilateral credit entities — the prospects were very somber.

I do not suggest that I was the only person capable of heading a reform program. But at that moment, it was I who had to decide. In retrospect, it becomes more and more obvious to me that I had no choice. Either we accepted an "institutional parenthesis" with all its risks, or we would surely change our course and perhaps never escape the past. The opposition, at least, had shown no desire to abandon the old mercantilist ways.

In Congress, Alan García was about to become leader of the opposition. Although many people rejected García, his influence within the power centers grew stronger every day. With his characteristic lack of responsibility, García was prepared to destabilize the government to give new life to the old populist demands. He would never have succeeded, but he would indeed have utterly ruined the country. Thus, I decided to be the first to oppose García. I had to ensure the viability of the economic program and collaborate with all initiatives geared toward institutional improvement.

In order to accomplish the first task, I sought to secure my position in the Cabinet. To achieve the second, I proposed the creation of a Constituent

Assembly. During the months of April and May 1992, I held meetings with leaders of the opposition and the major political parties. This solution was not accepted by the president until Hernando de Soto and I proposed the formation of a Constituent Congress, a proposal which was taken to the meeting of Latin American presidents held in the Bahamas. At the Chancellors' meeting, the president assumed responsibility for returning Peru to democratic rule within five months. In this way, we prevented Peru from becoming a "political pariah" in the international community.

These two motives guided my actions between April 5 and December 30, 1992. These were difficult months during which I endured pressure from the armed forces for increased expenditure, pressure from labor unions and other associations as well as mercantilist pressures of all kinds, even from Cabinet members. It is in such moments that one appreciates the importance of the system of balance of powers and the need to reaffirm the existence of the legislative branch. Despite these obstacles, the economic program was advanced, significant achievements were made with respect to structural reforms, and a concerted effort was made to reestablish the institution of democracy.

Beginning in April 1992, the country experienced a considerable fiscal surplus as a consequence of the accumulation of Treasury funds from the National Housing Fund (Fondo Nacional de Vivienda, FONAVI),[13] the National Tax Administration Superintendency (Superintendencia Nacional de Administración Tributaria, SUNAT), privatization funds, and the ministries' own incomes. This surplus amounted to 400 million soles as of June 1992. On the other hand, the recession was worsening due to the adverse climatic conditions (flooding in northern Peru and drought in the south) created by the El Niño phenomenon, the rationing of electricity due to the lack of rain, the restriction of vehicular traffic due to terrorist attacks), and the economic adjustments effected by the "fiscal package." Growth, initially estimated at 2.5 percent of GDP for 1992, registered negative figures. Thus, in August we formulated a series of benign policies to reduce the negative effects of the severe recession that we had been experiencing since April. This package included higher expenditures in public investment, the alleviation of extreme poverty, and support for the fight against terrorism. The General Sales Tax (IGV), which regulated exports, was reestablished; anti-technical taxes, such as the tax on checks, were eliminated; and the Selective Consumption Tax (ISC) was reduced by five percentage points. A sum of $100 million was appropriated for medium- and long-term financing, and bonds for financial restructuring were created. This benign package in no way threatened the viability of the economic program in that the package was being financed with the fiscal surplus that had been generated. However, the economic agents who had lobbied unsuccessfully for higher volumes of expenditure demonstrated their disappointment by deeming the package insufficient.

Pressure for a larger devaluation of the exchange rate began in September 1992, prompted by an increase in public expenditure of approximately 100 million soles, financed by the fiscal surplus that had been accumulated and spent. This injection of soles into the economy caused a reduction of the interest rate in soles, which in turn motivated the conversion of debts from soles to dollars, increasing the demand for dollars. This process triggered a devaluation of the exchange rate, which was reinforced by the modifications in SUNAT's deposit and payment system, extending these norms to regulate not only the National Bank (Banco de la Nación) but also the private banking system. All of these factors led to a 20 percent devaluation in 45 days, a gain of nine points in exchange parity. This devaluation continued accelerating and had to be controlled by means of the sale of dollars by the Treasury as further devaluation had put the economic program's anti-inflationary goals in jeopardy.

During the five quarters in which the Rights Accumulation Program (RAP) with the IMF was applied (1991-1992), joint evaluations showed a comfortable margin of compliance with fiscal and monetary goals, international reserves, and foreign indebtedness limits. These evaluations also reported significant advances as well as a deepening of the structural reforms. This was the first case of RAP compliance in the IMF and a great success for the country in its struggle to curb inflation and enhance its external credibility. For this reason, Peru obtained the right to clear arrears with the World Bank and the IMF.

THE EXTENDED FACILITY PROGRAM: 1993-1995

The program negotiated with the International Monetary Fund during November and December 1992 was an Extended Facility Program (EFP), which would have a duration of three years (1993-1995). This program had five primary objectives: 1) to control inflation, reducing it to 27 percent in 1993, and ultimately to 9 percent in 1995; 2) to achieve a growth rate of 3.5 percent in 1993, with a target of 5 percent annual growth as of 1995; 3) to ensure the viability of the balance of payments through the formation of a support group, the renegotiation of the foreign debt, and an increase in the level of international reserves; 4) to alleviate extreme poverty by dedicating 1 percent of the GDP to social expenditure; and 5) to continue deepening the structural reforms.

A number of advantages were obtained as a result of these negotiations: an increase in the fiscal deficit from 2.5 percent of GDP in 1992 to 2.9 percent in 1993, followed by a gradual decrease to 1.8 percent in 1995; an increase in tax levels from 9.5 to 10 percent of GDP between 1992 and 1993, followed by an increment of 1.5 percent during the following years; and the possibility of greater money supply margins in order to purchase dollars and maintain the exchange rate, provided this did not undermine the anti-inflationary goals. After the Letter of Intent was negotiated, it was not signed immediately for various reasons. First of all, it was deemed necessary that the program be approved by the Council of Ministers. Once this was achieved, it was to be made public and debated, which was also done, by unions, academics, and the representatives to the Annual Conference of Executives (Conferencia Anual de Ejecutivos, CADE). Subsequently, it was proposed that the Letter of Intent be made more flexible by including the concept of the "pacification of the country," a suggestion that was formulated in a letter addressed by the president of the Republic to the executive director of the IMF on December 13, 1992.

This impasse was overcome in the Washington negotiation by introducing a new paragraph stating that "donations and credits that are obtained with these ends will not be included in calculations regarding fiscal deficit."[14] Despite this effort, there seemed to be no greater intention to approve the Letter of Intent. A possible explanation for this could be that there was hope that Japan would finance the economic program, thereby making it unnecessary to resort to the IMF. This was not a feasible possibility, in my opinion, though some government officials mistakenly continued to believe this was the proper road to take. This situation worried me greatly as it was clear that the key requirements for the second economic reinsertion (i.e., the clearing of arrears with the World Bank and the IMF) had to be fulfilled before January 20, 1993, the date on which Bill Clinton would be inaugurated as president of the United States.

Nevertheless, President Fujimori's decision to exclude me from the Cabinet had already been made. On January 4, 1993, I therefore considered it my civic duty to write a letter of resignation, emphasizing the importance of refusing to give in to mercantilist or populist pressures and of not stopping half way on the road to prosperity and modernization. I concluded by urging that the Letter of Intent be signed as soon as possible so as not to endanger the process of economic reinsertion, which was the backbone of the economic program.

The macroeconomic projections of the Extended Facility Program for the period 1993-1995 are outlined below (see Appendix).

ECONOMIC POLICY GOALS

According to the Extended Facility Program, the economic policy goals for the period 1993-1995 are the following:

- Inflation should be reduced to 27 percent in 1993, 15 percent in 1994, and 9 percent in 1995.
- Net international reserves should grow by $170, $127, and $88 million, respectively, during each of these years.

- The fiscal deficit would be increased to 2.9 percent of the GDP in 1993, followed by a decrease to 2.3 percent and 1.8 percent of the GDP in 1994 and 1995, respectively. The fiscal deficit would be financed completely with foreign resources.

- The monetary supply should grow by 36, 22, and 17 percent, respectively, during the same period (1993 to 1995).

- The gross domestic product (GDP) should register the following gradual increases between 1993 and 1995: 3.5 percent, 4.5 percent, and 5 percent, respectively.

ECONOMIC POLICY INSTRUMENTS

Fiscal policy. Tax levies should increase to 10 percent of GDP in 1993 and 11.5 percent and 13 percent of the GDP in the following years, respectively. The tax policies that have been designed to achieve these goals are based on the broadening of the IGV and the income tax.

Income obtained by means of privatization should be equivalent to 0.6, 0.6, and 0.3 percent of the GDP for each year, respectively. This would represent a collection of $630 million for the three-year period.

Current expenditures should be reduced from 7 to 6.6 percent of GDP. The structural reforms would absorb the income from privatization. Capital expenditures would be increased from 3 to 4.7 percent of GNP, and the quasi-fiscal deficit would be eliminated by 1994.

Monetary policy. Monetary creation would be consistent with the inflationary goals and the growth of GDP. The required reserves ratio in foreign currency should not vary. In addition, interest rates should be free, and rediscounts should be given only in certain situations and for very short terms. The BCR should begin creating mechanisms with which to realize open market operations.

Trade policy. The advances and improvements already made regarding the reform of international trade should be maintained, and tariffs should be reduced to a uniform rate of 15 percent by June 1995.

Exchange policy. The exchange rate should continue to be determined by the market, with possible intervention by the BCR to manage international reserves or to avoid fluctuations in the interest rate, provided this does not interfere with the goals to control inflation.

Price policy. Prices should continue to be free and determined by supply and demand. Controlled prices should be adjusted to account for expected inflation and restructured according to international prices in order to allow for the privatization of the respective public enterprises.

Salary policy. Salaries in the private sector should be determined by the free market, and the government should refrain from establishing a minimum wage. Salaries in the public sector should be adjusted according to the availability of funds and, on average, should not exceed expected inflation.

KEY PRICES

The exchange rate is expected to register devaluations of 34, 16, and 7 percent, respectively, for the period 1993 to 1995, generating a real parity gain of 15 percent. The interest rate for loans in domestic currency could be reduced from a yearly rate of 63 percent in 1992, to 32, 14, and 10 percent during the next three years, with inflation rates of 27, 15, and 9 percent, respectively. These tendencies are not goals, but rather expected results of the economic program.

The program with the IMF for 1993 to 1995 should permit, through fiscal and monetary discipline, one-digit inflation, growth rates of 5 percent of the GDP, and international net reserves of $2.385 billion. In short, macroeconomic equilibria would be reached between 1993 and 1995.

KEY PRICES IN THE PERUVIAN ECONOMY

THE EXCHANGE RATE

The real exchange rate has been progressively deteriorating in Peru since accelerated inflation became hyperinflation. Thus, for instance, if the exchange rate had been equivalent to 100 in 1985, it deteriorated to 77 in 1987 and 54 in 1989. By July 1990, it had eroded to 46, and the August shock shrunk it even more, to a level of 33.

Deterioration of the real exchange rate indicates that devaluation of the sol has been slower than inflation. Thus, for instance, in 1988 inflation was recorded at 1700 percent, whereas devaluation amounted to 680 percent. The figures for 1989 and 1990 were 2800 and 1100 percent, respectively, and in 1990, 7600 and 3700 percent, respectively. In 1991, inflation was reduced to 139 percent, while devaluation continued its tendency to lag behind, reaching 87 percent. This tendency was reversed in 1992, with an inflation rate of 57 percent versus a devaluation rate of 63 percent.

When devaluation is slower than inflation, the exchange rate is "overvalued." As a result, domestic products become more expensive than imports, and exports are less competitive. This has been the case since 1986, but this phenomenon was disguised by means of exchange controls, the prohibition of imports, and controls in each of the principal markets.

Some exporters seek to accelerate the process of parity gain, that is, to cause devaluation to surpass inflation. This is not possible because in order to gain parity the BCR increases the money supply to buy more dollars in the economy and to raise or maintain the exchange rate. This process of acceleration has a limit that is reached very quickly, and if the policy remains in effect, inflation is reactivated. The process of exchange supervaluation developed over a period of five years; thus, it will take time to correct it. In fact, this correction will probably take a few more years, during which time exporters will have to adjust and restructure to become more efficient. Monetary policies alone will not correct the distortion of relative prices.

If the real exchange rate of August 1990 is taken as a base equivalent to 100, the exchange rate decreased to 86 in December 1991 followed by an increase to 91 in December 1992. Beginning in April 1992, there has been parity gain; devaluation has surpassed inflation in an attempt to correct exchange supervaluation. To correct this position, the government must work on the side of the exchange rate denominator, reducing a series of domestic surcharges on foreign trade in order to make exports and production more competitive for the domestic market. This adjustment is being accomplished by the structural reforms.

THE INTEREST RATE

The interest rate for foreign currency is equal to the international interest rate plus the "country risk" or the perception of how reliable a country is. The concept of "country risk" can be defined as the difference between the interest rate in foreign currency in the country in question and the London Interbank Offered Rate (LIBOR). This difference is that which motivates people to transfer their savings from Switzerland or Miami to Peru. In a politically and economically stable country, the country risk would fluctuate between 1 percent and 2 percent. When interest rates were freed up in Peru in March 1991, however, the country risk with respect to LIBOR fluctuated between 4 and 7 percent in 1991 and between 5 and 8 percent in 1992. The interest rate for loans in foreign currency is equal to the rate for foreign currency deposits plus the spread or financial margin for the banks or financial institutions.

In a free market, the interest rate for domestic currency deposits is at least equivalent to the inflation rate. If this were not so, no reasonable person would keep deposits in domestic currency as his or her money's value and purchasing power would decrease. The interest rate for domestic currency deposits is equal to the interest rate for foreign currency deposits plus the expected devaluation. The same is true in the case of loans. The expected devaluation depends on the inflation rate.

Interest rates for domestic currency deposits demonstrate the following behavior: to the degree that there is acceleration in the rate of inflation, as was the case in December 1990 and January 1991, the interest rate on deposits increases with a lag of two to three months. Later, when inflation presents a downward trend, the interest rate becomes closer to the inflation rate. The principle is very simple: no one saves in order to lose money. People learn to defend themselves from inflation and thus prefer to save in goods or other assets instead of in cash. The banks' spread reached 7 percent per month in 1990 and decreased to 4 percent per month in two years. It is still high.

On the other hand, as inflation and devaluation decrease and a greater degree of economic stability is observed, foreign currency interest rates gradually decline as well. The margin available to financial institutions for foreign currency operations has been reduced from 15 percent to 12 percent, which is still high.

Throughout 1991, interest rates in domestic and foreign currency demonstrated a downward trend inasmuch as inflation was diminishing. However, the relationship between interest rates in dollars and in soles showed an expected devaluation of 55 to 176 percent. Devaluation reached roughly 96 percent that year. During 1992, the relationship between the interest rates showed an expected devaluation of between 34 and 55 percent, while devaluation amounted to 65 percent due to government devaluation policies that were aimed at achieving exchange parity.

In sum, following a period of hyperinflation, interest rates reach high levels in both domestic and foreign currency and tend to persist at these levels even when inflation starts descending. Considering that a reduction of interest rates follows a decrease of inflation, the only way to lower interest rates is to reduce inflation and, consequently, the expectations for devaluation.

Just as inflation takes years to develop and years to control, it will also take years to reduce interest rates in both foreign and domestic currency. However, such a reduction must go hand in hand with a decline in the rate of inflation.

Implementing controls to lower the interest rate in domestic currency or establishing fixed rates at levels lower than the market value only creates currency black markets, raising interest rates and spreads even more. Controls also create incentives for capital flight when foreign currency interest rates are fixed. In order to contribute to a rapid decrease of interest rates, it is convenient to accompany inflation reduction with structural reforms in the financial sector, thereby making it more competitive and eliminating a series of added expenses which raise the cost of money.

SALARIES

For purposes of economic policy, the minimum wage has remained virtually unchanged. It has undergone almost no modification or the adjustments that have been made were designed in such a way that they have been practically irrelevant and have failed to contribute to the liberalization of the labor market. For instance, the minimum wage was increased from 4 to 25 soles per month in the second half of 1990. In January 1991, it was raised to 38 soles and was kept there for the entire year, while the inflation rate hit 139 percent. In 1992, the minimum wage was maintained at 72 soles, with an inflation rate of 57 percent, whereas in 1993 it should have been kept at 92 soles, following the trajectory of the expected rate of inflation for 1993.

In the private sector, wages were reduced as a result of hyperinflation from 100 in 1987 to 29 in 1990, subsequently rising to 34 at the end of 1992. Salaries were reduced to 32 and rose to 48, respectively. Finally, wages for government workers were reduced from 100 in 1987 to 14 in 1990. They later rose to 28 in 1992.

Hyperinflation is the worst enemy of remuneration. In a very short time, inflation shrinks purchasing power to extremely low rates. Stabilization programs also reduce salaries, but the primary cause for the reduction is hyperinflation. The cure must not be confused with the disease.

CONTROLLED PRICES

During Alan García's administration, regulated prices lagged so far behind international prices that a gallon of gasoline cost $.12, while in the United States it cost $1. An attempt was made to correct this price distortion in August 1990. Thus, for example, fuel prices rose sixfold; electricity, twofold; water, twofold; and telephone rates, fourfold. These price adjustments did not raise the prices of public services to international levels as the increases were made either for fiscal reasons or to balance each public enterprise's finances. Two and one-half years after the adjustments, fuels, potable water, and telephone rates were, in real terms, at half their August 1990 values, while electricity rates were 50 percent higher than the values they had reached at that time. This does not imply that regulated prices should be abolished but rather that it is necessary to determine the values of regulated prices according to international levels and to define a trajectory of adjustment for these prices in order to make public enterprises more efficient and thus suitable for privatization.

THE MICROECONOMIC REFORM OF MARKETS

Microeconomic reform encompasses the liberalization of the principal economic markets: the market of goods and services, the money market, and the labor market.

THE MARKET OF GOODS AND SERVICES

FOREIGN TRADE REFORM: IMPORTS

Policies implemented and perspectives regarding foreign trade reforms for imports were as follows:

- Import tariffs were reduced to only two levels, 15 percent and 25 percent, with the purpose of reaching a uniform 15 percent tariff as of 1995.

- Prohibitions, import restrictions, and tariff-like barriers (such as plant, animal, and other health regulations) were eliminated. It is still necessary to eliminate the discretionary power that exists in this regard in the Ministries of Health and Agriculture, however.

- Public enterprise importation monopolies, such as Empresa Nacional de Comercialización de Insumos (Enci), Empresa de Comercialización del Arroz (Ecasa), and Empresa de Petróleos del Peru (Petroperú), were eliminated. Regulations requiring the mandatory use of domestic materials in production and manufacturing process must be repealed.

- Tariff surcharges on four agricultural products — wheat, milk, rice, and sugar — have been restricted and are to be eliminated gradually by 1995.

- The free importation of second-hand goods was authorized with the exception of clothing, footwear, and personal care products. The fractioning of import duties on capital goods was permitted in order to stimulate investment and correct the "anti-investment" tendency.

- Import-supervisory agencies were contracted in order to reduce undervaluation and deter corruption. Customs reforms were aimed at facilitating procedures and reducing corruption and smuggling. Institutions that regulated foreign trade, such as the Foreign Trade Institute (Instituto de Comercio Exterior, ICE)) were also eliminated.

- Antidumping regulations and compensatory fees were approved and applied via an ad-hoc committee according to the guidelines established in the General Agreement on Tariffs and Trade (GATT).

FOREIGN TRADE REFORMS: EXPORTS

The policies implemented with respect to foreign trade reforms for exports were as follows:

- Taxes on traditional exports and subsidies on non-traditional exports (for example, Certex and the Fund for Nontraditional Exports [Fondo de Exportaciones No-Tradicionales, Fent]) were eliminated. The IGV was reinstituted for all kinds of exports, and the temporary admission mechanism became automatic.

- Several export monopolies and controls were eliminated, as well as export certificates and other surcharges, such as contributions to the Fishermen's Fund (la Caja del Pescador) as a prerequisite for exporting in the fishing sector.

- Existing export contracts must be renegotiated whether they are Certex's contracts or debt for products. New contracts must not be approved.

- Private mechanisms for the promotion of exports must still be identified.

GENERAL TRADE REFORMS

The following general trade reforms have been implemented:

- A reduction of port fees to international levels is in progress. The load reserve for maritime transport has been eliminated. An open-skies policy, the deregulation for air fares, and the deregulation of routes and fares for urban and inter-urban land transports have also been implemented.

- Various state merchandising monopolies have been eliminated. Ecasa has been liquidated, and Enci's activities should be oriented to channel food donations.

- Consumer defense, unfair competition, and antimonopoly regulation have been approved. A consumer protection agency, the Consumer Defense Institute (Instituto de Defensa del Consumidor, Indecopi), has been created.

These mechanisms must be applied carefully, however, inasmuch as the cure is often worse than the illness. The government is generally a poor watchdog of the quality of private sector production. Market sanctions for the sale of defective merchandise are more effective than state intervention. On the whole, governmental regulations fail to prevent errors and are a source of corruption. In addition, free trade zones must be eliminated in order to reduce unfair competition with the domestic market, and industrial export free trade zones should be promoted.

THE LIBERALIZATION OF THE MARKET OF GOODS AND SERVICES: RESULTS AND PERSPECTIVES

Tariff reductions to levels of 15 and 25 percent and the elimination of restrictions on foreign trade have meant that the maximum surcharge permitted in the Peruvian economy is 25 percent. Thus, any product that cannot be produced with an advantage margin of 25 percent compared to the imported product has no possibility of competing and surviving in the Peruvian market. Since two tariff levels exist, the maximum level of effective protection that is given to an industry whose product has a 25 percent tariff and whose raw materials have a tariff of 15 percent is 38 percent in terms of added value.

Smuggling causes a loss of protection as smugglers evade not only tariffs but also domestic taxes, such as the General Sales Tax (IGV) and the Selective Consumption Tax (ISC). Prompt correction of this distortion is urgently needed, preferably through market mechanisms rather than repressive measures. Possible instruments include reaching a uniform tariff of 15 percent as soon as possible, lowering the ISC on luxury goods (liquors, tobacco, jewelry, electric home appliances, and electronic appliances in general, for example) to 10 percent, and eliminating free trade zones in order to achieve tariff uniformity. Repressive measures such as the confiscation and destruction of smuggled goods must be implemented automatically, but these are less effective than market mechanisms.

The liberalization of foreign trade allows Peruvian consumers freedom of choice from among a great variety of domestic and imported goods offered at affordable and competitive prices. Before liberalization, for example, an auto buyer was limited to a selection of three models, the cheapest of which sold for the $25,000, payable in cash. At the present time, however, all types of cars are available, with the lowest prices ranging from $6,000 or $7,000, payable in monthly installments of $200 to $300. Why should Peruvian consumers have to pay three or four times the international price for a car? The fact that domestic producers have more direct access to bureaucratic channels or politicians does not give them the right to obtain monopolistic profits or to cover their inefficiency at the expense of the people.

The importation of consumer goods increased from $251 million in 1989 to $638 million in 1991. Imports of raw materials grew from $1.089 to $1.597 billion, while imports of capital goods rose from $666 to $934 million during the same period.

Positive results can also be appreciated in the transportation sector. Before urban transportation fares and routes were liberalized, price controls and a monopoly on the concession of routes produced a scarcity of transportation services, the deterioration of vehicles, and strikes every time a new fare increase was being negotiated. As a result of price deregulation, the number of vehicles in circulation grew significantly. Today, passengers travel comfortably in new vehicles, and fares have not risen significantly as a result of increased competition. Moreover, to the degree that the number of vehicles grows, the unions will progressively lose power; as of mid-1993, no strikes have been organized in the sector.

Periodic increases in fares are due to inflation, not liberalization. Critics claim that liberalization has caused a great deal of traffic, congestion, and pollution and that it will cause many new carriers to go bankrupt, but congestion or abundance is preferable to scarcity. If the government must intervene to resolve this problem, it should do so by applying free market norms, such as the opening of new access routes in congested areas. The market also regulates itself: many carriers will avoid congested areas to avoid losing money. Pollution is not limited to the transportation sector; it should therefore be combatted globally by the government through the application of market mechanisms. Regarding bankruptcies, insolvency is a risk every enterprise must take in a market economy. In a market economy, profits and losses are privatized. If things work, profits are generated. If there are no profits, the company either gets out of the market or reorients itself toward other activities.

The liberalization of routes and fares for domestic air transportation has permitted the operation of six airlines instead of the two that previously held an oligopoly. As a result of competitive pricing strategies, it is now cheaper, in relative terms, to use air rather than ground transportation. With respect to maritime transportation, the elimination of the "cargo reserve" — that is, the requirement that 50 percent of all Peruvian import or export cargo be transported by Peruvian flagships — has triggered competition between domestic and foreign freight carriers, resulting in a reduction of up to 50 percent in freight costs as well as the loss of domestic market for the domestic shipping companies, which can no longer count on legal advantages. Thus, freight exports decreased from $138 to $59 million between 1989 and 1991, while imports rose from $163 to $350 million. This situation favored both the domestic producer and the consumer, who received cheaper and more competitive service.

THE MONEY MARKET

FINANCIAL REFORM: POLICIES IMPLEMENTED AND PERSPECTIVES

The following measures have been implemented in carrying out financial reform:

- Various financial institutions were privatized and restructured. Institutions that had been expropriated were returned to their legitimate owners. Central Bank credits for the public and private sectors were eliminated, and the Banco de la Nación was significantly reduced. Insolvent financial institutions such as the Development Banking System (la Banca de Fomento) and several state and private banks, savings and loan associations, and cooperatives were methodically liquidated. In addition, the Finance Corporation for Development (Corporación Financiera para el Desarrollo, COFIDE) was converted into a second-tier bank.

- Savings in foreign currency which had been expropriated by the García administration were returned to their holders at the market exchange rate.

- Bias was eliminated by passing uniform legislation for all financial institutions. A new supervisory system was established to oversee financial institutions, and the Superintendency of Banking and Insurance (Superintendencia de Banca y Seguros, SBS) was restructured. An insurance fund, the Insurance and Deposits Fund (Fondo de Seguros y Depósitos), was created to guarantee savings and prevent bank runs.

- The process of restructuring the financial system's portfolios has begun, though the proper orientation must lead to frank and free negotiation between creditors and debtors. The state should avoid buying portfolios or granting subsidies.

- New legislation has guaranteed the autonomy of the Banco Central de Reserva del Perú, preventing its financing public sector expenditure. However, the BCR must still be recapitalized in order to eliminate the quasi-fiscal deficit.

- The insurance and reinsurance market has been liberalized, making it possible for the consumer to choose from both domestic and international insurance markets. A new law has liberalized the stock market, eliminating barriers to entering the market as well as taxes on capital gains in order to be competitive in international markets.

- Commercial loans to the agricultural sector have been facilitated by the elimination of the prerequisite of agricultural pledges (prenda agrícola).

- New legislation has been passed to regulate the system of cooperatives, and the National Institute for Cooperatives (Instituto Nacional de Cooperativas, INCOOP) has been liquidated.

Nevertheless, government guarantees on private sector transactions, such as Credit Insurance for Exports (Seguro de Crédito a la Exportación, Secrex), must still be eliminated.

The Results of Financial Reform

Remonetization

During the hyperinflationary period of 1988-1990, the accumulation of money intermediated by the system was reduced from 18 percent of the average GDP in 1983-1984 to 4 percent in August 1990. By December 1991, remonetization had increased this amount to 8 percent of the GDP. Following this gain, the twenty-seven existing financial institutions intermediated slightly over one-third of the amount they had previously managed. Considering that these institutions were operating with the same number of branches and employees, this situation was equivalent to a reduction in banking sales of 70 percent during this period. In comparison, financial intermediation in Chile is equivalent to 30 percent of the GDP, while in the United States, it is 80 percent of the GDP.

Remonetization has gradually taken place by means of the issuance of currency by the BCR. This currency has been used to buy dollars and obtain foreign currency, internally or externally, in order to satisfy the country's liquidity needs. Dollars that had been hidden under mattresses because of the loss of confidence created by the García administration's expropriation of savings began to reappear between September 1990 and May 1991.

Between May 1991 and December 1992, Peruvian capital started to return either to earn higher interest rates than in Miami or to recapitalize Peruvian enterprises. During the same period, "swallow" capital *(capital golondrina)* appeared due to investments made by Peruvian or foreign investors, mainly Latin Americans. By the end of 1992, $2.5 billion had entered the country from all of these sources.

Investments in the stock market, which are processed through the banking system, have been revitalized because of increased confidence in the economic reform program, the liberalization of the stock market, and the privatization process. The stock market has experienced strong growth and strong activity since 1991. Stock market investments convert the so-called "swallow" capital into investment capital. Stock market indexes increased over 100 in December 1991, reaching 373 in December 1992, when shares in banks and public services multiplied fivefold and sixfold, respectively. Trading volume grew from 51 million soles in December 1991 to 200 million soles in December 1992.

DOLLARIZATION

Dollarization has become more prevalent due to past hyperinflation. As of 1992-1993, 37 percent of total liquid assets are in soles, whereas 63 percent are in foreign currency. In terms of "quasi-money," 80 percent is in foreign currency, while the remaining 20 percent is in domestic currency. This tendency, which will continue for some years, will revert gradually as inflation falls and expectations of a significant exchange adjustment diminish.

SOLVENCY

During 1991 and 1992, the Peruvian financial system was extremely fragile. The Development Banking System was insolvent. Five banks with heavy portfolios — Banco Popular, Central de Cooperativas de Crédito (CCC), Caja de Ahorros de Lima, Surmeban, and Banco Central Hipotecario — registered great losses. These same banks failed in 1992. In addition, other financial institutions confront serious problems and are not considered to be adequately capitalized.

On the whole, the Peruvian financial system is going through a severe process of adjustment. Many banks are either bankrupt or in trouble; thus, they are reducing personnel and closing branches by more than 10 percent. Banks are also adjusting by investing in modernization: computers, information management systems, communications, the training and development of human resources, provisions for bad debts, and higher capitalization.

BANK PRODUCTIVITY

A bank's productivity can be measured by the amount of deposits handled by each employee. In 1992, each Peruvian bank employee managed an average of $135,000 in deposits. This figure was multiplied fourfold by the most efficient banks. In comparison, U.S. banks had an average productivity of $4 to $6 million per employee, while Chilean banks handled $1 million per employee.

INTEREST RATES AND BANK PROFITS

The distribution of rates and the foreign currency spread for 1992 are shown in Table 2.

Table 2.

Concept	Interest%
Savings income	8.0
Bank's margin	2.7
Treasury income	5.0
• ISC (15%)	3.2
• Assets tax (1%)	1.5
• Contribution to the Superintendency of Banking and Insurance (SBS)	0.3
Cash reserve cost	8.5
Total cost to client	24.2

The total cost to the client is 24 percent of the loan rate, of which 33 percent corresponds to the savings holder's income; 33 percent, to the cost of the BCR legal reserves; 20 percent, to Treasury income; and 11 percent, to the bank's margin.

The breakdown of a bank's margin for every $100 deposited is shown in Table 3.

Table 3.

Bank Margin per $100 Deposited		Percent
Cash reserve income	$50 x 4%	2.0
Loan income	$50 x 21	10.5
Gross income		12.5
Liability rate		8.0
Income before taxes		4.5
Less the following:		
Taxes on assets		(1.5)
Contribution to the SBS		(0.3)
Net margin		2.7

The less solvent banks are those which have higher deposit and loan rates with respect to those which have average solvency as well as the most efficient banks.

The informal banking system is not subject to cash reserve requirements, taxes, or contributions to the Superintendency of Banking and Insurance (SBS). In the informal system, deposit rates in foreign currency range from 12 to 20 percent, while interest rates on foreign currency loans run 30 percent or more. These institutions have margins that allow them to pay the formal loan rate (8-11 percentage points), taxes (5 points), plus legal reserves (8.5 points), that is, 21.5 to 24.5 percent of the liability rate. With a margin of 10 percent, they reach 30 or 35 percent.

Informal institutions make loans by means of systems such as compensatory deposits (3 to 1); that is, they lend S/.100 and deposit S/.33 as reserve. They also protect themselves with high guarantees and have enforceable collection mechanisms that do not apply to the formal banking system. These institutions are in permanent risk of repeating the Refisa phenomenon.[15]

CAN THE INTEREST RATE BE REDUCED?

A number of factors could contribute to the lowering of interest rates in Peru. First of all, a decline in inflation would allow the interest rate on deposits in domestic currency to be reduced by a similar magnitude and would be conducive to diminishing devaluatory expectations. Thus, the rates on deposits in domestic and foreign currency would tend to converge. Second, a reduction of the country risk, which could be achieved in the medium and long terms through political and economic stability, would lead to a decline in interest rates on foreign currency deposits.

A third factor which could contribute to lowering interest rates would be the reduction of the surcharges that the government charges the financial system. Thus, for example, regarding public finance, it was necessary to eliminate the tax on withdrawals or the 1.0 percent tax on checks so that banks could attract cheap money as well as eliminate the tax on loan interest payments (the ISC, which was 15 percent). Banks have also proposed to study the possibility of reducing or eliminating the 1 percent tax on assets as another way to achieve this goal. In monetary matters, they propose a gradual reduction of marginal cash reserves in foreign currency, which are presently at 50 percent. In addition, some analysts have suggested the elimination or significant reduction of the contribution financial institutions make to the Superintendency of Banking and Insurance (SBS).

A fourth element which would lead to a decrease in interest rates would be to disentangle the financial sector through the restructuring or eventual elimination of insolvent public banks in conjunction with intervention and the systematic liquidation of insolvent private banks and financial institutions. Furthermore, strict guidelines ensuring financial prudence should be applied by the SBS in order to make provisions for these institutions' bad debts and their capitalization.

Another contributing factor would be adjustments made by banks and financial institutions regarding the rationalizing of personnel, the number of branches in operation, and security and computing costs as well as the cost of product creation and innovation, marketing strategies, and new management. Finally, the fostering of further competition in the financial system, the attraction of foreign investment through the privatization of financial institutions, a reduction of the cost of foreign loans due to taxes, and the creation of new banks with higher capitalization levels would also lead to a decline in interest rates.

THE FOREIGN CURRENCY MARKET

The liberalization of exchange regulations has had the effect of attracting capital instead of promoting capital flight, as was the case in the past. Capital began to flow into the country in April 1991, reaching levels of $100 to $120 million a month. To date, some $2.5 billion in short-term funds (new money or money repatriated from abroad) has entered the country, a sum which is being used in the remonetization and recapitalization of the country.

THE LABOR MARKET

POLICIES IMPLEMENTED AND PERSPECTIVES

The following policies have been implemented in the area of labor reform:

- The system of occupational stability has been made more flexible. The application of the system of workers' community *(comunidad laboral)* has been limited to the distribution of profits under more uniform profit-sharing schedules.

- The authority to cancel the payment of compensation for time of service (Compensación por Tiempo de Servicios, CTS) has been established. A process of collective negotiations to foster direct communication between the employers and their employees has been established. Strikes have been regulated and democratized. In addition, the principle of "A day not worked is a day not paid" has been implemented with the object of significantly reducing the number of strikes organized by workers.

- The closing of workplaces is now permitted without previous authorization from the Ministry of Labor. Labor interests have been adjusted to market rates. Working hours have been made more flexible, and shifts and working conditions have been modified and improved.

- The state has discontinued the practice of fixing the minimum wage rate. Indexation of salaries has been eliminated, allowing salary levels to be determined by market and productivity criteria. The construction sector's "laborers' market" and similar practices have been eliminated.

- Monopolies such as the Maritime Work Control Commission (Comisión Controladora de Trabajo Marítimo, CCTM) have been eliminated.

- The concentration of power in the sector-based unions, entrepreneurial organizations, and in the government has been reduced.

- The concept of a three-party consensus between entrepreneurs, labor, and government has been replaced by a system of negotiation between entrepreneurs and the workers.

- A private retirement system, managed by Retirement Funds Management Enterprises (Administradoras de Fondos de Pensiones, AFPs) has been approved. This agency has been duly regulated and is overseen by an entity established for this purpose, the Superintendency of Retirement Funds Management Enterprises (Superintendencia de Administradoras de Fondos de Pensiones, SAFP).

State intervention must be avoided in areas that are characteristic of a "benefactor state," such as the creation of programs that would administer unemployment insurance, health insurance, supplementary allowances for families with small children, rental supplements, and so on. Programs such as these generate bureaucracy, and assistance rarely reaches those who genuinely need it (those who live in conditions of extreme poverty) as it tends to filter toward those in higher income sectors. In addition, people become accustomed to living on subsidies instead of working.

THE RESULTS OF LABOR REFORM

Labor reform has contributed to changing workers' attitudes and creating an awareness of the importance of keeping a steady job. The number of work-hours lost as a consequence of walkouts or strikes has been reduced considerably between 1988 and 1992, from 38 million hours lost in 1988 to 15 million in 1990, 10 million in 1991, and 1.2 million in 1992. The number of workers involved in strikes was reduced from 690,000 in 1988 to fewer than 136,000 in 1991. Thus, we have reached the lowest figures in many years.

Employment indexes have been reduced significantly, from 100 in 1980 to 84 in 1990 and 67 in 1992. The sectors most affected by labor reform have been commerce, industry, and services. These results are to be expected at the beginning of a stabilization and structural reform process, however. We must not forget that the ultimate cause of these effects was hyperinflation.

The reform of the national pension program encountered a very complex reality. At the onset of 1991, more than three million workers were contributing to the system. In 1992, this figure was reduced to 1.7 million as a result of the expansion of the informal sector and the downsizing of the productive sector.

In 1989, the National Pension System (Sistema Nacional de Pensiones, SNP), whose income had fallen from 2 percent to 1 percent of the GNP, collapsed when contributions failed to cover the payment of benefits. SNP reserves currently total $360 million, while obligations with pensioners and contributors amount to $29,500 billion. Fifteen percent of these obligations must be paid out to current pensioners until the term of obligation is completed, while the remaining 85 percent corresponds to the funds that will have to be paid to present contributors in the form of benefits already acquired within the system. Thus, the gap in the system amounts to $29.140 billion, which is the responsibility of the government. Given this bind, there are three alternatives which could impede the gap from growing wider: 1) reduce benefit payments even more, 2) increase contributions, or 3) close down the system. The third alternative is the most viable solution.

The Peruvian Social Security Institute (Instituto Peruano de Seguridad Social, IPSS) was inefficiently managed and thus showed negative results between 1985 and 1990. During this period, bureaucracy grew from 28,000 to 41,000 employees, administrative expenditure grew from 14 to 21 percent of total expenditure, and the population covered by Social Security increased threefold, while its income was reduced by half. In order to balance the budget, payments were reduced by 77 percent in real terms, and health benefits were so deficient that 20 percent of those who are insured now also have private insurance. Pension funds and the health care program were both plagued by poor management and corruption.

Luis Castañeda Lossio became director of the IPSS in 1990. He has reorganized the institution, reduced personnel, and improved the quality of medical care. Regarding pension payments, however, little can be done due to the insolvency of the National Pension System (SNP). The Peruvian Social Security Institute must be eliminated as a manager of retirement funds because of its insolvency. This should include the sale of its property. A private retirement system is the only effective solution to the problem.

The private pension system (Administradoras de Fondos de Pensiones, AFP) was to start operating in June 1993, with at least seven enterprises. It is essential that contributions to the AFPs be equal to those made to the IPSS. In addition, the retirement age should be increased to sixty-five years. The various retirement plans must be made uniform, eliminating privileges and personal gain. The new system should also include a number of the existing special retirement funds, such as the military, police, and the teachers' retirement plans.

REFORM OF THE PROPERTY STRUCTURE

PRIVATIZATION OF PUBLIC ENTERPRISES

One hundred eighty public enterprises, with approximately 200,000 employees and 1988 book-value assets (in the case of the nonfinancial enterprises) of $5.500 billion currently generate 15 percent of the GNP. The most important of these are in the oil, energy, mining, and telecommunications sectors. Between 1985 and 1989, public enterprises lost $1.685 billion.

In 1991, shares of two enterprises — Sogewiese Leasing S.A. and Compañías de Minas Buenaventura — were sold to the private sector in stock market auctions. A price of $2.3 million was paid for them. In 1992, ten additional public enterprises were sold either by public auction or in the stock market, for a total price of close to $247 million. These were Buses de Enatru ($11 million), Grifos de Petroperú ($37.4 million), Minera Condestable ($1.3 million), Banco de Comercio ($5.4 million), Química del Pacífico ($4.4 million), Industrias Navales S.A. ($807,000), Solgás ($7.3 million), Minpeco USA ($4.1 million), Hierroperú ($120 million), and Aeroperú ($55 million). Two financial enterprises that could not be privatized — Banco Popular del Perú and Surmeban — were liquidated that year. Moreover, the delay in the privatization of Aeroperú produced losses close to $50 million, which had to be covered by the Treasury. These sales were effected despite the events of April 5, 1992, which could have paralyzed the process due to the political and judicial instability that was created. The privatization schedule established for 1993 is shown in Table 4.

Table 4. Privatization Schedule 1993

January	Fibras, Cementos Lima, Renasa, and Flopesca
February	Empresa Siderúgica del Perú (Siderperú)
March	Petrolera Transoceánica, Refinería Conchán, Reaseguradora Peruana, Petróleos del Mar (Petromar), Servicios Petroleros (Serpetro), and Commsa
July	Sedapal, Compañía Peruana de Teléfonos (CPT).
August	Empresa Nacional de Telecomunicaciones (Entelperú)
December	Empresa Minera del Centro del Perú (Centromín), Electricidad de Lima (Electrolima), Electroperú, Papelera Peruana, Paramonga, Banco Continental, and INTERBANC
No fixed date	Cementos Yura, Cerper, Empresa de Sal (Emsal), Empresa Nacional del Tabaco (Enata), Empresa Nacional de Servicios Pesqueros (Epsep), Fertilizantes, S.A. (Fertisa), and Empresa Nacional Pesquera (Pescaperú)

However, this schedule was not met and had to be corrected. The best possible scenario would be that by December 31, 1994, some 180 public enterprises would be privatized. The most important hurdles the privatization process has encountered are the "loss of sovereignty" prejudice, bureaucratic opposition (due to loss of power and status), and the misconception that enterprises must not be sold while the market is depressed and that profitable enterprises should not be privatized.

Reforms Promoting Domestic and Foreign Investment

The following reforms have been implemented to promote domestic and foreign investment:

- Legislation providing a framework for domestic and foreign investment has been approved with the purpose of fomenting and attracting investments.

- Agreements that guarantee foreign investments, such as Miga and Opic, have been signed. The Paris Agreement and other bilateral agreements are still pending. The Ministry of Economy and Finance has been authorized to sign agreements to avoid tax duplication.

- Legislation regarding industrial property rights has been approved, including the concept of the patentability of medicines, inventions, and other activities for a one-year period.

- Litigation with several foreign investors has been resolved; these include Southern Peru Copper Corporation, Occidental Petroleum, and Japeco. Still pending are lawsuits with Belco-Aig and Petrolera Ganso Azul as well as an agreement for the exploitation of gas deposits in the Camisea region.

- Legislation regarding the concession of goods and services to the private sector has been ratified, along with sector-specific laws that permit sales or concessions for the exploitation of natural resources.

- Norms and agreements for migration-investment have been approved in order to promote foreign investment.

- Legislation regarding bankruptcies has been quickly approved so that insolvent enterprises can leave the market through clear procedures and within a very short time.

- Legislation has been provided to facilitate mergers and restructuring.

Foreign investment, which during García's five-year term reached the insignificant amount of $15 million, has grown to $600 million for 1991-1992, as a result of norms regulating and promoting foreign investment. Southern Peru Copper Corporation invested approximately $300 million after the conclusion of litigation, while OXY invested $60 million, and Newmond will invest about $35 million in the gold mines of Cajamarca over the next five years. Other investments include Televisa's investment in Channel 4 and foreign acquisition via the privatization process of companies such as Química del Pacífico, Solgás, Hierroperú, Aeroperú, and Quellaveco. Peruvian domestic investment is neither sufficiently ample nor capable of moving great amounts of money to finance projects. For these reasons, if a fast takeoff toward modernity is desired, Peru needs to act swiftly and vigorously to mobilize foreign investment.

PROPERTY BY SECTORS

With respect to agriculture, fishing, energy and mining, industry, housing, and infrastructure, it will be necessary to build upon the following measures, which have already been implemented:

AGRICULTURE

In the agricultural sector, free land transfers have been made available, land may now be used as collateral, subsidized credit has been eliminated, and domestic and foreign trade in agricultural products has been deregulated. The cost of water has been established at market levels. Agrarian reform must be terminated, and agricultural organizations (cooperatives, the Sociedad Agrícola de Interés Social, and so on) must be allowed to choose freely and democratically the entrepreneurial model they wish to follow.

FISHING

In the fishing sector, state intervention has been eliminated in the establishing of transformation coefficients, the use of different kinds of ships, and so on.

ENERGY AND MINING

Fuels and energy prices must be liberalized or regulated based on efficient international models in the case of state monopolies. The government should cease to engage in the exploitation of mining and oil reserves.

INDUSTRIES

In the industrial sector, norms and guidelines have been established for securing patents in order to protect the consumer.

HOUSING

The rental market of the housing sector has been liberalized, but it is necessary to deepen this reform and eliminate rent control. In addition, regulations governing new construction must be made more flexible.

INFRASTRUCTURE

Monopolies in the assignment of public works projects must be eliminated by means of domestic and international competition. The private sector must be in charge of the construction of public works. The polynomial formula in construction contracts linking the state and the private sector must be eliminated.

REFORM OF THE STATE

THE SIZE OF THE STATE

Very little has been done in relation to downsizing the state. The Ministry of Housing and Construction merged with the Ministry of Transportation and Communications; however, neither FONAVI nor Land Improvement Services was included in the merger. In fact, the Ministry of the Presidency now oversees land improvement matters, which directly contradicts the proposed restructuring. To date, only the National Planning Institute (Instituto Nacional de Planificación, INP) and the Foreign Trade Institute (Instituto de Comercio Exterior, ICE) have been eliminated.

Regarding personnel reduction, 70,000 employees out of a total of 645,000 active central government workers have been relocated at a cost of over $80 million. The central government should be reduced by decreasing the number of ministries from fourteen to eight. Only the following should remain: Foreign Relations; Defense; Interior; Economy, Finance, and Trade; Social Issues (Education, Health, Labor); Productive Issues (Industry, Tourism, Agriculture, Fishing, Mining, Oil); Infrastructure (Energy, Transports, Communications, Housing, and Sanitation); Presidency (Presidency, Justice, Regional Affairs).

There should be only one central entity with ministerial rank, the National Compensation for Social Development Fund (Fondo Nacional de Compensación para el Desarrollo Social, Foncodes), dedicated to the alleviation of extreme poverty. The National Institute for Public Administration (Instituto Nacional de Administración Pública, INAP) must be eliminated. Fifty-two out of a total of seventy decentralized public entities must be privatized or eliminated.

Six autonomous government institutions must be strengthened or created:

1. Central Bank of Reserves (Banco Central de Reserva del Perú, BCR);

2. General Controller's Office (Contraloría General de la República, CGR);

3. National Tax Administration Superintendency (Superintendencia Nacional de Administración Tributaria, SUNAT);

4. National Customs Administration Superintendency (Superintendencia Nacional de Administración de Aduanas, SUNAD);

5. Superintendency of Banking and Insurance (Superintendencia de Banca y Seguros, SBS); and

6. Superintendency of Retirement Funds Management Enterprises (Superintendencia de Administradoras de Fondos de Pensiones, SAFP).

Central government personnel would be relocated through the decentralization of health and education services, early retirement incentives, personnel selection by means of objective examinations, and privatization. This would permit the restructuring of the public sector's salary pyramid, the creation of permanent evaluation systems, and the establishment of public service as a profession.

TAX REFORM

The objectives of tax reform are to reach a tax rate of 13.5 percent of GDP by 1995 and 15 percent by the year 2000 and to levy taxes on consumption, not investment. In addition, the number of taxes should be reduced to five —

the General Sales Tax (IGV); the Selective Consumption Tax (ISC); the Imports Tax (Impuestos a la Importación); the income tax (Impuesto a la Renta); and the Estate or Assets Tax (Impuesto al Patrimonio o a los Activos). Taxes must not be exported; therefore, the IGV would not apply to exports. Tax relief and exemptions of all types (whether by sectors or geographic location) must be eliminated. The remaining taxes, tariffs, contributions, and regional taxes must be eliminated. Local taxes must be regulated. It is necessary to eliminate or renegotiate fixed-tax agreements in order to prevent the creation of monopolies and distortions in the allocation of resources or privileges.

The General Sales Tax should be collected at a rate of 18 percent without exonerations. The Selective Consumption Tax should be applied to gasoline, beer, soda, and automobiles only. The Imports Tax should be levied at a flat rate of 15 percent. Personal and corporate income tax would be based on a reduced number of rates without deductions. The ideal case would be to establish a uniform rate in the region of 20 percent. The tax on assets has been conceived as a minimum income tax that could gradually be eliminated due to its anti-investment bias. Exonerations on interest, stock market revenues, and capital gains should gradually be eliminated. To the degree that the cash supply allows it, taxes that distort economic activity must be eliminated. For that purpose, the 1 percent tax on debits or checks, the financial institutions' Selective Consumption Tax of 15 percent on active operations, and a series of taxes and levies that distort and add costs to economic transactions have been eliminated.

A modern and efficient tax administration system has been created. The administration is widely accepted and respected, which has resulted in an increase in the number of taxpayers.

Additionally, a new tax law has been formulated, thereby making it less expensive to pay taxes than to evade them. This law necessarily includes a clause specifying imprisonment for tax evasion. Tax declarations should be prepared honestly. The idea that only fools pay taxes in Peru must be challenged and discredited.

EXPENDITURE REFORM

Very little has been done to reform expenditures. The general budget law has been separated from the annual budget law in order to make this process more transparent and less troublesome. Some progress has been made with the general fund (Caja Unica), but the incomes generated by FONAVI, SUNAD, and SUNAT, and the ministries (for example, Fishing, Exterior Relations, and so on) are still not included in this general fund.

Regarding public investment, no major reforms have been accomplished. Projects are not prioritized according to their profitability, nor does the private sector participate in the construction of these projects so as to free up government resources for other activities. Irrigation and hydraulic projects continue to be top priorities. To date, $2.1 billion has been invested in them, with another $3.7 billion yet to be used.

Moreover, it is necessary to establish criteria for debt assumption by the state with respect to structural reforms. The most relevant areas are privatization, education, and retirement and housing funds.

ATTENTION TO THE POOREST SECTORS OF PERUVIAN SOCIETY

With respect to the alleviation of poverty, the Poverty Alleviation Program (Programa de Alivio a la Pobreza) was inaugurated in August-September 1990, but it was later suspended as a result of lack of funds and poor management. In 1991 and the first semester of 1992, very little was accomplished in this area due to these problems. As of August 1992, monthly expenditures for poverty relief programs increased from $4 million to $30 million, and these programs were administered by a new manager recruited from the private sector.

In the education sector, legislation has been passed in the areas of decentralization, financing, and the promotion of private investment in education. This legislation constitutes the foundation for the country's greatest structural reform. As yet, no advances have been made in the areas of higher education, health, or housing.

A National Compensation for Social Development Fund (Fondo Nacional de Compensación para el Desarrollo Social, Foncodes) has been created. In order to be effective, this program must be autonomous, efficient, and nonpolitical. It should also allow for the procurement of significant donations from abroad.

ENVIRONMENTAL PROTECTION

Little has been achieved in the areas of environmental protection and conservation. A new regulatory framework was approved in December 1990; however, this code is excessively restrictive, having been modeled on regulations implemented in developed countries. For example, it fails to consider market mechanisms, a very serious deficiency inasmuch as property rights are probably the best mechanism with which to achieve this goal.

INSTITUTIONAL REFORMS

Except for some aspects related to the judiciary and to the election of the Constituent Congress, little or nothing has been accomplished in the area of institutional reform.

RESISTANCE TO STRUCTURAL REFORMS

Inasmuch as those who seek to preserve the traditional socioeconomic order do not wish to lose subsidies, privileges, or immunity, the "tyranny of the status quo" is the major obstacle to the structural reform program. Any significant progress that has been attained in this area is due to the great economic, social, and political crisis that the country experienced between 1988 and 1990. This crisis allowed for significant changes and the breaking of the "Iron Triangle." Nonetheless, this triangle strengthens with the passage of time, making it more difficult to proceed with structural reforms.

The first wave of structural reforms met resistance on various fronts. Peruvian business associations, led by the National Society of Industries (Sociedad Nacional de Industrias, SNI), attacked the reduction of tariffs through the media. Through the General Confederation of Peruvian Workers (Confederación General de Trabajadores del Perú, CGTP), Peruvian trade unions expressed their opposition to the labor policies that had been adopted. APRA members and leftists in Congress or those Cabinet members who supported their point of view joined in opposition to the reform process, voicing particular discontent with the privatization policies.

During the second wave of structural reforms, the toughest opposition came from the various political parties, either institutionally or through their representatives in Congress and the Tribunal of Constitutional Guarantees (Tribunal de Garantías Constitucionales). Several Cabinet members and I approached the media and held meetings with different political groups in order to defend the structural reform package. It was hard to believe that opponents from the extreme Left to the extreme Right, including ex-FREDEMO supporters, had taken issue with education reform, arguing that it undermined free education in the country; that they denounced labor reform, claiming they sought to defend workers; that they opposed the elimination of agrarian reform because their own proposed reform had been tabled several years earlier; that they attacked the elimination of the Maritime Work Commission (Comisión Controladora de Trabajo Marítimo, CCTM) because a number of political parties protected the institution; and that they rejected the privatization and deregulation of routes and transportation fares, which were annulled by the Tribunal of Constitutional Guarantees. Even more unusual was the fact that the ability to restructure the state was denied to us by one vote from the Liberty Movement (Movimiento Libertad), a political organization that had advocated institutional reform during the 1989-1990 campaign.

The tax policies implemented between January and March 1992 encountered serious opposition from certain Peruvian business associations, which fought for the reduction of the IGV, the elimination of the tax on assets, and the reduction or elimination of the ISC on fuels. They also demanded a more favorable exchange rate and even proposed a generalized Certex.

The strongest pressure against the third wave of structural reforms came from the business associations, the professional associations (when contributions to professional associations were eliminated), jungle and border regions (when their respective exemptions were eliminated), and trade unions (when legislation was passed regulating strikes, collective negotiations, occupational stability, and indexation). Finally, government bureaucrats opposed the privatization of public enterprises and retirement funds.

How Long Does It Take for Structural Reforms to Bear Fruit?

Many people wonder how long it should take for an economic program like the one implemented in Peru to bear fruit. Some deem that the country should be functioning efficiently in one year or two. These estimates amount to little more than wishful thinking, however. How long would it take for an experienced entrepreneur to reestablish a bankrupt enterprise? The answer is from two to three years. Now, let us consider the case of a country that has been in total bankruptcy, a country that has been getting poorer for at least the last forty years, a country without growth because of Velasco's socialist reforms, García's populist and demagogic policies, and the war against terrorism. It would require stabilization and the implementation of structural reforms. It would need to become a relatively risk-free country for investors so that it could be the recipient of international credit, and peace would need to reign in all the land. These tasks could easily take from seven to ten years. In order to confirm this estimate, let us make a comparison with other countries that experienced similar circumstances.

In Chile, the stabilization process took five years. Inflation decreased from 503 percent in 1973 to 30 percent in 1978. Growth increased from (minus) -5.6 percent in 1973 to 1 percent in 1974, subsequently falling to (minus) -13 percent in 1975 and then growing after 1977 at a rate of 8 percent per year for several years. The fiscal deficit was reduced from 25 percent of GNP in 1973 to 1 percent of GNP in five years. Exports increased from $1.2 billion in 1973 (before falling in 1975), to $4 billion in 1979 and $8 billion in 1989. Interest rates for loans were reduced from 251 percent in 1973 to 62 percent in 1979 and 36 percent in 1989.

Chile initiated an intense structural reform program in 1980. Sustained economic recovery began after a severe crisis in 1992 and 1983 precipitated the collapse of the entire financial system. In 1992, the country grew at a rate of 11 percent and lowered its inflation rate by 11 percent. Today, after 20 years of political stability and fifteen years of economic stability, Chile is no longer considered underdeveloped; in fact, it is considered the most stable and developed country in Latin America. Thus, Chile is an example of the successful application of an economic stabilization and reform program based on the principles of a market economy.

Bolivia also suffered hyperinflation during the period 1984-1985. The hyperinflation rate decreased from 8,170 percent in 1985 to 66 percent in 1986 and 11 percent in 1987. Economic growth fell to (minus) -1 percent and (minus) -2.5 percent in 1985 and 1986, respectively, and later rose between 2.5 and 3.5 percent annually during the following six years. The public deficit was reduced from 44 percent of GDP to levels between 3.0 and 3.5 percent during the following years. While exports experienced a progressive decline from $628 million in 1985 to $543 million in 1988, they subsequently increased to $724 million in 1989. Interest rates remained high between 1985 and 1992. Loan rates remained above 40 percent, with deposit rates at 24 percent between 1989 and 1992. Though Bolivia is a successful case of macroeconomic stabilization, the country has sustained very little growth due to the fact that insufficient progress was made with structural reforms. This notwithstanding, Bolivia, a country which is now recording moderate growth, has enjoyed eleven years of political stability and seven of economic stability.

A third case is that of Mexico. While this country did not fall into hyperinflation, it reached an inflation rate of 102 percent in 1983. Five years of adjustment and structural reforms were needed to lower inflation to 20 percent beginning in 1989. During this period, Mexico experienced three years of falling GDP as well as a substantial reduction of exports in 1985 and 1986. The interest rate remained at high levels for more than five years. Because Mexico implemented a stabilization program and deep structural reforms which enabled it to grow and lower inflation significantly, it is another example of successful stabilization and economic growth today.

The World Bank has carried out numerous studies to determine the ideal timing and sequencing of reforms aimed at transforming an economy that is centrally planned into a market economy. According to the World Bank, to effect this transition, it is necessary for the country to implement unprecedented, complex reforms, and there is no unique order for economies in transition. Hungary, for instance, has been one of the most experienced countries with respect to decentralized decisions; the former Soviet Union is implementing its reforms within a framework of great macroeconomic instability, while the opposite is occurring in the former Czechoslovakia. Vietnam and China have allowed for greater presence of the private sector in comparison with other countries.

With respect to the reform process itself, the World Bank has arrived at a number of important conclusions regarding the phases of reform:

- Reforms can take up to ten years.
- Macroeconomic reform requires stabilization within the first three years and maintained stability during the following years.
- Market reform encompasses the following:

1. In the market of goods and services, prices should be liberalized within the first two years followed by the liberalization of the prices of basic commodities during the next seven years. Commercial restrictions should be eliminated the first year, and tariffs should be adjusted to a moderate level during the following five years. Regarding distribution, privatization and demonopolization are to take place during the first three years, and distribution is developed during the following five years.

2. In the labor market, contracts and dismissals should be deregulated during the first two and one-half years. Salary negotiations are to be liberalized during the following four and one-half years.

3. The financial market should be restructured and developed during the first three years. Over the following six years, it should be liberalized and privatized.

- Legislation regulating foreign investment should be revised during the first two years. Reform of ownership structures implies developing and privatizing small enterprises during the first three years. Large companies should be evaluated, restructured, and privatized over a ten-year period.

- Governmental reform requires the modification of the legal framework (mercantile, property, and tax legislation, for example) during the first three years. The institutional framework should be reformed over a period of ten years. Reform of the social security network should be effected within one year in order to provide for emergencies, and these changes should be institutionalized during the following seven years.

According to the World Bank, "The reforms will undoubtedly bring difficult adjustments with them. Inflation and unemployment will worsen when price controls are eliminated and the real economic losses in some activities become evident. The political opposition may grow in that situation, because of the more acute inequality in the income distribution that occurs after a radical modification of the incentive structure. However, very shortly afterwards exports could start to grow as well as the availability of consumer goods." [16]

Regarding structural reform, Peru is well ahead of the standard timetable because the country desires to achieve in five years what has taken ten years in other countries. However, passing reforms is one thing, and achieving results is another. Having reviewed other experiences in Latin America, we envision that it should take between seven and ten years to achieve stabilization and self-sustained growth, provided the process evolves within a framework of political stability where law and order prevail. The more precarious these conditions, the longer the program will take to bear fruit.

CONCLUSIONS AND RECOMMENDATIONS

THE PROGRESS OF THE ECONOMIC PROGRAM

Peru experienced the worst economic crisis in its history during the Alan García administration (1985-1990). The hyperinflation rate reached annual levels of 7,605 percent; the GDP fell 20 percent between 1988 and 1990; international reserves fell to (minus) $-100 million; the public and quasi-public debt reached 16 percent of GDP; and the money supply grew hand in hand with inflation. With respect to law and order, moreover, Peru was losing ground in the war against terrorism, and in political terms, the García administration had concentrated power to an excessive degree.

In July 1990, García was succeeded by an independent, Alberto Fujimori, who defeated all the traditional political parties. A short time after becoming president, President Fujimori decided to implement an adjustment program to control hyperinflation. His initial plan failed in December 1990, and inflation rose again to levels of 24 percent per month.

In February 1991, Fujimori began the consistent and integral implementation of an economic policy founded on five major structural reforms, a foreign policy characterized by openness, the country's participation in the global economy, and the maintenance of constitutional government. The following structural reforms were implemented by the Fujimori administration: 1) macroeconomic reform; 2) market reform involving the liberalization of the markets of goods and services, money, and labor; 3) reform of the property structure through the privatization of state assets; 4) reform of the state to reduce its size and functions; and 5) institutional reform in order to achieve stability.

These structural reforms were implemented in three phases. The first stage, which lasted from January 12, 1991, until April of the same year, included sixty-one executive orders that initiated market liberalization and privatization. The second phase, from May 18 to November 15, 1991, included 117 legislative decrees under the protection of powers delegated to the Congress. This phase reinforced the preceding reforms, defining the scope of the privatization process. During the third phase, from April 5 to December 30, 1992, the spectrum of the reforms was broadened by extending the program to areas such as retirement pensions and education.

The macroeconomic reforms implemented began registering positive results by December 1992. Inflation was reduced from 7,650 to 57 percent per year. Net international reserves rose from (minus) $-100 million to $2 billion, and the cash deficit was reduced from 16 to 2.5 percent of GDP. The money supply grew at rates lower than inflation, and tax levels rose from 5 to 9.5 percent of GDP. Zero GDP growth was recorded during the period 1991-1992, but this was the cost to be paid for controlling hyperinflation.

Market reforms have also shown significant progress. The prices of goods and services have been liberalized and are now determined by the market. The prices of public utilities are now undergoing a process of liberalization. Peruvian markets have been significantly deregulated, and artificial monopolies have been eliminated almost completely. Foreign trade has been liberalized through the reduction of tariffs to an average level of 17 percent (with two levels, 15 percent and 25 percent), the elimination of tariff-like policies, and the liberalization of the foreign exchange market.

Reform of the property structure has also effected important changes. During 1992, ten public enterprises were sold to the private sector, generating a total of approximately $247 million. Foreign investments were stimulated, growing from $5 million a year during the García administration to more than $100 million per year during 1992 and 1993, and commitments have been made for more than $600 million for the period 1993 to 1998. Finally, the government has approved the granting of concessions for infrastructure and public services.

The reform of the state also demonstrates important progress. The workers' retirement system is in the process of becoming private, education is being municipalized and privatized, and tax reform has progressed. Public expenditure for the purpose of alleviating extreme poverty has been prioritized, and in 1993 it should have been increased from 0.5 to 1 percent of the GDP. In the area of institutional downsizing, including the reduction of employment in the public sector, there is no evident progress, however.

With respect to foreign policy and international participation, 1991 witnessed a number of great achievements. First, the Support Group (which gave Peru more than $700 million) was created. The RAP agreement signed with the IMF was largely successful during the fifteen months that it was applied. Finally, renegotiations with the Paris Club were successfully completed, arrears with the IDB were cleared, and more than $300 million in fresh funds were obtained.

Thanks to the fulfillment of the RAP, arrears with the IMF and the World Bank were cleared on March 18, 1993. After having been isolated from the financial world for more than seven years, Peru has again become eligible for financial transactions. This is a great step in the economic reinsertion process. Also, there is already a three-year program with the IMF, and we can count on fresh money from both the IMF and the World Bank. The immediate task for the short term is to negotiate with the Paris Club and the commercial banking system.

Repatriation and the influx of short-term capital have reached levels of $2.5 billion. Financial reform has permitted the liberalization of depressed markets in the financial system and has improved the levels of insolvency and prudence in the system. Regarding restructuring of the state, little progress has been made toward reduction of its size; however, important achievements have been made in the area of privatization. State assets have been sold for more than $250 million. With tax reform, the country has instituted a more equitable system of taxation and achieved increased collections as well as improved tax management. As a result of labor reform, the labor market has been liberalized, which in the medium term will render better levels of employment and real compensation. In the areas of retirement funds and education, important legislation has been approved. Finally, as for institutional reforms, the area in which the least progress has been made is the judicial branch of the government.

Regarding law and order, significant progress has been made. Terrorism was severely set back in 1992 with the capture of the leaders of the most active subversive groups. Also, civil initiatives on the part of the armed forces and the reform of the judicial branch combined with the control of corruption and drug trafficking will permit the country to advance on the road toward peace.

In conclusion, during the García administration, Peru was sunk in chaos and despair. Today, thanks to the structural reform program, it is a country with a future. The economy is recovering as a result of the Peruvian people's efforts and hard work, together with increased domestic and foreign investment. We must understand very clearly, however, that we are only halfway along a long, rough road. We must persevere in the change of direction that was initiated with the economic program for the 1990s.

THE PENDING AGENDA

With respect to economic stabilization, inflation is not yet under control. The balance of payments is not in equilibrium, and the level of international reserves must be strengthened, albeit cautiously. The fiscal deficit is not yet under control, and the rate of tax collection is still low. Finally, the money supply is not necessarily aligned with the program's goals. Fiscal and monetary discipline continue to be necessary in order to consolidate the stabilization of macroeconomic variables.

With respect to modernization and structural reforms, a great deal still remains to be done. No progress has been made regarding the restructuring of the state, public expenditure, the health sector, housing, or the alleviation of extreme poverty. The same holds true for institutional reforms. The regulation and implementation of reforms in the areas of education and the retirement system are still pending, although the legal frameworks for these reforms have been established.

In addition, the privatization of state-owned assets must be accelerated significantly if the process is to be completed in 1995, and progress must still be made in the reform of the productive sectors.

Finally, it is necessary to complete foreign trade reform by liquidating Enci and eliminating the tariff surcharges on agricultural products and the restrictions on the utilization of powdered milk in industry. It is also important for the country to withdraw from the Andean Group and terminate any bilateral negotiations of a mercantilist nature. The promotion of foreign investment requires the resolution of litigation with foreign investors, such as the cases pending with AIG-Belco and Ganso Azul.

Financial reform requires reducing the Banco de la Nación to a minimum while fostering competition among the various financial institutions. Labor reform requires a change in the systems of occupational stability and workers' community. On the other hand, tax reform requires the cancellation of any tax stability agreements that would generate monopolies or privileges as well as the elimination of all exonerations.

Regarding Peru's reinsertion in the global economy, negotiations with the Paris Club in order to reduce the debt and make the payment situation more viable are indispensable. Also necessary is the formation of a group of foreign donors for social support matters. The country must also comply with the established requirements in order to obtain the release of pending credit disbursement from the Inter-American Development Bank and the World Bank. These credits are to be used in the areas of trade, finance, privatization, agriculture, health, sanitation, housing, social support, and structural adjustment.

Also pending is the renegotiation of the foreign debt with the former socialist countries, the Latin American Integration Association (Asociación Latinoamericana de Integración, ALADI), the commercial banking system, and our purveyors. The purpose of these negotiations would be to reduce the foreign debt through debt exchange instruments such as debt for privatization, investment, natural resources, and social services.

Regarding democratic governability, numerous short- and long-term goals remain to be undertaken. The effort directed toward the constitutional control and limitation of the government has not been entirely effective. Therefore, it is important to start considering the possibility of modifying the existing constitutional mechanisms. Regarding the maintenance of law and order, little headway has been made in the fight against drug trafficking and corruption.

RECOMMENDATIONS AND FUTURE RESPONSIBILITIES

A new course has been outlined for Peru, but, as we have pointed out, the country has gone only halfway. If the process is to be completed successfully, each of the branches of government must assume a series of responsibilities in the coming years.

First of all, the legislative branch must prove its autonomy as well as its capacity to oversee, understand, and defend a program based on a market economy. The Constitution must create an adequate framework to limit the power of the government and protect individual rights. Finally, the economic program must remain in effect, and more progress must be made in the area of structural reforms.

The executive branch must not succumb to the temptation of concentrating power. A broader degree of democratization must be sought in the country. The progress made over a period of two and one-half years must not be lost by giving way to populist or authoritarian temptations.

The judicial branch must show its autonomy vis-à-vis the other branches of government. It must lead the moralization process and zealously safeguard the modernization of the country.

In addition, we must counteract the influence of intellectuals who are out of touch with today's realities and prone to favor the concentration of power at the expense of individual freedom. Students do not have many alternatives in our restricted academic world, and it is precisely in this world where we must point out the roads to social well-being and freedom.

NOTES

1. This article is a compilation based on Carlos Boloña's *Cambio de rumbo* (Lima: Instituto de Economía de Libre Mercado, 1993).

2. See AGENDA 2000 1991.

3. From several speeches by Alan García, especially the press conference of October 5, 1985. For further information, see Alan García Pérez N.d., 337-387.

4. Editor's translation of the author's Spanish-language version.

5. Editor's translation of the author's Spanish-language version.

6. Editor's translation of the author's Spanish-language version.

7. No first name was provided.

8. The term "Special Drawing Rights" (Derechos Especiales de Giro) is a unit of account used by the International Monetary Fund. The relative value of this unit is established by means of an estimated average of quoted values for main currencies.

9. Increase in the price of gasoline.

10. Package of price increases.

11. Little Pentagon.

12. Shining Path.

13. The Banco de la Vivienda had been liquidated.

14. Editor's translation of the author's Spanish-language version.

15. When the Refisa Bank went bankrupt, officials did not return an estimated $200 million in deposits.

16. Editor's translation of the author's Spanish-language version. For further information, see Table 7.7 in World Bank 1990, 170-171.

REFERENCES

AGENDA 2000. 1991. *Boloña y Büchi. Estrategas de cambio.* Lima: Editorial Diana.

Boloña, Carlos. 1993. *Cambio de rumbo.* Lima: Instituto de Economía de Libre Mercado.

Cagan, Philip. 1956. "The Monetary Dynamics of Hyperinflation." In *Studies in the Quantity Theory of Money,* ed. Milton Friedman. Chicago: The University of Chicago Press.

Friedman, Milton, and R.V. Roosa. 1967. *The Balance of Payments: Free vs. Fixed Exchange Rates.* Washington, D.C.: American Enterprise Institute.

García Pérez, Alan. N.d. *A la inmensa mayoría* (Discursos). Lima: EMI Editores.

Taylor, ___1989. "Introducción a la escuela austríaca de economía." In *Escuela austríaca de economía* (Historia -Metodología - Actualidad), eds. Taylor and White. Mexico: Centro de Estudios en Economía y Educación.

von Hayek, Friedrich A. 1979. *¿Inflación o pleno empleo?* Mexico: Editorial Diana.

Williamson, John. 1991. "Exchange Reserves as Shock Absorbers." In *The Open Economy,* eds. Rudiger Dornbusch and F.L.C.H. Helmers. Washington, D.C.: World Bank.

World Bank. 1990. *Economic Reforms to Sustain Stabilization and Law.* The Foundation for Development (Preliminary Report). Washington, D.C.: World Bank.

Annex

Table 1.
Macroeconomic Projections 1993-1995

Peru: Aggregate Public Sector (Percent of Gross Domestic Product)

	Estimated		Projected		
	1991	**1992**	**1993**	**1994**	**1995**
Central Government					
Current revenues[2]	8.2[1]	9.4	10.0	11.5	13.0
Current expenditure[2] (excluding interest)	-6.0	-6.9	-7.0	-6.7	-6.6
Of which: PES	0.5	0.5	0.6	0.5	0.4
Current account (excluding interest)	2.2	2.5	3.0	4.8	6.4
Savings of the Rest of the Nonfinancial Public Sector	1.1	1.2	1.0	0.7	0.4
Current Account of the Nonfinancial Public Sector (excluding interest)	3.3	3.7	4.0	5.5	6.8
Revenue from privatization	0.0	0.1	0.6	0.6	0.3
Structural reforms	0.0	-0.1	-0.6	-0.6	-0.3
Capital expenditures[3]	-2.4	-3.0	-3.1	-3.9	-4.7
Quasi-fiscal deficit	-0.4	-0.1	-0.1	0.0	0.0
Deficit Excluding Interest	-0.5	-0.6	-0.8	-1.6	-2.1
Interest (due)[4]	-3.4	-3.0	-3.1	-3.9	-4.7
Global Deficit	-3.0	-2.5	-2.9	-2.3	-1.8
Financing	3.0	2.5	2.9	2.3	1.8
Internal	-0.3	-0.1	0.0	0.0	0.0
External	3.3	2.4	2.9	2.3	1.8

Sources: Banco Central de Reserva del Perú, Ministry of Economy and Finance, and
    International Monetary Fund estimates.
PES = Social Emergency Program (Programa de Emergencia Social.)
1 = Includes the yield collected through FONAVI (6% over payroll).
2 = Excludes privatization resources.
3 = Includes 1992 financial investments.
4 = Includes external debt.

Table 2.
Peru: Medium-Term Program
(Annual Rate of Growth)

	1991	1992	1993	1994	1995
Real GDP	2.6	-3.0	3.5	4.5	5.0
Consumer prices (average for period)	409.2	73.1	37.4	18.9	11.5
Consumer prices (end of period) (as percentage of GDP)	139.2	54.4	27.0	15.0	9.2
I. Balance of Payments					
Current Account Balance	**-4.6**	**-5.2**	**-6.0**	**-5.7**	**-5.5**
Net exports of goods and nonfinancial services	-1.9	-2.8	-3.2	-2.7	-2.4
Net balance of financial services	-3.3	-2.9	-3.7	-3.8	-3.7
Other service and transfers	0.6	0.5	0.9	0.8	0.6
Capital Account	**5.6**	**5.9**	**6.4**	**6.0**	**5.7**
Public sector	3.3	2.4	2.9	2.3	1.8
Private capital	2.3	3.5	3.5	3.7	3.9
Change in net international reserves (gain)	-1.0	-0.7	-0.4	-0.3	-0.2
II. Aggregate Public Sector					
Balance of the Aggregate Public Sector	**-3.0**	**-2.5**	**-2.9**	**-2.3**	**1.8**
Nonfinancial public sector savings	0.2	0.6	0.3	1.6	2.9
Capital expenditures	2.4	3.0	3.1	3.9	4.7
Central Bank losses	-0.4	-0.1	-0.1	-	-
Global Deficit	**-3.0**	**2.5**	**2.9**	**2.3**	**1.8**
External financing	3.3	2.4	3.1	3.9	4.7
Internal financing	-0.3	0.1	-	-	-
III. Savings and Investment					
Investment	**16.2**	**15.6**	**16.2**	**17.5**	**18.8**
Public sector	2.4	3.0	3.1	3.9	4.7
Private capital	13.9	12.6	13.1	13.6	14.1
Savings	**16.2**	**15.6**	**16.2**	**17.5**	**18.8**
External savings	4.6	5.2	6.0	5.7	5.5
Internal savings	11.6	10.4	10.2	11.8	13.3
Aggregate public sector	-0.6	0.5	0.2	1.6	2.9
Private sector	12.2	9.9	10.0	10.2	10.4

Sources: Banco Central de Reserva del Perú and estimates by the staff of the International Monetary Fund (IMF).

Continued on next page

Table 2—*Continued*

	1991	1992	1993	1994	1995
Memo					
Public sector interest	3.4	3.0	3.7	3.9	3.9
Primary surplus (aggregate public sector)	0.5	0.6	0.8	1.6	2.1
Outstanding external debt (as percentage of GDP)	42.3	43.5	51.2	50.8	48.1
External debt servicing (percentage of exports of goods and nonfinancial services)	58.8	49.5	36.5	38.6	34.3
Of which: interest	34.3	31.9	32.5	32.1	30.9

Table 3. Peru: External Public Sector Financing
Public Finances (Summary) (Billions of Dollars)

	1991	1992	1993	1994	1995
Public Sector — External Financing					
Current account (excludes public debt interest)	-0.711	-1.154	-1.036	-0.886	-0.873
Current account	-2.199	-2.505	-2.529	-2.479	-2.542
Public debt interest and IMF burden	1.488	1.351	1.493	1.593	1.669
Public debt servicing (includes IMF servicing)	-2.544	-2.109	-2.472	-2.475	-2.569
Multilateral	-0.436	-0.401	-0.555	-0.607	-0.650
Bilateral	-1.213	-1.185	-1.322	-1.300	-1.333
Paris Club	-0.915	-0.824	-0.968	-0.985	-1.039
Others	-0.298	-0.361	-0.354	-0.315	-0.294
Private creditors	-0.895	-0.523	-0.595	-0.568	-0.586
Gross exchange reserves	-0.422	-0.328	-0.323	-0.314	-0.314
Change in arrears					
Multilateral	0	-0.988	-0.870	0	0
IMF	0	0	-0.870	0	0
World Bank	0	-0.988	0	0	0

Continued on next page

Table 3—*Continued*

	1991	1992	1993	1994	1995
Total financial requirements	-3.677	-4.579	-4.701	-3.675	-3.756
Possible sources of financing	3.677	4.579	4.701	3.675	3.756
Private capital	0.676	1.732	1.445	1.563	1.802
Disbursements (nonconfirmed, commitments)	0.225	0.280	0.283	0.344	0.289
Multilateral	0.057	0.114	0.114	0.186	0.224
Paris Club	0.168	0.166	0.169	0.158	0.065
Multilateral disbursements (in cash)	0.325	1.138	1.343	0.445	0.268
IMF	0	0	1.032	0.185	0.208
World Bank	0	0.988	0.150	0.250	0.050
IDB	0.325	0.150	0.161	0.010	0.010
Relief (rescheduled)	2.081	1.1255	1.220	1.215	1.199
Multilateral	0.121	0	0	0	0
Bilateral	1.073	0.779	0.692	0.707	0.673
Paris Club	0.914	0.556	0.484	0.520	0.490
Other	0.159	0.223	0.208	0.187	0.183
Private creditors	0.887	0.476	0.528	0.508	0.526
Additional financial requirements	0.370	0.174	0.410	0.108	0.198
Possible multilateral financing	0.370	0.174	0	0	0
Earmarked for projects	0	0.042	0	0	0
Cash	0.370	0.132	0	0	0
Remaining gap	0	0	0.410	0.108	0.198
Memo:					
Payments to IMF	0.096	0.022	0.950	0.087	0.099
Interest	0.061	0.008	0.063	0.087	0.099
Principal	0.035	0.014	0.887	0	0
Current	0.035	0.014	0.017	0	0
Arrears	0	0	0.870	0	0
IMF access quotas	0	0	0.162	0.185	0.208

Table 4. Peru: Balance of Payments
(Billions of Dollars)

	1991	1992	1993	1994	1995
Current Account	-2.199	-2.505	-2.529	-2.479	-2.542
Trade balance	-0.165	-0.639	-0.609	-0.483	-0.378
Exports	3.329	3.333	3.466	3.711	4.046
Imports	-3.494	-3.972	-4.075	-4.194	-4.424
Services and transfers	-2.034	-1.866	-1.920	-1.996	-2.164
Nonfinancial services	-0.724	-0.726	-0.704	-0.673	-0.739
Transfers	0.268	0.283	0.338	0.312	0.295
Capital Account	1.008	1.296	0.858	1.081	1.191
Public sector	-0.816	-0.680	-0.538	-0.611	
Disbursements	0.205	0.280	0.283	0.344	0.289
Depreciation	-1.021	-0.743	-0.963	-0.882	-0.900
Private sector (includes errors and omissions)	1.824	1.579	1.535	1.619	1.802
Total Balance	-1.702	-1.209	-1.756	-1.454	-1.351
Changes in the net reserves of the Central Reserve Bank[1]	-0.457	-0.342	-0.178	-0.129	-0.106
Rescheduling	0.537	0.556	0.484	0.520	0.490
Change in arrears	-3.993	-0.317	0.729	0.695	0.709
Exceptional financing (World Bank, IDB, and Support Group)	0.715	1.312	0.721	0.368	0.258

1 = The rescheduling and the deferrals reflect the September 1991 Paris Club agreement.

Table 5. Peru: Principal Monetary Indicators
(Flows at a Constant Exchange Rate: In Millions of *Nuevos Soles*)

	1991	1992	1993	1994	1995
I. Central Bank of Peru					
Net international reserves[1]	351	428	356	317	288
(U.S. dollars)	(457)	(342)	(178)	(129)	(106)
Net domestic assets	19	-44.5	-	-38	-44
Credit to the SPNF	107	71.9	-118	-	-
Financial system credit	-56	-348.1	-	-54.5	-46
Other	-31	231.7	118	16.5	2
Money	370	384	356	279	244
Memo: swap requirements for deposits in foreign currency	-381	-207	-500	-554	-544
II. Financial System					
Net international reserves	1079	743.2	858	871	832
(U.S. dollars)	(1480)	(604)	(429)	(354)	(306)
Net domestic assets	952	656	1,007	1,083	1,010
Credit to the SPNF	-316	44	-105	-	-
Private sector credit	1,352	1,353	1,261	1,191	1,194
Other	-84	-741	-149	-108	-184
Liabilities with the private sector	2,031	1,399	1,865	1,954	1,842
III. Principal Indicators (Percentage of GDP)					
Money and demand deposits (M1)	1.9	1.9	1.9	2.0	2.1
M1 + quasi-money (M2)	2.8	3.1	3.2	3.3	3.5
Liabilities with the private sector (M3)	6.4	9.6	10.5	10.9	11.2
Credit to the private sector	4.3	6.1	7.7	8.7	9.5
(Percent growth, stocks measured at the same exchange rate)					
M1	124.7	52.9	36.0	21.9	16.8
M2	163.3	54.4	35.6	27.1	18.2
M3					
Valued at a constant exchange rate	150.8	31.2	23.6	19.9	14.7

SPNF = Nonfinancial Public Sector.

1 = Excludes reserve requirements in U.S. dollars.

Sources: Banco Central de Reserva del Perú and IMF staff estimates.

Continued on next page

Table 5—*Continued*

	1991	1992	1993	1994	1995
Valued at the end of period exchange rate	295.2	134.3	69.8	41.3	24.0
Monetary base	98.6	57.2	30.9	20.0	14.4
Money in circulation	135.7	59.7	34.6	20.2	14.7
Credit to the private sector					
Valued at a constant exchange rate	147.7	43.4	18.4	14.1	11.1
Valued at the end of period exchange rate	262.6	105.5	45.1	26.9	15.3
Of which: national currency	218.9	69.7	34.3	26.8	18.1
Memo:					
Rate of inflation:	139.0	53.9	26.9	15.0	9.2

Sources: Banco Central de Reserva del Perú and IMF staff estimates.

VII

THE DIFFICULT MOMENTS OF THE FUJIMORI ECONOMIC STRATEGY

Javier Iguíñiz Echeverría

INTRODUCTION

President Alberto Fujimori's original economic strategy was based on the assumption that Peru's adoption of the International Monetary Fund's (IMF) stabilization program would reduce inflation and ensure the procurement of foreign resources, and after stabilization, launch a long-run, export-oriented development process. My assumption is that these are still the points of departure and the expected results of the Fujimori administration. Obviously, the first challenge on the economic front was stabilization, while on the political front, it was the strengthening of personal authority. "Viability" refers to the process of reducing inflation as well as to achieving coherence between those policies which aim to stabilize the economy and those targeted at attaining long-term growth. Short-run management is not an easy task, and making short-run policies coherent with long-term goals is even more difficult. How has the Fujimori government fared in light of these goals?

The Peruvian experience in the area of stabilization is widely considered successful. Inflation has declined to a level fluctuating in the vicinity of 3 percent per month, and in 1993 the growth rate for the gross domestic product (GDP) will be positive. This paper will review some of the factors that have contributed to the viability of the adjustment policy which has been implemented in Peru since August 1990. I will examine the economic policy-making process which began in 1990 to show how much the Fujimori

Javier Iguíñiz Echeverría is professor and chair of the Department of Economics at the Catholic University of Peru (Pontificia Universidad Católica del Perú) and research associate at the Center for the Study and Promotion of Development (Centro de Estudios y Promoción del Desarrollo, DESCO) and the Bartolomé de las Casas-Rimac Institute (Centro de Estudios Rurales Andinos Bartolomé de las Casas.)

administration's economic strategy has advanced over the past three years. The following pages describe some of the crucial moments experienced during the stabilization process, but I will also suggest that the policies applied, in and of themselves, may not be conducive to a long-run process of economically sustainable growth and development.

Short-term viability does not necessarily coincide with viability for the long run. Macroeconomic adjustment to correct relative prices may still lie ahead. Current revenues of approximately 10 percent of the GDP and a huge current account deficit are not the best starting points for a long-run growth process. Only extremely rich and abundant natural resources will do the job. Positive economic and political conditions must be present to encourage exploration, and then if resources are found, their exploitation. In terms of macroeconomic policy, there are no easy ways out. The combination of lower inflation and more favorable exchange rate, when achieved, required the background of a recession and collaborated in deepening it. This was true in Peru during the second and third quarters of 1992.

The viability question arises partly because of the slow anti-inflationary process. After the initial shock (that is, anti-inflationary package of measures) in August 1990, when inflation was the overriding goal, the economic processes have also been guided by two other main objectives: 1) elimination of arrears with the IMF and the World Bank and 2) the reform of economic institutions and the "rules of the game." External conditionality pushed very strongly, as in other countries, in the direction of institutional change, particularly toward the opening of the internal market, a reduction of the state's intervention in the economy, the privatization of public firms, and the dismantling of labor protection laws. Consequently, efforts to curb inflation have competed with debt payments (Verdera 1992), and long-run strategy has concentrated on institutions rather than on relative prices and sectoral resource allocation. The assumption appears to have been either that more favorable relative prices could wait or that they were ineffective in the current institutional framework and political context. Indeed, the existing relative prices (appreciated local currency and high public prices) were favorable when it came to paying public external debt, selling utilities to foreigners, and financing education abroad, for example. Relative prices moved quite clearly to facilitate both debt payment and fiscal balance.

Viability is also a relevant question due to Fujimori's original isolation with respect to local business and technocrats; his only choice was a foreign capital and foreign management-based stabilization strategy. A national team of more than a few macroeconomists was not needed. In this context, the new government considered that foreign debt payment was the condition to obtain and maintain both. It is perfectly possible to interpret the evolution of the economic policy during the first two and one-half years of the Fujimori administration as having had among its most important goals the increase of reserves, the resumption of debt payment, and the elimination of arrears with the IMF and the World Bank. Indeed, the theoretically elegant and tacit ambivalence between money targets and exchange rate targets during this period can be read as a reflection of the difficulty of making debt payment and reserves growth compatible with lowering inflation. That is why, in my opinion, inflation took so long to decline. As is well known, foreign developments, particularly capital inflows, significantly contributed to the country's achievement of all short-term goals by providing cheap and abundant foreign money. In fact, the period 1990-1993 can be seen as a sum of short-run processes aimed at achieving these goals.

The task currently confronting the government is to move from an economic policy that to date has produced very limited results in terms of preparing the economy for the export-oriented development strategy to a plan which would accomplish three goals, perhaps simultaneously: 1) to maintain a low inflation rate with constant or increasing real exchange rates; 2) to reorient relative prices away from the still-important hostility toward the labor-intensive tradable sector without producing a financial crisis and a recession; and 3) to establish credible institutional and regulatory bases to promote social peace, new investment, and economically sustainable growth.

The Basis of Fujimori's Political Support

One of the most impressive feats of the current stabilization program is that it has won political support from the average Peruvian citizen. During most of the Fujimori administration, the economic program has rested primarily on the president's popularity since the program has been relatively slow in reducing inflation and promoting growth. In the first place, we have to consider the "García effect." As all interested in Peru know, from 1985 to 1987, Alan García symbolized the economic efficacy of nationalist pride. However, the frustration which prevailed at the end of his term was as deep as the seduction he generated at the beginning. The skyrocketing inflation, high unemployment, and sheer chaos that were the legacy of the García administration effected a 180-degree turnaround in public opinion across Peru's social strata.

The last years of the García administration plunged millions of Peruvians into squalor and discontent. In January 1993, the monthly income of a worker defined as "adequately employed" was $375 or more, the lower limit being very close to the most accepted poverty lines.[1] In 1987, 60 percent of the labor force fell within this category; in 1990, however, this figure plummeted to 18.6 percent. Before the August 1990 shock, moreover, real wages had fallen 35 percent below the level registered at the outset of the García government in 1985 and 59 percent below 1987 levels.[2]

As a result, the state was destroyed. Tax collection as a percentage of gross domestic product (GDP) fell to approximately 6.5 percent in 1989 (Webb and Fernández Baca 1994, 508). Social reactions were ineffective in light of such a vacuum. Also important was the belief — apparently shared by the president and the population — that the solution to the economic problem would have to come from abroad, as evidenced by the fact that Fujimori's popularity improved after his well-publicized trip to Japan and Korea.

Thus, García nearly destroyed all hope for immediate economic improvement as well as the possibility of a truly negotiated policy alternative with the IMF. Fujimori's isolation did the rest. The free fall in production, employment, and wages that characterized the economy from 1988 on produced a demoralized and passive civil society. Nonetheless, the power of the government allowed Alianza Popular Revolucionaria Americana (APRA) quite an impressive result in the 1990 election, though not enough to participate in the second round. Thus, Fujimori, an independent, became the alternative in the midst of an extremely aggressive campaign between the most powerful and financially sound candidates, Mario Vargas Llosa and Luis Alva Castro.

Demoralized by García's failure, the country had to depend more on foreign backing vis-à-vis multilateral organizations and private capital. García was associated with the "10-percent-of-exports" debt proposal, the attempted nationalization of private banks, the strong political party system, and the ensuing inflationary economic chaos. After winning the election, Fujimori changed his campaign policy proposals on all fronts. Thus, after the terrible September 1988 shock and the chaotic context of the June-July 1990 commercial and financial speculative process, the August 1990 shock was accepted with stoicism.

Once Fujimori had taken power, his well-known antiparty and anti-Congress campaign made the April 1992 coup extremely popular. This happened in spite of the fact that, one way or the other, nearly all the economic reforms that had been implemented had been passed by Congress. International pressures later impelled Fujimori to create a new legislative body, the Congreso Constituyente Democrático (CCD).

The most important event which contributed to Fujimori's popularity, however, was the capture of Sendero Luminoso leader Abimael Guzmán in September 1992. Fujimori linked this accomplishment to the April coup, justifying it. He also used Guzmán's capture to neutralize dissatisfaction during the 1992 recession and concentrate power. This can be considered the "Sendero component" of Fujimori's popularity.

At the end of 1992, the economic dilemma facing the country was evident: how to attack a 3 to 4 percent monthly inflation rate while at the same time providing employment. The political advantage that could be reaped by further lowering inflation was relatively minimal, whereas the popularity cost of permitting it to rise was enormous.[3]

THE STABILIZATION PROCESS:
FOUR "MOMENTS" AND VIABILITY

The viability and continuation of the Fujimori government vitally depend on the success of the short-run economic program. Obviously, the capture of Abimael Guzmán has also been crucial. With respect to macroeconomic policy, the period 1990 to 1993 can be viewed as a sum of short-run moments, some of which created difficulties for the program, while others reconstructed its viability. The program has still not been oriented to long-run criteria, nor have any significant policies been fully implemented for the long run. Relative prices, home savings rates, and current account deficits are not conducive to sustainable growth. To date, the assumption by the administration has been that the stabilization policy is technically independent and can therefore be separated from a long-run growth strategy. Ideally, after a relatively long period of stability, a growth strategy and the corresponding relative prices could be implemented. At that time, savings would supposedly be collected and managed by those who should have them, and investment would be decided according to comparative advantage rules.

During the first half of the Fujimori administration, the IMF and Peruvian policymakers were not interested in relative prices conducive to long-run growth. The government's philosophy, particularly while Carlos Boloña was the minister of economy and finance, was that there was no future for the Peruvian economy working within the existing institutional framework and economic power structure. This philosophy held that the state was too big and powerful and that business had to learn to compete without government assistance. Growth-oriented relative prices would allow the so-called "mercantilists" to survive, and survival would make the struggle against inflation more difficult. The full weight of the market had to be applied to the private sector so that the mercantilists would learn to survive.

During the first half of the Fujimori administration, the bulk of the academic debate regarding the reduction of inflation in Peru revolved around two issues: 1) management and coordination difficulties and 2) structural weakness inherent in the stabilization policy. The practical difference between the two is that in the case of management and coordination problems, the recommendation would be (and in fact was) to persist long enough to make the economic program credible. In the case of structural weaknesses, a modification would have to be made in the way the exchange rate, interest rates, and other relative prices were established. However, in academic and bureaucratic circles, the most important element distinguishing periods in the pre-1993 stabilization process has been the existence or absence of nominal monetary growth targets or the priority of impeding further appreciation of the exchange rate. Afterward, aside from problem-plagued 1992, the anti-inflationary objective dominated, and the exchange rate was allowed to move accordingly. At the same time, however, a number of minor alterations in the basic philosophy of the program have been introduced with no great fuss, including the de facto control of interest rates, temporary sectoral price controls, and so on. Nonetheless, the core of the stabilization program is clear: a floating exchange rate, monetary targets, market-determined interest rates and prices, a weakening of the labor movement, and an increase in taxes. The "dirty" element in the floating and the indexing of public prices (the price of potable water, electricity, kerosene, gasoline, and telecommunications) was necessary in order to allow the growth of reserves and payment of the debt. When the government violates any of these policies (i.e., before an election), sooner or later it reverts to applying them.

The core of the following discussion will be to describe the main challenges to the viability of the program during each stage of economic policy and to determine whether 1) the policies implemented have brought the economy closer to achieving the double (immediate and strategic) goal of low inflation and relative prices favorable to the tradable sector and 2) the strict implementation of the essence of the stabilization program leads to a stable economy, at least in the short run. Another reason for reviewing the first half (and most difficult period) of the Fujimori administration is that the Peruvian experience seems to be relatively peculiar even when compared to that of other Latin American countries. The difference between the European and Latin American stabilization experiences after very high inflations or hyperinflations is that the former did not include financial liberalization. The short-run Peruvian experience is original in other respects as well. As Peruvian economists Oscar Dancourt and Waldo Mendoza state:

> The Peruvian case is, however, peculiar. Differing from Argentina (under Cavallo) or Bolivia, or from the classic cases, it is the only case in which the posthyperinflationary stabilization was based on a monetary target and not on an exchange-rate target. It is the only case we know of where the end of hyperinflation was associated with a flexible exchange rate regime. The essential point is that the existence of a flexible exchange rate regime and a monetary policy regulating the supply of money through the buying and selling of dollars impedes the private sector from the automatic remonetization, dishoarding dollars accumulated during the hyperinflation once this has ended, as happened in the classic cases and in a more limited manner in Argentina and Bolivia (Dancourt and Mendoza N.d., 3).[4]

How has this experiment worked in practice? For analytical purposes, the current Fujimori administration can be divided into four periods corresponding to the evolution of the three most important variables in this analysis: inflation, relative prices, and growth. The viability of the economic program was enhanced during some of these periods; in others, it was damaged by economic policy. I will not deal with institutional reforms unless an analysis of this sort is absolutely essential to examining the viability of the economic program.[5]

AUGUST-DECEMBER 1990:
THE INITIAL SHOCK, INFLATION, POWER, AND THE EXCHANGE RATE

This section reviews the original stabilization package and the results of the policies implemented between August and December 1990 with respect to inflation and relative prices, including the real exchange rate. The meaning of this shock in terms of the relationship between Fujimori's economic power and relative prices is also analyzed. During this "moment," viability was built upon the political support of multilateral organizations and on the strengthening of state finances.

THE INITIAL ATTACK

A monetary approach dominated the original design of the stabilization package.[6] The program was structured so as to permit the Central Bank (Banco Central de Reserva del Perú, BCR) to acquire as much control as possible in order to control the money supply. To facilitate this process, government pressures had to be reduced; thus, the key components of the package were an impressive increase in public prices and the restoration of some fiscal sanity, resulting in greater monetary control. Relative (government/private) prices changed drastically and became a key element throughout the administration. Other decisive components were the floating of the exchange rate and control of the monetary base, making the money supply as exogenous as possible.

There is a growing consensus about what happened between August and October 1990. The most unexpected sequel to the August 8 shock was that the exchange rate resulting from the initial adjustment stayed well below the rate that had been expected in government circles. This was the first shock that caused an increase in real public prices (280 percent) and a reduction of the real exchange rate (-23.3 percent on average between July and August) (Webb and Fernández Baca 1991, 984).[7] In nominal terms, instead of the rate of 450,000 *intis* per dollar (I/$) that had been expected, two days after the package was implemented, the exchange rate was quoted at 290,000I/$. In contrast, in July 1990, the rate averaged 116,150I/$, whereas the day before the shock, it reached 330,000I/$. By the end of August 1990, the exchange rate had risen to 365,000I/$, still well below the level anticipated by the government (Webb and Fernández Baca 1991, 977). This huge increase in public prices and inflation induced the private sector to sell massive quantities of previously accumulated dollars. In the public's mind, it was not conceivable to have a shock without a devaluation. Transactions were in *soles*, but savings had been kept in dollars. The obvious result was an impressive appreciation of the domestic currency. Officials at the BCR wanted dollars to replenish reserves, but they also wanted to raise the exchange rate somewhat to promote exports. The result was a sixfold increase in the monetary base between August and October 1990, while inflation was declining and there was a relatively cheap increment in reserves in that very few *intis* were needed to buy a dollar.

It is still unclear whether the government wanted to supplement the original stabilization shock with exchange rate and public price targets or whether the attempt to increase reserves rapidly resulted in a deliberate policy mix with heterodox components. In fact, very early in the process, the government began claiming that the exchange rate was too low and that something had to be done[8] to remedy that original and, after more than four years, permanent sin of the adjustment program.[9] The government was clearly against further appreciation of the *inti* and wanted a rapid rise to the level of 450,000 per dollar. In any case, devaluatory expectations still dwelled in the back of all risk-averse minds in the aftermath of the previous September 1988 shock.

On the other hand, public prices were not in place according to previously established prices in dollars; they were far above the planned levels. The government therefore wanted them to decline. Modifying the exchange rate and public prices proved to be difficult,[10] however, and the result, deliberate or not, was a stabilization policy with typical exchange rate and price controls.[11] Whether the initial success of the program was due to the orthodox components of the program or to the heterodox aspects is an open question.[12] Indeed, such exchange rate and public price "anchors" were established after the impressive changes in relative prices, and they operated under a strict monetary policy, thereby allowing a more rapid recuperation of reserves.[13] The fiscal deficit was also previously reduced with the enormous increase in public prices.

In December 1990, however, the heterodox controls were abandoned, while monetary strictness was maintained within the guidelines provided by the desire not to let the exchange rate fall.[14] Why was the program modified? An abrupt increase in gasoline prices and a surprisingly high devaluation marked the end of this period. In December, inflation rose to 23.7 percent although it had been declining quite rapidly in previous months, from 397 percent in August 1990, to 13.8 percent in September, 9.6 percent in October, and 5.9 percent in November (Instituto Nacional de Estadística e Informática

1992, 36). Remonetization was going well (although it was not as impressive as in other countries at similar stages of the anti-inflationary program), and growth of the monetary base was "soft landing" nicely. However, reserves had grown very slowly in November 1990 and declined in December while debt payments were being made.[15] The decision to pay the debt became a self-imposed external restriction and, thus, an unnecessary fiscal overload. The "as if" anchors were probably removed as a consequence of fiscal and external problems rather than as a result of a freely decided change in the monetary-fiscal regime. This was, indeed, a well-known adjustment package with its external bottleneck, reserves crisis, devaluation, and increment of public prices. In the following months, policy was targeted at attempting to reduce the damage incurred in the month of December.

After the initial impact of the August 1990 shock, a new situation emerged with the legalization of deposits in dollars. Liquidity in dollars rose constantly and with fairly similar monthly increments. The April 1992 coup interrupted this trend for a short time, but after a few weeks, it continued (Campos 1993, 27). Why were transactions, at least out of current income, mainly in *soles*, while savings were mainly in dollars? The differential in interest rates in *intis* and in U.S. dollars cannot easily explain the dollarization process that occurred from then on.[16]

The Peruvian people seemed to be well prepared to accept very costly economic programs. The past two years have shown that the progress achieved in reducing inflation did in fact counteract the obvious dissatisfaction with increasing poverty. Nevertheless, if the adjustment program instituted by Alan García between 1988 and 1990 submerged millions below the water line, the Fujimori program did not provide any oxygen. Since 1990, the Peruvian people have been kept under water, to say the least. Moreover, in terms of quality of life, the conditions of those who were already living below the poverty line continue to worsen. For example, from June-July 1990, just before the new adjustment policy was implemented, to October-November 1990, the average per capita consumption in Lima fell by 26.4 percent. The largest decline was registered in the consumption of health services, with a drop of 88 percent (Instituto Cuánto 1991, 83).[17] This impoverishment was the direct result of the August shock.[18]

A POWER BASE FOR THE PRESIDENT AND RELATIVE PRICES

The political economy of this initial period suggests that the program had as an important result both the empowering and disempowering of the new president.[19] Politically speaking, two important by-products of the August 1990 shock and the liberalization of the economy were the improvement of fiscal accounts and the reduction of the maneuvering field in order to control the president's still uncertain behavior to meet the requirements of financial reinsertion. The first result ensured the survival of the state and that of the new president; the second guaranteed he would be under control. These two achievements (and perhaps also objectives) by the new president and the IMF, respectively, provide the background for the original basic structure of the stabilization program. An alternative would have been to devalue and then fix the exchange rate as Vargas Llosa's Frente Democrático (FREDEMO) had proposed. However, in that case, the shock would have empowered exporters and dollar owners who, at the time, opposed the new government inasmuch as they were bitter about having lost the 1990 election. If the Frente Democrático's suggestion had been implemented, money would have gone to the private sector, while the debtor was the state. A windfall tax would have been too indirect and risky a process. Moreover, a devaluation would have made it more expensive in domestic currency to pay public external debt. Other alternatives were discussed before the August 1990 shock, but these were also discarded after some last-minute consultations.

The significance of this aspect of Peruvian political economy is that alternative methods for changing relative prices and providing investment incentives will depend on a closer relationship between President Fujimori and the domestic business class. It would be difficult to force a change in relative prices in favor of Peruvian exporters in the absence of an alliance between this group and the president.

January-June 1991:
Debt Payments, Reforms, and Instability

The second stage of the macroeconomic reform program lasted from January to June 1991. The most pressing concerns of this "moment" were the difficulties confronted in undoing the damage caused in December 1990 and the offensive in the reform process.

Coordination Problems and Instability

Coordination problems were common after November 1990, but it is difficult to establish their importance in shaping the stabilization process. It could also be theorized that the management problems that occurred at the end of 1990 and during the first months of 1991 were the result of the particularly explosive situation created by the December 1990 minishock. These problems were common at the time, but they became especially evident in January when Banco de la Nación massively absorbed through tax payments the funds the Central Bank was trying to introduce into the economy (Centro de Investigaciones de la Universidad del Pacífico 1991). It was generally assumed by the supporters of the stabilization program that these coordination difficulties contributed to inflation due to the government's credibility problem.

However, the most important factor which accounted for the difficult transition to a declining monetary target regime was probably the "stop and go" monetary policy resulting from the high inflation rate experienced in December 1990 and the loss of reserves incurred from December 1990 to February 1991. After the inflation rate increased to 23.7 percent in December, the BCR reduced its acquisition of dollars and consequently money growth even more; nonetheless, reserves began to decline. As a consequence, policies were implemented to promote the recuperation of reserves and to impede a decline in the real exchange rate. The money supply increased again between February and March 1991, which led to the exchange crisis of April and May, at which time dollar purchases were again reduced. Debt payment with a strict money supply proved to be a risky business in this context.

A MULTITUDE OF REFORMS, A SMALL TEAM, AND STRATEGIC CHANGE

At this unstable moment in the life of a stabilization process character- ized by an undefined and uncoordinated short-run economic policy and the lack of a coherent blueprint for long-term sustainable growth,[20] a massive change in the institutional framework of the economy was launched in March 1991.[21] Strong external moral support and the even stronger pro-market ideological commitment by those in charge of implementation were all that were needed to start this period with great impetus. All reforms — the liberalization of the capital account, the opening of the internal market, and the liberalization of the labor market — were either started or deepened simultaneously. Around a dozen bureaucrats[22] were charged with the task of simultaneously managing not only this enormous institutional reform pro- gram but also debt repayment negotiations, and the stabilization policy. It should not be a surprise, therefore, that coordination and management problems ensued.

These institutional reforms, which at the time became more important than the stabilization program itself, were in fact strongly required by multilateral organizations, particularly by the Inter-American Development Bank (IDB), as a condition to the country's obtaining resources and ensuring its advance in the Accumulation of Rights project agreed upon with the IMF to eliminate arrears. However, the institutional reforms that were promulgated also served as the ground for building a new alliance between Fujimori, the Peruvian business class, and foreign investors, as local and international confidence has been strongly associated with the privatization of public firms. Finally, these reforms were essential for securing the business class' support of the stabilization program despite its recessive results.

July 1991-March 1992:
Perfect Monetarism Versus Relative Prices

The third phase of the Fujimori economic program comprises the period July 1991 to March 1992, when policy was closest to the basic plan. This period came to an end with a tax shock in March followed by the coup in early April. It is interesting to note that the August 1990 shock and the evolution of the economy from July 1991 to March 1992 are the two milestones that have best served as empirical references in the model-building effort in Peru.

The Stabilization of the Stabilization Policy

This third "moment" of the economic program, implemented in the second half of 1991, had as its most notable characteristic the relatively consistent use of declining monetary targets. The BCR was successful in gradually reducing the amount of money circulating in the economy. Inflation moved down smoothly from a level of 9.3 percent in June 1991 to 3.5 percent in January 1992.[23] During this period, public prices rose above inflation, the exchange rate appreciated, and real wages remained stagnant. In addition, the change in relative prices that resulted from the shock in August 1990 was reinforced. Monetary restriction occurred once more, though in a more gradual manner, and produced a similar pattern of relative prices. However, this time, the inflation rate declined slowly. In this way, one-half of the country's problem, that is, inflation, was solved; the other, relative prices, worsened. Success does not necessarily breed success; this period came to an end with the February 1992 rise in inflation to 4.7 percent and an aggressively resisted tax shock that pushed inflation to 7.4 percent in March 1992. As in December 1990, a fiscal problem put a halt to the anti-inflationary process. The tremendously popular April coup reduced the growing pressure against the government resulting from the tax shock, and a new phase began. Thus, a political move helped ensure the continuation of the program.

Modeling, Coincidences, and Paradoxes

The initial shock and the peculiar behavior of key variables during this period have prompted some creative explanations. One of the simplest ways of modeling this behavior is to consider that the short-run appreciation of the exchange rate was the direct result of domestic monetary restriction, while the composition of the public's portfolio of *soles* and dollars remained basically stable (Dancourt 1993). The peculiar decline in the real money supply and real liquidity that took place while inflation was falling was the consequence of the Ministry of Economy and Finance's increase of public prices. Prices rose enough to push the Consumer Price Index above the increment in money supply produced by the BCR's acquisition of dollars. In this context, as in August 1990, Peruvians were forced to sell dollars in order to secure the *soles* they required for operational purposes, and the exchange rate declined or rose less than inflation. Added to this monetary-fiscal combination was a policy controlling an increase in wages. In this way, the classic inverse relation between the real exchange rate and real wages was at least partly broken.

A common alternative explanation refers to the effect of high domestic interest rates on the inflow of dollars. If it is accepted that the reason for such rates is the monetary restriction, we find the same extremes and the same type of effects: an expanding money supply and a rising exchange rate or vice versa. In and of itself, the inflow of dollars does not appear to be sufficient to impact the exchange rate; the desire to acquire *soles* with dollars seems to be necessary. The same extreme points exist in the monetarist Simplest Excess Demand hypothesis, which is related to money expansion and inflation. In the case presented above, money control influences inflation by means of lowering the exchange rate rather than reducing aggregate demand. Inflation is more directly the result of the policies which increased public prices.

In spite of these coincidences, the need for original thinking is great. The end of the impressive, high-level inflations or hyperinflations of the late 1980s did not bring an end to dollarization or the remonetization of the economy. In Peru, the real monetary base fell to one-half the level it had registered during the worst previous inflationary episodes. Some recent models prepare us for several paradoxes. For instance, according to Peruvian economist Waldo Mendoza, in an economy "...with a banking system providing credit and accepting deposits in dollars, an expansive monetary policy raises the exchange rate, reduces the interest rate for domestic currency, and may raise the average cost of credit and reduce the level of activity."[24]

FOLLOWING THE APRIL 1992 COUP: A SMALL, ONE-SHOT CAPITAL OUTFLOW

April 1992 not only witnessed the "Fujicoup" but also marked another turning point for Peruvian economic policy. Though trying to operate always within the basic original framework of the stabilization program, the government's dominant objective after the first quarter of 1992 was the rise in the exchange rate.[25] This objective was successfully achieved with the "help" of the outflow of dollars after the coup, the reduction in new 1992 disbursements from $872 million in 1991 to $387 million (Banco Central de Reserva del Perú 1993, 44)[26] also due to the coup, and the growing domestic private demand for dollars due to the devaluation itself. In addition, dollar acquisitions by the BCR rose from $52 million in the first quarter of 1992 to $131 million in the second (Banco Central de Reserva del Perú 1993a, 45).

WRONG POLICY, RIGHT RESULTS?

During the second and third quarters of 1992, the Peruvian government achieved its two short-run goals: the inflation rate declined from 7.4 percent in March to 2.6 percent in September (Webb and Fernández Baca 1994, 440), its lowest point since May 1980, whereas the real exchange rate rose very quickly between those two months, recuperating a good part of what had been lost in the previous year. In addition, reserves rose. Behind this change in the inflation level, the exchange rate, and reserves, however, we find not only a recession within the recession (production declined 2.8 percent in 1992) and a financial crisis (fourteen financial institutions were intervened and dissolved during the year[27]) but also a worsening of the current account deficit. Are these the necessary costs of such an ideal evolution of absolute and relative prices?

During the first quarter of 1992 (that is, before the April coup), the inflow of capital was reducing its growth rate. In addition, monthly increments of liquidity in dollars averaged $62 million, well below the $126 million registered in 1991. April marked a change, however; there was a one-month decline of $158 million in the level of banking system reserves. Soon afterward, in June 1992, the previous level was regained (Banco Central de Reserva del Perú 1993b). We have therefore observed a "one-shot" process. This decline in reserves was due to the immediate drop in dollar deposits from $2.573 billion in March to $2.336 billion in April 1992. This $237 million decrease was recuperated only in September of that year, when deposits reached the level of $2.621 billion Banco Central de Reserva del Perú 1993b, 15). After the absolute fall in April, the level of dollar deposits started to rise again. Between May and August, the average monthly increment reached $38 million, and from September to December 1992, it rose to $100 million (Banco Central de Reserva del Perú 1993a, 53-54). This was the most immediate and visible effect of the Fujimori coup. The short-term nature of the problem showed that the international context was definitely favorable. In fact, in spite of the recession and the rising exchange rate, imports grew very rapidly, and trade and current account deficits worsened.

The immediate monetary consequences of this outflow of capital were the following:

1. The downward trend in nominal interest rates in dollars and for domestic currency deposits and loans ceased, while inflation was declining.

2. Real exchange rates stopped falling, and a continuous devaluation that would last the rest of the year began.

3. The real monetary base stopped declining and grew every month between April and September of that year.

4. Real liquidity in domestic currency decreased until June; after a brief recovery, it began another downward trend, which lasted until November.

5. The multiplier reached its highest value under Fujimori in April and then declined in spite of the reduction in reserves required by the BCR.

6. In spite of BCR policy, excess reserves grew continuously until September, reducing the amount of money available.[28]

In September 1992, devaluation reached 7.3 percent, followed by an increase to 12.9 percent in October. During the last quarter of 1992, inflation rates moved one point above the September level, marking a transitory end to declining inflation rates. This decline appears to be associated with the reduction in aggregate demand and its effects on the prices of nonprocessed food products. The more aggressive official deindexation of wages is also considered relevant to the lowering of demand,[29] but the previous increase in taxes was also important. The fiscal surplus was coupled this time with expenditure reduction, not only with rising public prices. In fact, these prices had a politically oriented trajectory since they rose during the second and third quarters but were frozen just before the November elections. It has been on this point that Minister Boloña received the most criticism about short-run management capabilities.

Higher taxes, public prices, and interest rates certainly did not favor business in the context of an economy with climatic and energy problems.[30] However, in spite of the devaluation, the prices of tradable goods grew very little, probably as a result of the declining internal demand. The prices of gasoline and transportation also rose less than inflation, but the Index of Real Public Prices as a whole rose during this period of disinflation.[31] Gasoline appears to be an especially important product when dealing with prices. Wholesale prices are very sensitive to variations in the exchange rate and also rose with the exchange rate. This ideal combination of declining inflation and rising real exchange rates came to a halt in the last quarter of 1992, when inflation started to grow again. The return to fiscal expansion after two quarters of strict austerity may be one element that accounts for this rise, but, as indicated, another relevant factor has been of a more speculative and financial nature.

A factor unrelated to policymaking — adverse climatic conditions — also contributed to the recession. Energy problems and drought affected most sectors of the Peruvian economy. Together, economic policy and climatic factors resulted in an important recession which started in February 1992, before the coup, but the rise of real interest rates in dollars as a result of the devaluation added coal to the fire. The real dollar lending interest rate rose from negative values to positive values, and the weighted average of the domestic and dollar-denominated real interest rate also rose sharply after April and remained at a high level throughout the year.[32] At the same time, banks did not want to lend money, creating some sort of rationing. Bad loans grew as a consequence of the recession and of higher average real interest rates. This situation in and of itself constituted a reason to raise excess reserves. The combination of an economy in recession and a rising real exchange rate seemed terrible for businesses indebted in dollars. The financial sector emerged from the 1992 experience smaller and more fragile than ever. Bad debts as a proportion of loans swelled from 12 percent in December 1991 to 21 percent in December 1992. Most of the increment was in the dollar component of the intermediation, rising from 13.4 percent to 23.4 percent (APOYO 1993, 24).[33]

In general, recession, growing unemployment, financial crisis and fragility, and the worsening of the trade balance implied a very high cost for these successful months in terms of inflation and relative prices. A prolongation of this situation would be very difficult politically. If these high costs were accepted at the time, it was for political reasons: the April 1992 coup and the capture of the leader of the Shining Path. Climatic factors, on the other hand, could not be attributed to the government, and were used to justify the new recession. In any case, such an interesting result in inflation and exchange rates was not achieved thanks to the maintenance of a very strict monetary policy. A stable and growing exchange rate was the goal in that period. After this experience, we should recognize that there is no easy way out of recession and antitradable relative prices at the same time.

Conclusion

Where Do We Stand?

The Peruvian economy is in a clear and definitive reactivation stage, but not necessarily on a long-run growth trajectory. After 1992, the level of economic activity fell 22.5 percent below that registered in 1987, a 30.3 percent decline in per capita terms (Banco Central de Reserva del Perú 1993a, 137).

In spite of the strictness in fiscal policy, tax pressure is still too low to sustain growing social expenditure. During the first full year of the Fujimori administration, that is, 1991, government income from taxes totaled 8.6 percent of GDP. In 1992, the percentage was 9.5 percent, increasing to 9.7 percent in 1993 (Banco Central de Reserva del Perú 1995).[34] Even in the case of an overvaluation of the GDP and a tax pressure that was higher than that registered, this trend does not correspond with the well-accepted improvements in the administration.

External accounts show a tendency that cannot last long in a normal international context. The figures presented in Table 1 provide us some bearing as to where we stand[35]:

Table 1.
External Accounts 1987-1992

	GDP (1)	DP/cap (2)	(Cur.Acc.) /GDP (3)	(Dom.Sav.) /GDP (4)	(Inv.) /GDP (4)
1987	4,348	215	-6.0	17.4	21.0
1988	3,965	192	-5.3	15.5	22.0
1989	3,504	166	0.0	17.8	17.6
1990	3,355	156	-3.6	14.1	15.5
1991	3,450	157	-5.1	13.2	16.6
1992	3,369	150	-6.6	12.4	16.6

Source: Banco Central de Reserva del Perú (BCR), *Memoria 1993*, (Lima: BCR, 1994).
1 = *Nuevos soles* of 1979. Annex I, 137.
2 = *Intis* of 1979. Annex I, 137.
3 = Percentages. Annex XIX, 155
4 = Percentages. Annex XIX, 155

The recuperation of previous levels of activity is at hand. Nonetheless, the current account deficit seems to be unsustainable. The worst economic crisis in the history of the country, that of 1987-1990, was precipitated by a smaller and shorter deficit than the current one.

A number of questions remain. Will foreign investment materialize soon enough to finance the current account and defend the level of reserves? Will the export sector grow soon enough to balance the trade and current account figures?

A Summary

Since 1990, the Peruvian economy has moved into another stage. High inflation and deep recession are now behind us. Macroeconomic policy, however, could not achieve these two goals and alter relative prices to promote exports and long-run viability at the same time. Comparatively speaking, the decline in inflation has been neither fast nor easy. Fiscal and external difficulties led the Fujimori administration to abrupt devaluations and increases in public prices that impeded a faster and more efficient anti-inflationary process. Multilateral organizations did not provide net resources to reduce the cost of adjusting. Indeed, among the fiscal problems facing the country, debt payment has been the most salient.

Economically, the riskiest moment in the economic program was the December 1990 affair. Politically, the most difficult period was that which transpired after the "Fujicoup" in April 1992. The August-December 1990 shock, which strengthened the state and provided Fujimori his own economic power base, putting the business sector under his rule, also proved to be crucial. In fact, the fiscal shock of December 1990 almost ruined the anti-inflationary process. The second challenge was the stabilization of the stabilization program, and coordination problems were also important. In 1995, the lack of management is still a weakness. Very few Peruvian economists have influenced or participated in the design and implementation of the stabilization program; perhaps fewer than ten individuals have served as full-time macroeconomists during the Fujimori administration.

It has become evident, moreover, that a strictly applied monetary policy leads to the overvaluation of the Peruvian currency. This problem, observed in the shock of August 1990, is registered once again, but in the context of more gradually applied medicine. The viability problem is therefore one of design. In a bimonetary economy, monetary restriction and higher public prices induce the selling of dollars and an appreciation of the *nuevo sol.* In 1992, for example, the viability of the economic program was negatively affected by a one-shot capital outflow produced by the reaction of foreign capital to the April coup, altering the volume of deposits in the banking system, international reserves, interest rates, and exchange rates for a month or more. Nonetheless, the international context continued to be favorable and normal trends were recuperated in the quarter following the coup. Interestingly enough, inflation declined and the *nuevo sol* depreciated during this period. In 1992, a recession precipitated by adverse climatic conditions was deepened by policy decisions, and a financial crisis caused more than a dozen banks, credit cooperatives, and other financial institutions to declare bankruptcy. Sendero Luminoso leader Abimael Guzmán was captured just in time to deflect the spotlight from the economic crisis, however.

Today, with an inflation rate of around 4 percent, the new issue has become employment. Notwithstanding the current low inflation rate and the resumption of growth, the design problem remains. This problem is not only one of international circumstances. A policy of active monetary restriction will appreciate the *nuevo sol* and endanger export expansion, reducing it to the richest mines and natural resources.

NOTES

1. The figure published by the Centro de Estudios y Promoción del Desarrollo (DESCO) for December 1993 was $340 (Centro de Estudios y Promoción del Desarrollo 1994). Other institutions produce similar figures.

2. The experience after September 1988 has shown Peruvians that the worst of all possible stabilization programs is a two-stage combination of an orthodox shock and the simultaneous announcement of a complementary heterodox package of policies to be implemented a few (ten in that case) days later. The inflation which ensued after the first stage aborted any gain in relative prices, and the subsequent price and income policies attempted to ensure the continuation of what was an unsustainable situation.

3. In a recent survey, 79 percent of those in favor of the government would change their opinion if prices get out of control. See *IMASEN confidencial* 1993.

4. Author's translation. A similar version can be found in Dancourt and Mendoza 1994. Other interpretations of the Peruvian experience characterize the 1988-1990 experience as a process of "high inflation," not hyperinflation. The relevance of the distinction is that the inertial aspects of the Peruvian economy cannot be assumed to have disappeared. See Gloria Canales and Alan Fairlie 1991.

5. Analysts have suggested different ways of dividing this period; mine corresponds to a greater degree with the periods suggested by Bruno Seminario and Elsa Galarza (1993).

6. For further details, see Iguíñiz, Basay, and Rubio 1993, 210-218.

7. See also Dancourt and Mendoza 1991, 144.

8. According to APOYO, "During the first months of the program some confusion existed in the management of the exchange rate policy. Authorities tried to correct the overvaluation of the domestic currency but resisted increasing their daily acquisitions of dollars because they were afraid of a resurgence of inflation" (APOYO 1993). Author's translation.

9. We consider that expectations of a devaluation are a permanent part of the scenario due to the somewhat mysterious origin of the continued overvaluation of the *nuevo sol* (i.e., Dutch disease, errors and omissions, and so forth), to the fact that the government does not appear to be happy with it, and to traumatic devaluatory experiences in the not-so-distant past.

10. One reason for this seems to be the ambiguity in the field of tariff reform. See Javier Escobal 1992, 249.

11. According to Oscar Dancourt, "En la práctica, el Banco Central de Reserva no operó durante los tres primeros meses del programa con una meta monetaria sino, por el contrario, con una meta cambiaria que era consistente con el rol asignado al

precio del dólar como ancla nominal del sistema de precios y salarios. De hecho, dada la ausencia de un mercado de bonos en la economía peruana, si el instrumento de la política monetaria — las operaciones de compra y venta de dólares — se utilizaba para fijar el tipo de cambio, la cantidad de dinero quedaba determinada por las decisiones de portafolio del sector privado" (Dancourt 1993).

12. According to this perspective, if the heterodox anchors had been maintained, the anti-inflationary program would have been far more efficient at reducing inflation. According to Oscar Dancourt, "Si la desinflación hubiese estado asociado a un tipo de cambio fijo, como lo estuvo durante algún tiempo después del Fujishock, no sólo la eficacia anti-inflacionaria del programa de estabilización hubiese sido bastante mayor, sino que también se hubiera posibilitado una mayor remonetización de la economía" (Dancourt 1993).

13. It should be stressed that in this case the increase in reserves was not related to the dollar acquisitions made by the BCR. As we will see, restrictive monetary policy and rising public prices lead to growing Central Bank reserves, but a less restrictive policy also leads to the same result when the banking system is reluctant to lend more or the economy has no productive use for those *nuevos soles*, and there is a dollar reserve requirement. The difference is that in the second case the exchange rate rises.

14. Referring to interest rates, Julio Velarde asserts, "Las tasas en *soles* continuaron altas en 1991, pero comenzaron a disminuir como consecuencia de la nueva política del BCRP: desde agosto dejó caer el tipo de cambio para controlar la inflación..." (Velarde 1995, 13).

15. According to Velarde, "A partir del 16 de octubre de 1990, el gobierno inicia el pago de la deuda externa con el Banco Mundial y el Banco Interamericano de Desarrollo, cuyos directivos se mostraron, por cierto, sorprendidos ante tal decisión del gobierno, pues iba mucho más allá de lo esperable.... La buena voluntad del gobierno, sin embargo, no fue igualmente correspondida pues los fondos de los organismos no llegaron con la rapidez que suponían en el MEF [Ministerio de Economía y Finanzas, *Ed.*].... El gasto no presupuestado y una situación aún precaria puso en apuros al MEF. Este se vio obligado a obtener recursos incrementando significativamente los precios de los combustibles y las tarifas por los servicios públicos" (Velarde 1992, 13).

16. The assumption is that since the beginning of the program, after the original decline in exchange rates, expectations of a devaluation are a permanent feature of the economy. Hence, the shorter the period one keeps money, the lower the risk of a loss due to a devaluation and the easier it is to deposit in *soles* and benefit from the higher interest rates. Transaction demand appears to be mainly in *soles*. Only expenditures that previously required some significant amount of savings, such as automobiles or real estate, are commonly made in dollars.

17. See also Franke 1993.

18. Added to the average per capita consumption decline experienced by the low and middle income groups under García (that is, from July 1985 to July 1986 and from June to July 1990, which amounted to 53.4 percent, the 1985-1991 cumulative figure is (minus) -64.4 percent (Instituto Cuánto 1991, 83).

19. This effort to control government's policy freedom is also expressed in the institutional reform process. After García, the lack of confidence in the government was so radical and the need to solve arrears so urgent that some policy tools had to be eliminated. It was not enough to persuade the new government of the need to improve its management; the state itself had to be changed institutionally, reducing government's freedom of action. Thus, institutional reform was perceived as a condition for stability. Apparently, such an abrupt and recent conversion to orthodoxy as Fujimori's did not appear convincing enough to multilaterals.

20. Some coordination problems are described in Centro de Investigaciones de la Universidad del Pacífico 1991, x-xi and 13-17.

21. For a fresh account, see Escobal 1992. See also Boloña 1993.

22. See Peñaranda 1993.

23. In general, the inflation rate was declining cyclically with high points corresponding to the variations in public prices and the exchange rate. See Seminario and Galarza 1993.

24. According to Mendoza, "In the first quarter [of 1992]...when the monetary policy was restrictive...due to the appreciation of the domestic currency, while the monthly rate of interest for loans in domestic currency was 10.4 percent, the average real interest rate was -1.9 percent" (Mendoza 1993a, 53). Author's translation. A less formal version is presented in Mendoza 1993b.

25. According to the Central Bank, "En el transcurso del año el tipo de cambio bancario registró una devaluación nominal de 62 por ciento y una ganancia real de 5 por ciento. Durante el primer trimestre el índice de tipo de cambio real disminuyó 20 por ciento, por lo que el énfasis del manejo cambiario a partir de abril se orientó a revertir esta pérdida de competitividad externa, lográndose revertir la tendencia decreciente y elevar el índice de tipo de cambio real en 31 por ciento entre abril y diciembre" (Banco Central de Reserva del Perú 1993a, 45).

26. Financial reinsertion was not a big help; net transfers were negative ($-338 million).

27. For further information, see the list in Banco Central de Reserva del Perú 1993a, 56.

28. According to the BCR, "Por el lado de las instituciones financieras, se mantuvo significativos superávits de encaje durante el segundo semestre. Ello se explicó por la fuerte reducción en las tasas de encaje exigible, y el comportamiento precautorio de los bancos asociado a los problemas en la recuperación de colocaciones y a la estacionalidad de las finanzas públicas" (Banco Central de Reserva del Perú 1993a, 60). Also, "La contracción real del crédito en moneda nacional al sector privado responde a la evolución de las captaciones en moneda nacional del sistema financiero que prácticamente no varió en términos constantes, así como a la mayor cautela de los intermediarios financieros en su política de colocaciones. Esa retracción crediticia se realizó a pesar de la política de encajes del BCRP, que redujo las tasas marginales y las exigibles de las obligaciones en moneda nacional sujeta a encaje" (Banco Central de Reserva del Perú 1993a, 62).

29. DL 757 canceled all the remaining wage indexation in mid-December 1991.

30. According to the Consorcio de Investigación Económica, "El Ministro Boloña, con plenos poderes...ejecuta una política fiscal que genera, en el segundo trimestre del año, un superávit fiscal de proporciones significativas. No reacciona contra la corrida de depósitos bancarios en moneda extranjera que se produce en el mes de abril. No asigna los fondos del FONAVI [Fondo Nacional de Vivienda, *Ed.*] en el sector productivo y, finalmente, aplaza los proyectos de inversión programados por el sector público" (Centro de Investigaciones de la Universidad del Pacífico [CIUP] 1993). See also Peñaranda 1993.

31. It appears that the price of gasoline influences the Consumer Price Index more than other public prices do.

32. The average is obtained using the percentage of deposits in dollars and *soles* as weights. It should be said that the nominal interest rates remained very stable. An agreement between the government and banks in September 1991 led to this stability and trend. See Dancourt, Mendoza, and Romero 1993, 156.

33. Provisions declined from 65.2 percent of bad loans to 60.1 percent.

34. In the fourth quarter of 1990, tax collection amounted to 10.3 percent of GDP. In the last quarter of 1991, collection declined to 8.7 percent, and in the last of 1992, it rose to 9.4 percent.

35. The estimated figures on the trade in coca derivatives are not figured in Current Account. We are assuming some sort of *ceteris paribus* when comparing different periods.

REFERENCES

APOYO (Lima). 1993. "Dinámica de tipo de cambio y políticas cambiarias alternativas/complementarias." March.

Banco Central de Reserva del Perú (BCR). 1995. *Nota semanal* 10, March 9.

Banco Central de Reserva del Perú (BCR). 1993a. *Memoria 1992.* Lima: BCR.

Banco Central de Reserva del Perú (BCR). 1993b. *Nota semanal* 4, February 1.

Boloña, Carlos. 1993. *Cambio de rumbo.* Lima: Instituto de Economía de Libre Mercado-SIL.

Campos, Alejandro. 1993. "Metamorfosis de la inflación: la dolarización." *Moneda* (Lima) V (56).

Canales, Gloria, and Alan Fairlie. 1991. "Hiperinflación y cambio de régimen en el Perú: Un análisis comparativo." Working Document 95. Lima: Centro de Investigaciones Sociales, Económicas, Políticas y Antropológicas, Pontificia Universidad Católica del Perú (CISEPA-PUC).

Centro de Estudios y Promoción del Desarrollo (DESCO). 1994. *Coyuntura laboral* 88 (May): 13-18.

Centro de Investigaciones de la Universidad del Pacífico (CIUP). 1991. *Informe de coyuntura: Primer semestre 1991. Evolución de la economía peruana.* Lima: CIUP.

Centro de Investigaciones de la Universidad del Pacífico (CIUP). 1993. "Informe sobre coyuntura económica peruana, 1992-IV." In *Boletín de opinión* 8 (May).

Instituto Cuánto. 1991. *Ajuste y economía familiar 1985-1990.* Lima: Cuánto S.A.

Dancourt, Oscar. 1993. "Desinflación, retraso cambiario y dolarización: Perú 1990-1992," *Foro económico* (Lima) (February).

Dancourt, Oscar and Waldo Mendoza. N.d. *Dolarización en el Perú: Causas y consecuencias.* Lima: Pontificia Universidad Católica del Perú.

Dancourt, Oscar, and Waldo Mendoza. 1991. "Perú. Situación económica." In *Situación latinoamericana* 4 (August). Madrid: Centro Español de Estudios de América Latina (CEDEAL).

Dancourt, Oscar, and Waldo Mendoza. 1994. "Agricultura y política de estabilización en el Perú: 1990-1992." In *Perú: El problema agrario en debate.* Lima: Sepia.

Dancourt Oscar, Waldo Mendoza, and Lucía Romero. 1993. "Perú: situación económica." In *Situación latinoamericana* 13 (February). Madrid: Centro Español de Estudios de América Latina (CEDEAL).

Escobal, Javier. 1992. "Marzo de 1991: ¿El mes de las reformas estructurales en el Perú?" In *¿Dónde va América Latina? Balance de las reformas económicas,* ed. Joaquín Vial. Santiago de Chile: Corporación de Investigaciones Económicas para Latinoamérica (CIEPLAN).

Franke, Pedro. 1993. "Variaciones del consumo de los hogares como efecto del ajuste de agosto de 1990," *Moneda* 56 (February).

Iguíñiz, Javier, Rosario Basay, and Mónica Rubio. 1993. *Los ajustes. Perú 1975-1992.* Lima: Fundación Friedrich Ebert.

MASEN confidencial (Lima). 1993. March.

Mendoza, Waldo. 1993a. "La política monetaria en el Perú: Metas versus discrecionalidad." Serie Documentos de Trabajo 110. (May) Lima: Centro de Investigaciones Sociales, Económicas, Políticas y Antropológicas, Pontificia Universidad Católica del Perú (CISEPA-PUC).

Mendoza, Waldo. 1993b. "Precios públicos, tasa de interés y retraso cambiario: Los dilemas de una economía dolarizadax." *Moneda* 57 (March).

Instituto Nacional de Estadística e Informática (INEI). 992. *Perú: Compendio estadístico 1991-92.* Vol. 3 (May). Lima: INEI.

Peñaranda, César. 1993. "Las reformas estructurales quedaron incompletas." *Expreso* (Lima), April 12.

Seminario, Bruno, and Elsa Galarza. 1993. "Informe sobre coyuntura económica peruana, 1992-IV." *Boletín de opinión* (May).

Velarde, Julio. 1995. "Liberalización del mercado financiero. El caso peruano." *Boletín de opinión* 16 (February).

Velarde, Julio. 1992. "El manejo económico de corto plazo durante los dos primeros años del gobierno de Fujimori." *Boletín de opinión* 6 (November).

Verdera, Francisco. 1992. "Del shock al golpe: La evolución de la economía peruana entre agosto de 1990 y junio de 1992." *Boletín de opinión* 6 (November).

Webb, Richard, and Graciela Fernández Baca. 1994. *Perú en números 1994.* Lima: Cuánto S.A.

Webb, Richard, and Graciela Fernández Baca. 1991. *Perú en números 1991.* Lima: Cuánto S.A.

VIII

ECONOMIC REFORM AND THE REAL EXCHANGE RATE IN PERU

John Devereux and
Michael Connolly

INTRODUCTION

This chapter examines the effects of consumption subsidies, public enterprise pricing, price controls, and informal markets on the real exchange rate with special reference to Peru. Under plausible assumptions, we show that economic reform in these areas can lead to a real exchange rate appreciation. While public sector price reform accounts for most of the real appreciation which accompanied the Alberto Fujimori reforms of August 1990, we find that it cannot explain Peru's recent real appreciation.

Consumption subsidies and public enterprise prices are important policy instruments in developing economies. Such policies are typically used for redistribution purposes and are especially important for populist governments.[1] The dramatic Latin American reforms of recent years have produced large reductions in consumption subsidies as well as huge increases in public enterprise prices. More generally, reform in these areas plays an increasingly important role in International Monetary Fund (IMF) and World Bank programs. As evidence of this, Sebastian Edwards (1989) found that public enterprise price increases and reductions in consumption subsidies were involved in 79 and 44 percent, respectively, of IMF programs between 1983 and 1985. Trade reforms, in contrast, were present in just 35 percent of the cases. Public sector price reforms have played an especially prominent role

John Devereux and Michael Connolly are professors of economics at the University of Miami.

The authors would like to thank Evan Tanner for his helpful comments and Mercedes Araoz, who provided data assistance.

in the economic policies of the Alberto Fujimori government in Peru. As this analysis will show, these policies have produced enormous changes in internal relative prices in Peru.

Thus, this chapter analyzes the real exchange rate effects of public sector price reforms. Surprisingly, given its practical importance to developing economies, this phenomenon has received no formal attention from economists.[2] Public sector price reforms produce, under plausible assumptions, a permanent real exchange appreciation. This finding has important policy implications as it may provide a partial explanation for some of the puzzling real appreciations that have accompanied economic reform. A noteworthy example is the real appreciation of the Peruvian *inti* (now the *nuevo sol*) following the Fujimori stabilization of August 1990. Typically, such real appreciations are attributed to lags in inflationary expectations or to credibility problems. Thus far, it is not widely understood that public sector reforms can permanently appreciate the real exchange rate.

We will examine the real exchange rate effects of public sector pricing in four areas. The first effects discussed are those resulting from consumption subsidies; examples for Peru include food and gasoline subsidies. The second group comprises subsidies which are implicit in public sector enterprise prices such as those charged for steel, fertilizers, and petrochemicals as well transport and public utilities.[3] Next are the effects of selective price controls, common in Peru under Alan García and a feature of populist regimes generally. Finally, we discuss the implications of the informal markets that characterize Peruvian factor and product markets for real exchange rate determination.

In the following section, we develop a benchmark model of real exchange rate determination. This model identifies the key parameters that shape the real exchange rate. We subsequently use the model to examine the real exchange rate effects of consumption subsidies, public enterprise prices, price control, and informal markets. First, a reduction in a consumption subsidy appreciates the real exchange rate in all cases. Second, the real exchange rate effects of public sector price rises as well as relaxations in price controls are uncertain. The direct effect of reform in each area is to raise the price level and hence to appreciate the real exchange rate. But the indirect effects of these policies are uncertain due to induced changes in the relative price of nontraded goods. Nonetheless, we show that in most cases the real exchange rate appreciates in response to public enterprise price increases. Finally, we argue that the influence of informal markets on the real exchange rate is ambiguous.

The concluding section applies these results to recent economic events in Peru, where the huge public sector price increases as well as the elimination or reduction in consumption subsidies associated with the August 1990 public sector price reforms appreciated the real exchange rate. However, such policies do not explain the continued real appreciation since October 1990.

A BENCHMARK MODEL OF REAL EXCHANGE RATE DETERMINATION

The model expounded in this chapter draws from the public finance literature and the pure theory of international trade. In particular, the approaches of Peter Neary (1988) and Avinash Dixit and Victor Norman (1980) are used. Accordingly, no money or other assets exist, and all markets are competitive. The model incorporates a general specification of tastes and technology, however. It is assumed that the economy is a price taker producing one nontraded good (services) and a large number of traded goods, some of which are produced by government enterprises. Later, the assumption that public sector output is traded is discarded. Without a loss of generality, let us choose one of the traded goods as our *numéraire*. Government enterprises are assumed to set marginal cost equal to price, which may include a subsidy or tax.

For convenience, we assume the economy consists of a single aggregate household. This allows us to model the demand side of the economy using the expenditure function $e(\cdot)$, given in equation (1). All goods are assumed normal. National income is given by the gross national product (GNP) or revenue function $r(\cdot)$. In equation (1), p_s equals the price of the nontraded good, p is a vector of traded goods prices, m is a vector of imports, U is a scalar representing welfare, V is a vector of factor endowments, t is a vector of trade taxes, and s is a vector of consumption subsidies. One element of p, the *numéraire*, is equal to one. The superscript "c" denotes prices faced by consumers. The first derivative of the expenditure and GNP functions with respect to the $i'th$ price provides compensated demand and output supply functions, respectively. Thus, the total demand and supply of tradables is given by $e_p(\cdot)$ and $r_p(\cdot)$, which are vectors of derivatives of the expenditure and revenue functions with respect to traded prices.

For equilibrium, income must equal expenditure and the nontraded goods market must clear. Equation (1) sets expenditure equal to national income plus tariff revenue minus consumption subsidies. We assume that subsidies are financed by lump sum taxes and that tariff revenue is also redistributed in a lump sum fashion.

$$\overline{\underline{\mathbf{1}}} \qquad e\left(p^c, p_s^c\,; U\right) = r\left(p, p_s; V\right) + tm - se_p$$

In (1), t is the tariff vector on net imports, and s is a vector of consumption on tradables. For the moment, we ignore subsidies on nontraded goods. Net imports are given by (2).

$$\underline{\overline{\overline{2}}} \qquad m = e_p\left(p^c, p_s^c; U\right) - r_p\left(p, p_s, V\right)$$

The second condition for equilibrium requires that the nontraded goods market clear, which is given by (3). In this expression $e_s()$ and $r_s()$ are the derivatives of the expenditure, and the GNP functions with respect to the price of nontraded goods.

$$\underline{\overline{\overline{3}}} \qquad e_s\left(p^c, p_s^c; U\right) = r_s\left(p, p_s; V\right)$$

The relationship between domestic and external prices in terms of the *numéraire* is given by (4) where p_i is the world price of the *i'th* good and t_i is the trade tax in this market. Equation (5) establishes the relationship between producer and consumer prices.

$$\underline{\overline{\overline{4}}} \qquad p_i = p_i^* + t_i$$

$$\underline{\overline{\overline{5}}} \qquad p_j = p_j^c + s_j$$

The GNP function provides a general specification of technology. In particular, no restrictions are placed on the number of goods and factors in this economy nor on the degree of vertical integration in production.[4] Finally, we assume that substitutability in supply and demand holds for all goods. This assumption is not unduly restrictive, however. In the more general case where complementarities exist, our results apply as correlations which hold on average. The real exchange rate, R, is given by (6) where P and P^* are the domestic and foreign price indices and E is the exchange rate.

$$\underline{\overline{\overline{6}}} \qquad R = \frac{EP^*}{P}$$

Equations (7) and (8) specify the price indices for the internal and external price levels. The domestic price index is given by the consumer price index, but the results are unchanged if the producer price index is used:

$$\underline{\overline{\overline{7}}} \qquad P = \prod_{i=1}^{n}\left(p_i^c\right)^{\alpha_i}$$

$$\frac{\overline{\overline{}}}{8} \qquad P^* = \prod_{i=1}^{n} \left(p_i^{c^*} \right)^{\alpha_i^*}$$

CONSUMPTION SUBSIDIES, PUBLIC SECTOR PRICES, AND THE REAL EXCHANGE RATE

This section analyzes the real exchange rate effects of reducing consumption subsidies as well as public enterprise price increases. We distinguish between subsidies on goods consumed by households, termed "pure" consumption subsidies, and those on goods which are consumed by households and used as inputs by firms. The latter case is referred to as "mixed" consumption subsidies.

CONSUMPTION SUBSIDIES ON TRADED GOODS

PURE CONSUMPTION SUBSIDIES

A reduction in a consumption subsidy on the j'th traded good raises prices faced by consumers, while producer prices are unaffected. The direct effect of reducing the subsidy is thus to increase the consumer price index. However, there are also indirect price-level effects working through induced changes in the nontraded price level.

Differentiating (3) and solving for the nontraded good price level yields (9) where $-\eta_{ss}$ is the compensated own elasticity of demand for services, η_{sj} is the compensated cross elasticity of demand for services with respect to the price of the j'th traded good, ε_{ss} is the elasticity of supply of the nontraded good, y is real income, and η_s^y is the income elasticity of demand for services. A "$\wedge$" denotes a proportional rate of change.

$$\hat{p}_s = \omega_j \hat{p}_j^c + \gamma \hat{y},$$

$$\frac{\overline{\overline{}}}{9} \qquad \text{where}$$

$$\omega_j = \frac{\eta_{sj}}{\eta_{ss} + \varepsilon_{ss}} > 0, \gamma = \frac{\eta_s^y}{\eta_{ss} + \varepsilon_{ss}} > 0$$

Changes in real income are defined as $dy = e_u dU$, where e_u is the inverse of the marginal utility of income. The first term in (9) is a positive substitution effect, while the second term is the income effect. From second-best considerations, the income effects of a subsidy reduction are uncertain in an economy with many distortions. For the special case assumed here, where all other distortions are zero, real income increases. More formally, this is established using (9) and (10). Thus, the income and the substitution effects of a decrease in the *j'th* subsidy cause a rise in the price level of nontraded goods.

$$\overline{\overline{10}} \qquad dy\left(1+\frac{s_j e_{ju}}{e_u}\right) = s_j e_{jj} ds_j + s_j e_{js} dp_s$$

Equation (11), obtained by combining (6), (7), (9), and (10), summarizes the relationship between a consumption subsidy and the real exchange rate. Inasmuch as reducing the subsidy increases the domestic price level relative to the foreign level, the real exchange rate must appreciate.

$$\overline{\overline{11}} \qquad \hat{R} = -\left(\alpha_j + \alpha_s \omega_j\right)\hat{p}_j^c - \alpha_{os}\gamma\hat{y} < 0$$

Proposition One: The elimination of a pure consumption subsidy on a traded good appreciates the real exchange rate.

MIXED CONSUMPTION SUBSIDIES

Subsidies are often placed on goods that are inputs, such as fertilizers, or on goods that are consumed by households and are inputs, such as gasoline or electricity. To examine the real exchange rate effects of a mixed consumption subsidy, let us assume that the economy has a fixed endowment of a mixed consumption good "oil."[5] The revenue function for this economy is given by (12), where p_o is the world price of oil and V is defined to exclude oil.

$$\overline{\overline{12}} \qquad r\left(p,p_s,p_o^c,p_o;V\right) = r'\left(p,p_s,p_o^c,p_o;V'\right) + p_o \overline{O}$$

The real income effects of a reduction in the oil subsidy, given in equation (13), are positive.[6] To obtain this result, other distortions in the economy are set to zero.

$$\overline{\overline{13}} \qquad dy\left(1+\frac{s_o e_{ou}}{e_u}\right) = s_o\left(e_{oo} - r'_{oo}\right)ds_o + s_o\left(e_{os} - r'_{os}\right)dp_s$$

Solving for the impact on the nontraded price level of an oil subsidy reduction, (14) is obtained.

$$\hat{p}_s = (\omega_o + \theta_o)\hat{p}_o^c + \gamma\hat{y}$$

<u>14</u>   where

$$\theta_o = -\frac{\varepsilon_{so}}{\eta_{ss} + \varepsilon_{ss}} > 0.$$

The oil price increase shifts demand toward nontraded goods while raising costs in the nontraded sector, but it also alters factor returns. This, in turn, has indirect effects on the supply of nontraded goods. Moreover, the factor price effect can reduce or increase the supply of nontraded goods. As a result, the overall effects on supply depend on whether the cost-increasing effects are outweighed by possible changes in factor rewards. If the cross elasticity of supply of services with respect to the price of oil (ε_{so}) is negative, then, as shown by (14), the nontraded price level increases and the real exchange rate appreciates.

<u>15</u> $$\hat{R} = -\left[\alpha_o + \alpha_s(\omega_o + \theta_o)\right]\hat{p}_o^c - \alpha_s\gamma\hat{y} < 0$$

Proposition Two: The removal of a subsidy on a good that is consumed and is used as an input produces a real exchange rate appreciation if nontraded goods and the subsidized good are substitutes in supply.

Consumption Subsidies on Nontraded Goods: The Case of Public Enterprise Prices

Consumption subsidies are often placed on nontraded goods. The implicit subsidies present in the prices of public enterprises are notable example of this. Large subsidies for electricity, transportation, and other public utilities were an important policy under the García regime. In this section, we examine the real exchange rate effects of public sector price increases. Let us assume that the good "electricity" is produced by a single state-owned enterprise. We further assume that electricity is a pure consumption good and that marginal cost is set equal to price with losses covered by lump sum transfers. The expenditure equal to output condition is given by equation (16), where p_g is the electricity price. All other distortions are set equal to zero.

<u>16</u> $$e(p, p_g^c, p_s; U) = r(p, p_g, p_s; U) - s_g e_g$$

Equation (17) represents the market-clearing condition for electricity.

<u>17</u> $$e_g(p, p_g^c, p_s; U) = r_g(p, p_g, p_s; V)$$

The system given by (3), (5), (16), and (17) can be solved for p_s and U. There are two nontraded goods, services and electricity, in this economy. Given our assumptions about technology and preferences, a reduction in the electricity subsidy raises the electricity price faced by consumers. Owing to income effects, however, consumer prices could increase by more than the reduction in the subsidy. The latter result, however, requires an implausible set of parameter values. Equation (18) captures the relationship between consumer prices and the electricity subsidy. The μ parameter is a complex function of elasticities of demand, supply, and income.

18 $$\hat{p}_g^c = \mu \hat{s}_g, \ \mu < 0$$

Reducing the electricity subsidy will raise welfare in the sense that everyone could be compensated and funds still be left over. This result, of course, depends on the assumption that the public utility sets price equal to marginal cost. If it acts as a monopolist, welfare can fall. Solving for the effects of a reduction in a consumption subsidy on the services price level, (19) is obtained.

19 $$\hat{p}_s = \omega_g \hat{p}_g^c + \theta_g \hat{p}_g + \gamma \hat{y}$$

From this expression, the public enterprise price increase influences the service price level through three channels. First, it shifts demand toward services. This effect is given by the first term. Second, it alters the supply of services. The sign of the supply effect depends on the relationship between services and the subsidized activity in supply, ε_{sg}. By assumption, this is negative.[7] Finally, the increase in income raises the demand for services. The income effect is given by the final term. In sum, the impact of a public sector price increase on the service price level is uncertain as demand and supply effects work in different directions. Turning to the real exchange rate effects of public sector price increases, in (20) note that the direct effect is to appreciate the real exchange rate.

20 $$\hat{R} = -\left(\alpha_g + \alpha_s \omega_g\right) \hat{p}_g^c - \alpha_s \theta_g \hat{p}_g - \alpha_s \gamma \hat{y}$$

However, the overall effects are uncertain as the nontraded goods' price-level effects are ambiguous. In practice, however, an increase in the supply of services due to reductions in public sector subsidies are probably minor. In the first place, public sector enterprises are typically capital intensive. Thus, any increase in service employment will be small. Also, public enterprise output is an important input into the nontraded sector. So price increases will directly raise the nontraded price level. Consequently, there is a presumption that a public sector price increase appreciates the real exchange rate.

Proposition Three: A public enterprise price increase will usually appreciate the real exchange rate.

PRICE CONTROLS AND THE REAL EXCHANGE RATE

P rice controls were a prominent feature of economic policy under Alan García as under most populist regimes. With generalized price controls, official prices do not reflect scarcity, and black markets appear. The removal of such controls will almost certainly be accompanied by an increase in the measured price level and hence a real exchange rate appreciation. A more common situation in developing economies occurs when price controls are selectively applied to certain goods or services.[8] This section provides a general equilibrium treatment of the relationship between selective price controls and the real exchange rate.[9]

Let us assume that price control is imposed on a nontraded good z that is produced by the private sector.[10] We assume that price control is costlessly imposed and perfectly monitored, that no black markets emerge, and that quality is unchanged. We also assume that the controlled good is allocated to its highest-value users and that rents arising from rent control are distributed in lump sum fashion. Admittedly, these assumptions, associated with traditional textbook treatments of price control, are unrealistic. They do, however, allow us to isolate the economic forces which determine the impact of price controls on the real exchange rate. The more realistic case, where rents are dissipated, is considered later.

CASE 1: NO WAITING IN LINE

Given these assumptions, the demand side of the economy can be represented by the restricted expenditure function as defined in equation (21). In this function, the rationed quantity of the nontraded goods appears as an additional argument. The controlled price does not appear.[11]

21 $$e(p, p_s; \overline{z}; U) = \text{Min } px + p_s x_s + p_z z \text{ s.t. } U = U(x, x_s, z), z = \overline{z}$$

Virtual prices, as developed by E. Rotbarth (1940-1941) and especially Peter Neary and Kevin Roberts (1981), simplify the analyses. The virtual price is defined as that price which induces consumers to purchase just the rationed amount.[12] There are two nontraded prices in this economy: 1) the price of the controlled good and 2) the price of services. The virtual price for z is obtained from equation (22), where e_z is the derivative of the restricted expenditure function with respect to the *quantity* of the rationed good (see Neary and Roberts 1981 for a proof). From the properties of the restricted expenditure function, e_z is negative. Intuitively, a relaxation in the rationing constraint reduces the cost of obtaining a given level of utility.

22

$$\tilde{p}_z = \overline{p}_z - e_z$$

where $\tilde{p}_z$ indicates the virtual price,

$\overline{p}_z$ indicates the controlled price.

Equation (23) modifies the income equal to expenditure condition to allow for price control. In the modified budget constraint, consumer expenditure evaluated at virtual prices is equal to output.

23

$$e(p, p_s, \tilde{p}_z; U) = r(p, p_s, \overline{p}_z; V) + (\tilde{p}_z - \overline{p}_z) r_z$$

The market-clearing condition for the price-controlled good is (24).

24

$$e_z(p, p_s, \tilde{p}_z; U) = r_z(p, p_s, \overline{p}_z; V)$$

Equation (25) solves for the impact of a relaxation in price control on the price level of services. A relaxation of price control increases the producer price of z, reduces its virtual price, and raises income (which can be verified by totally differentiating (3), (24), and (25) and assuming substitution in supply and demand). As a result of the lower price, consumers substitute toward z. This effect is captured by the first term. The overall effects on demand are ambiguous, however, because real income increases. On the supply side, the supply of services is reduced as the z sector expands. Consequently, the overall impact on the nontraded price level, and hence the real exchange rate, is ambiguous.[13]

25

$$\hat{p}_s = \omega_z \hat{\tilde{p}}_z + \theta_z \hat{\tilde{p}}_z + \gamma \hat{y}$$

CASE 2: WAITING IN LINE

In practice, rents due to price control are not transferred in a lump sum fashion, rationed goods do not always go the highest-value users, and resources are used up in black markets and waiting in line. We now examine how our results are changed when rationed goods are allocated by time expenditures. This allows us to introduce the rent-seeking behavior of Anne Krueger (1974) and Jagdish Bhagwati (1980) into the model.

The income equal to expenditure condition for this economy is given by (26), where L is the endowment of labor, L_z is labor used up waiting in line, and w is the wage rate. Waiting in line, in effect, reduces the effective labor force available to the economy. Note that we have redefined V, the vector of factor endowments, so as to exclude labor.

$$\textbf{26} \qquad e(p,p_s,\tilde{p}_z;U) = r(p,p_s,\overline{p}_z,w;V) + (\tilde{p}_z - \overline{p}_z)r_z + w(\overline{L} - L_z)$$

The labor market condition is given by (27), which sets the demand for labor equal to its endowment less labor used up waiting in line. Recall that the first derivative of the revenue function with respect to the wage rate is the demand for labor.

$$\textbf{27} \qquad r_w(p,p_s,\overline{p}_z;w;V) = \overline{L} - L_z$$

Since individuals are identical, rents due to price controls are completely dissipated. This condition is given by equation (28).

$$\textbf{28} \qquad wL_z = (\tilde{p}_z - \overline{p}_z)r_z$$

Waiting in line changes our results in two ways. First, an easing of price controls increases the effective labor force available to the economy as time wasted in line falls. Consequently, the real income gains of price decontrol are greater. Second, the increase in the effective labor force changes the supply of nontraded goods. The sign of this effect, which is uncertain, depends on the Rybcznski term (g_{sL}) for services. Solving for the nontraded price level, we obtain (29), where p_L, the elasticity of the nontraded price level with respect to the effective labor, is equal to $g_{sL}(g_s/L)$. It can be positive, negative, or zero.

$$\textbf{29} \qquad \hat{p}_s = \omega_z \hat{\overline{p}}_z + \theta_z \hat{\tilde{p}}_z + \pi_L \hat{L} + \gamma \hat{y}$$

A relaxation in price control directly increases the measured price level, as shown by the first term in (30), and appreciates the real exchange rate. The overall effects are, however, uncertain. In contrast to public enterprise price increases, moreover, there is no presumption that the real exchange rate appreciates.

Proposition Four: The direct effect of a reduction in price control is to appreciate the real exchange rate, but indirect effects working through the nontraded price level may offset the direct effect.

$$
\boxed{30} \qquad \hat{R} = -\left(\alpha_z + \alpha_s\theta_z\right)\hat{\bar{P}}_z - \alpha_s\left(\omega_z\hat{\bar{P}}_z + \pi_L\hat{L} + \gamma\hat{y}\right)
$$

INFORMAL MARKETS AND THE REAL EXCHANGE RATE

One consequence of the extensive governmental regulation historically present in Peru is informal or black markets in many areas of the economy. The work of Hernando de Soto (1990), in particular, has drawn attention to this phenomenon. Peru, as well as other Latin American economies, is introducing broad-based reforms based on the removal of government-imposed distortions in factor and product markets. Examples of this are the privatization of government enterprises, the reform of labor market regulations, and the easing of entry barriers. This section sketches some of the avenues through which such reforms affect the real exchange rate. Informal markets take many forms, but all have a common characteristic: they emerge to avoid high taxes or to escape onerous government regulation. In most cases, moreover, government policies increase formal sector prices above their free market levels. We shall focus on both features to provide a simple example which captures many of the issues involved in an informal market.

Let us assume that the government levies a tax on the consumption of the $i'th$ traded good and that informal producers subsequently emerge to avoid the tax. Let us assume that firms in the informal sector produce a nontraded good, denoted by p_j. This good is a perfect substitute for the taxed good in consumption. Therefore, its price is equal to the tax-inclusive price of the $i'th$ good.

Within an informal sector, the income equal to expenditure condition is given by (31). Note that p_j may be omitted from expenditure function because of our assumption of perfect substitutability. Tax revenue is equal to domestic consumption of this good (e_i) less production of the informal sector (r_j) multiplied by the tax rate. Finally, (32) is the market-clearing condition for services.

$$
\boxed{31} \qquad e\left(p_i^c, p, p_s; U\right) = r\left(p_j, p_i, p, p_s; V\right) + t_i^c\left(e_i - r_j\right)
$$

$$
\boxed{32} \qquad e_s\left(p_i^c, p, p_s; U\right) = r_s\left(p_j, p_i, p, p_s; V\right)
$$

Two issues must be addressed in regard to the real exchange rate effects of the informal sector. First, given that distortions exist, what are the effects of the informal sector on the real exchange rate? And, second, does the informal sector change our results concerning economic reform and the real exchange rate? Each question is addressed in turn.

Using (31) and (32), it can be shown that the informal sector reduces real income so long as tax revenue is positive and there are no other distortions in the economy. Intuitively, income is lower because the informal sector reduces tax revenue without affecting the consumption distortion. On the supply side, the expansion of illegal trade draws resources from the nontraded sector while the fall in income reduces demand. Thus, the impact of the informal sector on the real exchange rate, holding existing distortions constant, is ambiguous.

Let us turn to the second issue: Does the informal sector alter our analysis of economic reform? Here we define reform as a reduction in the consumption tax. Using (31) and (32), it can be shown that income increases with a reduction in the consumption tax and that the informal sector contracts. Solving for the effects of the consumption tax on the nontraded price level we obtain (33).

$$33 \qquad \hat{p}_s = \left(\omega_i + \theta_j \right) \hat{p}_i^c + \gamma \hat{y}$$

The fall in the traded price level shifts compensated demand away from services, but the increase in income raises demand. On the supply side, the contraction of the informal sector increases the supply of services. Therefore, the overall effects on the nontraded price level and the real exchange rate are uncertain. Moreover, the existence of an informal sector does not change this result. With no illegal sector, the θ_j is zero, but this does not alter our conclusions. It does, however, make it more likely that the nontraded price level will fall. This gives us our final result.

Proposition Five: The real exchange rate effects of a decline in informal markets are uncertain.

This result continues to hold if we allow for taxes on the consumption of nontraded goods or if informal producers exist because of barriers to entry or other government regulations. These modifications, however, make it more likely that the informal sector will increase income.

PUBLIC SECTOR PRICES AND THE REAL EXCHANGE RATE IN PERU: 1985-1993

To conclude, we analyze the public sector pricing policies associated with the Alan García and Alberto Fujimori governments in Peru and discuss their role in explaining real exchange rate movements. Throughout this section, we emphasize the enormous changes in relative prices that resulted from public sector pricing policies. In particular, we focus on the real exchange rate effects of the August 1990 reforms and, second, on whether public sector prices have played a role in the sustained real appreciation since then.

The Alan García administration took office in August 1985. García's economic program called for a partial suspension of payments on international debt, expansionary demand policies, and greater restrictions on international trade. After an initial growth spurt in 1986-1987, the economy ran into current account problems, experienced an acceleration in inflation, and suffered a rapid fall in output and real wages. However, our attention is confined to developments in the areas of interest to the subject matter of this paper: subsidies and public sector pricing. Before the 1990 reforms, Peru had 135 state enterprises. These enterprises were the sole producers of electricity, gas, oil, and telecommunications and had roughly a one-third share in mining and transport. In 1982, state enterprises accounted for 32 percent of gross national product (GNP) (Balassa et al. 1986).

Table 1 presents data on the real prices of public sector products in Peru from 1985 to 1993. The public sector price index is constructed using the prices of 22 important publicly provided goods. Altogether, these items have a weight of 21 percent in the consumer price index. The entries in the first part of the table were formed by deflating each price by the consumer price index and then expressing the result as a percentage of the corresponding level for July 1985. Table 1 also provides the public sector price index in terms of all other goods.

From 1985 onward, public sector prices lagged behind inflation. Indeed, the nominal prices of many public sector prices were reduced as part of the government's heterodox strategy. Furthermore, the administration placed large subsidies on rice, potatoes, milk, and gasoline products. By 1987, implicit and explicit consumption subsidies amounted to at least 7 percent of GNP (World Bank 1989, 52). By then, the relative price of public sector goods was at only one-third of its original level. As a result of depressed prices, public enterprise revenue as a percentage of GNP decreased from 26 percent of GNP in 1985 to 10 percent in 1989. The budget deficit almost doubled over the same period, reaching 11 percent of GNP in 1989.[14]

On August 8, 1990, just days after succeeding the García administration, the Alberto Fujimori government introduced its economic program. Price

Table 1.
Real Public Sector Prices in Peru
1985-1992

	July 1985	July 1986	July 1987	July 1988	July 1989	July 1990	Aug 1990	Aug 1991	Aug 1992	Mar 1993
Gasoline (84 octane)	100	82	66	40	29	8	49	36	32	28
Kerosene	100	53	33	29	29	20	96	56	60	55
Electricity (residential)	100	60	41	25	9	7	60	33	58	43
Bus fare	100	86	79	75	58	55	75	91	101	n.a.
Local phone call	100	84	75	51	28	8	45	32	63	42
Whole milk powder	100	85	66	77	37	53	71	43	40	41
Drinkable water	100	96	114	56	19	30	53	48	51	30
Wheat (common bread)	100	79	58	33	57	55	79	30	32	35
Rice (common)	100	74	63	57	54	51	47	35	39	42
Public sector price index	100	76	66	58	32	35	59	40	45	42

Sources: Compiled data from Instituto Nacional de Estadística; Coyuntura Económica; Universidad del Pacífico, Lima; and Banco Central de Reserva del Perú.

Note: The public sector price index is computed in terms of all other goods, that is, all nonpublic sector goods.

controls were lifted, the exchange rate was unified, and large increases in public sector prices were enacted. Altogether, the nominal price of public sector goods increased by 654 percent in August while the relative price of public sector goods in terms of all other goods, as shown by Table 1, increased by 69 percent. In September, quantitative restrictions on foreign trade were removed, and a new tariff regime was initiated with tariff rates set at 15, 25, and 50 percent.[15] A temporary surcharge of 10 percent was placed on the two highest rates.

To the surprise of most observers, the stabilization plan was accompanied by a significant real appreciation. Figure 1 and Table 2 traces the evolution of the trade-weighted real exchange rate for Peru from January 1990 to March 1992. Because of the complex system of multiple exchange rates and

Table 2.
The Real Exchange Rate in Peru
(July 1990=100)

1990												1991							
1	**2**	**3**	**4**	**5**	**6**	**7**	**8**	**9**	**10**	**11**	**12**	**1**	**2**	**3**	**4**	**5**	**6**	**7**	**8**
58	48	59	54	65	100	75	58	64	59	56	52	42	44	40	42	50	48	43	39

1991				1992												1993			
9	**10**	**11**	**12**	**1**	**2**	**3**	**4**	**5**	**6**	**7**	**8**	**9**	**10**	**11**	**12**	**1**	**2**	**3**	**4**
38	42	46	44	42	39	36	37	40	41	42	43	45	49	48	46	46	46	47	47

Sources: For 1990, the real free rate and the real export rate were provided by the Departamento de Investigaciones, Banco Central de Reserva del Perú. For 1991, the real export rates are from Banco Central de Reserva del Perú, *Nota semanal*, various issues.

Note: For January to August 1990, the real free rate and the real export rate were averaged. In August 1990, the exchange rate was unified and floated. Thus, the export rate and the free rate are the same after August 1990.

controls, pre-August 1990 real exchange rate measures should be treated with great caution. However, with the unification of exchange rates in August, the real exchange rate is measured precisely.

We shall use a simple approach to determine the effects of public sector price increases on the real exchange rate. Recall from (6) that the real exchange rate is the ratio of the external to internal price levels denominated in domestic currency. Using (6), (7), and (8), we obtain the following decomposition, where E is the nominal exchange rate which is used to convert external prices into domestic prices.

$$\overline{\overline{34}} \qquad \hat{R} = \alpha_g\left(\hat{E} - \hat{p}_g\right) + \alpha_s\left(\hat{E} - \hat{p}_s\right) + \alpha_t\left(\hat{E} - \hat{p}_t\right) + \hat{P}^*$$

We aggregate traded goods into a composite commodity, tradables, denoted by p_t. Observe that all the variables in (34) are measurable. This expression splits changes in the real exchange rate into changes due to public sector, traded, and nontraded price movements. We first look at real exchange rate movements from June 1990 to December 1990, thereby capturing the effects of the August 8, 1990 Fujimori plan. Subsequently, we examine real exchange rate developments since then.

Figure 1.
The Real Exchange Rate in Peru: 1990-93
July 1990 = 100

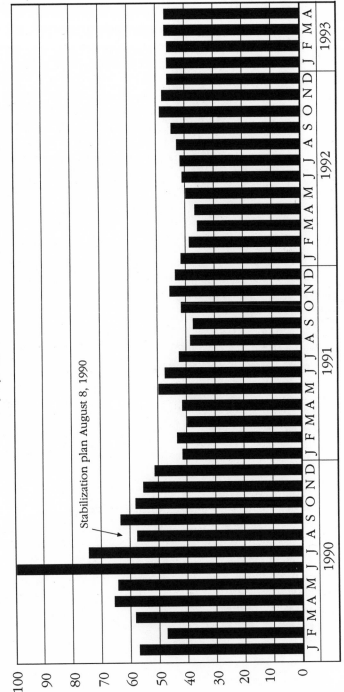

THE FUJIMORI PLAN

Table 3 reports the percentage changes in prices for the nominal exchange rate, tradables, nontradables, public sector prices, and the overall domestic price level, P. Again, public sector prices were increased in August 1990 by 654 percent, that is, by seven and one-half times their July levels! The export and import exchange rates were unified and floated, while the exchange rate depreciated by 378 percent. Overall, inflation was 397 percent in August. Also noticeable is the fall in the relative price of nontraded goods in August. This is less of a puzzle once it is realized that the currency depreciation and the rise in consumer prices reduced the real money supply by 40 percent, having a negative liquidity effect on the relative price of services (for a model of this process, see Connolly and Taylor 1976). Finally, the trade liberalization accounts for the relatively low rate of increase in the price of tradables in September and October, when the traded price level fell by 38 percent in terms of the exchange rate.

Table 4 identifies the sources of the real exchange rate changes. The final column shows that changes in the external price level had no role in explaining real exchange rate developments over this period. The large real exchange rate appreciation of 36 percent in August 1990 is explained by public sector price increases. The real depreciation of September 1990 appears to be due primarily to the trade liberalization.

REAL EXCHANGE RATE DEVELOPMENTS SINCE DECEMBER 1990

To conclude, we shall provide a brief summary of real exchange developments since December 1990. Table 3 highlights changes in prices since 1990. It is noteworthy that the pace of inflation did not slow after the first six months of 1991. Indeed, if anything, inflation appears to have strengthened in the first quarter of 1993. However, public sector prices are now adjusted at regular intervals.

In Table 4, the real exchange rate appreciation apparent in the last quarter of 1990 continued into 1991. In the first quarter of 1991, the real appreciation totaled more than 20 percent. Only from the second quarter of 1992 has a real depreciation taken place. Even so, the real exchange rate remains greatly appreciated compared to its September 1990 value. As the table makes clear, most of this real appreciation can be ascribed to an increase in the relative price of nontraded goods. Public sector prices have no role, however, in this recent real appreciation.

Table 3.
Changes in Prices in Peru: June 1990 to April 1993
in % per month

	$\hat{E}$	$\hat{P}_g$	$\hat{P}_s$	$\hat{P}_t$	$\hat{P}$
June 1990	62.90	49.00	33.60	47.00	42.60
July 1990	85.90	74.50	41.10	77.50	63.20
Aug. 1990	378.10	654.00	272.20	412.70	397.00
Sept. 1990	43.50	4.10	32.10	5.40	13.80
Oct. 1990	2.80	6.00	11.80	9.60	9.60
Nov. 1990	-1.50	4.80	4.40	7.70	5.90
Dec. 1990	18.30	27.70	27.40	19.10	23.70
Jan 1991	4.50	12.20	33.10	9.50	17.80
Feb 1991	1.90	4.60	19.60	4.20	9.40
Mar 1991	3.60	0.90	16.60	4.30	7.70
April 1991	12.30	2.40	11.20	3.40	5.80
May 1991	25.00	7.10	6.48	8.90	7.60
June 1991	6.35	9.90	13.20	6.00	9.30
July 1991	-2.40	11.10	11.20	6.50	9.10
Aug 1991	-3.60	4.60	13.00	4.00	7.20
Sept 1991	0.00	7.50	5.70	4.60	5.60
Oct 1991	15.00	5.60	1.90	4.90	4.00
Nov 1991	12.00	7.10	0.70	5.20	4.00
Dec 1991	-1.90	7.40	-1.20	6.00	3.70
Jan 1992	-2.00	1.80	4.80	3.30	3.50
Feb 1992	-1.00	0.60	9.60	2.90	4.70
Mar 1992	-2.00	0.30	13.00	6.60	7.40
April 1992	6.30	2.70	5.30	1.80	3.20
May 1992	10.80	15.50	-2.00	2.40	3.40
June 1992	4.40	3.40	6.50	1.40	3.60
July 1992	5.10	2.70	3.80	3.60	3.50
Aug 1992	4.00	3.90	2.30	2.70	2.80
Sept 1992	6.20	3.30	0.60	3.90	2.60
Oct 1992	13.10	6.00	0.10	5.40	3.60
Nov 1992	4.50	5.70	-1.30	6.50	3.50
Dec 1992	0.60	3.60	2.30	5.20	3.80
Jan 1993	3.70	3.30	6.50	4.30	4.90
Feb 1993	4.10	2.80	5.10	1.30	2.90
March 1993	4.50	3.10	3.20	5.60	4.20
April 1993	3.80	3.20	5.30	4.30	4.40

Sources: Banco Central de Reserva del Perú, *Nota semanal*, various issues; authors' calculations.

Table 4.
Decomposition of the Change in the Real Exchange Rate in Peru
June 1990 to April 1993

	$\hat{R}$	$\alpha_g\left(\hat{E}-\hat{P}_g\right)$	$\alpha_s\left(\hat{E}-\hat{P}_s\right)$	$\alpha_t\left(\hat{E}-\hat{P}_t\right)$	$\hat{P}*$
June 1990	20.3	2.9	10.2	7.0	0.20
July 1990	21.9	2.4	15.7	3.7	0.20
Aug 1990	-35.9	-57.9	37.1	-15.2	0.20
Sep. 1990	31.0	8.3	4.0	16.8	1.90
Oct 1990	-6.4	-0.7	-3.2	-3.0	0.50
Nov 1990	-5.1	-1.3	-2.1	-4.1	2.40
Dec 1990	-3.3	-2.0	-3.2	-0.4	2.20
Jan. 1991	-18.4	-1.6	-10.0	-2.2	-4.60
Feb. 1991	-6.5	-0.6	-6.2	-1.0	1.30
Mar. 1991	-2.9	0.6	-4.5	-0.3	1.30
Apr. 1991	4.7	2.1	0.4	3.9	-1.60
May 1991	17.2	3.8	6.5	7.1	-0.10
June 1991	-4.3	-0.8	-2.4	0.1	-1.20
July 1991	-11.9	-2.8	-4.8	-3.9	-0.40
Aug. 1991	-10.7	-2.8	-4.8	-3.9	-0.40
Sept. 1991	-5.9	-1.6	-2.0	-2.0	-0.03
Oct. 1991	11.7	2.0	4.6	4.4	0.70
Nov. 1991	8.1	1.0	3.9	3.0	0.20
Dec. 1991	-6.0	-2.0	-0.2	-3.5	-0.30
Jan. 1992	-5.2	-0.8	-2.4	-2.3	0.30
Feb. 1992	-6.5	-0.3	-3.7	-1.7	-0.80
Mar. 1992	-10.6	-0.5	-5.2	-3.8	-1.00
Apr. 1992	3.7	0.7	0.3	2.0	0.70
May 1992	8.4	-1.0	4.5	3.7	1.20
June 1992	2.2	0.2	-0.7	1.3	1.40
July 1992	3.7	0.5	0.5	0.7	2.00
Aug. 1992	2.1	0.0	0.6	0.6	0.90
Sept. 1992	4.0	0.6	1.9	1.0	0.40
Oct. 1992	8.2	1.5	4.6	3.4	-1.30
Nov. 1992	-1.5	-0.3	2.0	-0.9	-2.40
Dec. 1992	-3.2	-0.6	-0.6	-2.0	0.00
Jan. 1993	-1.8	0.1	-1.0	-0.03	-0.70
Feb. 1993	1.2	0.3	-0.3	1.3	0.00
Mar. 1993	1.0	0.3	0.5	-0.5	0.70
Apr. 1993	1.5	0.1	-0.5	-0.2	2.10

Where α_g = 0.21, α_s = 0.35, and α_t = 0.44

Sources: Authors' computations from data from the Instituto Nacional de Estadística; Coyuntura Económica; Universidad del Pacífico; and Banco Central de Reserva del Perú, *Nota Semanal*, various issues.

CONCLUDING COMMENTS

This chapter has examined the effects of consumption subsidies, public enterprise pricing, price controls, and informal markets on the real exchange rate with special reference to Peru. Under plausible assumptions, reform in these areas can lead to a real exchange rate appreciation. The public sector price reforms of Peru in August 1990 were followed by a large real appreciation. As an empirical matter, comprehensive public sector price reforms that are not reversed tend to appreciate the real exchange rate permanently. These factors cannot explain Peru's most recent real appreciation, however.

NOTES

1. On economic populism, see Dornbusch and Edwards 1990 and 1991 and Sachs 1989.

2. Dornbusch, Sturzenegger, and Wolf (1990) and Buffie (1992) examine macroeconomic issues arising from public sector pricing but do not mention the exchange rate.

3. For developing countries, state enterprises typically produce between 10 percent and 20 percent of GNP. Short (1984), for example, found that the average share of public enterprises in Africa was 18 percent, while Balassa et al. (1986) estimated that the average for large Latin American economies was 19 percent.

4. Following Neary (1985), the model can be extended to allow for unemployment. This would complicate the model but not change the results.

5. We adopt this assumption for expository purposes. When the supply of oil is variable, a separate revenue function must be specified for the oil economy. The results would still hold.

6. From Shepard's Lemma, the first derivative of the revenue function with respect to the price of oil gives the demand for oil as an intermediate input in the nonoil domestic economy.

7. The ε_{sg} term is negative in the specific factor model but can be positive or negative in the Heckscher-Ohlin model. In general, there is a presumption that it is negative.

8. Selective price controls have long been a feature of Latin American economies (see Balassa et al. 1986).

9. For partial equilibrium approaches, see Barzel 1974, Cheung 1974 and Sah 1987.

10. Our results are readily generalized to cover 1) shortages which arise when public sector prices lag behind inflation or 2) the imposition of price controls on traded goods.

11. For details on the restricted expenditure function, see Deaton and Muellbauer 1980 and Cornes 1992.

12. For an alternative treatment of price control in general equilibrium, see Helpman 1988.

13. If trade ceases, price controls on importables and exportables have identical real exchange rate effects. If trade continues for an export good, an easing of price controls raises the nontraded price level.

14. The García administration intensified trade restrictions. By 1987, all imports required a license, and the average effective rate of protection arising from trade restrictions and multiple exchange rates was estimated by the World Bank (1989) to be 141 percent.

15. The 50 percent rate was abolished in April 1991.

REFERENCES

Balassa, Bela, Gerardo Bueno, Pedro-Pablo Kuczynski, and Mario Henrique Simonsen. 1986. *Towards Renewed Economic Growth in Latin America.* Washington, D.C.: Institute for International Economics.

Barzel, Yoram. 1974. "A Theory of Rationing by Waiting." *Journal of Law and Economics* 17:73-95.

Bhagwati, Jagdish. 1980. "Lobbying and Welfare." *Journal of Public Economics* 14:355-363.

Buffie, Edward F. 1992. "Stabilization and Public Sector Prices." *Journal of Monetary Economics* 29:253-276.

Chandra, Vandana, and M. Ali Khan. 1993. "Foreign Investment in the Presence of an Informal Sector." *Económica* 60:79-104.

Cheung, Steven. 1974. "A Theory of Price Control." *Journal of Law and Economics* 17: 53-71.

Connolly, Michael, and John Devereux. 1992. "Commercial Policy, the Terms of Trade, and Real Exchange Rates." *Oxford Economic Papers* 44:507-512.

Connolly, Michael, and Dean Taylor. 1976. "Adjustment to Devaluation with Money and Non-traded Goods." *Journal of International Economics* 6:289-298.

Cornes, Richard. 1992. *Duality and Modern Economics.* New York: Cambridge University Press.

Deaton, Angus, and John Muellbauer. 1980. *Economics and Consumer Behavior.* Cambridge: Cambridge University Press.

De Soto, Hernando. 1990. *El otro sendero: La revolución informal.* Lima: Instituto Libertad y Democracia.

Devarajan, Shantayanan, Christine Jones, and Michael Roemer. 1989. "Markets under Price Controls in Partial and General Equilibrium." *World Development* 12:1881-1893.

Dixit, Avinash, and Victor Norman. 1980. *The Theory of International Trade: A Dual, General Equilibrium Approach.* Cambridge: Cambridge University Press.

Dornbusch, Rudiger, Federico Sturzenegger, and Holger Wolf. 1990. "Extreme Inflation: Dynamics and Stabilization." *Brookings Papers on Economic Activity* 2: 1-84. Washington, D.C.: The Brookings Institution.

Dornbusch, Rudiger, and Sebastian Edwards. 1990. "Macroeconomic Populism." *Journal of Development Economics* 32:247-277.

Dornbusch, Rudiger, and Sebastian Edwards. 1991. *The Macroeconomics of Populism in Latin America.* Washington, D.C.: The Brookings Institution.

Edwards, Sebastian. 1989. *Real Exchange Rates, Devaluation, and Adjustment: Exchange Rate Policy in Developing Economies.* Cambridge: MIT Press.

Fallis, George, and Lawrence Smith. 1984. "Uncontrolled Prices in a Controlled Market: The Case of Rent Controls." *American Economic Review* 77:193-200.

Gould, John, and Steven Henry. 1967. "The Effects of Price Control in a Related Market." *Económica* 54:411-429.

Helpman, Elhanan. 1988. "Macroeconomic Effects of Price Controls: The Role of Market Structure." *Economic Journal* 98: 340-354.

Krueger, Anne. 1974. "The Political Economy of the Rent-Seeking Society." *American Economic Review* 64:291-303.

Neary, J. Peter. 1985. "International Factor Mobility, Minimum Wages and Factor Price Equalization: A Synthesis." *Quarterly Journal of Economics* 100:551-570.

Neary, J. Peter. 1988. "Determinants of the Equilibrium Real Exchange Rate." *American Economic Review* 78:210-215.

Neary, J. Peter, and Kevin Roberts. 1981. "The Theory of Household Behavior under Rationing." *European Economic Review* 87:25-42.

Pastor, Manuel, and Carol Wise. 1992. "Peruvian Economic Policy in the 1980s: From Orthodoxy to Heterodoxy and Back." *Latin American Research Review* 27:83-118.

Paus, Eva. 1991. "Adjustment and Development in Latin America: The Failure of Peruvian Heterodoxy 1985-1990." *World Development* 19:411-434.

Rotbarth, E. (1940-1941). "The Measurement of Changes in Real Income under Rationing." *Review of Economic Studies* 8:100-107.

Sachs, Jeffrey. 1989. "Social Conflict and Populist Policies in Latin America." National Bureau of Economic Research (NBER) Working Paper #2897. Cambridge: NBER.

Sah, Raj. 1987. "Queues, Rations, and the Market: Comparisons of Outcomes for the Poor and Rich." *American Economic Review* 74:69-76.

Short, R. Peter. 1984. "The Role of Public Enterprises: An International Statistical Comparison." In *Public Enterprise in Mixed Economies: Some Macroeconomic Aspects*, eds. R. Peter Short, Robert H. Floyd, and Clive S. Gray. Washington, D.C.: The International Monetary Fund.

Tobin, James, and Henrik Houthakker. 1950/51. "The Effects of Rationing on Demand Elasticities." *Review of Economic Studies* 18:140-153.

Webb, Richard. 1987. "Stabilization Policy: Peru 1980-1985." Unpublished manuscript.

World Bank. 1989. *Peru: Policies to Stop Hyperinflation and Initiate Economic Recovery.* Washington, D.C.: World Bank.

IX

ALTERNATIVE SCENARIOS FOR THE PERUVIAN ECONOMY

Santiago Roca

INTRODUCTION

O ver the past three years (1990-1993), the Peruvian economy has undergone a drastic economic stabilization program, the most salient characteristic of which has been the reorganization of state finances through a severe reduction in pre-debt public spending, increased tax collection, and a modification of the prices of public utilities. Accompanying this reorganization is an essentially restrictive monetary and exchange policy in addition to a set of structural reforms designed at the spur of the moment and carried out without regard to sequence or timing. Forming a backdrop to the program are the fetters and trammels established by the International Monetary Fund (IMF), which limit government and private sector spending, thus generating a surplus that is then spent to comply with debt obligations that the government has fulfilled with great stoicism.

Though the program sought to slash inflation with "one blow," the inflation rate has decreased only gradually. It first fell to an average of 10 percent monthly during the months following the 1990 shock and then to 7 to 8 percent throughout 1991, 4 to 5 percent in 1992, and 3 to 4 percent during the first half of 1993. These results have been achieved at an unnecessarily high cost: production, employment, and the standard of living have fallen much further than expected. Likewise, the principal relative prices — salaries, the exchange rate, interest rates, tax rates, and the main public prices — have not managed to align themselves at levels coherent with the country's medium- and long-term possibilities. Though the government has restored the equilibrium in domestic public finances, this equilibrium becomes precarious

Santiago Roca, Ph.D. in economics, Cornell University, is professor of economics and finance at the Graduate School of Business Administration (Escuela Superior de Administración de Negocios, ESAN) in Lima, Peru.

315

as foreign payment commitments increase. With respect to external sector equilibrium, the dangerous balance of trade deficit has been financed with incoming short-term capital. Though this inflow of short-term capital may increase reserves, its real impact is not yet fully clear.

With these indicators in mind, Peru's future prospects are fraught with uncertainty. The government asks for more time and for perseverance in the program's grand design, arguing that the structural changes will eventually bear fruit and encouraging the notion that its program is the only one that is feasible. Nevertheless, various economic groups believe that the stabilization program needs modification in order to obtain more balanced levels of inflation and of economic activity. Some call for a more flexible monetary policy. Others suggest a reorganization of public finances to give preference to internal spending. Many maintain that the effective rates on taxpayers are too high and that these rates should be reduced and the tax base broadened. There are also those who call for ceilings on public utility prices. Some bolder proposals suggest 1) completely "dollarizing" the economy by having the Central Reserve Bank (Banco Central de Reserva del Perú, BCR) purchase all the *soles* in the system, thereby eliminating the domestic currency; 2) remonetizing the economy with *soles* through a massive purchase of dollars, causing an abrupt devaluation, and then freezing exchange rates and public prices; and 3) attacking the inflationary expectations and lack of credibility in the program. Clearly, these proposals vary depending upon the impact of the structural reforms and externally based shocks.

Capitalizing on the Graduate School of Business Administration's (Escuela Superior de Administración de Negocios, ESAN) long experience with various kinds of macroeconomic models for the Peruvian economy (Roca and Prialé 1986; Roca and Prialé 1988; Roca and Cáceres 1989; Roca and Simabuko 1990a; Roca and Simabuko 1993), the organizers of the international conference "The Peruvian Economy and Structural Adjustment: Past, Present, and Future" have requested that we simulate several scenarios of alternative economic policies for 1993 and 1994 and analyze and discuss the principal conclusions and recommendations.

Thus, this chapter aims to analyze alternatives for Peruvian economic policy for the years 1993 and 1994. To this effect, we briefly review the financial programming model used for these projections and evaluate the degree to which the model's projections and the real course of the Peruvian economy are in agreement for the year 1992. The selected scenarios and present projections for 1993 and 1994 are then defined. The final section outlines major conclusions and recommendations.

SUMMARY OF THE FINANCIAL PROGRAMMING MODEL

The financial programming model MOPRE I was designed in mid-1989 (Roca and Simabuko 1990a) and has passed through the progressive modifications and expansions of MOPRE II and MOPRE III to arrive at the present model, MOPRE IV (Roca and Simabuko 1993). Basically, the model analyzes the Peruvian economy by disaggregating it into four interrelated economic sectors: 1) the external sector, 2) the public sector, 3) the monetary sector, and 4) prices and production. In each of these sectors, the structural equations and the diverse mechanisms of transmission that link the model's variables and blocs together are specified. At first, from 1989 to 1990, we designed a model based on a small and open economy with a fixed exchange rate, precarious financial development, state control over certain goods and services, and a productive apparatus dependent on imports. Our subsequent updated versions take into account the existence of a free and floating exchange rate, the impossibility of financing the fiscal deficit through inflation, and the liberalization of basic prices and financial markets.

In simplified terms, the model allows us to observe the manner in which sectoral disequilibria are simultaneously determined by including the following fifteen elements:

1. The public sector's economic result (deficit or surplus) is broken down into the central government, state-owned enterprises, and the rest of the public sector. The impact of major spending or income is separated out by origin, whether in domestic or foreign currency. The model also takes into account the nominal and real effect of any variation in the economy's basic prices. It takes the following points into consideration:

   a. The positive effect of increases in public rates and prices both on the state-owned enterprises, which produce the goods or provide the services, and on the central government's income (e.g., the effect of price changes on the collection of the fuel consumption tax);

   b. Internal spending by the central government, state-owned companies, and the rest of the public sector, adjusted according to the economy's average price increase based on predetermined criteria of indexed wages, salaries, and other current spending;

   c. Inflation's negative impact on income from taxes, through the Olivera-Tanzi effect, which causes prices to rise faster than collection;

   d. The government's capital income and spending, caused by the sale of state enterprises and by public investment decisions; and

   e. The ambiguous impact of devaluation, which ultimately depends on the structure of external spending and income as well as on the price and the elasticity of both.

2. The model consistently links the results of the balance of payments current account with the economic results of the nonfinancial public sector. Variations in the former are figured into the latter and vice versa by accounting for the following:

a. Public sector imports and interest payments on the foreign debt and their impact on the balance of payments, which are linked with current public sector spending; and

b. Public sector exports with foreign sales by public enterprises; the value of external transactions is linked with the taxes on exports and imports.

3. Incoming funds for the public sector are measured in both the balance of payments and the public accounts by figuring net external financing of the public sector and making it compatible with the balance of payments capital account. This rubric considers the following:

a. Amortization of foreign debt principal;

b. Refinancing agreements, regularization, and nonpayment; and

c. External disbursements, including those of the Support Group, the International Development Bank, the World Bank, and others.

4. The government's economic results are figured on a budget and a cash basis. The budget accounting includes current interest due on the foreign debt, as defined by the negotiations that restored Peru's status in the international financial system. The cash accounting method shows the sum of actual revenue and disbursements, allowing us to obtain net results and to calculate net transfers abroad.

5. Once the nonfinancial public sector economic result is obtained, the model links it to the monetary bloc using the BCR's net internal credit to the public sector.

6. In order to determine the BCR's net internal credit to the public sector, we first subtract from the public sector deficit all net external and internal financing provided by the private sector and the rest of the financial system (excluding the BCR). Once this variable is determined, we add to it BCR credits to the National Bank (Banco de la Nación), the development banks, private banks, and "others" (promissory notes, rediscounts, and so on). The result gives us the total of the internal source of the monetary base (money creation).[1]

7. The capital account balance is consistently registered with the banking system's monetary accounts, and the shortfall or gap is covered under the rubric of "short-term capital and errors-omissions" in the balance of payments.

8. Concerning the entry of capital and deposits in foreign currency into the financial system, the model takes into account the banking system's reserve policies and remunerations on those reserves, regulated by the BCR.

9. The external source of the monetary base (dollars purchased by the BCR with a national currency counterpart) is made consistent with changes in the BCR's net reserves by registering the entry of foreign currency that has a national currency counterpart (BCR's net foreign currency purchases, for example).

10. Once primary issuance (the monetary base) has been determined by source (internal or external), the program determines the banking multiplier, which indicates the system's capacity to expand primary credit. This multiplier is disaggregated into a) the average effective level of reserves that financial institutions (banks and others) set within the margins allowed by the Central Bank[2] and b) the preference for cash, which is determined by the portfolio decisions of private agents.

11. Interest rates on national currency are determined by monetary policy and by the money's opportunity cost so that they respond to currency decisions over time and become a variable of adjustment between the economy's current level of liquidity and expectations of inflation and devaluation.

12. To determine the exchange rate, the model analyzes both supply and demand elements in the exchange market. To do so, the demand equation includes the real amount of money and the level of reserves. The real amount of money basically considers "financial" demand created by the quantity of money available in national currency, which measures the ceiling or maximum level of "dollarization" and "real" demand determined by imports and the level of economic activity (gross domestic product, GDP). The latter takes into account the level of international reserves, quantifying the Central Bank's capacity to meet the demand for foreign currency and deal with the risk of the foreign exchange collapse. The supply conditions are determined by that part of the quasi-money in foreign currency that could potentially enter the exchange market and by the BCR's capacity to sell reserves in the free market. The impact of devaluation expectation has been included in these variables.

13. The model generates prices consistent with sectoral results as these respond to variations in the money supply, the exchange rate, controlled prices, past inflation, and inflationary expectations. In this sense, inflation occurs because of cost and demand pressures, with the particularity that the expectations variable incorporates changes in the behavior of economic agents, which have been entered into the equation through the use of a moving coefficients model. The model assumes that inflationary expectations adjust asymmetrically as a result of distortions in relative prices and past inflation, acting as an "information filter" for the referential and observable

variables (money supply, exchange rate, controlled prices, inertia), thus configuring a "process which unfolds over time (and) which is characterized by constant transformation" (Roca and Simabuko 1990b).

14. Product is determined using the economy's real liquidity, public and private spending, the import capacity as set by the level of reserves, and price stability.

15. Once inflation and GDP levels are determined, these variables once again enter into the determination of each of the model's blocs, constantly repeated until consistent and coherent results are obtained.

Though possibilities abound for closing the model (see Roca and Simabuko 1990a, 1993), two basic mechanisms are proposed that make it possible to adjust supply and demand simultaneously. The first ties money creation (from internal and external sources) to cost variations (controlled prices, public utilities prices, exchange rates, and tax rates). This mechanism tends to balance demand with aggregate supply, either shrinking or expanding it depending on the characteristics of the initial adjustment. The second mechanism forces exchange rates to be determined by the supply and demand pressures that affect the exchange market.

For example, though a strategy incorporating an increase in tariffs and controlled public prices would have an inflationary effect on the supply side, its effect on the demand side would be contractive and deflationary as it would reduce the fiscal deficit and the internal source of money creation. On the other hand, a devaluation would have, *ceteris paribus*, three effects. One would be a cost-pushed inflationary effect. Second, a devaluation would be expansive as well as inflationary because of the increase in the external source of money creation. Third, it could have a contractive and deflationary effect on the internal source of money creation if its effects on public sector revenues were greater than its effects on spending. Conversely, it could have an expansive and inflationary effect if its effects on spending exceeded its effects on revenue.

In addition to the shifting of aggregate supply and demand noted above, variations in public pricing and in the exchange rate indirectly influence prices by sparking inflationary expectations and by changing the behavior of economic agents. Thus, a contractive fiscal policy will have a different inflationary effect depending on whether it seeks to fight inflation by increasing revenues or by reducing expenditures. Efforts to increase public revenues by adjusting public rates directly affect costs, demand, and inflationary expectations, while reducing expenditures affects only demand, leaving costs and expectations intact.

THE MODEL'S PROJECTIONS AND THE COURSE OF THE PERUVIAN ECONOMY IN 1992

Since 1985, ESAN has systematically made projections on the Peruvian economy, first using annual data and subsequently, over the last four years, using monthly and quarterly data. In this section, we will review the course of the Peruvian economy and the *ex-ante* and *ex-post* predictions of the MOPRE IV model for 1992.

THE COURSE OF THE ECONOMY, THE ASSUMPTIONS, AND THE MODEL'S EX-ANTE PROJECTIONS FOR 1992

If we observe the evolution of the principal economic variables in 1992, we can see that the stabilization program has not remained unchanged throughout the year. On the contrary, it has seesawed in such a way as to affect the final results for 1992. For example, the growth in public prices was frozen during certain periods and then readjusted (see Figure 1). Likewise, the levels of issuance and liquidity for national currency were not stable even though the program did consider growth objectives for the monetary base (see Figure 2).

These frequent economic policy changes not only responded to internal and external conditions (the April 1992 coup, decreased disbursements from abroad, constant changes in the law, the congressional elections, and so on) but also to changes in priorities and objectives in the program itself, design problems, management shortcomings, and the program's own erratic motion.

In order to describe the course of the economy, we will locate ourselves in time by using quarterly reports on the Peruvian economy in 1992[3] (ESAN 1992). In the first module, January, we presented a preliminary look at what might happen in 1992. The scenario that proved closest to reality established the following assumptions: declining indexing schemes for controlled prices, increased collection of sales and property taxes, public sector austerity, a net foreign currency inflow of approximately $550 million, and a severe restriction of the monetary base and local money supply, compensated with a considerable increase in foreign currency deposits.[4]

The general results for late 1992 projected an economy with an inflation rate of nearly 55 percent, an exchange rate of S/1.55, and 3.4 percent GDP growth (see Table 1). The facts later showed that during the first quarter some of our assumptions materialized, while others, such as the declining indexing scheme for public prices, were replaced by a price freeze through March. Contrary to all assumptions, a tax shock was applied, causing an inflationary "bump" and a tendency toward declining economic activity.

Figure 1.
Diverse Prices

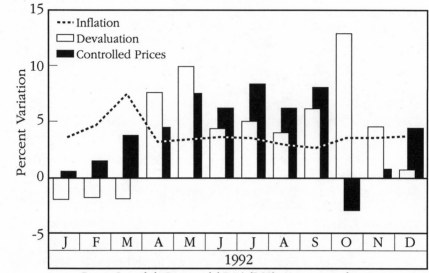

Source: Banco Central de Reserva del Perú (BCR), *Nota semanal,* various issues.

Figure 2.
Liquidity in M/N and Primary Issue

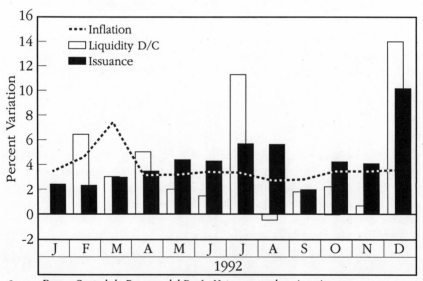

Source: Banco Central de Reserve del Perú, *Nota semanal,* various issues.

Table 1.
Ex-Ante Economic Projections for 1992

Trimester or Projection Module	I	II	III	IV
Inflation (%)	53.1	63.5	60.7	57.4
Interest rates in national currency (%)				
Lending nominal annual rate		142.4	130.4	132.3
Lending real annual rate		48.3	43.4	47.6
Exchange rate[1]	1.55	1.63	1.47	1.61
Production (% variation)	3.4	0.8	0.1	-0.7

Source: Escuela Superior de Administración de Negocios (ESAN), *Riesgo y futuro: Servicio de asesoría en proyecciones económicas y decisiones estratégicas; Reportes trimestrales de enero, abril, julio y octubre 1992*, (Lima: ESAN, 1992).

1 = December average

The events of April 1992 completely altered the assumptions in the second module, which had to take into account that the "Fujicoup" would lead to cuts in the foreign inflows of funds and increases in military spending.

With this exercise, we demonstrated that the effect of the smallest amount of external financing would depend on the adjustment of internal variables. Thus, for example, we discussed both an inflationary option, which issued *soles* to cancel the foreign debt, and a recessive option, which reduced pre-debt public spending or increased taxes in order to meet the debt. A third, less recessive alternative was to follow the second option while proportionally reducing debt payments. In this latter case, for late 1992, we projected an inflation of approximately 63 percent, an exchange rate of S/1.63, a real lending interest rate of 48 percent, and a stagnant GDP (0.8 percent) (see Table 1).

As it turned out, the government opted for an indexed adjustment in public prices, severe spending cuts, and a severe restriction of local currency supply, without including any mechanisms for reducing debt payments. At the same time, the economy experienced a retraction of deposits in foreign currency and an increase in the exchange rate as well as increased interest rates on foreign currency. Inasmuch as the government chose the path of recession rather than that of reduced debt payments, the economy suffered a larger degree of paralysis than had been projected. To this we must add the initial impact of the rationing of electricity and the drought that the country suffered.

By mid-1992, the economy was already clearly showing the recessive effects of the program the government had chosen, and these effects were deepened by inconsistencies in the treasury's management of public funds. This mismanagement had generated a public sector surplus of 400 million *soles,* which were neither reinvested in the economy nor recirculated in the financial system. It was precisely these surpluses, generated by the fiscal overadjustment, that the government later pointed to in its first announcements of economic reactivation.

Thus, in the third module, programs were implemented in a manner that allowed the existing economic policy to continue. Proposals to reactivate the economy were analyzed, including increased public expenditures, reductions in the tax rate, and the first suggestions that the government provide credits to refinance bad debts in the private sector (carried out in part through the monetary program). Income from the sales of state-owned companies, and the potential effect of the new private pension funds (Administradoras de Fondos de Pensiones, AFPs), were also figured in.

Though the proposals for reactivation proved relatively effective in avoiding a decline in GDP, they were not so useful in fighting inflation. Thus, the classic tradeoff between inflation and production arose, bringing with it the governmental dilemma of having to choose between them. The second scenario's projection for late 1992 estimated 60 percent inflation, an exchange rate of S/1.50, a real interest rate of 43 percent, and 0 percent growth (see Table 1).

If we look at what the Peruvian economic authorities actually did, we find that the program became somewhat more flexible in fiscal terms during this third quarter inasmuch as government spending on public investment rose slightly but remained rigid in monetary terms, except in July, for seasonal factors. As a result, the GDP fell much more than projected, and inflation remained below 3 percent monthly despite increases in the exchange rate.

By the fourth quarter, the short-term projections indicated that the recessive tendency for 1992 would be difficult to overcome. Greater public spending and an extension through December of the price freeze for public rates (because of the November elections) would not have a major impact on 1992's final results. Thus, independent of any scenario (or economic management), the model projects 57 percent inflation, an exchange rate of S/ 1.61, a real lending interest rate of 47 percent, and a 1 percent drop in production (see Table 1).

OBSERVED RESULTS AND EX-POST PROJECTIONS

The general results for 1992 are undoubtedly related to the erratic management of economic policy. During the first trimester, the public price freeze and the stillborn tax package destabilized prices early on. The measures taken on April 5, with the resulting cutback in foreign aid and credit, added to the fiscal overadjustment and the monetary contraction to produce the severe recession, which appeared at mid-year. Later, after recognizing the existence of an unused public surplus, the government tried a belated, short-lived, and timid reactivation through spending. The effort did not bear fruit thanks to rigid monetary management. In the final trimester, the exchange rate's tendency to rise for seasonal reasons revived inflation, which at the end of the year had returned to roughly 4 percent monthly.

The chief results observed in 1992 were the following:

1. The government managed to cut inflation from 139 percent in 1991 to 57 percent in 1992 but paid the cost with a 3 percent decline in production, which squashed per capita income down to 1960 levels. The exchange rate recovered a few points of the parity lost in 1990 and 1991, while still achieving only 70 percent of the parity of September 1990. Urban public transportation and electricity rates rose faster than inflation, displaying a tendency to reach international levels. Fuel prices fell behind inflation, reaching 77 percent of their 1990 level, and Petroperú's prices remained far below international prices. Lastly, interest rates displayed a highly elevated real price (see Table 2).

2. As for credits and loans, we can observe that it was cheaper to go into debt in dollars (99 percent) than in *soles* (144 percent). Both levels greatly exceeded inflation, however. The greatest profit on deposits also went to foreign (76 percent) rather than national (47.6 percent) currency, and interest on the latter fell below annual inflation (see Table 3). This points to a severe distortion in the spread of interest rates on national currency.

Table 2.
1992 GDP and Prices

Inflation (%)	56.70
GDP (e)[1] (%)	-3.00
Exchange rate[2]	1.63
Devaluation	63.00
Interest rates (%)	
Nominal	143.00
Real	55.10
Relative prices (Real indicator 100=9/90)	
Fuels	77.00
Electricity	101.00
Urban transportion	132
Exchange rate	70

Sources: Banco Central de Reserva del Perú (BCR), *Memoria 1992.* (Lima: BCR, 1992); Instituto Nacional de Estadística e Informática (INEI), *Informe económico mensual,* various issues.

1 = Estimate.

2 = December average.

Table 3.
Cost and Profitability Equivalent in Foreign
and Domestic Currency (1992)

	(%)
I. Cost:	
a. National Currency	143.8
b. Foreign Currency	98.8
II. Profitability:	
a. National Currency	47.6
b. Foreign Currency	75.7

Source: Banco Central de Reserva del Perú (BCR), *Nota semanal,* various issues.

3. In the central government's accounts, we noted a deficit of 1.7 percent of GDP, slightly higher than the previous year's. The income side showed the progress made by the tax agency, the National Tax Administration Superintendency (Superintendencia Nacional de Administración Tributaria, SUNAT), in collecting sales and income taxes. Spending was still below 1990 levels and showed a changed structure, which prioritized interest payments on the foreign debt. Capital spending remained depressed (see Table 4). The economic results of state-owned companies and the rest of the public sector were practically balanced. The public sector's net foreign transfers totalled (minus) $-37 million in 1991, rising to (minus) $-338 million in 1992.

4. The BCR's net reserves reached $2.001 billion, an increase of $697 million over the previous year (see Table 5). This sharp rise breaks down into a) $497 million in net foreign exchange purchases by the BCR; b) $362 million in banking reserves to cover obligations, which the financial system deposits in the BCR; and c) (minus) $-125 million in net payments on the public foreign debt paid with BCR resources.

5. The balance of payments presented an accumulated $518 billion in reserves. This figure can be broken down into (minus) $-2.029 billion in the current account, $612 million in long-term capital, and $1.935 billion in short-term capital (see Table 6). Thus, the existing balance of payments is utterly dependent on short-term capital flows, whose highly volatile nature is cause for concern. The trade balance showed a deficit of (minus) $-567 million, interest on the public foreign debt amounted to (minus) $-782 million, and nonfinancial services generated a net outflow of (minus) $-850 million in reserves.

Table 4.
Public Sector Accounts
(Percent of GDP)

	1990	1991	1992
Economic result			
A. Central government	-3.6	-1.5	-1.7
Revenues	9.1	8.6	10.3
IGV	1.5	1.8	2.7
ISC fuel	2.3	2.2	1.8
Income tax	0.5	0.7	1.4
Expenditures	12.7	10.1	12.0
Current, pre-debt	9.3	6.8	8.1
Capital	1.2	1.7	1.9
B. State-owned enterprises	-0.7	-0.5	-0.1
C. Other public sector	0.0	0.5	0.0
Total public sector	-4.3	-1.5	-1.8
Net foreign transfers (millions of dollars)	5.0	-37.0	-338.0

Sources: Banco Central de Reserva del Perú (BCR), *Memoria 1992*, (Lima: BCR, 1992); Banco Central de Reserva (BCR), *Nota semanal*, various issues.

Table 5.
Net Central Bank Reserves
(Billions of Dollars)

	1991	1992
BCR net international reserves (flow)	0.773	0.697
Purchases-sales	0.940	0.497
Intervention	0.926	0.659
Other	0.140	-0.162
Financial system reserve Deposits	0.511	0.362
Foreign debt net payments	-0.511	-0.125

Source: Banco Central de Reserva del Perú (BCR), *Nota semanal*, various issues.

Table 6.
Balance of Payments
(Billions of Dollars)

	1991	1992
Current account balance	-1.584	-2.029
A. Trade balance	-0.165	-0.567
Exports	3.329	3.484
Imports	-3.494	-4.051
B. Financial services	-1.011	-0.910
Public	-0.888	-0.872
Private	-0.123	-0.128
C. Nonfinancial services	-0.724	-0.850
D. Transfers	0.316	0.298
Long-term capital	0.705	0.612
E. Public	0.824	0.475
D. Private	-0.119	0.137
Short-term capital		
Errors and omissions	2.130	1.935
Balance of payments	1.251	0.518

Source: Banco Central de Reserva del Perú (BCR), *Nota semanal*, various issues.

Table 7.
Monetary Accounts
(% of GDP)

	1991	1992
Money creation (monetary base)	2.400	2.400
National currency liquidity	4.400	4.400
Quasi-money in foreign currency		
(billions of dollars)	2.391	2.845
Total liquidity	11.000	12.900
Nominal GDP (millions of *soles*)	34.930	54.872

Source: Banco Central de Reserva del Perú (BCR), *Nota semanal*, various issues.

Table 8.
Observed Data and Ex-Post Projections (1992)

	Observed	Ex-Post
Inflation (%)	56.7	60.1
Exchange rate (*soles*)		
Annual average	1.25	1.23
December average	1.64	1.62
Interest rate on national currency (%)		
Annual lending rate	143.0	125.2
Annual deposit rate	47.6	48.5
Banking system net international reserves (billions of dollars)	2.451	2.319
Liquidity in national currency (billions of *soles*)	2.462	2.274
Quasi-money in foreign currency (billions of dollars)	2.845	2.776
Production (% variation)	-3.0	-1.4

Sources: Banco Central de Reserva del Perú (BCR); Escuela Superior de Administración de Negocios (ESAN), *Riesgo y futuro: Servicio de asesoría en proyecciones económicas y decisiones estratégicas; Reportes trimestrales de enero, abril, julio y octubre 1992* (Lima: ESAN, 1992).

6. Lastly, monetary accounts showed no progress in the remonetization of the economy since the levels of national currency issue and liquidity remained depressed as a percentage of GDP (see Table 7). Only total liquidity showed some recovery due to the growth in foreign currency deposits.

In summary, the Peruvian economy's relative price structure (interest and exchange rates, public sector prices, and taxes) is still very much out of alignment, while the public and external sectors enjoy only precarious equilibrium with an extremely low level of national currency monetization. Inflation has dropped to half its 1991 level, but the GDP has fallen roughly 3 percent. The BCR has continued to recover reserves through a policy of currency purchases and the financial system's reserve deposits. Public sector pre-debt expenditures are extremely low, while payments abroad on interests and amortization have grown. Net resource transfers in 1992 reached (minus) $-338 million. Incoming foreign exchange through short-term capital and the "errors and omissions" line item continue to be significant, causing negative effects on production and the exchange rate.

Comparing the data from Table 2 to that of the ex-ante projections in Table 1, we can conclude that the scenarios conducted throughout 1992 corresponded reasonably well to reality. The only variable that was out of context was the projection for the GDP. Inflation as well as the interest and exchange rates all closely approximate the observed amounts.

To be more exact and learn to what degree the model for 1992 fit, we ran the program again using as assumptions the economic policy measures implemented in reality (exogenous or policy measures in the model), obtaining the results shown in Table 8. Thus, ex-post we can state that the model produced a good adjustment.

SCENARIOS FOR THE PERUVIAN ECONOMY 1993-1994

In the preceding two sections of this chapter, we reviewed the principal characteristics of the macroeconomic programming model, MOPRE IV, and the course observed in the Peruvian economy with relation to the ex-ante and ex-post projections for 1992. In this section, a simulation exercise will be carried out by feeding the model's exogenous variables with different kinds of economic policies throughout 1993 and 1994.[5] We propose four scenarios:

- Scenario I — Strict controls on money creation and on the quantity of money.

- Scenario II — Flexible monetary policy.

- Scenario III — Greater expenditures in public investment financed with accelerated privatizations and greater foreign disbursements.

- Scenario IV — Abrupt devaluation and frozen exchange rate policies.

Scenario I gives us the basis upon which we define the principal variables of economic policy. Using it as our basis, we partially modify some of the assumptions in order to create the other scenarios. After feeding in the assumptions for each of the scenarios, the model resolves its simultaneous system of equations and the national accounting framework as we have explained above in the section on the model's structure, repeating until it converges and produces results. The model reproduces the country's economic-financial accounting on a monthly, quarterly, and annual basis.

Table 9.
Assumptions

	Scenario I	Scenario II*	Scenario III *	Scenario IV *
Controlled prices and utility rates	Fuels: Jun.-Dec.: Deval(-1)+1; 1994: Deval (-1) Electricity: Jun.-Dec.: Infl(-1)+3; 1994: Infl (-1) Urban public transportation: 90% average (devaluation, fuel prices) (every five months)			Fuels: adjusted and floated at international levels Electricity: adjusted and floated at international levels Urban public transportation: 70% average (devaluation, fuel prices) (every 9 months)
Nonfinancial public sector	Central government income Selective Consumption Tax (ISC) on fuel (average rate): 1993: constant fall up to 50% rate; 1994: 50% rate Other ISC: 100% inflation General Sales Tax (IGV): 18% fuel + 13% of imports + 1.6% of GDP (internal sales) Income tax: 1.4% of GDP		Central government income	

* = Changes versus Scenario I.

1 = Includes financial cost of unpaid debt service with the Paris Club.

2 = See Figure 3. 3 = See Figure 4.

Continued on next page

Table 9—*Continued*

	Scenario I	Scenario II*	Scenario III *	Scenario IV *
Nonfinancial public sector (Continued)	Property tax: 100% inflation Import tariffs: 9% of total imports Other: For immigrants' nationalization $30 million Privatization (cash income): 1993: $203 million; 1994: 0.6% of GDP Central government spending Wages and salaries (total amount): Jul.-Dec.: Monthly increase of S/0.32 million Christmas bonus S/0.50 million 1994: Increase by S/0.23 million (Jan)+ S/0.30 million (June) + bonus S/0.55 million Goods and services: 100% inflation Transfers: 90% inflation + salary homologation		Central government income (Continued) Other: Privatization (additional): 1993: $74 million 1994: 0.9% GDP ($367 million) Central government spending	

Table 9—*Continued*

Nonfinancial public sector (Continued)		
S/0.32 million + bonus S/0.40 million		
Foreign debt interest: [1,2]		
Amount due 1993: $1.53 billion		
Amount due 1994: $1.512 billion		
Payments 1993: $633 million		
Payments 1994: $722 million		
Other:		
Social security pension payments 1993: S/0.170 million 1994: S/0.420 million		
Capital spending: 1993: $815 million 1994: $1.08 billion	Capital spending (additional): 1993: $340 million 1994: $760 million	
Amortization of the foreign debt[2]: Amount due: 1993: $957 million 1994: $600 million Payments: 1993: $639 million 1994: $262 million		

Continued on next page

Table 9—*Continued*

	Scenario I	Scenario II*	Scenario III *	Scenario IV *
Nonfinancial public sector (Continued)	Foreign disbursements[3]: 1993: $1.423 billion 1994: $486 million Treasury bond issues to pay social security pensions: 1993: S/0.170 million 1994: S/0.420 million Income from state-owned enterprises: Petroperú: Overseas sales: $16 million monthly Domestic sales: Adjusted nominally with the fuel price plus real growth according to Petroperú projections Electricity: Adjusted by the average rate plus real growth of 0.25% monthly Spending by state-owned enterprises Current expenses: 55% inflation Capital expenses: $35 million monthly		Foreign disbursements (additional): 1993: $261 million 1994: $363 million	

Table 9—*Continued*

Nonfinancial public sector (Continued)	Adjustment of income and spending with sale of state-owned enterprises: Impact of private pension funds (AFPs) on the Social Security Institute (IPSS): net loss of $9 million per month		
External sector (net BCR reserves)	Exchange balance: Net foreign currency purchase: 1993: $116 million 1994: $20 million Objective: Monetary base grows at average monthly rate of 1.5% Net flow on the public debt: Jun.-Dec.: 0; 1994: 0	Exchange balance: Net foreign currency purchases: 1993: $294 million 1994: $423 million Objective: Monetary base grows at average monthly rate of 4.7%	Exchange balance: Net foreign currency purchases: 1993: $642 million 1994: $70 million Objective: Abrupt devaluation in July 1993 and freeze until mid-1994
Monetary sector	Internal BCR credits (net): To the National Bank: 0 To the development banks: 0 To the commercial banks: 1993: S/-0.14 million; 1994: S/0.4 million Promissory notes (net flow): 1993: S/-0.28 million 1994: S/0.28 million		

Continued on next page

Table 9—*Concluded*

	Scenario I	Scenario II*	Scenario III *	Scenario IV *
Monetary sector (Continued)	Purchase of treasury bonds: 1993: 40% of the bonds issued 1994: 22% of the bonds issued Financial intermediation: Domestic currency bank reserves: 1993: 22%; 1994: 25% Foreign currency bank reserves: 1993: 44%; 1994: 44%	Financial intermediation: Domestic currency bank reserves: 1993: 18%; 1994: 11% Foreign currency bank reserves: 1993: 47%; 1994: 48%		Foreign currency deposits exit the banking system. Financial intermediation: Domestic currency bank reserves: 1993: 29%; 1994: 24% Foreign currency bank reserves: 1993: 45%; 1994: 31%

SCENARIO I:
STRICT CONTROL ON MONEY CREATION AND ON THE SUPPLY OF MONEY

CHARACTERISTICS OF SCENARIO I

In this first scenario, we assume that after June 1993 Peru's economic policy is managed in the following manner (see Table 9):

1. From a partial freeze on public rates and prices, we move to a system of re-adjustments above the level of devaluation and/or inflation in an effort to overcome the rate lag.

2. The average tax, the Selective Consumption Tax (Impuesto Selectivo al Consumo, ISC) on fuels is reduced by 25 percentage points over the year, from 75 percent to 50 percent, raising Petroperú's net income.

3. The tax system increasingly depends on the General Sales Tax (Impuesto General a las Ventas, IGV) and the income tax.

4. From the sale of state-owned companies, the treasury obtains roughly $203 million in cash in 1993 and 0.6 percent of the GDP in 1994.

5. The government slowly assumes the cost of retirement pensions as current workers switch to the private pension system, financing these expenditures with medium-term treasury bonds.

6. The rest of pre-debt current spending remains austere, growing less than inflation.

7. Expenditures on public investment drop as a proportion of the GDP.

8. The schedule for disbursements and payments on the public foreign debt follows the referential program signed with the IMF and the Paris Club and the recent agreements with the American International Group (AIG) and JAPECO, with predictions for a net negative transfer of (minus) $-750 million in 1993 and (minus) $-498 million in 1994 (see Figures 3 and 4).

9. Current spending by state enterprises continues to fall, and income continues to increase, indexed to changes in public prices and higher goals of physical production.

10. A net purchase of foreign exchange by the BCR of $116 million in 1993 and $20 million in 1994 is assumed, thus providing one of the mechanisms used to determine the variation in money creation.

11. The model sets a goal of 1.5 percent monthly growth in the monetary base, adjusting the internal and external sources of money issue simultaneously.

Figure 3.
Public Sector Foreign Debt

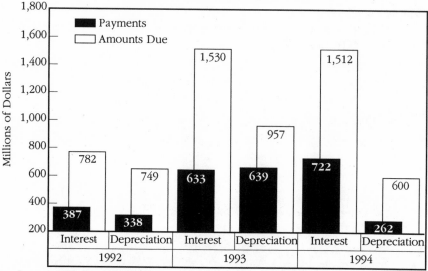

Sources: 1992: Banco Central de Reserva del Perú (BCR), *Nota semanal*, (Lima: BCR, 1992), various issues.

1993: International Monetary Fund, *IMF Referential Program*.

1994: N.n. Hendrix, and N.n. Pereda, *Dueda externa, privatización y estrategia de negociación con la banca comercial*, (Lima: BCR, 1993).

Figure 4.
Net Public Sector Foreign Transfers

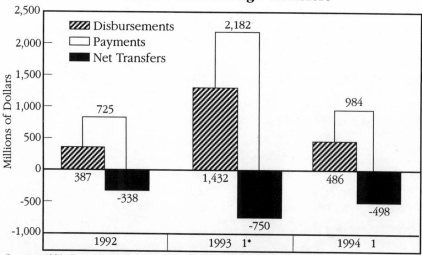

Sources: 1992: Banco Central de Reserva del Perú (BCR), *Nota semanal*, various issues.

1993: International Monetary Fund, *IMF Referential Program*.

1994: N.n. Hendrix, and N.n. Pereda, *Dueda externa, privatización y estrategia de negociación con la banca comercial*, (Lima: BCR, 1993).

1 = Assumption Scenario I.

* Includes back debt registered with the World Bank.

12. The average level of local currency reserves which commercial banks must deposit in the BCR rises slightly, especially in 1994, thus restricting liquidity.

13. The average rate of foreign currency reserve deposits continues at the December 1992 level.

14. The BCR buys a percentage of the treasury bonds issued by the government to pay retirement pensions, but always in harmony and consistent with the monetary objectives mentioned above (see Table 9 and Figures 3 and 4).

PROJECTIONS

Using the characteristics and assumptions listed above for Scenario I, below we present the model's principal annual projections (see Table 10). When necessary, we will also use available monthly and quarterly internal printouts to enrich our description of the economy's course over 1993 and 1994.

We observe a reduction in inflation from 1992's 57 percent, to 38 percent in 1993 and 23 percent in 1994. These results are partly due to the fact that the severe monetary controls slow down the exchange rate and cause less inflationary pressure. Likewise, the direct impact of a smaller quantity of money, like that of the lower adjustment in public rates (which are indexed to the exchange rate), helps achieve this reduction.

Fuel prices, however, rise faster than the exchange rate in 1994 because they do not decline in the months when the exchange rate appreciates, allowing Petroperú to recover the parity lost since October 1992, when prices were frozen. At the same time, the cost of electricity rises faster than inflation in 1993 and at the same rate in 1994.

The exchange rate, one of the economy's key variables, loses some parity in 1993 and falls behind significantly in 1994, as it depreciates only 14 percent versus an inflation, which reaches 23 percent. Bank lending real interest rates, though they remain high compared to international standards, continue on a downward course, reaching 33.8 percent in 1993 and 24 percent in 1994, as inflation declines.

Economic activity, which through May 1993 showed signs of recovery, is somewhat slowed by the restrictive monetary policy, growing only 3 percent in 1993, with the result that production levels are similar to those of 1991. The restrictive policies are much more strongly felt in 1994, when gross internal product falls by (minus) -1 percent.

The nonfinancial public sector produces economic results of (minus) -3.1 percent of GDP in 1993 and (minus) -4.4 percent in 1994, figures much greater than those obtained in 1992. The responsibility for this increased deficit lies principally in the central government's negative balance inasmuch

Table 10.
Projections for the Peruvian Economy 1993-1994

| | Scenarios | | | | | | | |
| | I | | II | | III | | IV | |
Period	1993	1994	1993	1994	1993	1994	1993	1994
Inflation (%)	37.6	23.4	52.7	52.0	39.5	30.0	105.6	18.3
Public prices (% variation)								
• Fuel	36.4	35.9	54.4	53.3	37.7	37.9	102.0	22.2
• Electricity	51.3	24.6	64.4	50.8	53.2	28.7	70.8	18.2
• Urban public transport	31.5	29.7	49.2	49.5	35.5	41.0	104.4	18.3
Exchange rate[1]	2.19	2.50	2.71	4.13	2.31	3.01	3.84	4.48
% variation	34.6	14.0	66.0	52.5	41.7	30.5	135.5	16.6
Real interest rates on domestic currency								
• Loans (at 360 days)	33.8	24.0	36.2	53.6	36.4	34.5	107.0	23.2
• Deposits (savings)	-5.0	-2.4	-9.6	-4.3	-4.9	-1.7	-6.4	-0.3
GDP (% change)	3.0	-0.9	4.4	1.4	4.1	0.3	3.8	2.0
Public sector economic results								
Non-financial (% GDP)	-3.1	-4.4	-2.8	-3.3	-3.6	-5.0	-2.1	-3.5
• Central government	-2.5	-3.8	-2.5	-3.3	-3.1	-4.7	-2.4	-3.7
Income	10.4	10.4	10.5	10.5	10.6	11.3	10.9	10.4
Spending	12.9	14.1	13.0	13.9	13.7	16.1	13.3	14.1
Foreign debt[2]	3.2	3.3	3.3	3.7	3.2	3.6	3.7	4.1
Capital	1.9	2.4	1.9	2.7	2.6	4.4	2.1	2.9
• State-owned enterprises	-0.5	-0.6	-0.2	0.2	-0.4	-0.3	0.5	0.4
• Other	-0.1	0.0	-0.1	-0.1	-0.1	-0.0	-0.2	-0.2
Net financing:								
• External[3]	1.8	2.2	2.0	2.5	2.5	3.3	2.3	2.7
• Internal[3]	1.2	2.1	0.8	0.8	1.1	1.7	-0.2	0.8
Bond issuance[3]	0.2	0.4	0.2	0.3	0.2	0.4	0.1	0.3
Memo: Gross domestic product								
(billions of *soles*)	83,958	105,495	88,060	138,201	85,364	113,882	106,907	158,932
(billions of dollars)	44.340	45.945	42.508	41.037	43.825	41.882	38.867	37.047
Banking system's net international reserves[3]	3,085	3,218	3,404	4,220	3,121	3,400	2,623	2,749
Balance of payments[3]	634	132	953	815	670	280	172	126

1 = Average December exchange rate.
2 = Includes the financial cost of unpaid debt service with the Paris Club.
3 = Numbers in millions of dollars.

Continued on next page

Table 10—*Continued*

					Scenarios			
	I		II		III		IV	
Period	1993	1994	1993	1994	1993	1994	1993	1994
• Balance of								
current account[3]	-2,555	-2,288	-2,647	-2,784	-2,588	-2,469	-2,414	-1,665
Commercial balance[3]	-430	-207	-517	-678	-461	-381	-286	421
Financial services[3]	-1,638	-1,620	-1,638	-1,620	-1,638	-1,620	-1,638	-1,620
Public sector[2,3]	-1,530	-1,512	-1,530	-1,512	-1,530	-1,512	-1,530	-1,512
Private sector[3]	-108	-108	-108	-108	-108	-108	-108	-108
Nonfinancial services[3]	-771	-745	-776	-770	-773	-752	-774	-750
Transfers[3]	284	284	284	284	284	284	284	284
• Long-term capital[3]	1,020	1,158	1,020	1,158	1,281	1,521	1,020	1,158
Public sector[3]	780	1,014	780	1,014	1,041	1,377	780	1,014
Private sector[3]	240	144	240	144	240	144	240	144
• Short-term capital, errors, and omissions[3]	2,170	1,263	2,581	2,441	1,976	1,227	1,566	633
BCR net international reserves[3]	2,527	2,610	2,905	3,650	2,553	2,743	2,295	2,004
Exchange balance	526	83	904	745	552	190	294	-290
Public debt (net)[3]	-24	0	-24	0	-24	0	-24	0
Net purchase of foreign currency[3]	116	20	294	423	116	20	642	70
Bank reserve deposits[3]	339	138	544	419	365	251	-435	-348
Money creation (Monetary base)	1,737	2,137	2,127	3,784	1,699	2,095	3,582	4,015
% real variation	-6.5	-0.3	3.2	17.0	-9.7	-5.1	29.1	-5.2
% GDP	2.1	2.0	2.4	2.7	2.0	1.8	3.4	2.5
Domestic currency liquidity	2,989	3,720	4,080	7,524	2,928	3,647	5,356	7,046
% real variation	-11.8	0.9	8.5	21.3	-14.7	-4.2	5.8	11.2
% GDP	3.6	3.5	4.6	5.4	3.4	3.2	5.0	4.4
Quasi-money in foreign currency								
Millions of dollars	3,561	3,874	3,770	4,564	3,621	4,190	1,889	1,957
Total liquidity	10,802	13,415	14,282	26,362	11,291	16,279	12,606	15805
% real variation	10.5	0.6	31.7	21.5	14.0	10.9	-13.6	6.0
% GDP	12.9	12.7	16.2	19.1	13.2	14.3	11.8	9.9
Average rate of bank legal reserves								
Domestic currency	0.21	0.24	0.17	0.10	0.21	0.24	0.29	0.24
Foreign currency	0.43	0.44	0.45	0.48	0.43	0.44	0.42	0.29

2 = Includes the financial cost of unpaid debt service with Paris Club.

3 = Numbers in millions of dollars.

as both state enterprise and the rest of the public sector are projected to be in equilibrium. Analyzing the central government's account, we detect that this additional deficit arises from the greater burden of interest (currently due) on the foreign debt and the new expenditures to cover retirement pensions.[6] The remainder of the government's current pre-debt spending continues to be austere compared to 1992 levels. With this general result in the public sector, given the (net) external inflow of roughly 2 percent of GDP, internal financing tends to grow nearly one percentage point of GDP.

The balance of payments is projected as positive in 1993 ($634 million) and 1994 ($132 million); hence, the banking system's reserves reach $3.085 and $3.218 billion, respectively. The current account presents sustained deficits of over $2.3 billion, balanced by surpluses in the long-term capital account and the line item for short-term capital and errors and omissions.

In the Central Bank, reserves grow $526 million in 1993 and only $83 million in 1994. The 1993 increase comes from the commercial banks' reserve deposits and from the purchase of foreign currency. These sources grow more slowly in 1994 as the rate of growth in foreign currency quasi-money declines — given the reduced differential between domestic and foreign interest rates — and because the restrictive monetary policy limits the accumulation of reserves through money creation.

The monetary policy behind this scenario is so tough that in 1993 both money creation and liquidity in national currency fall notably in real terms. Neither recovers in 1994. Money creation and liquidity in national currency fall as a percentage of GDP, from 2.4 percent and 4.4 percent (respectively) in 1992 to 2 percent and 3.5 percent (respectively) in 1994, while foreign currency liquidity continues to grow in spite of their decreasing rates.

In summary, this first scenario succeeds in reducing inflation at the expense of a new fall in production in 1994. The real exchange rate progressively falls behind. This seems to have no major impact in the model, however, since the trade balance does not deteriorate. Although the economy's monetization would be at its lowest level, the interest rate would continue to fall in real terms due to the decline in inflation. In percentage terms, the economy's "dollarization" would have increased. The balance of payments accumulates foreign currency at a declining rate, with a much greater current account deficit than in 1992 and with a reduction in short-term capital for 1994. Quasi-money in foreign currency continues to enter but at a much slower pace than during the three previous years as a result of the decreased relative profitability of foreign financial assets. Peru does not resolve its precarious national and foreign equilibria, which are influenced by the public sector's significant net foreign transfers and the weakness of the production sector (Figure 4).

Scenario II: Monetary Flexibility

Characteristics of Scenario II

This second scenario maintains the same assumptions as Scenario I, with the exception of those regarding monetary policy. In broad terms, monetary policy can be divided into two stages. The first, throughout 1993, has the objective of raising the exchange rate, but within certain limits on increased money creation (not more than 5 percent per month). In this case, fundamentally through the BCR's purchases of foreign currency, money issue becomes partially endogenous to the system, conditioned by the exchange rate goals. In addition, the average banking reserve deposits are reduced substantially, whereas the banking reserve deposits in foreign currency rise slightly. In the second stage, for 1994, the exchange rate goals are abandoned, and a rigid and unvarying scheme of money creation returns with issuance running at an average level of 5 percent per month. In practical terms, the government returns to a constant increase in the monetary base but at levels far higher than the 1.5 percent per month proposed in the first scenario (see Table 9).

Projections

This scenario produces 52 percent annual inflation for both years, higher than the 38 percent and 23 percent of the first scenario. However, in exchange, it offers GDP growth of nearly 4.4 percent in 1993 and 1.4 percent in 1994. This represents 1.4 percent and 2.5 percent of GDP more than in Scenario I (see Table 10).

Public prices, especially fuels, recover and rise a few points above inflation. The exchange rate recovers a few points of parity in 1993 but stagnates in real terms in 1994, as the government refuses to take a more active policy of money creation. Interest rates rise in real terms compared with the first scenario, above all in 1994, reflecting the Fisher effect. In the short term, however, because of the expansion of the monetary base and of the money supply, interest rates fall between July and October 1993.

The public sector's economic performance is better than in the first scenario, largely because the state-owned enterprises earn higher monthly incomes thanks to readjustments in public prices, thus reducing the public sector's net demand for internal financing.

As a result of the significant increase in short-term capital and the errors and omissions line item, the balance of payments accumulates more foreign currency even though the current account deteriorates. The trade balance deteriorates in comparison with the first scenario because of the impact of GDP growth on imports and the limited short-term elasticity of real exchange rate on exports and imports. The BCR accumulates greater reserves by buying more foreign currency, as the more expansive monetary policy allows. Also, as quasi-money in foreign currency increases much more than in the first scenario, the banking reserve deposits in the BCR also rise.

In this scenario, the economy is monetized through the increase in the monetary base and the reduction of the reserve requirements in national currency, reaching by the end of 1994 a level of 5.4 percent of GDP. Total liquidity — national and foreign — reaches almost 20 percent of GDP.

In summary, Scenario II generates greater inflation than Scenario I, but it allows a greater recovery in production and thus in employment. The real exchange rate recovers some of its lost parity, as do fuel prices, but the real interest rate is distorted by a significant increase. Public accounts improve, and together with the effect of the increased exchange rate, the demand for internal financing diminishes. Both the Central Bank and the banking system accumulate much greater reserves due to the growth of foreign currency quasi-money and the BCR's currency purchases policy. This is also reflected in the greater growth of short-term capital. The economy ends with a much greater quotient of financial intermediation as a result of the existing remonetization.

SCENARIO III: INCREASED INCOME THROUGH PRIVATIZATION AND EXTERNAL DISBURSEMENTS AND GREATER GOVERNMENT SPENDING ON INVESTMENT

CHARACTERISTICS OF SCENARIO III

Scenario III follows the major assumptions of the first scenario but differs from it in that it proposes to reactivate the economy with greater public investment financed by means of greater cash income from the privatization of state-owned enterprises; greater disbursements from the World Bank, IMF, and the Support Group; or a new refinancing with the Paris Club and other foreign creditors[7] (see Table 9). The BCR's purchases of foreign currency remain at the amounts stipulated in the first scenario, but they no longer have a specific goal for the monthly monetary base, which is left to the results of the system.

PROJECTIONS

With these changes, the model projects 39 percent inflation in 1993 and 30 percent in 1994, levels somewhat higher than those obtained in the first scenario, especially for 1994. The higher inflation for 1994 occurs because the exchange rate rises in both nominal and real terms more than in the first scenario, and the increased public investment exceeds by nearly $30 million the greater income from privatization and foreign relief (see Table 9), thus requiring additional inflationary financing.

Clearly, increased public investment has a positive effect on production, which grows 4.1 percent in 1993 and 0.3 percent in 1994. These increases represent growth of more than one percentage point over the first scenario. The real exchange rate ends up in better shape than it did in the first scenario, although its impact on the trade balance is hardly significant. Instead, imports increase, and the trade balance deteriorates — compared with the first scenario — due to the increased GDP growth. Long-term public sector capital inflows are greater because of the additional foreign aid assumed for this scenario.

The Central Bank accumulates more reserves than in Scenario I due to the greater relative profitability of foreign financial assets, motivating the entry of foreign currency deposits and increasing the respective commercial bank reserves deposited in the BCR. Given that this scenario has no explicit exchange rate or anti-inflationary objectives, the monetary policy turns out to be extremely restrictive.

In summary, we can conclude that if the government received greater income from the sale of public companies or greater debt relief, it could spend more on public investment, revitalizing economic activity. Compared to the first scenario, this revitalization would have the effect of increasing imports and thus the demand for dollars, thereby improving the real exchange rate. Though inflation rises in 1994, this increase is due to the fact that the simulated external relief is insufficient to cover the increased spending on investment, originating inflationary financing. If external relief were greater, more resources would be freed up, and the rate of inflation could be even lower than it was in the first scenario. Obviously, if the foreign debt is not paid through money issue but rather with decreased internal government spending or higher taxes on the private sector, this relief nonpayment would result in greater GDP growth.

Scenario IV: Abrupt Devaluation and a Frozen Exchange Rate Through Mid-1994

Characteristics of Scenario IV

Unlike Scenario I, this fourth exercise posits that in July 1993, the BCR begins an aggressive policy of foreign currency purchases to elevate the exchange rate abruptly until it reaches S/3.90 and then freezes the rate for approximately twelve months, after which it is allowed to fluctuate freely without Central Bank intervention. At the same time as the exchange rate adjustment occurs, public service prices are fixed at international levels in dollars, allowing them to float. Given the exchange rate freeze, the prices for these services would only reflect variations in their international prices, which for this specific case we assume to be constant.

In addition, we assume that these exchange rate measures cause a flight of foreign currency deposits from the banking system, which is compensated with the reduction of the foreign currency reserve requirements during 1994. Since the Central Bank has used foreign currency purchases to adjust the exchange rate, it is advisable to increase reserve requirements in national currency during the rest of 1993 and then gradually reduce them as the economy stabilizes (see Table 9).

PROJECTIONS

According to our monthly printouts, the July 1993 exchange rate and public price shock greatly increase that month's inflation, causing minor lags in the two months that follow, after which inflation has practically ended, settling at levels fluctuating between 0.3 percent and 1.3 percent per month. Thereafter, as the exchange rate is gradually freed in mid-July 1994, it does not take off but continues to fluctuate in the same range. The annual projected inflation reaches 105 percent in 1993 and 18.3 percent in 1994.

As for production, the final result is positive as GDP grows 3.8 percent in 1993 and 2 percent in 1994, over four percentage points above the results of the first scenario. Unlike Scenario II, in which the devaluation as a whole fails to have a positive effect on significantly increasing exports and reducing imports, in this scenario, the effect is visible: exports increase by over $420 million, while imports decline by $200 million. The trade balance for 1994 is thus a positive $421 million.[8]

The exchange rate that results in this scenario is the highest of all in the simulation exercises, whereas basic prices appear to be practically stabilized. The new relative price structure (with September 1990 as a base) indicates that throughout 1994 (monthly data), the exchange rate remains at 82 percent, while fuel prices hold steady at 77 percent, electricity rates at 83 percent, and public transportation stabilizes at 125 percent. This could represent the new alignment of the economy's basic prices.

Even though the real interest rate continues to be high in absolute terms, it is nevertheless the lowest of all the scenarios for 1994. The spread between active and passive interest rates is also the lowest. Moreover, the passive interest rate is the only one in all the scenarios that hardly loses anything against inflation.

Obviously, both the monetary base and national currency liquidity grow significantly and remonetize the economy in 1993. This remonetization retreats somewhat in 1994 because the policy is not finely tuned to increase liquidity as production grows. Nevertheless, the economy approaches the end of 1994 more solidly monetized than in any of the other scenarios.

A number of obvious, unanswered questions remain about Scenario IV. A crucial question relates to how the high current rate of "dollarization" in deposits and credits in the financial system could be dealt with once the exchange rate increased. Would the financial system be able to survive? Coherent alternatives to devaluation would have to be devised, but this is an issue to discuss at some other time.

CONCLUSIONS AND RECOMMENDATIONS

The primary purpose of this chapter has been to present some exercises in economic simulation using the MOPRE IV financial programming model developed at ESAN. We have first reviewed the model's principal characteristics and then evaluated the course of the Peruvian economy during 1992, comparing it with the model's ex-ante and ex-post projections. Lastly, we have described and analyzed four alternative scenarios for economic policy. Four principal conclusions are derived from these exercises.

First of all, there is no single way to resolve the problem of inflation and stabilization in Peru. For example, Scenario I stabilizes the economy little by little, possibly in two more years, if it manages to have the relative price of the exchange rate (which is heavily undervalued) perceived as permanent in the medium and long terms.[9] At the other extreme, Scenario IV manages to stabilize the economy almost immediately after the shock, originating a new relative price structure more compatible with current productive activity.

Second, the first two scenarios clearly present evidence of a trade-off between inflation and production, which will be resolved by the value judgments of economic policy decisionmakers. A more flexible monetary policy, as that presented in Scenario II, would lead to higher production and a better exchange rate but higher levels of inflation. A restrictive monetary policy, as in Scenario I, reduces inflation, drags down the exchange rate, and stagnates production. However, real interest rates achieve more moderate levels in the contractive scenario, which implies that lowering the interest rate under current conditions would make it necessary to reduce inflation.

Third, paying less on the debt or receiving greater foreign relief, as depicted in Scenario III, has expansive effects on production without necessarily increasing inflation if public finance is managed appropriately. If public finances are mismanaged and the government goes too far in spending, inflation would continue at current levels (50 percent annually). Too many commitments on overseas payments contract production.

Seen from a different angle, paying less on the debt could help reduce inflation. If the government were buying dollars with BCR money creation in order to pay the debt, paying less would obviously reduce inflation. This conclusion would become relevant if there were any pressure from international commercial banks for the government to assume back payments on the debt using BCR money creation. It is also important to point out that speeding up the sale of state enterprises and the use of the Central Bank's accumulated reserves to pay the debt have different effects. In the first case, the government trades property for debt, while in the second, it causes an overseas "binge" paid for by sacrificing internal productive potential.[10]

Fourth, it is interesting to highlight that Scenario IV is the only one of the four simulations which brakes the trade-off between inflation and production. After the initial devaluatory shock, the economy (in 1994) is able to slow inflation and initiate GDP growth. Surprisingly, even in 1993, production, which was negatively affected by the shock, begins to recover after two months and in the end grows more than it does in the first scenario. In addition, the real interest rate falls, and relative prices stabilize and maintain their alignment throughout 1994. Note that the 1994 current account improves significantly, though it remains negative.

Evidently, not all the scenarios we have run are mutually exclusive. There is a chance for renegotiating better terms for the debt payment commitments or speeding up the sale of public companies while carrying out Scenarios I or IV, and doing so would produce different results. Other possibilities might also be evaluated, such as a scheme of lower public price increases, an additional tax shock, an external investment shock, and so on. One might even study the effects of completely dollarizing the economy, making the Central Bank buy all the national currency in the system (a feasible proposal, since the BCR has accumulated more than $2.5 billion in reserves, and its exchange holdings have improved significantly). What is important is to make it clear that once the decisions of economic policy have been made, the country must accept the costs and benefits that implacably will occur. There is no single way of doing business. Today's decisions always compromise tomorrow's, and the rumination that having done things differently would have had less costly results is always present.

Notes

The author is especially grateful for the comments and assistance provided by Luis Simabuko Nako, ESAN research associate.

1. In recent months, current regulations and policies have kept the Central Bank (Banco Central de Reserva del Perú, BCR) from providing credit to the public sector, but this has not prevented operations through which the BCR withdraws or injects money in the system by receiving larger or smaller deposits from the National Bank (Banco de la Nación) or the Peruvian Social Security Institute (Instituto Peruano de Seguridad Social, IPSS). In addition, the development banks (Banco Agrario, Banco Central Hipotecario, and so on) have been deactivated, cutting still further the sectors that received primary credit from the Central Bank.

2. The average effective reserve considers both funds reserved in the Central Bank's vaults as well as deposits in each institution. Moreover, a distinction is made between National Bank (Banco de la Nación) reserves, which in some way respond to government monetary policy, and the rest of the banking system's reserves.

3. Each quarterly report analyzes various alternatives for economic policy in the next twelve months. For purposes of this chapter, we have selected those scenarios that ex-ante were closest to reality, revising only the consolidated annual projections.

4. We describe only those assumptions that either characterize or differentiate among the different scenarios.

5. We conducted these simulation exercises in mid-June 1993.

6. After 1994, when current contributors to the national pension system have switched to the private pension system, the central government has to spend approximately 1 percent of GDP covering pensions for retired persons. This cost will decrease over approximately 20 years, as current pensioners pass away.

7. We may also assume that the funds come from a group of donors or another mechanism that the government can activate in order to obtain overseas funding in support of the social investment program. We should recall that funds obtained through a "donors' board" and destined to social programs are not considered within the limits of indebtedness set by the Letter of Intent signed with the International Monetary Fund (IMF).

8. Exports would respond to the real exchange rate after nine months, giving rise to the validity of the J curve in the trade balance.

9. This would require profound transformations in the productive sector. In the interim, internal productive activity would continue to be relatively stagnant.

10. We should note that the Central Bank manages the country's monetary policy independently from the treasury's debt payment problems. Therefore, there is no

direct link between money creation and debt payment. Likewise, there is no link between BCR's loss of reserves and debt payments; if there were a link, the Constitution and the law would be broken. The debtor is the treasury, not the BCR.

REFERENCES

Banco Central de Reserva del Perú (BCR). 1992. *Memoria 1992.* Lima: Banco Central de Reserva del Perú.

Banco Central de Reserva del Perú (BCR). *Informe económico mensual.* Lima: Banco Central de Reserva del Perú. Various issues.

Banco Central de Reserva del Perú (BCR). *Nota semanal.* Lima: Banco Central de Reserva del Perú. Various issues.

Escuela Superior de Administración de Negocios (ESAN). 1992. *Riesgo y futuro: Servicio de asesoría en proyecciones económicas y decisiones estratégicas; Reportes trimestrales de enero, abril, julio y octubre 1992.* Lima: Escuela Superior de Administración de Negocios.

Hendrix, N.n., and N.n. Pereda. 1993. *Deuda externa, privatización y estrategia de negociación con la banca comercial.* Lima: Banco Central de Reserva del Perú.

Instituto Nacional de Estadística e Informática (INEI). *Informe económico mensual.* Lima: Instituto Nacional de Estadística e Informática. Various issues.

Roca, Santiago, and Rodrigo Prialé. 1986. "La devaluación y los programas de estabilización en el Perú." *El trimestre económico,* 53, 212 (October-December).

Roca, Santiago, and Rodrigo Prialé. 1988. *Informe final del proyecto "Perfeccionamiento y desagregación de un modelo macroeconómico para la economía peruana".* Unpublished. Lima: Escuela Superior de Administración de Negocios (ESAN).

Roca, Santiago, and Armando Cáceres. 1989. *Reporte final del modelo de fuentes y usos de fondos para la economía peruana.* Unpublished. Lima: Escuela Superior de Administración de Negocios (ESAN).

Roca, Santiago, and Luis Simabuko. 1990a. *Especificación de un modelo básico de precios para la economía peruana, MOPRE.* Unpublished research report. Lima: Escuela Superior de Administración de Negocios (ESAN).

Roca, Santiago, and Luis Simabuko. 1990b. *Dinámica inflacionaria en el Perú 1986-1990.* Unpublished. Lima: Escuela Superior de Administración de Negocios (ESAN).

Roca, Santiago, and Luis Simabuko. 1993. *Perfeccionamiento del modelo básico de precios para la economía peruana: Del MOPRE I al MOPRE IV.* Unpublished. Lima: Escuela Superior de Administración de Negocios (ESAN).

Appendix

THE PERUVIAN ECONOMY AND STRUCTURAL ADJUSTMENTS: PAST, PRESENT, AND FUTURE

June 28 and 29, 1993 / Coral Gables

CONFERENCE OBJECTIVES

The Peruvian economy is now at a crossroad — perhaps a true historical turning point. The dominance of the import substitution model appears to have ended, and the prospect of an export-led economy remains a distant possibility. Forging solutions to Peru's development problems is complicated by modest results of the current stabilization program and the persistence of political violence.

The Fujimori government instituted various structural reforms in 1991 (privatization of state-owned enterprises, liberalization of the rural land market) simultaneously with the economic adjustment program. Short-term austerity policies combined with institutional reforms have not improved economic performance (inflation rate, GNP growth, employment, income distribution, and poverty). Therefore, the Peruvian economy continues to be in transition — relative prices are still unaligned, inhibiting economic recovery and growth.

These matters will be discussed by a group of outstanding economists from Peru, the United States, and other countries. The main objectives of the Conference are 1) to evaluate the Peruvian economy in the long, medium, and short terms; 2) to discuss the economic and political viability of the current adjustment policies and institutional reforms; and 3) to propose major or minor corrections in Peru's economic policy to improve the results of the ongoing program, without losing positive outcomes attained in the past two years.

MONDAY, JUNE 28, 1993

Morning Program

BACKGROUND

The Current Economic Situation in Long-term Perspective

Shane Hunt, Professor of Economics, Boston University (paper)

Javier Iguíñiz, Professor of Economics, Pontifica Universidad Católica del Perú (discussant)

Efraín Gonzales de Olarte, Research Associate, North-South Center/Instituto de Estudios Peruanos (IEP) (discussant)

Seventeen Years of Failure: Stabilization Policies, 1976 to 1993

Rosemary Thorp, Professor of Economics, Oxford University, England (paper)

Manuel Pastor, Jr., Professor of Economics, Occidental College, Los Angeles (discussant)

Francisco Verdera, Research Associate, Instituto de Estudios Peruanos (IEP) (discussant)

Afternoon Program

CURRENT STABILIZATION POLICY, STRUCTURAL ADJUSTMENT, AND INSTITUTIONAL REFORMS

The Economic Structure of Peru in the 1990s

Daniel Schydlowsky, Professor of Economics, American University, Washington, D.C. (paper)

Andrew Morrison, Professor of Economics, Tulane University/ New Mexico University (discussant)

Javier Escobal, Research Associate, Grupo de Análisis para el Desarrollo (GRADE) (discussant)

External Constraints on Institutional Reforms, Privatization, Deregulation and Liberalization

Teobaldo Pinzás, Research Associate, Instituto de Estudios Peruanos (IEP) (paper)

Richard Weisskoff, Professor of Economics, University of Miami (discussant)

John Sheahan, Professor of Economics, Williams College, Massachusetts (discussant)

TUESDAY, JUNE 29, 1993

Morning Program

The Economic Consequences of the "Peruvian Disease": Dutch Disease + Drug Traffic + Insurgency

Elena Alvarez, Professor of Economics, State University of New York at Albany (paper)

Francisco Verdera, Research Associate, Instituto de Estudios Peruanos (IEP) (discussant)

Humberto Campodónico, Research Associate, Centro de Estudios de Promoción y del Desarrollo (DESCO) (discussant)

The Viability of the Fujimori Economic Strategy

Carlos Boloña, Former Minister of Economy and Finance of Perú (paper)

Javier Iguíñiz, Professor of Economics, Pontificia Universidad Católica del Perú (paper)

Rudiger Dornbusch, Professor of Economics, Massachusetts Institute of Technology (discussant)

Julio Velarde, Professor of Economics, Universidad del Pacífico (discussant)

Afternoon Program

ALTERNATIVE SCENARIOS FOR THE PERUVIAN ECONOMY

Santiago Roca, Professor of Economics, Escuela Superior de Administración de Negocios (ESAN) (paper)

Bruce Kelley, Professor of Economics, Florida International University (discussant)

Javier Escobal, Research Associate, Grupo de Análisis para el Desarrollo (GRADE) (discussant)

Round Table Discussion

Discussion, all participants

Concluding Remarks

Efraín Gonzales de Olarte, N-SC/IEP

For further information please contact:

Dr. Efraín Gonzales de Olarte Conference Organizer

Dr. Steve Stein, Director Peru Working Group North-South Center University of Miami 1500 Monza Avenue Coral Gables, Florida 33146-3027 U.S.A. Tel (305) 284-2144 Fax (305) 284-6370

Index

A

Acción Democrática (Venezuela) 52
Acción Popular 46
Accumulation of Rights project 275
Aeroperú 240, 242
AFP (Administradoras de Fondos de Pensiones) 238, 240, 324
Africa 23, 35, 50, 310
Agreement of Amplified Facility 187
AIG (American International Group) 337
AIG-Belco 254
ALADI (Latin American Integration Association) 254
Allende, Salvador 52, 143
Alva Castro, Luis 268
Andean Development Corporation 115
Andean Group 217, 254
Andean Reserve Fund 115
Antióquia 52
APRA (Alianza Popular Revolucionaria Americana) 46, 50, 64, 123, 207, 217, 247, 268
April 1992 coup 133, 134, 268, 273, 277, 280, 321
Arequipa 103
Argentina 9, 12, 15, 16, 17, 18, 19, 21, 143, 218, 270
Asia 14, 15, 23, 34, 35, 43, 50
Austria 193
Austrian School 6, 189

B

Bahamas 187, 221
balance of payments 3, 60, 62, 65, 79, 80, 81, 85, 86, 101, 111, 112, 113, 115, 116, 131, 134, 185, 188, 189, 196, 197, 216, 222, 253, 318, 326, 342, 343
Banco Agrario (Agrarian Bank) 186, 349
Banco Central Hipotecario 234, 349
Banco Continental 241

Banco de Comercio   240
Banco de la Nación (National Bank)   143, 222, 232, 254, 274, 318, 349
Banco Popular del Perú   234, 240
Barahona Act   217
BCR (Banco Central de Reserva del Perú)   23, 24, 45, 48, 50, 64, 68, 69, 122,
    134, 189, 190, 191, 197, 198, 199, 213, 214, 224, 225, 232, 233, 234, 235,
    244, 271, 272, 274, 275, 276, 277, 278, 279, 280, 281, 284, 285, 316, 318,
    319, 326, 329, 337, 339, 342, 343, 344, 345, 346, 347, 348, 349, 350
Belaúnde Terry, Fernando   18, 44, 66, 70, 86, 112, 196
    government   45, 69, 86, 102, 107, 112, 133, 151, 196
Beltrán, Pedro   62, 65, 121
Bhagwati, Jagdish   40, 299
Bolivia   37, 47, 62, 141, 143, 148, 175, 176, 249, 270
    government   61
Boloña, Carlos   5, 6, 7, 14, 50, 132, 184, 213, 256, 269, 279, 285, 286
Booz-Allen & Hamilton   144
Brazil   12, 15, 16, 17, 18, 19, 20, 43, 44, 51, 52, 69
Büchi, Hernán   184
Buses de Enatru   240
Bustamante, José Luis   52
    APRA-Bustamante period   17, 44, 123

C

CADE (Conferencia Anual de Ejecutivos)   144, 223
Cagan, Philip   192
Caja de Ahorros de Lima   234
Cajamarca   103, 242
Camdessus, Michael   218, 219
capital flight   67, 157, 163, 164, 210, 227, 237
capitalism   39, 48
Caracazo   128
Castañeda Lossio, Luis   240
Castro, Fidel   52
CAT Colombia's (Certificado de Ahorro Tributario)   86
Cavallo, Domingo   218, 270
    Cavallo model   9
    Cavallo Plan   218
CCC (Central de Cooperativas de Crédito)   234
CCD (Congreso Constituyente Democrático)   268
CCTM (Comisión Controladora de Trabajo Marítimo)   238, 247
Cementos Lima   241
Cementos Yura   241
CEMLA (Centro de Estudios Monetarios para Latinoamérica)   147
Centromín (Empresa Minera del Centro del Perú)   241

Cerper 241

Certex (Certificado de Reintegro Tributario a las Exportaciones) 79, 86, 89, 217, 218, 229, 230, 247

CGR (Contraloría General de la República) 244

CGTP (Confederación General de Trabajadores del Perú) 247

Chile 7, 13, 17, 18, 19, 35, 44, 51, 52, 62, 71, 89, 128, 130, 132, 134, 139, 143, 144, 184, 192, 234, 235, 248

China 14, 200, 249

civilismo 17

CLAE (Centro Latinoamericano de Asesoría Empresaria) 37

Clinton, Bill 223

coca 5, 78, 79, 89, 100, 108, 122, 141, 147, 148, 149, 150, 151, 152, 153, 154, 155, 156, 163, 164, 171, 173, 174, 175, 176, 207, 286

cocaine 5, 68, 69, 147, 148, 149, 151, 152, 153, 154, 175

CODELCO (Corporación Nacional del Cobre de Chile) 89

COFIDE (Corporación Financiera para el Desarrollo) 232

Colombia 17, 18, 19, 35, 43, 44, 50, 51, 59, 86, 108, 123, 134, 148, 153, 217

Commsa 241

communism 39, 47, 130

Compañías de Minas Buenaventura 240

comunidad laboral (workers' community) 87, 119, 133, 210, 238, 254

Congressional Commission on the Economy 214, 215

Constituent Assembly 220

Constituent Congress 221, 246

Constitution of 1979 207

Consumer Defense Institute (Instituto de Defensa del Consumidor, Indecopi) 230

consumer price index (CPI) 276, 286, 292, 293, 302

conversion mechanisms. *See* Chapter IX

COPRI (Commission to Promote Private Investment) 139, 144

Corbo, Vittorio 52, 134, 140, 143

CPT (Compañía Peruana de Teléfonos) 241

CTS (Compensación por Tiempo de Servicios) 238

Cuajone mines 27, 28, 51, 89

Czechoslovakia 249

D

Dancourt, Oscar 270, 276, 283, 284, 286

DD (Dutch Disease) 5, 38, 79, 118, 121, 147, 148, 156, 163, 164, 171, 173, 174, 176, 283

DDRC (domestic resource cost) 90, 91, 100, 118, 121

De Melo, Jaime 134, 140, 143

De Soto, Hernando 118, 187, 221, 300

DEA (U.S. Drug Enforcement Administration) 149, 152

DEM (Distrito Electoral Múltiple)   208
DEU (Distrito Electoral Unico)   208
Development Banking System   232, 234
development model   2, 40, 41, 43, 44, 45, 46, 47, 49, 52
Dixit, Avinash   291
dollarization   68, 217, 234, 273, 277, 319, 342, 347
Dornbusch, Rudiger   8, 43, 143, 310
Drake, Paul   37, 52
drug trafficking   8, 147, 149, 155, 156, 188, 217, 253, 254

E

East Asia   14, 23, 39, 41, 42, 43, 44, 45, 50
Ecasa (Empresa de Comercialización del Arroz)   229, 230
Economic Commission for Latin America and the Caribbean (ECLAC)   9
economic determinism   39
economic liberalization   201
Edwards, Sebastian   43, 289, 310
EFP (Extended Facility Program)   222
Electrolima (Electricidad de Lima)   241
Electroperú (Electricidad del Perú)   241
Emergency Agrarian Law   216, 218
Emsal (Empresa de Sal)   241
Enata (Empresa Nacional del Tabaco)   241
Enci (Empresa Nacional de Comercialización de Insumos)   229, 230, 254
Entelperú (Empresa Nacional de Telecomunicaciones)   241
Entramsa   209
Environmental protection   207, 246
Epsep (Empresa Nacional de Servicios Pesqueros)   241
ERBS (Exchange-Rate-Based Stabilization)   59, 60, 62, 69, 70, 72
ESAN (Escuela Superior de Administración de Negocios)   315, 316, 321,
   347, 349
estabilidad laboral   87, 210, 238, 248, 254
estate or assets tax (Impuesto al Patrimonio o a los Activos)   235, 245
Europe   12, 19, 34, 35, 50, 189, 215, 270
exchange rate   3, 4, 5, 9, 42, 60, 62, 68, 70, 71, 72, 79, 80, 81, 84, 85, 86, 87,
   89, 101, 102, 103, 104, 106, 107, 108, 109, 110, 111, 112, 115, 116, 118, 119,
   121, 123, 141, 157, 190, 191, 194, 196, 197, 198, 202, 210, 214, 222, 224,
   225, 226, 232, 247, 266, 267, 269, 270, 271, 272, 274, 276, 277, 278, 279,
   280, 282, 283, 284, 285, 292, 303, 304, 306, 310, 311, 315, 316, 317, 319,
   320, 321, 323, 324, 325, 329, 330, 339, 342, 343, 344, 345, 346, 347
   real exchange rate   6, 101, 102, 103, 109, 110, 116, 117, 121, 134, 156, 157, 164,
   171, 173, 191, 225, 226, 267, 271, 275, 277, 278, 279, 280, 289, 290, 291, 292,
   293, 294, 295, 296, 297, 298, 299, 300, 301, 302, 303, 304, 306, 309, 310, 343,
   344, 345, 349

F

Fable 209

Fent (Fondo de Exportaciones No-Tradicionales) 229

Fertisa (Fertilizantes, S.A.) 241

Fishermen's Fund (la Caja del Pescador) 229

Flopesca 241

FONAVI (Fondo Nacional de Vivienda) 221, 243, 245, 286

Foncodes (National Compensation for Social Development Fund) 244, 246

foreign debt 3, 4, 9, 51, 78, 101, 141, 199, 214, 216, 222, 254, 266, 318, 323, 326, 337, 342, 345

Four Tigers (Korea, Taiwan, Hong Kong, and Singapore) 41

FREDEMO (Frente Democrático) 130, 131, 247, 274

Friedman, Milton 197, 212

Friedman, Rose 212

Fujimori, Alberto 4, 6, 8, 47, 71, 127, 131, 132, 141, 142, 144, 183, 187, 215, 219, 251, 265, 266, 267, 268, 271, 274, 275, 279, 282, 285
  administration 6, 7, 70, 131, 144, 183, 197, 212, 217, 219, 223, 251, 265, 266, 267, 268, 269, 270, 271, 273, 276, 280, 281, 282, 290, 302
  Fujicoup 278, 282
  Fujishock 284
  reforms of August 1990 289, 290, 302, 304, 306
  self-coup (auto golpe) 133, 134, 140

G

García, Alan 69, 79, 112, 191, 214, 215, 219, 220, 234, 248, 251, 256, 268
  administration 4, 6, 39, 69, 70, 77, 80, 86, 87, 101, 102, 104, 105, 107, 112, 113, 122, 130, 131, 140, 143, 196, 197, 199, 200, 228, 232, 242, 251, 252, 253, 267, 268, 273, 284, 285, 295, 297, 302, 311
  García effect 267, 290

GATT (General Agreement on Tariffs and Trade) 229

GDP (gross domestic product) 14, 16, 17, 23, 26, 28, 29, 30, 31, 35, 51, 66, 67, 70, 122, 153, 163, 173, 175, 176, 189, 199, 200, 213, 218, 221, 222, 224, 225, 233, 234, 244, 249, 251, 252, 265, 266, 268, 280, 281, 286, 319, 320, 321, 323, 324, 326, 329, 330, 337, 339, 342, 343, 344, 345, 346, 348, 349

Germany 50, 51, 192, 193

GNP (gross national product) 35, 37, 100, 102, 116, 185, 194, 198, 200, 218, 224, 239, 240, 248, 291, 292, 302, 310

Grados, Alfonso 69

Great Britain 192

Great Depression 17, 19, 30, 31, 147

Greece 192

Grifos de Petroperú 240

Guano Age 12, 13, 19, 31, 33

Guerra del Pacífico (La) 192

Guzmán, Abimael 220, 268, 269, 282

H

Harrod-Domar framework   20
Haya de la Torre, Víctor Raúl   217
Hierroperú   240, 242
Hirschman, Albert   21, 52
    Hirschmanian linkages   31
Hungary   192, 249
Hurtado Miller, Juan Carlos   212
Hussein, Saddam   219
hyperinflation   37, 131, 140, 184, 185, 189, 190, 192, 193, 194, 196, 199, 200,
    225, 227, 228, 233, 234, 239, 249, 251, 270, 277, 283

I

ICE (Instituto de Comercio Exterior)   229, 243
ICOR (incremental capital-output ratio)   28
IDB (Inter-American Development Bank)   6, 51, 78, 143, 187, 214, 215, 252,
    254, 275
Iglesias, Enrique   214
IGV (Impuesto General a las Ventas, general sales tax)   111, 214, 215, 217,
    219, 221, 224, 229, 231, 245, 247, 337
IMF (International Monetary Fund)   6, 7, 59, 60, 62, 64, 128, 137, 143, 187,
    188, 197, 212, 215, 216, 218, 222, 223, 225, 252, 256, 265, 266, 267, 268,
    269, 274, 275, 289, 315, 337, 344, 349
    IMF Letter of Intent   133
import substitution   20, 40, 41, 42, 44, 45, 46, 100, 114
imports tax   245
INAP (Instituto Nacional de Administración Pública)   244
income tax   206, 214, 219, 224, 245, 326, 337
INCOOP (Instituto Nacional de Cooperativas)   233
Indecopi (Instituto de Defensa del Consumidor)   230
Index of Real Public Prices   279
India   50
Indonesia   62
Indumil   209
Industrias Navales S.A.   240
INEI (Instituto Nacional de Estadística e Informática)   23, 24, 27, 28, 51, 272
inflation   3, 6, 7, 8, 9, 40, 43, 47, 60, 61, 64, 68, 70, 71, 72, 78, 100, 103, 104,
    105, 106, 107, 108, 109, 111, 112, 116, 122, 131, 133, 134, 157, 163, 164,
    171, 173, 176, 184, 185, 188, 189, 190, 191, 192, 193, 194, 195, 196, 199,
    200, 207, 210, 212, 213, 214, 215, 222, 223, 224, 225, 226, 227, 228, 231,
    234, 236, 248, 249, 250, 251, 253, 265, 266, 267, 268, 269, 270, 271, 272,
    273, 274, 275, 276, 277, 278, 279, 280, 281, 282, 283, 284, 285, 302, 306,
    310, 315, 316, 317, 319, 320, 321, 323, 324, 325, 329, 330, 337, 339, 342,
    343, 344, 345, 346, 347, 348

informal economy 130
informal market 85, 88, 106, 289, 290, 300, 301, 309
informal sector 4, 67, 79, 80, 82, 83, 87, 88, 100, 104, 105, 106, 114, 130, 155, 209, 239, 300, 301
INP (Instituto Nacional de Planificación) 243
institutional reforms 1, 2, 4, 6, 7, 8, 9, 207, 246, 253, 271, 275
Instituto Cuánto 153, 175, 176, 273, 284
Instituto de Economía de Libre Mercado 183, 256
Insurance and Deposits Fund 233
INTERBANC 241
interest rate 3, 20, 42, 61, 68, 69, 70, 71, 72, 80, 83, 84, 85, 87, 110, 120, 131, 134, 140, 141, 157, 190, 191, 194, 196, 200, 201, 206, 210, 222, 224, 225, 226, 227, 234, 235, 236, 237, 248, 249, 269, 270, 273, 277, 278, 279, 280, 282, 284, 285, 286, 315, 319, 323, 324, 325, 339, 342, 343, 344, 346, 347, 348
international reserves 6, 115, 128, 163, 164, 171, 185, 189, 191, 196, 197, 198, 202, 218, 222, 223, 224, 251, 253, 282, 319
IPSS (Instituto Peruano de Seguridad Social) 239, 240, 349
Iraq 219
ISC (Impuesto Selectivo al Consumo) 216, 221, 231, 235, 237, 245, 247, 337
ISI (import-substituting industrialization) 60, 78, 85, 88, 89

J

Japan 6, 41, 50, 51, 84, 214, 223, 268
Japeco 242, 337
Joint Budget Committee 218

K

Kaufman, Robert 41, 44, 47, 52
Kenya 50
Keynes, John M. 1, 20, 194
    Keynesian foreign trade multiplier 14, 31
    Keynesian policies 189, 194
    Keynesian theories 189
Korea 38, 41, 42, 43, 50, 268
Kuomintang 42
Kwan Yew, Lee 48

L

labor market 81, 82, 85, 88, 114, 119, 133, 186, 190, 201, 202, 205, 209, 210, 227, 228, 237, 250, 253, 275, 299, 300
Latin America 12, 13, 14, 15, 16, 17, 18, 19, 23, 34, 35, 38, 39, 41, 42, 43, 44, 48, 50, 51, 52, 59, 60, 68, 71, 86, 128, 130, 131, 139, 144, 157, 184, 221, 234, 248, 250, 270, 289, 300, 310

LDCs (less developed countries)   35, 131, 132
Leguía, Augusto   17
Letts, Ricardo   217
Lewis, W. Arthur   2, 11, 12, 13, 23, 33, 34, 35, 37, 46
liberalization   6, 7, 8, 69, 71, 100, 128, 130, 131, 132, 133, 134, 141, 142, 143,
    185, 186, 187, 201, 210, 220, 227, 228, 230, 231, 232, 234, 237, 250, 251,
    252, 270, 273, 275, 306, 317
Liberty Movement (Movimiento Libertad)   247
LIBOR (London Interbank Offered Rate)   226
Lima   13, 80, 110, 118, 217, 234, 241, 256, 273, 281, 315

M

macroeconomic stability   7, 139, 140, 201, 249
Maddison, Angus   12, 14, 15, 17, 19, 28, 50
Malawi   23, 50
Malaysia   200
Marcos, Ferdinand   48
marginal social costs   80, 81, 87, 88
    utility   80, 81, 84
market of goods and services   190, 201, 209, 228, 230, 250
Mendoza, Waldo   270, 277, 283, 285, 286
Mexico   12, 17, 18, 19, 43, 44, 68, 71, 249
Miami   1, 110, 111, 147, 175, 226, 234, 289
Miga   241
Minera Condestable   240
Ministry of Agriculture   229
Ministry of Economy and Finance   191, 212, 241, 276, 284
Ministry of Health   229
Ministry of Housing and Construction   243
Ministry of Labor   238
Ministry of Transportation and Communications   243
Minpeco USA   240
MNCs (multinational corporations)   38, 39, 52
monetary emission   6, 188, 189, 192, 194, 196, 199
money market   72, 190, 201, 209, 210, 211, 228, 232
MOPRE I   317
MOPRE II   317
MOPRE III   317
MOPRE IV   317, 321, 330, 347
Morales Bermúdez, Francisco   65, 67, 150
Moreyra, Manuel   112
MRTA (Movimiento Revolucionario Tupac Amaru)   155
MUC (Mercado Unico de Cambios)   81, 107, 112, 122

Mulford, David   214
multiclass elitism   44
multilateral institutions   132

N

narcotics trafficking   130
Neary, Peter   176, 291, 297, 298, 310
neo-Confucianism   41
neoliberalism   2, 4, 47, 48, 49, 128
Nepal   35
Newmond   242
NIR (net international reserves)   185, 189, 191, 196, 197, 198, 223, 251
non-traditional exports   78, 86, 110, 115, 116, 121, 229
Norman, Victor   291
North America   12, 19, 30

O

Occidental Petroleum   242
OECD (Organization for Economic Cooperation and Development)   50
oligarchy   46, 52
Olivera-Tanzi effect   104, 116, 317
Opic   241
OXY   242

P

Pakistan   23, 50
Panama Canal   17
Papelera Peruana   241
Paramonga   241
Paredes, C.   72
Pareto, Vilfredo   119
Pareto, Vilredo
   Pareto conditions   83
Paris Agreement   241
Paris Club   6, 187, 188, 215, 252, 254, 337, 344
Pastor, Manuel   2
Paz Estenssoro, Víctor   47
Pescaperú (Empresa Nacional Pequera)   241
Petrolera Ganso Azul   242, 254
Petrolera Transoceánica   137, 241
Petromar (Petróleos del Mar)   241
Petroperú (Petróleos del Perú)   101, 139, 144, 214, 229, 325, 337, 339
Pinochet, Augusto   44, 52, 128, 139, 143, 144

Plan Austral   62
Plan Cruzado   62
political economy   11, 40, 61, 67, 68, 273, 274
Popular Unity (Unidad Popular)   18, 139, 143
populism   4, 9, 43, 44, 52, 195, 310
poverty   7, 31, 80, 88, 114, 140, 149, 150, 154, 187, 204, 205, 207, 221, 222,
     239, 244, 246, 252, 253, 267, 273
Poverty Alleviation Program (Programa de Alivio a la Pobreza)   246
PPC (Partido Popular Cristiano)   207
Prebisch, R.   37
presidential elections of 1990   131
PRI (Partido Revolucionario Internacional)   52
price controls   5, 6, 70, 107, 194, 209, 231, 250, 270, 272, 289, 290, 297, 298,
     299, 300, 302, 309, 310
private sector   7, 65, 67, 70, 85, 104, 108, 111, 113, 115, 117, 140, 143, 144,
     186, 188, 189, 190, 197, 198, 199, 200, 201, 202, 203, 205, 206, 211, 225,
     228, 230, 232, 233, 240, 242, 243, 245, 246, 249, 252, 269, 270, 272, 274,
     297, 315, 318, 324, 345
privatization   6, 131, 132, 133, 137, 139, 144, 186, 203, 221, 224, 228, 234,
     237, 240, 241, 242, 244, 246, 247, 248, 250, 251, 253, 254, 266, 275, 300,
     330, 344
PROEM (Programa Temporal de Empleos)   130
public expenditure   6, 62, 101, 189, 190, 191, 196, 204, 211, 213, 215, 216,
     222, 252, 253, 324
public sector   35, 37, 45, 48, 66, 67, 108, 112, 113, 117, 130, 140, 141, 143,
     190, 200, 201, 225, 233, 244, 252, 289, 290, 291, 293, 295, 296, 302, 303,
     304, 306, 309, 310, 317, 318, 320, 321, 324, 326, 329, 339, 342, 343, 345,
     349

Q

Quellaveco   242
Química del Pacífico   240, 242

R

RAP (Rights Accumulation Program)   6, 187, 215, 216, 222, 252
   RAP agreement   252
real exchange rate   176
Reaseguradora Peruana   241
Refinería Conchán   241
Refisa Bank   256
reform
   agrarian   150, 151, 242, 247
   armed forces   6

commerce 213
economic 74, 139, 213, 217, 219, 220, 234, 266, 268, 289, 290, 301
education 6, 34, 142, 205, 247, 253
electoral college 6, 208
expenditure 245
financial 132, 134, 143, 213, 232, 233, 252, 254
governmental 250
health care 6, 34, 206
housing 6, 206, 243
institutional 1, 2, 4, 6, 7, 8, 9, 49, 185, 246, 247, 251, 253, 271, 275, 285
investment 133, 241
judicial branch 6, 208, 253
labor 213, 237, 239, 247, 253, 254
labor market 202, 210, 253, 275, 300
legal 188
legislative branch 6, 207
local governments 208
macroeconomic 139, 212, 249, 251, 274
market 201, 249, 251, 252, 275
microeconomic 228
peacekeeping forces 209
political parties 6, 208
property rights 185, 209
property structure 6, 203, 240, 251, 252
public administration 213
public expenditure 204
regional governments 208
retirement system 202
state 6, 185, 204, 205, 243, 251, 252
structural 6, 7, 8, 127, 131, 132, 133, 139, 143, 183, 185, 186, 187, 188, 201, 207, 209, 211, 213, 217, 221, 222, 224, 226, 227, 239, 246, 247, 248, 249, 250, 251, 253, 255, 315, 316
tax 62, 64, 65, 66, 71, 194, 204, 213, 215, 244, 252, 253, 254
trade 7, 131, 133, 134, 137, 143, 224, 228, 229, 230, 254, 289
relative prices 3, 4, 5, 7, 40, 62, 78, 87, 89, 101, 105, 106, 107, 108, 112, 116, 122, 194, 195, 226, 266, 267, 269, 270, 271, 272, 273, 274, 276, 278, 280, 281, 283, 290, 302, 315, 319, 348
Renasa 241
Renovación Democrática 143
República Aristocrática 31, 46
Ricardo, David 121
Rivas Dávila, Carlos 217
Roberts, Kevin 297, 298
Rodríguez Pastor, Carlos 69
Roldán, Mary Jean 44, 52
Roosa, R. V. 197
Roosevelt Recession 17
Rotbarth, E. 297

S

Sachs, J.   72, 310
SBS (Superintendencia de Banca y Seguros)   233, 235, 236, 237, 244
Secrex (Seguro de Crédito a la Exportación)   233
Sedapal   241
Serpetro (Servicios Petroleros)   241
Sheahan, John   7, 44, 143
Shining Path (Sendero Luminoso)   79, 100, 102, 103, 108, 113, 117, 122, 155, 220, 256, 268, 280, 282
Siderperú (Empresa Siderúgica del Perú)   241
Silva Ruete, Javier   112
Simplest Excess Demand hypothesis   277
Singapore   41, 50
Smith, Adam   47
SNI (Sociedad Nacional de Industrias)   247
SNP (Sistema Nacional de Pensiones)   239, 240
Social Emergency Program (Programa de Emergencia Social)   187
social time preference   84, 85, 120
socialism   47, 48, 139, 189
Sociedad Agrícola de Interés Social   243
Sociedad Paramonga   137
Sogewiese Leasing S.A.   240
Solgás   240, 242
Southern Peru Copper Corporation   242
Soviet Union   50, 249
Special Drawing Rights (Derechos Especiales de Giro)   197, 256
stabilization policies   4, 5, 59, 62, 101, 116, 128, 143, 269, 272, 275, 276
Stallings, Barbara   44, 52
staple theory   21, 31
structural adjustment   2, 3, 4, 5, 8, 9, 128, 202, 254
   programs   6, 7
subsidies (subsidy)   6, 42, 69, 70, 102, 142, 186, 201, 205, 206, 212, 229, 233, 239, 247, 289, 290, 291, 293, 294, 295, 296, 302, 309
SUNAD (National Customs Administration Superintendency)   244, 245
SUNAT (National Tax Administration Superintendency)   48, 221, 222, 244, 245, 326
Superintendencia de Administradoras de Fondos de Pensiones, AFP   238, 244
Superintendency of Banks (Superintendencia de Bancos)   48
Support Group   6, 187, 188, 214, 215, 222, 252, 318, 344
Surmeban   234, 240
Switzerland   226

T

Taiwan   41, 42, 43
Televisa   242
terrorism   47, 117, 188, 208, 209, 221, 248, 251, 253
Thailand   200
third world   34, 35, 37
Toquepala mines   28, 31, 62, 89
Torres y Torres Lara, Carlos   213
trade   34, 37, 38, 51, 52, 65, 84, 89, 101, 102, 111, 112, 116, 119, 122, 133, 134, 137, 164, 173, 195, 196, 229, 230, 244, 254, 278, 281, 289, 291, 293, 294, 300, 301, 303, 304, 306, 310, 311, 347, 348
  balance   280, 316, 326, 342, 343, 345, 346, 349
  coca   147, 286
  foreign   31, 61, 132, 134, 186, 202, 209, 210, 226, 228, 229, 230, 231, 242, 252, 254, 303
  free trade zones   230, 231
  illegal drug   68, 130, 134, 155
  international   100, 197, 224, 291, 302
  liberalization   7, 69, 71, 100, 131, 133, 134, 143, 306
  policy   224
  taxes   81, 85, 291, 292
  unions   211, 247, 248
Tribunal of Constitutional Guarantees   247
Trujillo, Perú   184

U

U.S. Department of State   149, 152
U.S. Treasury   214
Ulloa, Manuel   69
UNDCP (United Nations International Drug Control Programme)   152
UNDP (United Nations Development Programme)   153
United States   6, 15, 16, 17, 19, 48, 50, 51, 108, 122, 149, 152, 192, 223, 228, 234
Universidad Agraria   33
Uruguay   143
USAID (United States Agency for International Development)   152, 155

V

Vargas Llosa, Mario   130, 268, 274
VAT (valued-added tax)   105
Velarde, Julio   7, 284
Velasco Alvarado, Juan   3, 18, 45, 89, 150
  government   27, 44, 45, 46, 89, 101, 112, 144, 207, 248
Venezuela   35, 43, 44
Verdera, Francisco   5, 143, 151, 266

Vietnam   249
Von Hayek, Friedrich A.   6, 193, 194

W

War of the Pacific   30, 31
War of the Thousand Days   50
Washington Consensus   127
Webb, Richard   35, 45, 69, 70, 73, 74, 131, 176, 268, 271, 272, 278
Western Hemisphere   15, 17, 19, 49
Williamson, John   197
World Bank   21, 26, 27, 51, 78, 188, 216, 218, 222, 223, 249, 250, 252, 254,
   256, 266, 267, 289, 302, 311, 318, 344
World War I   11, 31, 33, 34, 35
World War II   31

PRODUCTION NOTES

This book was printed on 60 lb. Glatfelter Supple Opaque Natural text stock with a 10 point C1S cover stock, film laminated.

The text was set in Garamond for the North-South Center Press, using Aldus PageMaker 5.0a, and the figures were created in Aldus Freehand 4.0, on a Macintosh IIci computer. It was designed and formatted by Susan Kay Holler, who also created the index.

The cover was created by Mary M. Mapes using Adobe Illustrator 5.5 to create the illustration and exported to Quark XPress 3.3 for the composition and color separation.

The book was edited by Cynthia L. Jenney, Jayne M. Weisblatt, and Kathleen A. Hamman.

Cynthia L. Jenney also re-translated large sections of Carlos Boloña's chapter and selected the terms for the index.

It was printed by Thompson-Shore, Inc. of Dexter, Michigan, U.S.A.